American Women Authors and Literary Property, 1822–1869

Through an exploration of women authors' engagements with copyright and married women's property laws, *American Women Authors and Literary Property, 1822–1869*, revises nineteenth-century American literary history, making women's authorship and copyright law central. Using case studies of five popular fiction writers – Catharine Sedgwick, Harriet Beecher Stowe, Fanny Fern, Augusta Evans, and Mary Virginia Terhune – Homestead shows how the convergence of copyright and coverture both fostered and constrained white women's agency as authors. Women authors exploited their status as nonproprietary subjects to advantage by adapting themselves to a literary market in which unauthorized reprinting was the norm and to a copyright law that privileged readers' access to literature over authors' property rights. Homestead's inclusion of the Confederacy in this work sheds light on the centrality of copyright to nineteenth-century American nationalisms and on the strikingly different construction of author-reader relations under U.S. and Confederate copyright laws.

Melissa J. Homestead is associate professor of English at the University of Nebraska–Lincoln. She held the Mellon Post-Dissertation Fellowship at the American Antiquarian Society. Her work has appeared in *Prospects*, *New England Quarterly*, *Catharine Maria Sedgwick: Critical Perspectives*, and *Jewett and Her Contemporaries*. In 2003, she directed the third Catharine Maria Sedgwick Symposium.

This book is published in association with the American Antiquarian Society (AAS), in Worcester, Massachusetts, which supported the author's research and writing through a Mellon Post-Dissertation Fellowship, funded by a grant to AAS by the Andrew W. Mellon Foundation.

AMERICAN WOMEN AUTHORS AND LITERARY PROPERTY, 1822–1869

MELISSA J. HOMESTEAD
University of Nebraska–Lincoln

CAMBRIDGE
UNIVERSITY PRESS

CAMBRIDGE UNIVERSITY PRESS
Cambridge, New York, Melbourne, Madrid, Cape Town, Singapore,
São Paulo, Delhi, Dubai, Tokyo, Mexico City

Cambridge University Press
32 Avenue of the Americas, New York, NY 10013-2473, USA

www.cambridge.org
Information on this title: www.cambridge.org/9780521154758

First published 2005
First paperback printing 2010

A catalog record for this publication is available from the British Library

Library of Congress Cataloging in Publication data

Homestead, Melissa J., 1963–
American women authors and literary property, 1822–1869 / Melissa J. Homestead.
p. cm.
Includes bibliographical references and index.
ISBN 0-521-85382-6
1. American literature – Women authors – History and criticism. 2. Women and literature – United States – History – 19th century. 3. American literature – 19th century – History and criticism. 4. Copyright – United States – History – 19th century. I. Title.
PS217.W64H66 2005
810.9′9287′09034 – dc22 2005015907

ISBN 978-0-521-85382-8 Hardback
ISBN 978-0-521-15475-8 Paperback

Contents

Preface: "Imperfect Title"

In 1830, a Congressional committee recommended the extension of the term of copyright protection in the United States, and in its report the committee reasons, "If labor and effort in producing what before was not possessed or known will give title, then the literary man has title, perfect and absolute, and should have his reward."[1] To have "perfect title" to property is to have an ownership right that cannot be challenged. This 1830 Congressional report was one of very few during the middle years of the nineteenth century to issue such a ringing endorsement of authorial proprietorship, however. Instead, Congress adopted the logic of copyright opponents, who criticized such natural rights arguments for the expansion of copyright, arguing instead that the primary purpose of the copyright law was to serve the interests of readers and publishers. Following this logic, Congress rebuffed repeated attempts to amend the law so that authors who were not citizens or residents of the United States could claim the protection of the U.S. law for their works. Not until 60 years after the passage of the 1831 Copyright Act (extending the term of protection for American authors) did Congress pass an international copyright law at least partially recognizing by statute what the 1830 Congressional report considered natural and inevitable. Although the American "literary *man*" deserved (according to copyright advocates) a perfect title to his literary productions, his title, not recognized in other countries and devalued on the American market, remained "imperfect."

If the relationship of the claim of the literary *man* to his literary property was imperfect, then what are we to make of the relationship of literary *women* to this regime of property, especially considering the notably successful exploitation of the American literary market by American women authors in the nineteenth century? In legal decisions and in the copyright debates, judges, Congressmen, authors, and publishers drew on the discourses of paternity, commerce, and landed property to define and create the legal rights of authors under copyright, and all of these discourses brought with them their own gendered values and expectations, reinforcing the ambiguous status of women as authors. How could a woman be an author under copyright when copyright advocates claimed for the author status as or equivalent to a father, a farmer working his fields, a professional

1 House Committee on the Judiciary, *Copyright*, 21st Cong., 2nd sess., 10 Dec. 1830, H. Rep. 210, 2.

man selling his services, a tradesman selling his labor, or a businessman trading his goods in the marketplace? Such questions presuppose, however, that nineteenth-century American men who wrote had precisely the same relationship to their literary property as did fathers to their children, farmers to their fields, professional men and tradesmen to their services and labors, and merchants to their goods. Instead, when copyright advocates used these analogies, they inevitably revealed the gap between what they believed the law *should* do for authors and what it *did* do. For most of the century, copyright advocates failed in their attempts to fully invest the author with the legal rights to which they claimed authors as male citizens of the republic were entitled.

Women (and especially married women) also could not claim many of the rights of citizens. Most notably, under the common law doctrine of coverture, married women could not own property. Thus for much of the nineteenth century, both married women under coverture and authors under copyright could possess property and the fruits of their labors imperfectly or not at all. Nineteenth-century copyright advocates argued that the copyright law's failure to grant authors full proprietary status discouraged them from producing, but women authors, doubly distanced from authorial proprietorship, were not discouraged from producing, nor were their works excluded from the market. Instead, I argue, the convergence of literary property laws and married women's property laws, of copyright and coverture, was productive for the women (mostly white and middle class, and mostly married) whose successes transformed the terrain of the American literary marketplace.

Drawing on and contributing to scholarship in literary, legal, cultural, and book history and using a variety of nineteenth-century sources, I reconstruct in this book the engagements of Catharine Maria Sedgwick, Harriet Beecher Stowe, Fanny Fern, Mary Virginia Terhune, and Augusta Jane Evans with the law and with competing visions of the possibilities and limitations of American authorship articulated in the copyright debates. These case studies document women authors' efforts to expand the proprietary reach of both women and authors, but even when their efforts failed to achieve the desired results, they did not stop writing. As nonproprietary subjects, women adapted themselves to a literary market in which unauthorized reprinting was the norm, making the most of their "imperfect" proprietary status of American authorship and working astutely within the constraints imposed by a law that privileged readers' access to literature over authors' property rights.[2]

2 I adapt Meredith McGill's helpful restatement of my argument: "In her dissertation . . . Melissa Homestead argues that as nonproprietary subjects women more easily adapted themselves to unauthorized reprinting." *American Literature and the Culture of Reprinting, 1834–1853* (Philadelphia: University of Pennsylvania Press, 2003), 286n.

Acknowledgments

This book began as a dissertation in the English Department at the University of Pennsylvania. Although the book has taken a considerably different shape from the original project, I owe my primary scholarly debt to my dissertation committee, Peter Conn (director), Nancy Bentley, and Christopher Looby, and to my dissertation writing group, Jeannine DeLombard, Leigh Edwards, and Ashley Montague Row.

I am also heavily indebted to the American Antiquarian Society (AAS), where I thrice attended the Summer Seminar in the History of the Book in American Culture (in 1995 under the direction of Robert Gross and Mary Kelley, in 1997 under the direction of Meredith McGill and Joan Shelley Rubin, and in 2003 under the direction of Barbara Hochmann and David Stewart) and where I was twice awarded fellowships (a month-long Petersen Fellowship in 1997 and a year-long Mellon Post-Dissertation Fellowship in 2000–1). At the beginning of my second residence, the AAS arranged for Meredith McGill, Grantland Rice, and Elizabeth Waning Harries to read my unrevised dissertation, and I thank them all for their comments. The AAS also gave me access to a network of scholars who have been essential to many elements of this project, and I cannot praise enough the legendarily helpful staff, past and present, including Nancy Burkett, Joanne Chaison, John Hench, Thomas Knoles, Marie Lamoureux, Philip Lampi, Dennis Lurie, Russell Martin, Caroline Sloat, and Laura Wasowicz. Without the AAS, this book might have been written, but it would have been a much poorer effort and much less fun to write.

Other libraries whose collections and staff have been crucial to the research for this project include Alabama State Department of Archives and History; American Philosophical Society; Beinecke Library at Yale University; Bizzell Memorial Library at the University of Oklahoma; Boston Athenaeum; Boston Public Library; Duke University Library Special Collections; Firestone Library Special Collections at Princeton University; Free Library of Philadelphia; German Society of Pennsylvania Library; Georgetown University Law Center Library; Haverford College Library Special Collections; Harvard Law Library; Historical Society of Pennsylvania; Historic Mobile Preservation Society; Hoole Alabama Collection at the University of Alabama; Houghton Library at Harvard University; Library Company of Philadelphia; Library of Congress; Massachusetts Historical Society; New York Public Library; National

Archives (in DC and the Mid-Atlantic and Great Lakes Regional Branches); Trinity College Library Special Collections; United States Supreme Court Library; University of Massachusetts Library; and Van Pelt Library, Rare Books and Special Collections, and Law Library at the University of Pennsylvania.

A portion of Chapter 4 appeared in the *New England Quarterly* as "'Every Body Sees the Theft': Fanny Fern and Literary Proprietorship in Antebellum America," 74, no. 2 (2001): 210–31, and is reproduced with the permission of the copyright holder, *New England Quartlery*. An earlier version of Chapter 3 appeared in *Prospects: An Annual Journal of American Cultural Studies* as "'When I Can Read My Title Clear': Harriet Beecher Stowe and the *Stowe v. Thomas* Copyright Infringement Case," 27 (2002): 201–45, and is reproduced with the permission of the copyright holder, Cambridge University Press. A small snippet of Chapter 1 appeared as part of "Behind the Veil?: Sedgwick and Anonymous Publication," in *Catharine Maria Sedgwick: Critical Perspectives*, ed. Lucinda L. Damon-Bach and Victoria Clements (Boston: Northeastern University Press, 2002), 19–35, and is reproduced with the permission of the copyright holder, Northeastern University Press.

The Nineteenth-Century American Women Writers Study Group has been a crucial resource since I first attended a meeting in 1997. Our reading and discussion of women's texts and the historical and theoretical issues impinging on them have enriched and complicated my approach to this project. Particularly important was a 1999 meeting facilitated by Laura Hanft Korobkin and Elizabeth Maddock Dillon focusing on the topic of "women and property," the secondary readings for which crucially shifted my thinking on gender and property.

Individual scholars have been generous in sharing resources and expertise, and others have read and responded to portions of the manuscript. In alphabetical order, I acknowledge my indebtedness to Paula Bernat Bennett, Richard Chused, Patricia Cline Cohen, Gayle Harris, Cheri Larsen Hoeckley, Amy Hudock, Rita Keresztesi, Leon Jackson, Barbara Ryan, Francesca Sawaya, Martin Schultz, Robert Shalhope, Jean Silver-Isenstadt, Karen Manners Smith, Naomi Z. Sofer, Amy Thomas, Siva Vaidhyanathan, Joyce Warren, Karen Woods Weierman, and Elizabeth Young. I also thank my Cambridge University Press readers, Sandra Zagarell and Ezra Greenspan, for their comments on and support of my project.

The University of Oklahoma provided research support on several occasions, namely a College of Arts and Sciences Junior Faculty Summer Research grant, a Research Council Junior Faculty Summer Research grant, two College of Arts and Sciences Faculty Enrichment grants, two semesters of graduate research assistant support from the Department of English (funding the labors of Kimberly Martinson and Steven Salaita), and an undergraduate research assistant for a semester funded by the Honors Research

Assistant Program (Clinton Stevens, who assisted with translations from the German for Chapter 3).

When I was hired as a paralegal in the Intellectual Property Group at the Philadelphia law firm of Dechert, Price & Rhoads in 1990, I am sure that partner Glenn A. Gundersen did not intend to train me for a return to my abandoned doctoral study to become a hybrid scholar of law and literature, but he did in spite of himself. I outlasted associate Thomas H. Speranza (now of Kleinbard, Bell & Brecker), but when I began this project with a seminar paper on *Stowe v. Thomas* in 1994, he graciously took phone calls from me about such arcane matters as the distinctions between forms of legal remedies for copyright infringement.

Last, but not least, I thank my parents, John and Carolyn Homestead, for their extraordinary understanding and patience with my long and arduous path to the Ph.D. and then the grueling years of the academic job market. Even though they happily concede that they don't understand a word of what I've written, they have fully supported my endeavors as worthwhile because they want for their daughter whatever their daughter wants for herself. Every junior academic in the humanities should have such parents.

Introduction: "Lady-Writers" and "Copyright, Authors, and Authorship" in Nineteenth-Century America

Not pay us for our toils of thought!
The struggling of our brains!
By old George Fox, the indignant blood
Is lava in my veins!
Shame on our country and its laws!
Strike, let the Bastile [*sic*] fall!
Down with the tyrant Publishers!
Hurrah for Faneuil Hall!

On October 10, 1847, the *Saturday Evening Post* published on its front page a group of poems, tales, and letters under the title "Copyright, Authors, and Authorship" by one of its regular contributors, Grace Greenwood (pseudonym of Sarah Jane Clarke, later Sarah Jane Lippincott).[1] As the headnote "explains,"

> A short time since a friend of ours, a gentleman connected with the press, being in favor of an International Copyright Law, and feeling an interest in the encouragement of native genius by adequate pecuniary compensation, applied to many of our first authors for their opinions concerning these subjects, leaving them at liberty to embody their sentiments in the form of poems, letters, or sketches. But our friend, being called to the defence of his country, in the midst of his labors of love, left in our hands the important documents. It will be seen that the collection was not complete, several authors of note not having reported themselves; but such as it is, we give it to the public, to read and ponder and inwardly digest.[2]

What follows is actually a group of pieces written by Greenwood in the style of famous American writers of the era, most of them with the "author" identified only by initials that clearly correspond to the name of one those

1 For an overview of her life and career, see Donna Born, "Sarah Jane Clarke Lippincott (Grace Greenwood)," in *American Newspaper Journalists, 1690–1872*, ed. Perry J. Ashley, vol. 43 of *The Dictionary of Literary Biography*, 303–8 (Detroit: Gale, 1985).

2 Grace Greenwood, "Copyright, Authors, and Authorship," in *Greenwood Leaves: A Collection of Sketches and Letters* (Boston: Ticknor, Reed and Fields, 1850), 283. For materials included in the original publication in the *Saturday Evening Post* and added subsequently, I hereinafter cite this edition in the text. The original appearance, including some items not included in *Greenwood Leaves*, is "Copyright, Authors, and Authorship," *Saturday Evening Post*, 9 Oct. 1847, [1].

famous writers. The series leads off with the rousing call to authorial action quoted above by "JGW" (John Greenleaf Whittier), summoning all American authors (or at least all Northeastern authors) to a meeting at Faneuil Hall, the scene of many meetings in support of the American Revolution, to discuss the question of international copyright. "Whittier's" call is relatively inclusive, going out to Henry Wadsworth Longfellow at Harvard, William Cullen Bryant at his editorial desk for the *New York Evening Post*, FitzGreene Halleck at his counting house in New York, Lydia Huntley Sigourney in Connecticut mourning over a dead friend, and even the "Corinnes and Sapphos fair,/In Lowell factories dwelling," who may have published works in the *Lowell Offering*. "Whittier" includes all of these authors because, according to the poem, they have one thing in common – they have not been adequately paid for their "toils of thought" and "struggling of [their] brains," and rather than accept their martyrdom, they should stage a revolutionary overthrow of the law that oppresses them, the copyright law. Although "Whittier's" call is gender inclusive, Greenwood tellingly partitions off "contributions" from women authors under the heading "Lady-Writers" (including her "own" contribution, the last item in the group, a "Letter from the West" signed "Grace Greenwood"). She thus suggests that gender potentially inflected the questions presented by copyright reform and that women writers had a different relationship to the law than did their male peers.

My study of women authors and literary property in the United States from the 1820s through the 1860s aims to answer precisely the question posed by Greenwood's gender segregation of her parodies: what relationship did women authors have to the copyright law and to debates about its reform in the nineteenth century? If international copyright was, as many of the parodies of the male writers suggest, to be justified on the ground that men laboring in the field of letters should be able to provide financially for their wives and children, where did "lady-writers" fit in? More specifically, what are we to make of a seeming paradox at the heart of the relationship between women and the law: if, as nineteenth-century copyright advocates often insisted, the weak copyright law frustrated the development of American literature because it provided inadequate protection for and incentives to authors, how do we account for the spectacular commercial and popular successes of American women in the American literary market at midcentury?

The figure of the writing woman as a successful commercial agent in the literary market troubled and repulsed many nineteenth-century critics and continues to trouble and challenge modern literary historians. Did nineteenth-century women authors wholeheartedly and successfully exploit, and even help invent, the structures of commodity capitalism, or did they maintain a psychological and emotional detachment from the market in which their texts circulated? That is, should we read nineteenth-century American women's popular authorship through Ann Douglas's *Feminization of American Culture* (and, more recently, Lori Merish's *Sentimental Materialism*) or through Mary Kelley's *Private Woman, Public Stage*?[3]

Recognizing copyright law as a crucial mechanism structuring the literary market and authors' relations to it complicates the question of how women authors engaged the market for literature. Copyright grants literary texts legal status as property – a peculiar kind of property, but property nonetheless. Thus laws regulating the ownership and control of property more broadly applied to copyrights, and under broader property law principles, women (and especially married women) had a profoundly different relationship to property than that enjoyed by their male peers. Whether or not women authors distanced themselves psychologically and emotionally from the market, the law effectively created a distance by refusing to grant most women the legal status of proprietors. One might expect the nonproprietary status of many women to discourage them from producing literary texts, but their productivity in the face of their dispossession belies the logic of copyright advocacy. Their rights to property, their labors, and their very persons often in doubt, women wrote and published anyway, and readers purchased their works in unprecedented numbers.

Concurrently with this burst of women's production and readers' consumption, advocates and opponents of international copyright argued in print over the law's allocation of power between authors and readers, with the anticopyright position and readers' interests effectively holding sway for most of the century. The questions raised by the copyright debates were thus part of every author's "scene of writing," to use Richard Brodhead's useful phrase from *Cultures of Letters*. As Brodhead argues, "A work of writing comes to its particular form of existence in interaction with the network of relations that surround it: in any actual instance, writing orients itself in or against some understanding of what writing is, does, and is good for that is culturally composed and derived."[4] In the copyright debates, American culture attempted to compose just such formulations of what writing is, does, and is good for, and American writers who hoped to reach an audience and succeed would ignore such formulations at their peril. Publishers, who decided which works to circulate and how to circulate them, necessarily

3 Ann Douglas, *The Feminization of American Culture* (New York: Knopf, 1977); Lori Merish, *Sentimental Materialism: Gender, Commodity Culture, and Nineteenth-Century American Literature* (Durham: Duke University Press, 2000); Mary Kelley, *Private Woman, Public Stage: Literary Domesticity in Nineteenth-Century America* (New York: Oxford University Press, 1984; reprinted University of North Carolina Press, 2003).

4 Richard Brodhead, *Cultures of Letters: Scenes of Reading and Writing in Nineteenth-Century America* (Chicago: Chicago University Press, 1993), 8.

tried to gauge which works met certain audience expectations and thus would be commercially successful; but publishers also played an important role in setting those expectations by, for most of the century, loudly and publicly arguing *against* the expansion of authorial rights through international copyright. Finally, the copyright debates were as much a part of the various "scenes of reading" in nineteenth-century America, scenes that structured readers' individual experiences of literary texts, as they were part of authors' "scenes of writing." Especially at the dawn of the age of literary celebrity, readers read not just literary texts but authors, too, and the copyright debates contributed to the symbolic construction of American authorship.

For the remainder of this introduction, I continue to tease out the implications of the copyright debates for nineteenth-century scenes of reading and writing. I first continue my analysis of Greenwood's parodies as a concrete and particular interpretation of the gendered implications of the copyright debates. I then use this particular instance to sketch out the broader claims of my project and its relationship to previous scholarship on copyright and literature and on women's authorship in nineteenth-century America. Examining women's authorship through the lens of copyright history and vice versa, I locate a convergence between women's self-fashionings as authors and readers' expectations and desires as both expressed through and shaped by the copyright debates. By locating such a convergence between women authors and a mass readership, I do not simply relocate the supposed easy triumph of popular women's authorship to a slightly different location within the market, nor do I entirely re-distance them from the market, thus preserving them from the contamination of trade. Instead, I seek to recover and revalue the complex and contested nature of their engagements. Although the women I study attempted to exploit literary proprietorship as a mode of authorship, U.S. copyright statutes and their legal status as women sometimes subverted their aims and at times enabled other authorial modes. The recovery of these women's experiences contributes to literary history, but it also can teach us about the present and the future of copyright as a mechanism structuring the relationship between cultural producers and consumers.

"National necessity" versus "sweating wages": Readers and authors at odds in the antebellum copyright debates

For anyone who has not spent time browsing nineteenth-century periodicals, the pervasiveness of the copyright debates across the cultural spectrum can come as a surprise. The *Saturday Evening Post*, for instance, which published Grace Greenwood's parodies, was a widely circulated weekly, published every Saturday night for appropriate reading Sunday in the family circle.[5] When Greenwood wrote the parodies and when the *Post* accepted them for publication, both author and publisher clearly believed that moderately well informed readers, both men and women, and perhaps even older children, would understand and appreciate them. Not only did the editor assume a basic level of understanding, he assumed a great enough level of interest to devote almost the entire front page to the parodies, a space usually reserved for the fictional tales and novelettes that were the *Post*'s bread and butter. Indeed, nowhere in the parodies, not in the headnote or in the parodies themselves, are the bare facts of the international copyright controversy even explained for readers. The U.S. copyright statute specified that its provisions protected only works authored by citizens of the United States or "residents therein." Rather than leaving the unprotected status of works authored by noncitizens or nonresidents implicit, the law specifically permitted and even encouraged the appropriation of such works by U.S. publishers: "[N]othing in this act shall be construed to extend to prohibit the importation or vending, reprinting or publishing within the United States, of any map, chart, book or books, written, printed, or published by any person not a citizen of the United States, in foreign parts or places without the jurisdiction of the United States."[6] In response to this open invitation, publishers legally could, and did, publish cheap, unauthorized editions of works by English and other European authors (across the Atlantic, the British copyright law did not specifically exclude from protection works authored by persons who were not British subjects or residents, but as a practical matter, most American authors could not secure copyright protection for their works in Britain).[7] According to U.S. copyright advocates, the exclusion of British-authored works from copyright protection caused American-authored works protected by copyright to be sold at much higher prices than "unbought" reprints of British works, and this price disparity made it difficult for American authors to find an audience and receive adequate compensation for their labors. Opponents of international copyright successfully argued that the law and its positive promotion of reprinting should remain undisturbed. The *Post* and Greenwood, however, assumed that average readers knew both these facts and the typical arguments for and against international copyright. By the time the *Post* published the parodies

5 On the history of the *Post* and other "story papers," see Mary Noel, *Villains Galore: The Heyday of the Popular Story Weekly* (New York: Macmillan, 1954). On family reading of weekly literary magazines in newspaper format (focusing on a Southern paper, the *Spirit of the Age*), see Amy M. Thomas, "Literature in Newsprint: Antebellum Family Newspapers and the Uses of Reading," in *Reading Books: Essays on the Material Text and Literature in America*, (Amherst: University of Massachusetts Press, 1996), 101–16.

6 Copyright Act of 1790, in Thorvald Solberg, ed., *Copyright Enactments of the United States*, 1783–1906 (Washington, DC: Government Printing Office, 1906), 32, 34. Although Congress enacted many additions and amendments over the course of the nineteenth century, this section remained in effect.

7 This brief description of the law and trade practices for transatlantic authorship necessarily oversimplifies a very complex topic. See Chapter 5 for a more in-depth discussion.

in 1847, both American and British authors had been petitioning Congress for ten years, urging the passage of an international copyright law that would better protect the "rights" of *all* authors by granting U.S. copyright protection to both resident and nonresident authors, while copyright opponents had mounted and maintained an effective defense against these efforts.

Authors rarely made copyright the direct subject of imaginative literature (which is precisely the source of the parody collection's humor – who writes poems about copyright reform?), but readers of Greenwood's parodies would have encountered more serious discussions of the question in many print media of the day – daily and weekly newspapers, popular monthly magazines like *Graham's*, and high-toned quarterlies like the *North American Review*. Such discussions framed the question of copyright reform not as a specialized issue of concern only to lawyers and to a few interested parties in the publishing industry, but as a question with possible profound and immediate effects for all concerned – for readers, authors, and publishers, and for the American nation. Although some argued that *all* parties would benefit from reciprocal copyright arrangements with England and other countries, most recognized international copyright as a field of struggle between competing interests.[8] Greenwood's parodies frame the struggle as one between authors and publishers (in "Whittier's" poem, authors plan to revolt against "tyrant publishers"), but more often the issue was framed as a struggle between authors and readers. Did copyright law protect absolute property rights of authors, or did the superior right of reader access (and the necessary corollary, the right of publishers to publish) trump authors' rights? Should readers have to pay authors more or less than they were being paid, or did truly great authors not write for money at all?

About six months before it published Greenwood's parodies, the *Post* published a long and vigorous anticopyright editorial tackling just such questions, framing the struggle over copyright as a struggle between authors greedy for more money and power and American readers craving knowledge. Copyright advocates often accused copyright opponents of "literary agrarianism," associating their lack of respect for literary property with contemporary radical critiques of property ownership and attempts to give the poor access to farmland.[9] The *Post* editorial does not deny this characterization but embraces it, claiming that reader "hunger" for books trumped

8 Throughout this study, I adopt and adapt the terminology of Pierre Bourdieu's sociology of literary production, particularly the notion of "the field of cultural production" as structured by conflict. "The Field of Cultural Production, or: The Economic World Reversed," in *The Field of Cultural Production: Essays on Art and Literature*, ed. Randall Johnson (New York: Columbia University Press, 1993), 34.

9 See, e.g., Cornelius Mathews's labeling anticopyright "an allowable agrarianism of ideas." *The Better Interests of the Country, in Connexion with International Copy-right* (New York: Wiley & Putnam, 1843), 9. As Martin Buinicki argues in his analysis of James Fenimore Cooper's dual engagements in debates over rights in real property (land) and literary property, land was hardly an unproblematic ground from which to figure the stability of literary property during the "Anti-rent wars" of the 1830s

even the author's property rights in his literary crops: "Now, granting that an author has as much and the same right to his book, as the farmer has to the products of his orchard or his field, it does not follow from this, that his right is absolute and without limitation. As the rights of property in the latter, may justly upon occasion be made to yield to the strong demands of bodily hunger, or national necessity; so may the right of an author in his works, be made to yield before the mental hunger of the masses of society."[10] Although each of Greenwood's parodies takes on the particular style and subject matter of the author parodied, almost all of the pieces focus on the pathos of authorship in a nation that privileged readerly voraciousness over authorial property rights, particularly the pathos of the author and the author's family starving for lack of adequate financial return for his literary labors. That is, whereas the *Post* claimed that the law should first and foremost allow readers to satisfy their mental hunger, the "authors" argued that the law should protect authors and their families from physical starvation.

Of Greenwood's thirteen parodies (including "Whittier's"),[11] the first nine parodies are of male authors, and of those nine, only the Whittier parody reaches beyond the situation of the male author to include women. Instead, the "authors" repeatedly focus on the inability of male authors to support their wives and children through writing. A macabre tale by "EAP" (Edgar Allan Poe) tells of an author immolated in a garret, having abandoned his wife and family. As the ghastly Adolphus Twiggs tells the narrator, "You see before you the victim of the miserable compensation awarded to native genius, and *of the want of a law of International Copyright!*" (p. 290).[12] A narrative poem by "FGH" (FitzGreene Halleck) describes the situation of a poet who awakens from a dream of the glories of the court minstrel's life to the reality of the sheriff banging on his door, the poet's creditors having sent the sheriff to collect debts (pp. 292–3) (a parody ironically appropriate to a man who was lauded as "the American Byron" for his satiric long poem "Fanny," but who also worked in the banking industry for most of his adult life in order to earn a living). While his wife distracts the sheriff, the poet hides in his meal-chest and plans to leave the country on the morning boat. The remaining pieces by the "men" comment on

and 1840s. "Negotiating Copyright: Authorship and the Discourse of Literary Property Rights in Nineteenth-Century America," PhD diss., University of Iowa, 2003, 63–5.

10 "International Copy-Right," *Saturday Evening Post*, 10 Apr. 1847, [2].

11 When the pieces were published in *Greenwood Leaves* in 1850, Greenwood added an additional parody by "OWH, MD" (Oliver Wendell Holmes), changed the byline on one of the lady writers' poems from "Kate Carol" to "FSO" (Frances Sargent Osgood – "Kate Carol" was an identifiable psuedonym and persona of Osgood – thanks to Eliza Richards for explaining this puzzling change), and removed her own "Letter from the West," replacing it with a new "Fable from the Burmese" by "FF" (Fanny Forrester – "Fanny Fern" had not yet begun her pseudonymous career in 1850).

12 For Poe's complex and contradictory relationship to the sort of literary nationalistic rhetoric that Greenwood puts in his mouth, see Meredith McGill, *American Literature and the Culture of Reprinting, 1834–1853* (Philadelphia: University of Pennsylvania Press, 2003), chap. 5.

the immense gulf between some ideal of authorial eminence and power and the reality of American authorship. For instance, "The Author of 'Typee'" (Herman Melville) describes the glories of the life of a poet on the island of Typee (the best lodge on the island, food and precious oils supplied through voluntary taxation, the prettiest maiden for a bride, and even the choicest enemy for his cannibalistic pleasure), so that American Christians "might learn a lesson from the savages" about how authors should be treated (p. 294). Although copyright reform was not the direct subject of *Typee*, Melville's book, as well as two volumes of Poe's poems and tales, were published in Wiley & Putnam's "Library of American Books," a series that linked its American literary nationalist project with copyright reform by featuring a quotation from the *Address of the American Copy-Right Club* on the paper cover of each book: "Sundry citizens of this good land, meaning well, and hoping well prompted by a certain something in their nature, have trained them selves to do service in various Essays, Poems, Histories, and books of Art, Fancy, and Truth."[13] By featuring this motto on the covers, George Palmer Putnam, a publisher exceptional during the 1840s for his strong public support of international copyright, meant to frame *Typee* as a service to American readers, but in Greenwood's parody, "the author of 'Typee'" seems more interested in what his countrymen and -women can do for him than in what he can do for his countrymen and -women.

In the small subsection titled "Lady-Writers," Greenwood includes only four authors, and without the same tight unanimity of theme found in the generic, unmarked section of (male) authors. In a "Letter from New York" in the style of her widely read and reprinted columns for the *National Anti-Slavery Standard*, "LMC" (Lydia Maria Child) expresses faith that copyright reform is "one of the reforms of the age," as important as the abolition of war and capital punishment (p. 303). In a brief lyric, "Kate Carol" (Frances Sargent Osgood) poetically protests that "precious poetesses" should be protected from "vulgar wants and harsh distresses" of common life, that their clothing should be as pretty and bejeweled as their verses (pp. 304–5). "LHS" (Lydia Huntley Sigourney) poetically laments that she cannot publish a collection of a dead female friend's poetry because a publisher tells her, "It would not pay" (p. 306). Finally, Grace Greenwood, adopting her most typical newspaper genre of the letter, writes a "Letter from the West" addressed to the fictional man who "collected" the pieces, balancing Child's "Letter from New York" geographically and in content. Greenwood begins

13 Herman Melville, *Typee a Peep at Polynesian Life During a Four Months' Residence in a Valley of the Marquesas* (New York: Wiley & Putnam, 1846). Reading Greenwood's parody of Melville out of context, John Evelev suggests she is castigating him for insufficient professionalization in his early career. "'Every One to His Trade': *Mardi*, Literary Form, and Professional Ideology," *American Literature* 75, no. 2 (2003): 305–33. On Putnam's publishing and copyright activities, see Ezra Greenspan, "Evert Duyckinck and the History of Wiley and Putnam's Library of American Books, 1845–1847," *American Literature* 64, no. 4 (1992): 677–93; and Greenspan, *George Palmer Putnam: Representative American Publisher* (University Park: Pennsylvania State University Press, 2000).

her letter with the anticipated benefits to readers of copyright reform, claiming that it will be both "an immeasurable benefit to the native genius" and a benefit to readers, who will be delivered "from foreign stupidity and mediocrity – what Coleridge calls 'brain-dribble.'" However, she quickly turns to more self-interested motivations, lampooning the arguments of copyright opponents (such as her editor at the *Post*) who claim that authors should write not for dollars but for "pleasure," "fame," or "posterity." If America wants its authors to work hard enough at their labors to "sweat" so that their poetic products will be good, says Greenwood, it must pay authors "sweating wages."

As Greenwood's parodies suggest, when authors sat down to write, they confronted a vision of the tenuous position of American authors in a culture that refused to give legal protection to their literary property fully commensurate with the protection given to other forms of property. The copyright debates suggest that both authors and readers understood that to take on the role of author was to subject oneself to dispossession at the hands of publishers and readers and to lose (or be denied access to) certain forms of cultural power. The specter of the powerless author as slave, stripped of his rights in his own person, his labor uncompensated and his property turned into public property, haunts antebellum copyright advocacy. By framing her copyright parodies with a poem in the persona of abolitionist poet John Greenleaf Whittier, Greenwood hints at this figure of the author as slave. One of the poets "Whittier" calls to Faneuil Hall, the scene of the revolutionary overthrow of the "enslavement" of American colonists to the British crown, is a fellow abolitionist poet, William Henry Burleigh:

> Ho, brother Burleigh, leave "the cause" –
>   Slaves, masters, chains and all!
> Let's battle for *ourselves* awhile –
>   Be off, to Faneuil Hall!
>
> (p. 284)

That is, rather than battle for the right of the slave to himself and to the fruits of his labor, the abolitionist poets should join together to abolish authorial slavery, the taking of "the toils of thought" and "struggling of [the] brains" by "tyrant Publishers" (and the readers they serve) in the absence of international copyright.

The (white) male authors ventriloquized in Greenwood's parodies consistently rail against the constraints imposed by a copyright law that did not allow them to claim the perfect title to their literary properties that they believed was theirs by right. Greenwood's "ladies," however (with the exception of Greenwood herself), do not represent themselves as wronged literary proprietors. "Sigourney" worries about the effects of the law not on herself but on her poor dead friend, whose poetry will fail to find an audience; "Child" seeks reform for the benefit of others, whether they be murderers condemned to die or dispossessed authors; and "Osgood" gestures toward the literary market as a source of wealth while disdaining to engage its mechanisms – "precious poetesses" should simply *have* beautiful things *before* warbling their songs rather than worrying about whether or not their warblings will pay.

How should we read this refusal of Greenwood's "ladies" to argue for a stronger copyright law on their own behalf? Are they merely genteelly avoiding the taint of trade? Are they enacting a genuinely different mode of authorship in which they understand their literary labors to be a form of disinterested service on behalf of others? Are they strategically effacing authorial self-interest at a time when readers were not disposed to look kindly on the demands of greedy authors? Greenwood's parodies of the "lady-writers" hint at one or more of these motives, singly or in combination, for each woman author she targets, and in my subsequent case studies of actual women authors, I find them similarly various in their methods of authorial self-representation and in their motives. Crucially, however, in Greenwood's parodies, the apparent distance of each woman from the market created by her refusal to argue on her own behalf also registers, I propose, the legal status of women as nonproprietary subjects. The (male) authors, as proprietary subjects in other spheres of activity, have clear cause for indignation at being "enslaved" by readers and publishers, but the legal status of the ladies excludes them from even the possibility of such indignation at being dispossessed. If, as popular feminist antebellum reform rhetoric would have it, women become the property of their husbands upon marriage (little more than slaves), the ladies are already slaves, with no ground for common protest with their male peers.

Greenwood's own pointed call for "sweating wages" for authors significantly departs from this norm, but she subsequently distanced herself from this public articulation of a strong proprietary position. Greenwood eliminated her "Letter from the West" when she reprinted her parodies in *Greenwood Leaves* in 1850 (and she misleadingly claims in her introduction to the appearance of the parodies in this book that she published them anonymously in the *Post*). These revisions suggest that she came to understand the power that the seemingly marginal position of "lady-writer" offered in the face of continuing mass resistance to international copyright law. What could be gained by publicly castigating her readers on her own behalf when accommodating herself to readers' desires might be more profitable? Rather than include her sarcastic personal letter arguing that publishers and readers would have to pay her much more if they wanted her to write better poetry and sketches, she substituted a sentimental and gently humorous sketch by "FF" (Fanny Forrester) about a female fairy leaving the paradise of fairyland to devote herself to the plight of poor (male) poets on earth. Crucially, the absence of her own voice as a strong advocate of copyright reform transforms the parodic aim of the collection as a whole. In the *Post*, she seems to be gently mocking each author's style, typical subject matter, and persona (including her own), while supporting the cause of international copyright. In its revised form in *Greenwood Leaves*, "Copyright, Authors, and Authorship" more broadly lampoons the authors *and* the cause they support, an international copyright law.

The story of Grace Greenwood's engagement with copyright does not end in 1850, however. In both 1847 and 1850, Greenwood controlled the fruits of her authorial labors, her paltry "sweating wages," but when she married Leander K. Lippincott in 1853, she discovered in very concrete terms what a difference marriage made to her status as an author. Her earlier copyrights were registered by Greenwood herself or by her publishers, but from 1853 on, Leander Lippincott became the registered proprietor of his wife's copyrights. By 1853, Greenwood had thus lost her ground for protest against readers' and publishers' incursions into her proprietary domain because, although she was still an author, she was no longer a literary proprietor. She continued to "sweat" at the labor of literary production after marriage, but her "sweating wages" legally belonged to her husband.

Reading nineteenth-century literary history through copyright

When I began this project more than a decade ago, the intersection between copyright and literature in nineteenth-century America remained virtually untouched by literary historians, an anomalous absence considering the volume of commentary published in the nineteenth century – Greenwood's parodies are but a drop of ink in the sea spilled on the topic.[14] Standard literary histories say relatively little about copyright, and what they do say sometimes uncritically reproduces the arguments of nineteenth-century copyright advocates, complete with the righteous indignation Greenwood captures in her Whittier parody. They emphasize the difficulties American authors faced in the American market (because of competition from cheap reprints of English works) and in the English market (where they could

14 James J. Barnes brilliantly reconstructs these debates and efforts for and against reform on both sides of the Atlantic, but his work is political and cultural history rather than literary history. *Authors, Publishers, and Politicians: The Quest for an Anglo-American Copyright Agreement, 1815–1854* (Columbus: Ohio State University Press, 1974). Furthermore, because women were largely absent from organized efforts on behalf of copyright in the United States during the antebellum years, American women are also largely absent from his study. Aubert J. Clark's published dissertation covers the sweep of the entire century but lacks the methodological sophistication and deep research of Barnes's study. *The Movement for International Copyright in Nineteenth Century America* (Washington, DC: Catholic University of American Press, 1960). Clark places the blame for everything wrong with the nineteenth-century American literary market squarely on the shoulders of women novel readers and "militant female[s] clutching . . . bulky manuscript[s]" (p. 34).

seldom and only with great difficulty obtain copyright protection for their works). In the words of the influential *Literary History of the United States* published in 1948, "Under piracy the printers made money, and from them came the specious cry of free books for free men and the foolish charge that international copyright would turn the native business to foreign control. Not until 1891 was a comparatively decent copyright act written into American Law."[15] The message is clear: the lack of international copyright frustrated the development of American authorship and American literature.

In *American Literature and the Culture of Reprinting* (2003), Meredith McGill has effectively overturned these pieties, analyzing "unauthorized" reprinting as a system functional on its own terms rather than criticizing it as dysfunctional in contrast to the later proprietary system imagined as perfectly functional. McGill persuasively argues that the "culture of reprinting" that structured the literary market in the antebellum era reflected both a "republican understanding of print as public property" and a Jacksonian valuation of "local over national authority."[16] Rather than a disorganized preview of the eventual nationalization of print and the proper recognition of authors' rights, McGill finds an exuberant reprint culture that is both regional and transatlantic. In chapters in broader studies of eighteenth- and nineteenth-century authorship, Grantland Rice (*The Transformation of Authorship* [1997]) and Michael Newbury (*Figuring Authorship in Antebellum America* [1997]) are equally skeptical of proclaiming the full instantiation of the proprietary model of authorship a triumph, as is Martin Buinicki in an article on Walt Whitman's reconciliation of copyright ownership with his radically democratic poetics.[17] In *Copyrights and Copywrongs: The Rise of Intellectual Property and How it Threatens Creativity* (2001), Siva Vaidhyanathan

15 Robert E. Spiller et al., eds., *Literary History of the United States* (New York: MacMillan, 1948), 621. The *LHUS* also notes, however, that the "injustice" of the lack of copyright was somewhat ameliorated by the earnings authors made through the American magazines (p. 622). See also William Peterfield Trent et al., eds., *Cambridge History of American Literature* (New York: MacMillan, 1944), 545–6, 550–1. The most recent *Cambridge History*, following William Charvat, takes a more moderate position, recognizing negative and positive results of the copyright situation. Sacvan Bercovitch and Cyrus K. Patell, eds., *The Cambridge History of American Literature*, vol. 2, *1820–1865* (New York: Cambridge University Press, 1995), 14. Charvat, *The Profession of Authorship in America, 1800–1870* (Columbus: Ohio State University Press, 1968), 31–2.

16 McGill, *American Literature*, 14. Unfortunately, these pieties are so entrenched that even scholars who have read McGill continue to criticize "piracy" as an imposition against "major" American and British authors. See, e.g., Jennifer Phegley, "Literary Piracy, Nationalism, and Women Readers in *Harper's New Monthly Magazine*, 1850–1855," *American Periodicals* 14, no. 1 (2004): 63–90 (on Melville and Dickens in *Harper's*).

17 Grantland Rice, *The Transformation of Authorship* (Chicago: University of Chicago Press, 1997). Michael Newbury, *Figuring Authorship in Antebellum America* (Stanford: Stanford University Press, 1997). Martin Buinicki, "Walt Whitman and the Question of Copyright," *American Literary History* 15, no. 2 (2003): 248–75. Buinicki's unpublished dissertation includes additional chapters on James Fenimore Cooper, Harriet Beecher Stowe, and Mark Twain.

primarily analyzes the twentieth and twenty-first centuries and the implications of copyright in the digital age, but he also includes Mark Twain as a primary figure in his chapter surveying the history of American copyright.[18] All of these studies explore and value what a literary cultural landscape in the absence of international copyright enabled rather than simply lamenting what it frustrated. However, they focus primarily on male authors (McGill on Charles Dickens, Edgar Allan Poe, and Nathaniel Hawthorne; Rice on Washington Irving and Joel Barlow; Newbury on Hawthorne, Poe, and Fanny Fern; Buinicki on Whitman; and Vaidhyanathan on Twain).

This study thus seeks to extend and complicate these accounts by focusing on what the nineteenth-century copyright climate enabled for women authors, particularly authors of novels and other prose fiction. This focus on novels and novelists is somewhat arbitrary, but it also has a historical logic. Paula Bernat Bennett has recently reminded us that poetry, including poetry by women, was everywhere in nineteenth-century America, in daily and weekly newspapers, in magazines, and in books, and that women were authors of much of that poetry (and Greenwood's parodic targets, both male and female, are split about evenly between writers of poetry and prose).[19] However, the most commented-on commercial successes in the American literary market were novels, and the status of novels and novelists also became the center of the literary property debates, both the status of British novelists whose works were widely reprinted in the United States (especially Walter Scott and Charles Dickens) and American novelists who achieved American success and whose works were reprinted in England (James Fenimore Cooper and most especially Harriet Beecher Stowe as author of *Uncle Tom's Cabin*).

"No more separate spheres" has recently become the rallying cry of nineteenth-century American literary history,[20] but a careful separate study of women authors' engagements with literary proprietorship is necessary on two grounds.[21] First, as my analysis of Greenwood's parodies suggests, the problematic status of women authors as proprietors provides an illuminating

18 Siva Vaidhyanathan, *Copyrights and Copywrongs: The Rise of Intellectual Property and How it Threatens Creativity* (New York: New York University Press, 2001).

19 Paula Bernat Bennett, *Poets in the Public Sphere: The Emancipatory Project of American Women's Poetry, 1800–1900* (Princeton: Princeton University Press, 2003).

20 See especially Lora Romero, *Home Fronts: Domesticity and Its Critics in the Antebellum United States* (Durham: Duke University Press, 1997); and "No More Separate Spheres," a special issue of *American Literature* (Sept. 1998), published with additional essays as *No More Separate Spheres: A Next Wave American Studies Reader*, ed. Cathy Davidson and Jessamyn Hatcher (Durham: Duke University Press, 2002). See also Monika Elbert, ed., *Separate Spheres No More: Gender Convergence in American Literature, 1830–1930* (Tuscaloosa: University of Alabama Press, 2000).

21 Carla Hesse, examining similar questions in the context of Revolutionary-era France, admirably defends the necessity of historical inquiry into the specific conditions of women's literary production against poststructuralist critique. "Reading Signatures: Female Authorship and Revolutionary Law in France, 1750–1850," *Eighteenth-Century Studies* 22, no. 3 (1989): 469–87.

angle for viewing the structures of a literary market only partially open to authorial proprietorship. Second, comparisons of the works and careers of men and women that fail to fully appreciate the specificity of women's experiences risk reproducing old critical dichotomies that remain intransigent despite decades of canon revision. For much of the twentieth century, the view prevailed in literary history that nineteenth-century women writers were scribblers, writers, or hacks and their works subliterary pabulum designed to cater to the debased tastes of a mass audience, while canonical male authors were truly "authors" and their texts complex and subtle works of art designed to challenge readers.[22] In his chapter on the copyright debates and authorship in antebellum America, Michael Newbury reproduces this dichotomy in his comparative reading of Poe, Hawthorne, and Fern. He reads Poe's "Purloined Letter" and Hawthorne's "Artist of the Beautiful" as subtle and creative meditations on the nature of literary property as not entirely reducible to commodity status, whereas he reads Fanny Fern's *Ruth Hall* as "radically conventional and even unimaginative in its understanding of literary value that seems to have no existence beyond the commercial terms of copyright."[23] Newbury even enlists Fanny Fern's prenuptial agreement with her third husband, James Parton, as evidence of her unimaginative acceptance of the commodification of literature by copyright law, proof that in Fern's mind, "literary property stands undifferentiated from other possessions."[24] Fern entered into such a prenuptial

22 On this critical tradition, see Paul Lauter, "Melville Climbs the Canon," *American Literature* 66, no. 1 (1994): 1–24 (and although I find Brodhead's terminology useful, in a number of ways, he participates in this critical tradition in *Cultures of Letters*). Romero also powerfully and succinctly limns these entrenched assumptions about women's popular authorship and the difficulties of not reinforcing these assumptions even in feminist criticism of women's works. *Home Fronts*, 71. However, she also argues that women writers and texts really *didn't* dominate the popular literary market, arguing instead that modern criticism has inaccurately replicated the nineteenth-century perception of a "flood" of women's texts and women's values overrunning the literary market (pp. 12–13). Her primary evidence for this revisionary claim is a statistic cited by David S. Reynolds. *Beneath the American Renaissance: The Subversive Imagination in the Age of Emerson and Melville* (Cambridge: Harvard University Press, 1988), 337–8. Reynolds's statistics are problematic in their own right, and Romero misrepresents them (e.g., Reynolds's makes a quantitative claim about percentages of male- and female-authored "volumes," which Romero takes to be a statistic about male and female authored "fiction"). I believe that it is possible to acknowledge *both* that women and their texts predominated *and* that such a phenomenon need not be interpreted negatively. I am more persuaded by Susan Coultrap-McQuin's summary of evidence of the centrality of women to the popular literary market, particularly fiction. *Doing Literary Business: American Women Writers in the Nineteenth Century* (Chapel Hill: University of North Carolina P, 1990), 2.

23 Newbury, *Figuring Authorship*, 193.

24 Ibid., 195. Newbury's criticism of Fern as unimaginative points to the continuing challenges of working on writers like Fern. He more easily locates complexity in Hawthorne and Poe, in part, because nearly a century of sustained critical attention (and the availability of multiple biographies, bibliographies, and editions of works and correspondence) makes that complexity more easily accessible and legible.

agreement so that she could maintain control of all of her property and assets, including her copyrights, after marriage (a situation never faced by male authors such as Poe and Hawthorne). To expect such an agreement to characterize her literary texts as anything other than property makes no sense. As Chapter 4 makes clear, such a reading fails to understand the complex interactions in Fern's career and works between literary proprietorship and married women's property law, settling instead for reinscribing a literary historical narrative that finds canonical male writers to be in opposition to the market while popular women are unthinkingly complicit.[25] For women such as Fern, their practices of engagement with the market, and especially with literary proprietorship, were differentiated from those of their male contemporaries precisely by their legal status as women. Far from being "unimaginative," Fern and her female peers deeply and imaginatively, if sometimes obliquely, engaged literary property issues in their careers and in their works in ways inextricably tied to their legal status as women.

This study begins with a chapter surveying and analyzing in more depth the theoretical and practical implications of married women's property law for women authors: "Authors, Wives, Slaves: Coverture, Copyright, and Authorial Dispossession, 1831–1869." Spanning decades and authors and using Mary Virginia Terhune's novel *Phemie's Temptation* (1868–1869) as a frame, I review the history of married women's property law, providing brief case studies of legal difficulties experienced by three authors (Mary Gove Nichols, Lydia Maria Child, and E. D. E. N. Southworth). Analyzing the overlapping rhetorics of feminist reformers (who claimed that the law "enslaved" married women to their husbands) and advocates of copyright reform (who saw authors as "enslaved" by readers who appropriated their literary property without remuneration), I place these concerns in a transatlantic context through a discussion of the participation of British women authors (particularly Lady Caroline Norton and Elizabeth Barrett Browning) in efforts to reform coverture in Great Britain. The popular feminist trope of the (white) wife as slave plays an important role in my reading of the legal situation of married women authors, but, as the in-depth case studies presented in the succeeding chapters amply demonstrate, the analogy between white married women and slaves was always misleading and incomplete because white married women had ways of exercising agency

25 I adopt the description of this binary as "opposition" versus "complicity" from a proposition in Meredith McGill's dissertation not included in her book: "Contrary to the image frequently summoned or assumed by critics, the market for books in antebellum America was not a monolithic, totalizing structure which demanded extremes of opposition or complicity. It was a remarkably differentiated set of practices, the configuration of which was the subject of considerable struggle." "Poe's Plagiarisms: Literary Property and the Authorial Self in Antebellum America," PhD diss., Johns Hopkins University, 1993, 3.

within the constraints of marriage unavailable to most black women, slave or free.

Chapter 2, "'Suited to the Market': Catharine Sedgwick, Female Authorship, and the Literary Property Debates, 1822–1842," features the only subject of this study who never married, Catharine Sedgwick. Examining Sedgwick's engagements with copyright advocacy in light of the ambiguous status of all women in the early nineteenth century (married and unmarried) as citizens of the American republic, this chapter considers the import of Sedgwick's decision to sign a petition to Congress in favor of international copyright in 1838 (she was the only American woman author to sign a petition to Congress on the subject of copyright reform before the Civil War). Following Sedgwick's career chronologically, the chapter reads Sedgwick's public and private constructions of herself as an author in the context of the copyright debates, arguing that Sedgwick helped to construct and then embraced a particular vision of republican authorship in sync with the logic of the existing law rather than in opposition to it. Responding to the sometimes conflicting discourses of literary nationalism and republican citizenship, she shifted her authorial ground in ways that allowed her to remain salable and relevant in a literary market that disenfranchised authors.

Chapter 3, "'When I Can Read My Title Clear': Harriet Beecher Stowe and the *Stowe v. Thomas* Copyright Infringement Case (1853)," turns from the international copyright debates to the law of infringement, analyzing Harriet Beecher Stowe's copyright suit against a Philadelphia publisher who published an unauthorized German translation of *Uncle Tom's Cabin* for the American market. Stowe publicly and privately denigrated and minimized her personal authorial agency in the composition of *Uncle Tom's Cabin*, representing herself as a passive conduit for divine truth compelled to speak for the benefit of slaves. The context of *Stowe v. Thomas*, however, reveals Stowe to be an aggressive proprietary author attempting to push the law further in support of authors' "rights" than any other American author had asked it to go before. Ironically, the judge who decided the case, Robert Grier, was also a prominent enforcer of the Fugitive Slave Law, and, I argue, Grier's opinion (especially its unusual incorporation of slave characters from the novel, Tom and Topsy, into its legal reasoning) was designed to undermine Stowe's authority and the abolitionist message of her novel. I consider the implications of Stowe's aggressively proprietary stance in relation to the social and economic critique of the marketplace offered in *Uncle Tom's Cabin*, and I read the novel as encoding Stowe's fantasies of an author's truly perfect and inviolable title to her literary "children."

Chapter 4, "'Every body sees the theft': Fanny Fern and Periodical Reprinting in the 1850s," turns from a legal dispute over rights to sell copies of a book to a literary market largely unregulated by copyright – the free-wheeling world of periodicals, a chaotic literary market that Fanny Fern negotiated as successfully as any other writer at midcentury. Although scholars have traditionally claimed that the rampant unauthorized reprinting of articles from one periodical to another made it difficult for authors to succeed professionally, Fanny Fern cleverly exploited the wide unauthorized circulation of her works through reprinting in locally and regionally circulated weeklies, building a national audience for her works that successfully enabled her to enter the more remunerative national book market. Once she had successfully negotiated the transition to the book market and stable proprietary authorship, however, Fern began to rewrite the history of her early career and her creative exploitation of reprinting. I argue that her autobiographical novel *Ruth Hall* was, in part, an attempt by Fern to anchor a stable authorial persona in the past to secure future proprietary claims.

Chapter 5, "A 'Rank Rebel' Lady and Her Literary Property: Augusta Jane Evans and Copyright, the Civil War and After, 1861–1868," serves as a companion piece to my chapter on Catharine Sedgwick and the antebellum international copyright debates. In it, I reconstruct Augusta Jane Evans's behind-the-scenes lobbying for passage of a copyright law in the Confederate States of America, including provisions for international copyright, exploring how by so doing, Evans sought to promote both a new Confederate literary nationalism and her own interests as a proprietary author. The publishing history of her arch-Confederate novel *Macaria* (published in Richmond in 1864 and republished quickly in New York and England) further situates Evans as a proprietary author both negotiating her interests in the Confederacy and attempting to negotiate her interests in the North, a region that she and other Confederates insisted was a separate, foreign nation. After Southern defeat, Evans reintegrated herself into U.S. culture by producing a new literary property, her hugely successful novel *St. Elmo*. My reconstruction of Evans's activities during the 1860s reveals that Evans was a canny player in the literary field, who understood and exploited the possibilities of shifting national narratives shaped by copyright law. Furthermore, by including Evans and the Confederate States of America, I throw into sharp relief the ideological underpinnings of U.S. copyright law and the gendered and racialized implications of its proprietary logic.

In Chapters 3, 4, and 5, the legal status of married women recurs as a shaping force in each woman's engagements with literary property. Calvin Stowe, not Harriet Beecher Stowe, was the plaintiff in *Stowe v. Thomas*. Fanny Fern's estranged second husband makes an important (and unwelcome) appearance at the height of her newly won success as an author, and, as I mentioned earlier, she made special legal arrangements with her third husband that protected her ability to own and control her literary property after that marriage. The contrasting marriage plots of Augusta Evans's novels illuminate her own decision to become Mrs. Lorenzo Wilson shortly after the stunning success of *St. Elmo*, a novel whose heroine is both a single woman and a popular author for most of the novel, but who, in the final pages, marries and, at her husband's direction, forswears authorship.

In the epilogue, I bring back Mary Virginia Terhune, author of *Phemie's Temptation*, to reflect on an 1892 Supreme Court decision, *Belford v. Scribner.* Well after statutory reform supposedly made the question of whether or not a married woman could own and control property separately from her husband a moot point, the Supreme Court was asked to decide whether or not Terhune's transfer of one of her copyrights to her publisher many years before was valid without the consent of her husband. Although the U.S. Congress passed the International Copyright Act in 1891 and state legislatures had passed laws allegedly making coverture obsolete, *Belford v. Scribner* points to the persistence of the intersection between coverture and copyright. From the vantage point of this dispute, I briefly look forward from 1892 to consider the implications of my study for literary history and for the future of copyright law in the twenty-first century.

The events that feature prominently in my case studies (particularly in my chapters on Stowe, Fern, Evans, and Terhune) do not appear at all in *Private Woman, Public Stage*, Mary Kelley's influential collective biography of a group of nineteenth-century women popular novelists and their perceptions of themselves as authors, even though all of my primary figures are also primary figures in her study. One can find few or no traces of the events I reconstruct and analyze in the authors' diaries and letters that are the primary source materials of Kelley's study (in the case of Augusta Evans, Evans used letters artfully and strategically to obscure her proprietary activities, traces of which can be found in other print and manuscript sources). Kelley emphasizes the conflict women writers felt between their domestic values and the values of the marketplace – a conflict which, in Kelley's reading, led women to attempt to deny and disguise their very public roles as producers of culture. Reframed in the context of the constructions of authorship produced in the copyright debates, even such denials take on a very different resonance than they do in Kelley's study (see especially my analysis of Catharine Sedgwick). In *Doing Literary Business* (1990), Susan Coultrap-McQuin examines the careers of some of the same writers as Kelley (and shares only one primary figure in common with my study, Harriet Beecher Stowe), but she emphasizes the affinity between women writers and the market, arguing that the market may have been more congenial to women writers than to men, especially in the 1850s and 1860s. Drawing on correspondence between female authors and their publishers, Coultrap-McQuin finds that these women experienced the market as a sort of domestic space in which they visited their "gentlemen publishers," who they believed were paternalistic friends protecting their interests.

In the interstices between these two interpretations of women's experiences of authorship, I locate a productive friction in women's engagements with the market, engagements mediated both by copyright law and by laws affecting the status of women. Coverture as a legal doctrine and an ideology shaped the status of all nonslave women, and as a result, women authors faced challenges not faced by their male peers. However, the intersection between coverture and copyright proved both limiting *and* productive for women authors, with the same legal limits against which each woman struggled also providing opportunities for success within the system that constrained her. The effects of this gendered legal nexus were, however, far from uniform, with each woman's experiences shaped by her particular circumstances, as well as by shifting attitudes about the function of literature and the role of women in American culture.

Drawing on scholarship in literary, legal, cultural, and book history, as well as a wide variety of nineteenth-century sources (including legal decisions and court records, legal treatises, newspaper and magazine articles, books and pamphlets, government documents, publishers' catalogs, copyright registration records, and authors' letters), I seek to reconstruct the complex discursive and material web that both enabled and constrained each woman's authorship. In the process, I shuttle back and forth between the overstuffed universe of public discourse on the topics of literary and married women's property and a careful, factual reconstruction of each woman's activities. In reconstructing both public debates and authorial activities, I aim to recover how readers and the authors themselves understood and interpreted women's authorial proprietorship. These reconstructions contribute to literary history both transferable insights about the cultural meanings of authorship in nineteenth-century America and more local, factual knowledge about each woman's career. Scholarship on nineteenth-century American women authors has relied too frequently on unsubstantiated anecdotes, reminiscences, and received wisdom rather than on research into available sources contemporaneous to important events. Anecdotes and reminiscences can be revealing – for instance, the anecdote that Stowe said "God wrote" *Uncle Tom's Cabin* tells us a great deal about how some nineteenth-century reading publics interpreted Stowe's authorship, and publisher J. C. Derby's reminiscence about how Augusta Jane Evans's novel *Macaria* came to be "pirated" in the North during the Civil War reveals how Northern readers constructed Evans as an author after the South's defeat. However, interpretation of and theorizing concerning the cultural meanings of women's authorship and texts should be built on research into contemporaneous sources rather than on anecdote alone – my reconstruction of Stowe's role as a plaintiff in *Stowe v. Thomas* uncovers the ways that Stowe and others understood her agency as the author of *Uncle Tom's Cabin* quite differently than the "God wrote the book" anecdote suggests, and Derby's tale conceals far more than it reveals about Evans's proprietary activities during the war.

In the course of each case study, I practice my craft as a literary critic and historian by reading literary texts backward and forward as emanations from the structures of copyright and property law and as commentary on them. In this respect, I follow in the footsteps of McGill (especially her readings of Dickens's *American Notes for General Circulation* and Hawthorne's *House of the*

Seven Gables) and Newbury.[26] In *No Trespassing: Authorship, Intellectual Property Rights, and the Boundaries of Globalization*, Eva Hemmungs Wirtén has advocated that literary critics and historians engage in what she characterizes as "a reading of legal doctrine as cultural text,"[27] and in my interpretation of legal doctrine, I often read it as text encoding broad ideological and cultural meanings. However, as someone who trained and worked for many years as a paralegal, I believe that it is equally important to understand how legal doctrine worked on the ground in ways that distinguish it from other forms of cultural text. That is, I seek to understand how individual actors experienced and negotiated legal doctrine in their attempts to achieve particular ends. My understanding of the pragmatics of the law resembles that of legal historian Hendrik Hartog as he articulates it in *Man and Wife in America*, his history of nineteenth-century marriage and divorce. He identifies the responses of particular husbands and wives to shifting legal doctrines as "improvisations," but not as entirely free improvisations. Rather, reciprocal exchanges between individuals and the law produce these improvisations. Thus, in Hartog's view, both inside and outside the courtroom, husbands and wives "were coerced and molded in the law as they molded and transformed themselves."[28] In court, judges and lawyers similarly "had to improvise solutions to immediate and intractable conflicts, using the imperfect materials of an inherited and changing legal order."[29] Thus I map out a broader theory of how the convergence of these two sets of legal doctrine, copyright and coverture, symbolically constructed The Woman Author, but I also reconstruct the improvisational responses of individual women authors (as well as their husbands and their lawyers) on and against this ground of legal doctrine. The authors whose lives and works I analyze in the following pages shared a legal and cultural status as (white) women, but within such structures, each performed the role of "lady-writer" differently, belying the assumption that there was a single authorial mode practice by women in the antebellum United States.

26 See also Paul K. Saint-Amour's description of his method in his analysis of late nineteenth- and early twentieth-century British texts, analyzing "copyright's presence *within* literary texts" rather than as something primarily external to the texts and regulating their circulation and evaluation. *The Copywrights: Intellectual Property and the Literary Imagination* (Ithaca: Cornell University Press, 2004), 12.

27 Eva Hemmungs Wirtén, *No Trespassing: Authorship, Intellectual Property Rights, and the Boundaries of Globalization* (Toronto: University of Toronto Press, 2004), 13.

28 Hendrik Hartog, *Man and Wife in America: A History* (Cambridge: Harvard University Press, 2000), 2.

29 Ibid., 4.

Chapter 1

Authors, Wives, Slaves: Coverture, Copyright, and Authorial Dispossession, 1831–1869

In Mary Virginia Hawes Terhune's novel *Phemie's Temptation* (serialized in 1868 in *Godey's Lady's Book* under the less provocative title of *Phemie Rowland*, published in book form in 1869, and published in both instances under her long-time pseudonym "Marion Harland"), the intersection of two forms of property law, the law of coverture and the law of copyright, drives the novel's plot.[1] The eponymous heroine's bankrupt husband, James Hart, abandons her, and in order to support herself and her daughter, she resumes the career as an author she had abandoned when she married. As she begins to put a new life together for herself, Phemie faces the intersection between her legal disabilities under the common law doctrine of coverture and her literary proprietorship in an extreme form. Not only is James Hart her husband, he is also her publisher. Early in her marriage, without her husband's prior knowledge or consent, she publishes a novel under the pseudonym "Epsilon," hoping he will be pleased after the fact. Instead, he is outraged. Her husband's publishing house, through his partner Mallory, published Phemie's book without Mallory knowing the identity of "Epsilon" (although Mallory does find out after Phemie reveals her authorship to her husband). After Hart absconds and Mallory fails to produce the royalties due to Phemie for the considerable sales of the book, Joe Bonny, her sister's husband, suggests that she sue. Her friend Miss Darcy (a spinster, an advocate of women's rights, a writer, and a magazine editor) explains Phemie's dilemma this

1 Although Terhune consistently published under the pseudonym "Marion Harland," her true identity was widely known. For the sake of consistency and to accurately reflect her legal identity in her engagements with the law of copyright in the period after her marriage to the Reverend Edward Payson Terhune, I will refer to her as "Terhune" throughout. She and her works are included in Nina Baym, *Woman's Fiction: A Guide to Novels by and About Women in America, 1820–1870* (Ithaca: Cornell University Press, 1978); Mary Kelley, *Private Woman, Public Stage: Literary Domesticity in Nineteenth-Century America* (New York: Oxford University Press, 1984); and Elizabeth Moss, *Domestic Novelists in the Old South: Defenders of Southern Culture* (Baton Rouge: Louisiana State University Press, 1992). For her relationship to slavery, abolitionism, and the Union, see Moss, Terhune's own autobiography (*Marion Harland's Autobiography* [New York: Harper & Brothers, 1910]); Karen Manners Smith, "Marion Harland: The Making of a Household Word," PhD diss., University of Massachusetts, 1990 (also treating extensively her relations with her husband); Smith, "Half My Heart in Dixie: Southern Identity and the Civil War in the Writings of Mary Virginia Terhune," in *Beyond Image and Convention: Explorations in Southern Women's History*, ed. Janet L. Coryell et al. (Columbia: University of Missouri Press, 1998), 119–37; and Elizabeth R. Varon, *We Mean to Be Counted: White Women and Politics in Antebellum Virginia* (Chapel Hill: University of North Carolina Press, 1998).

way: "[W]hom does she prosecute? Her husband, as one of the firm who defrauded her. And if he were not concerned in any manner in the iniquitous transaction, she could not sue the authors of the injury. The prosecution must originate with him."[2] After a lengthy digression calling for reform of the married women's property laws right out of feminist reform literature (complete with a vignette of a poor laundress whose drunken husband steals all of her wages), Miss Darcy returns to Phemie's particular case: "Mr. Hart should bring a suit against those who have ploughed with his heifer, and kept back her hire from his lordly palm; but when the unrighteous husbandmen are the respectable firm of Mallory & Hart, the complication is more than discouraging. It is simply and ludicrously hopeless!" (p. 235).

To my knowledge, there were no actual instances in nineteenth-century America in which a married woman author's situation was quite so ludicrously and intricately hopeless as that of Phemie, a married woman abandoned by a man who is both her husband and her publisher; but by pushing her fictional situation to the logical extremes of the law, Terhune exposes the ludicrous logic of far more mundane marital situations. Terhune herself suffered no such conflicts with her own husband, who was a Presbyterian minister, not a publisher, and who never attempted to interfere with the literary career that she had established before their marriage or with her management of her literary properties. Terhune, like many married women writers, claimed the legal benefits of copyright for herself and thus seemingly asserted herself as full legal subject capable of owning property; however, as her novelization of a married woman author's literary proprietorship demonstrates with excruciating clarity, Terhune simultaneously confronted her own disappearance into the single legal subject of marriage, her husband. If possession of a legally recognizable self was a prerequisite to acquiring and holding property, could a married woman legally own the literary property she created? If, as Terhune describes the relationship between Hart and Phemie, implicitly invoking the language of master and slave, "he was her legal proprietor" (p. 296) – and she was thus his property, his "heifer" (p. 235) – could Phemie (or any other married woman author, since married women were little more than property in marriage) own literary property?

Although the answer to these questions is a qualified no, it is precisely dispossession rather than secure possession that characterized authorship in nineteenth-century America. American authors were not "lords" in secure possession of property and able to sue to protect proprietary interests. They were, in the absence of international copyright, unlordly lords with no right to recover damages when others ploughed with their heifers outside the national boundaries of the United States. In the extreme case of Phemie

2 Mary Virginia Terhune, *Phemie's Temptation* (New York: Carleton, 1869), 234. Hereinafter cited in the text.

as an author, this dispossession occurs even within the boundaries of the American nation, where she is the heifer who cannot even sue for self-protection against the man who "owns" her.

This chapter maps out the gendered legal terrain of literary proprietorship in nineteenth-century America, the bumpy and shifting terrain over which Terhune herself traveled over the nearly twenty years of her career before textualizing it in *Phemie's Temptation* and over which she continued to travel for twenty more years. A number of recent critical studies have analyzed coverture in relation to women's literature of the period, as a structure of female subjectivity for both authors and readers, as an explicit subject of literary texts that aim to motivate reform, and as a legal condition affecting women authors.[3] However, such studies have not fully engaged the complexities of both copyright law and married women's property law as they intersected in the larger culture and in the careers of particular authors. In an attempt to reconstruct these intersections as both experienced by women authors and perceived by the larger culture, I necessarily shift between legal technicalities and larger theorizing, between the behind-the-scenes mundanities of publishing contracts and copyright registrations and the public debates over the status of married women and the status of authors under the American law. The chapter begins with a brief analysis of the place of gender in the antebellum international copyright debates and a discussion of the specifics of married women's property law and modern scholarly debates about the law and its reform. This overview lays the groundwork for an analysis of coverture and copyright in the lives of three antebellum women writers, Lydia Maria Child, Mary Gove Nichols, and E. D. E. N. Southworth. From this analysis of the largely private experiences of three women, I return to the public debates over international copyright and the ways that copyright advocates figured (white male) authors in the absence of international copyright as "enslaved" to readers.

Phemie's Temptation is a key text in this chapter because it makes the intersection between coverture and copyright the subject of explicit public

3 On the early American novel as "privileging the *feme covert*," see Cathy N. Davidson, *Revolution and the Word: The Rise of the Novel in America* (New York: Oxford University Press, 1986), chap. 6. For coverture as enforcing a sense of female disembodiment and thus driving women authors and readers to seek the pleasures of embodiment through the scenes of masochism in sentimental fiction, see Marianne Noble, *The Masochistic Pleasures of Sentimental Literature* (Princeton: Princeton University Press, 2000). For Elizabeth Stoddard's short-circuiting of the intersection between coverture and copyright by theorizing an alternative economy of authorship, see Ellen Weinauer, "Alternative Economies: Authorship and Ownership in Elizabeth Stoddard's 'Collected by a Valetudinarian'," *Studies in American Fiction* 25, no. 2 (1997): 167–82. For women's literary texts as advocating reform, see Paula Bernat Bennett, *Poets in the Public Sphere: The Emancipatory Project of American Women's Poetry, 1800–1900* (Princeton: Princeton University Press, 2003), chap. 2; and Barbara A. Bardes and Suzanne Gossett, *Declarations of Independence: Women and Political Power in Nineteenth-Century American Fiction* (New Brunswick: Rutgers University Press, 1990), chap. 3.

analysis. Most married women authors (at least in the United States) who actually experienced the sort of marital rupture experienced by Phemie kept such ruptures private, making the results of such ruptures the subject of gossip and speculation rather than a platform for reformist rhetoric. Terhune's happy marriage was widely publicized, and no reader would have been in danger of thinking that the novel represented her life. Readers may, however, have been rightly tempted to read the novel as a roman à clef about some other woman author, particularly Terhune's fellow popular novelist E. D. E. N. Southworth, whose tragic history as a deserted wife was part of her public persona (even if the desertion was only obliquely hinted at). There being no clearly public factual analogue to the fictional Phemie, the situation of women authors was largely absent from both the literary property debates and the married women's property debates. Instead, in discussions of copyright reform, all authors are assumed to be men, and in discussions of married women's property reform, the female victims of the law labor at everything but literature and the properties seized by their husbands are everything but copyrights.[4]

Despite this relative scarcity of public analysis, no married woman author could avoid such an analysis in private, and this publicly unarticulated yet powerfully present intersection between coverture and copyright structures possibilities for reading the situation of American authorship in the nineteenth century. Before I return to *Phemie's Temptation* at this chapter's conclusion, I consider the instructively different situation in England, where poet Lady Caroline Norton made her disastrously unhappy marriage and her conflicts with her husband over her literary properties the subject of public comment. In her pleas for reform of the laws of coverture, divorce, and child custody, she detailed her conflicts with her husband at great length and explicitly analogized her legal status as a married woman author to that of an American slave. *Phemie's Temptation* similarly demonstrates that the intersection between coverture and copyright inescapably circuited through the popular trope of the (white) wife as slave, but with significantly different results in the American context than in the British.

The trope of the (white) wife as slave has a long and contested history, and the accuracy of the underlying analogy continues to be the subject of scholarly debate. As Karen Sánchez-Eppler rightly observes, even when abolitionist feminists expressed their sympathy with slaves, their claims of a common experience of dispossession and abuse at the hands of white men

4 The intersection of patent law and coverture represents a striking contrast, with feminist reformers specifically calling for reform and married women's patent proprietorship made the subject of special legislation in several states. Zorina B. Khan, "Married Women's Property Laws and Female Commercial Activity: Evidence from United States Patent Records, 1790–1895," *Journal of Economic History* 56, no.2 (1996): 363. See also Anne L. Macdonald, *Feminine Ingenuity: Women and Invention in America* (New York: Ballantine, 1992).

generally "tend toward asymmetry and exploitation," making the experiences of slaves a pretext for protest against the oppression of white women.[5] Diane Roberts observes of this dynamic that by employing the slave-wife analogy to attempt to write themselves "out of a kind of slavery," white women have "sometimes tried to write black slaves out of slavery as well."[6] Terhune was neither a feminist nor an abolitionist, and her use of the trope clearly serves to write black slaves out of slavery. Terhune wrote *Phemie* after the Union victory in the Civil War and the emancipation of the slaves. Born and raised in Virginia in a Whig family, she moved North when her Northern husband accepted a call to a church in New Jersey, and during the war she supported the Union. However, she did not support abolition, and she indignantly portrays Phemie as her husband's chattel not to protest the injustice of the abolished institution of chattel slavery (she did not believe the institution to be unjust – at least when the chattel were persons of African descent in the southern states). Instead, she figures Phemie as a slave-wife in protest against a white woman of culture and education like Phemie being treated as little more than property. And, ultimately, despite her obvious indignation, Terhune seems unable to narrate Phemie's "emancipation" from marriage. As I discuss in greater detail at the close of this chapter, having brought together the figures of author, wife, and slave in the person of Phemie, Terhune cannot separate them. This inextricable tangle speaks not only to the dispossession of married women authors by the law but to the cultural power paradoxically conferred on (white) women authors by their status as nonproprietary subjects in a nation that refused to grant full status as proprietors to authors.

"[N]o property [is] more peculiarly a man's own than that which is produced by the labour of his mind" and "[T]he husband and the wife are regarded as one person": Authors, wives, and property law

From the origins of copyright law and continuing into the nineteenth century, writing women had a problematic relation to the analogies and metaphors used to explain and justify the legal protection of literary texts as property. As Mark Rose has argued, in eighteenth-century England, those who successfully advocated for the creation of statutory copyright relied on John Locke's theory of the origins of property to explain and justify authorial proprietorship. In Locke's theory, the foundation of all property

5 Karen Sánchez-Eppler, *Touching Liberty: Abolition, Feminism, and the Politics of the Body* (Berkeley: University of California Press, 1993), 15.

6 Diane Roberts, *The Myth of Aunt Jemima: Representations of Race and Region* (London: Routledge, 1994), 6–7.

and of government is each person's property in his own person. That self-possession then allows a man to acquire property through his labors: "The *Labour* of his Body, and the *Work* of his Hands, we may say, are properly his. Whatsoever then he removes out of the State that Nature hath provided, and left it in, he hath mixed his *Labour* with, and joyned to it something that is his own, and thereby makes it his *Property*."[7] Thus, according to Locke, man acquired property rights by mixing his labor with common materials, and civil government had a fundamental duty to protect those property rights acquired through labor. Advocates of copyright transformed Locke's laboring body and hands into the author's laboring mind. Similarly, they transformed Locke's material objects removed from the state of nature and made a man's own through physical labor (such as trees transformed into lumber to build a house) into words and ideas from the common store transformed by the author's intellectual labors of invention, arrangement, and selection into works of literature.

The Lockean influence on copyright law survived the Atlantic crossing and dominated much analysis of copyright in the nineteenth-century United States, particularly analysis supporting an expansion of legal protection for authors as proprietors. Several of the copyright statutes passed by the individual states during the early 1780s before the ratification of the U.S. Constitution clearly reflect this Lockean heritage (and the masculine bias inhering in that heritage). Adopting and adapting Locke's language and ideas, the prologues to the statutes proclaim, with slight variations in language, their rationale for granting legal protection to literary property:

> As the improvement of knowledge, the progress of civilization, and the advancement of human happiness, greatly depend on the efforts of ingenious persons in the various arts and sciences; as the principal encouragement of such persons can have to make great and beneficial exertions of this nature, must consist in the legal security of the fruits of their study and industry to themselves; and as such security is one of the natural rights of all men, there being no property more peculiarly a *man*'s own than that which is produced by the labour of *his* mind.[8] [emphasis added]

One might argue that the drafters of this statute intended the masculine pronoun to be generic and inclusive. However, the drafters of New York's

7 Mark Rose, *Authors and Owners: The Invention of Copyright* (Cambridge: Harvard University Press, 1993), 5.

8 All statutes relevant to this study are collected in Thorvald Solberg, ed., *Copyright Enactments of the United States, 1783–1906* (Washington, DC: Government Printing Office, 1906). The quoted language is from New Hampshire Act of 1783 (p. 18). Close variants are the Massachusetts Act of 1783 (p. 14) and Rhode Island of 1783 (p. 19). For an abbreviated Lockean prologue, see the North Carolina Act of 1785 (p. 25).

copyright statute clearly signal their belief that such language was not inclusive and that their statute should similarly "encourage" women to produce by specifying that an author might be a "he" or a "she":

> Whereas it is agreeable to the principles of natural equity and justice that every author should be secured in receiving the profits that may arise from the sale of *his or her* works; and such security may encourage persons of learning and genius to publish their writings, which may do honour to their country and service to mankind.[9] [emphasis added]

While "mankind" as the object of authorial beneficence is inclusive, the statute's drafters understood that "he" and "his" with reference to "author" required the supplement of "she" and "her" in order to unambiguously secure proprietary rights to women authors.

In his famous *Commentaries on American Law*, first published more than four decades after these state copyright statutes, American jurist James Kent clearly shows the influence of Locke's principles in his analysis of copyright. In his analysis of the law of personal property, Kent observes that the laws of "civilized" societies have severely limited the circumstances under which a man may lay claim to property by virtue of "original acquisition"; instead, most men in civilized societies acquire property through transfer of the title from one man to another.[10] Kent places copyrights and patents under the category of "Original acquisition by intellectual labor," commenting, "It is just that they [ingenious men] should enjoy the pecuniary profits resulting from mental as well as bodily labour."[11] While recognizing the limits that statutory copyright places on the author's property rights in his published works, he describes the author's right in his manuscript as both natural and reasonable: "It is clearly the author's exclusive right, inasmuch as it is created by his own labor and invention; and the reason and moral sense of mankind acquiesce in the solidity of the title."[12]

As Ellen Weinauer writes of such formulations of the author as a Lockean possessive individual, "By codifying literary labor *as* labor, copyright laws effectively ratified the author's status as a proprietary subject. Secure title to the literary text meant secure title to the self."[13] As Kent makes clear in his larger analysis of property law, however, at the common law under the

9 Ibid., 29. New York's statute, passed on 29 April 1786, was the last such pre-Constitution state statute.

10 *Commentaries on American Law*, 2nd ed. 4 vols. (New York: O. Halstead, 1832), II:355–6. Because Kent does not include the sentence (discussed later) about the "solidity" of the author's title in the first edition of the treatise (the first volume of which appeared in 1826), I quote from the second edition, the first in which this sentence appears. Perhaps the very early public debates about the desirability of international copyright spurred by the 1830 copyright term extension prompted him to be more adamant in his support of copyright.

11 Ibid., II:366.

12 Ibid., II:280.

13 Weinauer, "Alternative Economies," 169.

doctrine of coverture, married women are not "persons" capable of acquiring property, either by original acquisition or by transfer. Paraphrasing English jurist William Blackstone's influential summary of the common law tradition, Kent infamously claims that "the husband and the wife are regarded as one person, and her legal existence and authority [are] in a degree lost or suspended, during the continuance of the matrimonial union."[14] As one legal historian has remarked of this formulation, "Essentially, husband and wife were one flesh; but the man was the owner of that flesh."[15] A married woman who wrote was thus doubly barred from access to the status of proprietary subject – she could not claim her literary labors as her own, nor could the property produced by those labors, legally recognized or not, ratify her status as proprietary subject because title to that literary property vested in her husband, not her.

Kent does not bring together his analyses of the legal logics of coverture and copyright, leaving his legal narrative of the origins of literary property and its implicitly masculine creator undisturbed by the potentially disruptive figure of the writing woman. The 1831 domestic copyright act, which extended the right to renew copyright registrations to an author's heirs, more explicitly wrote the masculine gendered author into the law in two ways. First, throughout the act, the masculine pronoun "he" appears with "the person entitled to protection by this act" as its referent (and, indeed, Congress consistently used the masculine pronoun in this way for the remainder of the century). Second, the act specifies that "the widow, or child, or children" of a deceased author were the heirs entitled to exercise the right to renew the copyright registration for a second fourteen-year term after the expiration of the initial twenty-eight-year term.[16] Although the word "widow" potentially applied equally to male and female surviving spouses, the committee report in support of the act leaves no doubt as to the gender identity of that imagined surviving spouse, reasoning that "by the very event of the death of the author, *his* family stand in more need of the only means of subsistence ordinarily left to them" (emphasis added).[17] The committee assumes that the death of a wife will not disturb a husband and father's economic status, but that a woman who loses her

14 James Kent, *Commentaries on American Law*, 1st ed. (New York: O. Halstead, 1827), II:109.

15 Lawrence M. Friedman, *A History of American Law*, 2nd ed. (New York: Touchstone/Simon & Schuster, 1985), 208.

16 Solberg, *Copyright Enactments*, 37–8. The masculine pronoun similarly appears in earlier federal acts, as well as in pre-Constitution state laws, with the exception of New York (as discussed earlier). Note that this gender-specific language does *not* appear in the patent act, which is both specific and inclusive in its pronouns: "That upon the petition of any person or persons that he, she, or they, hath invented or discovered any useful art, . . . it shall be lawful . . . to cause letters patent to be made out in the name of the United States." United States Patent Act of April 1790, quoted in Khan, "Married Women's Property," 365.

17 House Committee on the Judiciary, *Copyright*, 21st Cong., 2nd sess., 10 Dec. 1830, H. Rep. 3, 1.

author-husband has no means to feed and clothe her family, except royalties earned from the continuing sales of her dead husband's works. While Congress needed to specify that the widow of a male author had the right to renew her dead husband's copyright, the surviving husband of a dead female author needed no such congressional intervention because his wife's copyrights were, in the case of most marriages in 1831, always his in the first place. The congressional committee played knight errant to helpless widows and children of male authors in need of protection, but it failed to account for women who themselves might be authors and for the effects of disruptions of marital unity caused by events other than the death of a husband. It is precisely such a disruption to marital unity that befalls the fictional Phemie and that befell actual women authors in less extreme forms.

So what, legally speaking, was the status of a married woman author under the laws of coverture and copyright? When Harriet Beecher Stowe began publicly supporting women's suffrage and reform of married women's property laws after the Civil War, she succinctly summarized the legal disabilities suffered by married women whose identities coverture obliterated by invoking the standard slave-wife analogy of feminist reform rhetoric. In an article published in 1869 (the year that *Phemie* was issued in book form) in *Hearth and Home*, a periodical she also edited, Stowe describes how under the common law of coverture inherited from English legal tradition

> the position of a married woman . . . is, in many respects, precisely similar to that of the negro slave. She can make no contract and hold no property; whatever she inherits or earns becomes at that moment the property of her husband, who can take and use her wages without consulting her. Her children are not (in law) *her* children, but *his* – he can separate them from her, and put them under the guardianship of any other woman he may choose. Though he acquired a fortune through her, or though she earn [*sic*] a fortune through her talents, he is sole master of it, and she cannot draw a penny. . . . In the law of slavery, a human being is considered as a *thing* simply; but in the English common law a married woman is nothing at all. She passes out of legal existence.[18]

Stowe, like other advocates for the statutory reform of the status of married women, invoked the slave-wife analogy in order to disrupt the "one flesh" trope of the common law coverture tradition. By analogizing the legal situation of the married woman (a "generic" woman often clearly assumed to be white) to that of a slave, while analogizing her husband to a slave master, advocates of reform demonstrated with painful clarity the ways in which married women could be the objects of abuse by their husbands rather than being merged into them, even as the law insisted that wives did not exist separately from their husbands and thus could not be abused in this way.

18 Harriet Beecher Stowe, "The Woman Question," *Hearth and Home*, 7 Aug. 1869, 520–1.

The story of the married woman as slave or nonentity entirely at the mercy of an abusive, spendthrift husband, while dramatic and appealing as an instrument of feminist reform, was, in some respects, a caricature. As legal historian Hendrik Hartog argues, feminist reformers intentionally misrepresented coverture as "descriptive of social reality" rather than as a legal fiction, a misrepresentation that "animated the law with demonic power."[19] Instead, Hartog argues, "The merger – the near obliteration of the female self – implicit in the oneness of 'one flesh' was always contradictory and inconclusive in the law, radically incomplete. If wives became their husbands' property legally, it was in a more complicated sense than the apparent analogies to trees and fields and pets and slaves that both feminist and misogynist literature raised" (p. 135). "Wives were never things in the law," he cautions his readers; "dependent, unequal, subordinate, surely. Often legally unable to act as competent legal subjects. At the same time, a wife always remained a person in the law, separable from her husband" (p. 125). One of the most powerful proofs of the inaccuracy of the slave-wife analogy is the law of marriage as it applied, or rather did not apply, to slaves. A slave could never be a wife – or a husband – under the law (p. 93). A "wife" did have a separate, if limited, legal status under the law as a person, and slave women had no access to that legal status.

Stowe's dramatic and damning summary of the law presents the effects of the common law of coverture in its purest form, but as Stowe also acknowledges elsewhere in her article, statutory reform of the common law had been in progress for decades by 1869 on a state-by-state basis – the first wave of reform occurred primarily in the 1840s, and such reforms were largely complete by 1870 in the northern states and by the 1880s in the South. Stowe asks her readers to educate themselves about the laws in their own states and to recognize their indebtedness to the work of feminist reformers. Before statutory reform of coverture, the primary instrument for recognizing this status of wives as separate persons was the law of equity. However, Stowe does not account for these exceptions, which the U.S. law inherited from the English legal tradition along with coverture.[20] Courts exercising their equitable rather than legal jurisdiction carved out many exceptions to the

19 Hendrik Hartog, *Man and Wife in America: A History* (Cambridge: Harvard University Press, 2000), 123. Hereinafter cited in the text.

20 Two complex exceptions to coverture also existed at the common law, the concepts of "dower" (for wives) and "curtesy" (for husbands). However, these doctrines applied to real property, not personal property, and dower rights had little effect on women while they were still married. The doctrines would not have applied to a married woman's literary properties that came into existence either before or after she contracted marriage. For discussions of dower and curtesy, see Marylynn Salmon, *Women and the Law of Property in Early America* (Chapel Hill: University of North Carolina Press, 1986), chaps. 2 and 7, and Norma Basch, *In the Eyes of the Law: Women, Marriage and Property in Nineteenth-Century New York* (Ithaca: Cornell University Press, 1982), chap. 2.

legal fiction of marital unity under the common law. As Joseph Story notes in his influential *Commentaries on Equity Jurisprudence* (1836), courts of equity "for many purposes, treat the husband and wife, as the Civil Law treats them, as distinct persons, capable (in a limited sense) of contracting with each other, of suing each other, and having separate estates, debts, and interests."[21] Prior to marriage, a man and his intended wife could agree to allow the woman as wife ownership of a "separate estate," property reserved for her own use, and equity courts would enforce such contracts (courts also allowed third parties, normally the wife's blood relations, but sometimes also the husband, to "settle" property "on the wife" for her sole use before or after marriage). Through such an agreement, a husband could also allow his wife to conduct business independently as a "*feme sole* trader" (a *feme sole* being the common law term for an unmarried woman); in addition, a court in equity could confer such feme sole trader status on a woman whose husband had abandoned her.[22] As long as a marriage continued to function to the satisfaction of both parties, even such sharply defined legal exceptions to marital unity might be beside the point if a husband chose not to exercise the power over his wife that the law allowed. As the example of Mary Virginia Terhune's marriage attests and as Hartog argues more broadly, the law vested such rights in a man as a husband, but the law did not compel him to actually exercise those rights within the private sphere of marriage (p. 109).

As legal historian Norma Basch notes, however, all of the equitable exceptions to coverture required the married woman to be "consistently dependent on others: on her husband, for an antenuptial agreement, on relatives for a trust estate, and on the state in abandonment, separation, and divorce."[23] Furthermore, as feminist contract theorist Carole Pateman notes, arguments such as Hartog's tend to "confuse examples of married couples with the *institution* of marriage.... [E]ven if a husband renounces his power, his wife's freedom is always contingent on his willingness to continue the

21 *Commentaries on Equity Jurisprudence*, 2 vols. (Boston: Hilliard, Gray & Co., 1836), II:597.

22 Tapping Reeve, *The Law of Baron and Femme; of Parent and Child; of Guardian and Ward; of Master and Servant; and of the Powers of the Courts of Chancery* (New Haven: Oliver Steele, 1816), 182; John Edward Bright, *A Treatise on the Law of Husband and Wife, as Respects Property*, ed. Ralph Lockwood, 2 vols. (New York: Banks, Gould & Co., 1850), chap. 9, sec. 1. As Reeve notes, however, the husband's consent is necessary because "it would operate as a fraud upon her intended husband, and disappoint his just expectations" to set herself up to do business on her own account (although his consent may be assumed "if she do so openly, and with his knowledge, and he marries her") (p. 182). As Richard H. Chused points out, states did not uniformly recognize equity law, and many did not create chancery courts, a form of specialized equity courts. In such states, equity was dispensed by law courts, or even by state legislatures, which passed private legislation regulating matters such as feme sole trader status or equitable settlements for the benefit of married women. "Married Women's Property Law: 1800–1850," *Georgetown Law Journal* 71 (1983): 1368–72, 1384–97.

23 Basch, *In the Eyes of the Law*, 27.

renunciation."[24] Even women such as Terhune, who appear to have lived their lives and managed their literary affairs with a great deal of freedom and autonomy, were doubly dependent on the continuing goodwill of their husbands. While property might be settled on a woman after marriage, she had no independent power to contract with her husband after she was married. Even if a husband and wife privately agreed after marriage to allow the wife to control property during her coverture, if the couple separated, courts routinely declined to enforce such contracts on the ground that, the wife's legal existence being suspended during her coverture, a court could not enforce a nonexistent contract between a husband and himself. Courts could only enforce such arrangements if the husband created a trust for his wife's benefit and granted her power to control the property included in that trust. Once the states enacted statutory reforms that (at least hypothetically) made these limited equitable exceptions to coverture accessible to all without special contractual provisions or the creation of trusts, courts across the country nevertheless interpreted the statutes very narrowly, treating them as extremely limited exceptions to a still existing common law of coverture.[25] Even when statutes granted women the ability to *hold* separate property, courts were reluctant to allow married women full rights to *dispose* of that property as they pleased.[26]

Furthermore, married women's property laws were just that – laws concerning ownership of property, and thus laws that had very little effect on the lives of many working- and middle-class women, who did not bring large property holdings to marriage. Courts consistently held that a wife's earnings and property purchased with a wife's earnings did not constitute separate property under the common law or under married women's property statutes, because these assets came into existence after the woman contracted a marriage.[27] Even after state legislatures late in the nineteenth century passed earnings laws designed to allow married working women to maintain control over their own earnings from nonhousehold labor, courts again construed statutes extremely narrowly, finding that, as legal historian Amy Dru Stanley describes it, "though the wife gained a contractual right

24 Carole Pateman, *The Sexual Contract* (Stanford: Stanford University Press, 1988), 158.

25 Sara L. Zeigler, "Uniformity and Conformity: Regionalism and Adjudication of the Married Women's Property Acts," *Polity* 28, no. 4 (1996): 469–70.

26 Richard H. Chused, "Late Nineteenth Century Married Women's Property Law: Reception of the Early Married Women's Property Acts by Courts and Legislatures," *American Journal of Legal History* 29, no. 1 (1985): 3–35 (focusing on Oregon, and citing many examples of courts' severely limiting married women's dispositional rights even after legislation specifying that married women could hold property for their "sole and separate use").

27 Zeigler, "Uniformity and Conformity," 490–3. On the common law, see Reeve, *Baron and Femme*: "The ground, on which the husband is joined with the wife, is this: the wife, by marriage, is entirely deprived of the use and disposal of her property, and can acquire none by her industry" (p. 3).

to her wages, her husband retained his proprietary claim both to her person and to her domestic labor."[28] Unless a woman performed the labor for which she was paid entirely outside the home and kept all of her earnings entirely separate from general household accounts, the courts would not protect the woman's wages from her husband or her husband's creditors.[29]

"*[H]is right* in my *brains*": The intersection between coverture and copyright in the careers of married women authors

If a woman's household labor remained the "property" of her husband even after the passage of married women's property laws and earnings laws, what was the status of property created through a married woman's literary labors? Copyrights were, in Kent's words, "property originally acquired through intellectual labor," and thus were not treated like land (real property); and although copyrights fell into the other major legal category of property, "personal property," the means through which they came into existence made them a peculiar form of personal property. A cookstove (legally speaking, an item of personal property) might be "settled on" a married woman by her family as part of her separate estate, or a married woman might attempt to purchase a cookstove with her earnings from churning butter. In the first instance, a court would recognize the cookstove as hers, but in the second instance, the outcome is less clear. Because the woman purchased the stove with earnings from what could be construed as household labor to which her husband had a proprietary claim, a court might determine that he, not she, had title to the cookstove. A wife's acquisition of such personal property with her wages more closely resembles a married woman author's acquisition of a copyright than a third party settling an item of property on a woman. A copyright is, once it comes into existence, personal property, but the authorial labor required to create it is labor. Even after the statutory reform of coverture, courts were reluctant to grant married women control over their own persons and their labors, especially labors in the home, and the home was, of course, for the nineteenth-century woman author, the primary site of literary production.

These questions had implications for the largely private negotiations between husband and wife, but they also had implications for the public life of woman-produced literary properties as registered with federal authorities and protected by statute. The copyright registration process was (and is) largely formal and administrative, with federal authorities conducting no

28 Amy Dru Stanley, "Conjugal Bonds and Wage Labor: Rights of Contract in the Age of Emancipation," *Journal of American History* 75, no. 2 (1988): 495.

29 Ibid., 497.

examination of the legitimacy of claims by the registrant, who simply paid a small fee and presented a printed title page of the work before publication of the work as a whole. Federal district courts, and later the Library of Congress, simply recorded registrations and accepted deposits of works after publication rather than accepting applications and subjecting them to examination. Publishers were the registered proprietors of the overwhelming majority of published works rather than authors, making the scope of the effect of the law of coverture on copyright registration practices difficult to trace, but the variety of practices traceable in the copyright registers suggest both confusion and conflict. Some married women could and did register copyrights in their own names (e.g., Harriet Beecher Stowe's name appears on the registration for *Uncle Tom's Cabin*), but the presence of married women authors' names in the copyright register books as proprietors of their own works did not necessarily grant them the ability to enforce their copyrights or to dispose of them at will. If a court were asked to determine who held legal title to such a copyright, a judge would likely have declared it the property of the author's husband, not the author herself. And even if a married woman author defended her right to hold her copyright separately from her husband, she still would have confronted laws that gave a married woman standing to file a lawsuit only when joined in the action by her husband or another man serving as her "next friend." A number of men married to women authors removed all ambiguity from this relation by registering their wives' copyrights in their own names. For instance, Daniel Holmes registered the copyrights in his wife Mary Jane Holmes's novels as proprietor; Edward Stephens registered some, but not all, of the copyrights in his wife Ann Sophia Stephens's novels; the Reverend Charles W. Denison registered the copyright in *The Crown Rule in Boston*, a serialized novel by his wife Mrs. Mary A. Denison; and, as I mentioned in my introduction, Leander K. Lippincott became the registered proprietor of Grace Greenwood's copyrights after their marriage.[30]

30 For Greenwood's husband's registrations of her works, see the copyright notices in her books from the 1850s after the marriage. For copyrights in Stephens's works, see the following in the Southern District of New York registers: 14 June 1850, Edward Stephens as proprietor of *Julia Warren: A Sequel to Palaces and Prisons*, by Ann S. Stephens; 10 Apr. 1852, Edward Stephens as proprietor of *The Gipsey's Legacy*, by Ann S. Stephens; 13 Dec. 1853, Edward Stephens as proprietor of *The Orphans from the Alms House*, by Mrs. Ann S. Stephens; 21 Jan. 1856, Edward Stephens as proprietor of *The Wife's Trial*, by Mrs. Ann S. Stephens; 6 Aug. 1855, Mrs. Ann S. Stephens as author and proprietor of *The Old Homestead*, by Mrs. Ann S. Stephens; 29 June 1856, Mrs. Ann S. Stephens as author and proprietor of *Lost Jewels, A Novel*, by Mrs. Ann S. Stephens. In the District of Massachusetts register, see 6 Jan. 1858, Rev. Charles W. Denison as proprietor of *Crown Rule in Boston; or The Days and Ways of the Cocked Hats*, by Mrs. Mary A. Denison. The Rare Books Division of the Library of Congress holds all nineteenth-century copyright register books, with microfilm copies at the Copyright Office. Ellen Weinauer also notes that Elizabeth Stoddard's husband signed the publishing contracts for her first and third novels, although she does not comment on whether or not he registered the copyrights in those novels in his own name. "Alternative Economies," 170.

These copyrights in women's literary works registered by their husbands as proprietors tell a relatively unambiguous story of coverture asserted in ongoing, functional marriages, but some married women authors and their literary properties occupied a far more ambiguous legal terrain. Lydia Maria Child, Mary Gove Nichols, and E. D. E. N. Southworth provide concrete examples of the legal maneuverings of women authors facing difficulties as they attempted to separate their financial affairs from those of destitute, or even devious, husbands. This task was made particularly complex for the women themselves and their legal advisors because the application of married women's property law to copyrights was never made the subject of specific legislation, of a published judicial decision, or of commentary in a legal treatise.[31] The difficulties presented by U.S. federalism would have only complicated an already complex situation. As Joel Prentiss Bishop observes in his influential nineteenth-century legal treatise *Commentaries on the Law of Marriage and Divorce*, "All our marriage and divorce laws, and of course all our statutes on the subject, so far as they pertain to localities embraced within the territorial limits of particular States, are State laws and State statutes; the national power, with us, not having legislative or judicial cognizance of the matter within these localities."[32] The Constitution reserved the power to grant copyrights for published works exclusively to the federal government. The common law, however, which varied from state to state, granted a limited form of protection to unpublished works; and married women's property laws, both common law and statutory, also varied from state to state.

In 1841, several years before statutory reform of coverture by individual states began in earnest, health reformer and author Mary Gove (later, Mary Gove Nichols) was forced to confront the opaque tangle of the federal statutory law of copyright, the common law of copyright in unpublished works, and the state common law of coverture when she sought to publish her first book, a compilation of her lectures on women's anatomy and physiology. In July of 1841, in the midst of a lecture tour that included stops in Baltimore, Philadelphia, and New York, she wrote to her friend, author and reformer John Neal, about writing and delivering a lecture on the topic of "the Rights of Woman" at the solicitation of friends in Baltimore. Her

31 See the epilogue for *Belford v. Scribner*, a case in which the infringers asserted the intersection of coverture and copyright as a defense; however, the courts did not actually rule on the question. I have examined a very large number of treatises on the law of marriage and on married women's property law from the period, and while they comment in depth on a number of forms of property and contracts and how the laws would regulate them, none of them addresses copyrights and author-publisher contracts about copyrights.

32 Joel Prentiss Bishop, *Commentaries on the Law of Marriage and Divorce, of Separations without Divorce, and of the Evidence of Marriage in All Issues* (Boston: Little, Brown & Co., 1864), 74. For recent historical commentary on the complex implications of the control of marriage by the states rather than the federal government during the nineteenth century, see Hartog, *Man and Wife*, chap. 1.

speech advocated "the right of property for married women," "the right of freedom of tho't and action," and "the education of women."[33] Indignantly describing the status of a married woman under coverture as "a thing – a chattel, only a chattel her husband has no right to sell," she also writes of her conversations in New York City with Judge Thomas Herttell, an early advocate of married women's property reform in New York State, and of her desire to see statutory reform.[34] While her letter ends on a self-described "ugly" note as she recounts opposition to her ideas and to her lecturing before "promiscuous" (mixed-gender) audiences, her postscript reports a more hopeful prospect. "A printer in Boston," she reports, "an honest man tells me he will get up my Lectures into a 'book' – 1000 copies worth a dollar a copy for $300, – I think I shall have the work done this winter."[35]

Assuming that she is describing the typical "half-profits" financial arrangement, in which she and the publisher would split the proceeds from sales after the publisher recouped his $300 cost for producing the edition, her hopefulness stemmed from the prospect of earning $350 on the sales of the pamphlet,[36] a financial windfall that would have enabled her to forego the strains of traveling the lecture circuit. Her buoyant mood did not last long, however, as she confronted the effects of the law of coverture in a concrete, material, and personally pressing way. Gove faced a seemingly insoluble legal problem as she sought to publish her book without the consent or assistance of her estranged husband, Hiram Gove. As she wrote to Neal a month later in August, smarting at the insult to her pride from the situation and asking him to burn the letter after reading it,

> I want to publish my book and I want it secured to me. I called on [attorney Robert] Rantoul and gave him two dollars to tell me that my manuscript was not mine or rather that a woman's manuscript was not hers for I did not let him know that I wanted the information for myself. Since then I have been assured that a manuscript is not property and is only made property

33 Mary Gove to John Neal, 3 July 1841, in Irving T. Richards, "Mary Gove Nichols and John Neal," *New England Quarterly* 7, no. 2 (1934): 349.

34 Ibid. New York State did not enact reform until 1848, but Herttell publicly advocated reform in 1837, using the slavery analogy and the vignette about a poor woman with a drunken husband drinking up her wages that continued to be standards of reformist rhetoric through the end of the century. See *Remarks Comprising in Substance Judge Herttell's Argument in the House of Assembly of the State of New-York, in the Session of 1837, in Support of the Bill to Restore to Married Women 'the Right of Property,' as Guaranteed by the Constitution of this State* (New York: Henry Durell, 1839).

35 Mary Gove to John Neal, 3 July 1841, in Richards, "Mary Gove Nichols," 351.

36 Susan Geary explains half-profits publishing and the transition to the royalty system in the 1850s through the example of Harriet Beecher Stowe's dispute with her publisher about her proceeds from the sales of *Uncle Tom's Cabin*. "Harriet Beecher Stowe, John P. Jewett, and Author-Publisher Relations in 1853," *Studies in the American Renaissance*, 1977, 345–67. Thanks to Leon Jackson for identifying this arrangement as a half-profits contract. A full $350 profit would actually have been unlikely because review copies and other marketing costs would also have been deducted from the $700; nevertheless, Gove stood to make a fairly substantial sum of money.

> by the copy right and that whoever takes out the copy right will own the book. Rantoul told me the woman's husband must transfer his property in the manuscript to the man who took out the copy right or the man could not hold it. My husband is absent. I have no certainty that he will transfer *his right* in my *brains*, for he thinks the doctrine that gives woman the right of property a doctrine of Devils. . . . Years before my marriage my husband failed in business. Since my my [*sic*] marriage, by my pen, I have paid the larger portion of these debts contracted when I was a child. A part remains due. I am willing to pay them, and have written to my husband that I will do it, if I receive enough for my book past paying expenses, that is if he will relinquish *his right* (?) to my manuscript, to some one in trust for me, who shall take out the copy right. I have received no answer from him and I know his views about women, their right to property, ability to take care of it etc.[37] [emphasis and parenthetical question mark Gove's]

Gove's letter represents a rare recorded instance of a lawyer's advice on the effects of coverture on a married woman's literary proprietorship. Without case law or treatises to guide him, Robert Rantoul advised Mary Gove on the "hypothetical" situation described to him by recurring to first principles in each relevant area of the law. Before a work was published, an author had very limited common law property rights in the manuscript, sometimes referred to as "common law copyright." Common law copyright consisted of the right to decide whether or not the manuscript would be published, and once the work was published, the federal copyright statute, rather than the common law, applied.[38] In order for the work to be protected by the copyright statute, the author or the person to whom the author transferred her or his rights had to register the copyright before publication, include a copyright notice in proper form in every copy published, and deposit copies of the published work with federal authorities within three months of publication.[39] If these formalities were not strictly observed, a published work was considered to be "dedicated to the public" and became public property open for appropriation by anyone rather than private property under control of an individual author or proprietor. However, as Rantoul advised Mary Gove, under the common law doctrine of coverture, the common law right to authorize publication of her manuscript belonged to

37 Mary Gove to John Neal, 10 Aug. 1841, in Richards, "Mary Gove Nichols," 351–2.

38 For antebellum discussions of the limited scope of common law protection for manuscripts, see Story, *Equity Jurisprudence*, II:218; and George Ticknor Curtis, *A Treatise on the Law of Copyright* (Boston: Charles C. Little and James Brown, 1847), 83–9.

39 These provisions originated in this combination with the 1831 copyright act. See Solberg, *Copyright Enactments*, 37–41. Several alterations to deposit requirements followed, with the most significant change being the shifting of registration and deposit functions from the district courts and the State Department to the Library of Congress in 1870. See Solberg, *Copyright Enactments*, 46–52; and John Y. Cole, "Of Copyright, Men, and a National Library," *Quarterly Journal of the Library of Congress* 28, no. 2, (1971): 114–36.

Hiram Gove, not to her, because she had no independent legal identity. If a husband refused to be a party to such a transfer, he could sue any publisher who published on his wife's authorization alone for violating his common law rights in the manuscript, or he could demand that any profits on sales be paid to him.

In her autobiographical novel *Mary Lyndon, or, Revelations of a Life* (1855), written after Hiram Gove divorced her and she had married fellow progressive reformer Thomas Low Nichols, she repeats the story and gives it a public life (in the process discounting the value of Robert Rantoul's legal advice by fifty percent and making herself more direct and forthright in seeking advice about herself):

> According to the law of the land, this man owned me, body and soul, and my child. In Boston, I could not sell a book that I had written, because he was legally its owner. When I doubted this fact, I went to Robert Rantoul, and asked him if it were indeed true that I had no property in my work, and no right to sell it. He said, "Madam, you have no legal right to it, and therefore you can not sell it." He received a dollar for this information. Through every act of my life ran this thread of wrong and misery – the idea of the public that a man owned me – that I had no right to the friendship, love, or sympathy of any other man for this reason.[40]

As a wife, Gove, in her own reading of her legal situation, is her husband's "property" and little more than a slave (he "owns" her "body and soul"); she cannot own literary property, even property she creates, any more than she can "own" her own child. In both her life and her novelization of it, her struggles with her husband over property and over child custody

40 *Mary Lyndon, or, Revelations of a Life* (New York: Stringer and Townsend, 1855), 314–15. Prior to book publication, the novel was serialized in *Nichols' Journal*, a water cure journal published by Mary Gove and Thomas Lowe Nichols. In the *Journal* the novel appeared under her signature, but in book form it appeared with no author's name but the designation "an autobiography." Despite the absence of her name on the book, her authorship was widely known (and harshly criticized). See, e.g., the review "A Bad Book Gibbeted," *New York Times*, 17 Aug. 1855, 2. Baym briefly discusses Gove Nichols in *Woman's Fiction* (pp. 255–8) in a chapter titled "Other Novelists of the Fifties," which addresses women novelists who do *not* fit the "woman's fiction" rubric. *Mary Lyndon* has received some attention from modern critics for its intertwined critiques of medicine and of marriage as an institution. See, e.g., Joel Myerson, "Mary Gove Nichols' *Mary Lyndon*: A Forgotten Reform Novel," *American Literature* 58, no. 4 (1986): 523–39; Susan Steinberg Danielson, "Healing Women's Wrongs: Water-Cure as (Fictional) Autobiography," *Studies in the American Renaissance* (1992): 247–60; and Dawn Keetley, "The Ungendered Terrain of Good Health: Mary Gove Nichols's Rewriting of the Diseased Institution of Marriage," in *Separate Spheres No More: Gender Convergence in American Literature, 1830–1930*, ed. Monika M. Elbert (Tuscaloosa: University of Alabama Press, 2000), 117–42. For Gove Nichols's unsettled relationship to feminism and abolitionism, see Jean Silver-Isenstadt, *Shameless: The Visionary Life of Mary Gove Nichols* (Baltimore: Johns Hopkins University Press, 2002), 6–10, 28–9, 232–5. For her lecturing activities and the life context in which her dispute with Hiram Gove over her book occurred, see ibid., 54–62. Patricia Cline Cohen graciously shared her ongoing research for a book on Mary Gove Nichols.

are virtually inseparable. In *Mary Lyndon*, "Mary's" struggles with "Albert" over the custody of their daughter repeatedly intertwine with her struggles to gain control over her literary property. In life, Mary Gove followed up her letter to John Neal about her copyright troubles with a long letter seeking advice about "the Law respecting *Divorce* and *children*."[41] In this letter (dated February 1842), she segues abruptly from her discussion of her custody struggles with Hiram over daughter Elma to a report on the status of her book, which is "nearly out of Press. . . . It will be got up well."[42] Coverture as the law structuring the marital relation troubled her rights to both her biological child and the child of her brain.

Her report that her book was in press was not, however, a sign that she and Hiram had resolved their conflict over the book's publication. Recall that Mary herself sought advice from an attorney concerning the status of her literary property, that she asked for that advice as if the advice did not apply to her personally, and that she clearly indicated to John Neal that she did not want him to publicize Rantoul's advice. Either she chose not to inform her publisher, David H. Ela, of her husband's likely opposition to the publication of the book and his legal right to interfere with that publication, or Ela was willing to risk it. Ela registered the copyright in *Lectures to Ladies on Anatomy and Physiology* "by Mrs. Mary A. Gove" in Massachusetts federal district court on February 14, 1842, indicating his own status as proprietor. By March 1842, the book was being reviewed in the press.[43]

Clearly, Hiram Gove was not pleased and attempted to claim Mary's profits on sales of the book. On June 6, 1842, in a document witnessed by David H. Barlow (editor of the *Essex County Washingtonian*, a reform newspaper to which Mary began contributing articles in the same month), Hiram Gove implicitly acknowledges his attempts to claim his wife's literary earnings and disavows future claims: "I hereby relinquish to my wife Mary S. Gove all claims to her Mental and personal labours, and do hereby agree with her and whom this may concern *never* to claim any of her earnings."[44] Although only Hiram signed the document, it is essentially a contract, a document memorializing an agreement between Hiram and Mary. It is doubtful that a Massachusetts court in 1842 would have enforced such a contract between husband and wife. The legal institution of marriage and the rights of husbands under the common law of coverture continued to exist whether Hiram claimed to "renounce" those rights or not, and most judges would have been reluctant to prevent Hiram from reasserting his

41 Mary Gove Nichols to John Neal, 1 Feb. 1842, in Richards, "Mary Gove Nichols," 353.

42 Ibid., 354.

43 For reasons not clear from the surviving evidence, another printer/publisher's name actually appears on the title page, but Ela's name appears in the copyright notice, and he is identified as the printer. Mary S. Gove, *Lectures to Ladies on Anatomy and Physiology* (Boston: Saxon & Pierce, 1842).

44 Declaration of Hiram Gove, 6 June 1842, private collection of Charles Letchworth, England. Quotations by permission of Charles Letchworth (Mary Gove Nichols's great-great-grandson).

rights. As long as Hiram Gove behaved as if he were legally bound by its terms, however, Mary could exercise control over her literary properties and profits (much as Terhune did in the context of her functional marriage to a noninterfering husband). For years, Hiram, a Quaker, resisted legally ending their marriage, but in 1848 he reversed course and divorced Mary on the ground of her desertion of him. From 1848 on, her copyrights in her newly created works were no longer subject to *Hiram's* claims but may have been subject to her *second* husband's claims if they did not make proper legal arrangements *before* their marriage to establish a separate estate for Mary.

Lydia Maria Child, who appears as one of the "lady-writers" in Grace Greenwood's 1847 copyright parodies in her guise as promoter of reform in her *Letters from New York* (see Introduction), faced the questions posed by the intersections of copyright and coverture in a crucially different marital situation from that of Mary Gove. While Gove spent years unsuccessfully trying to dissolve her marriage to Hiram Gove, finally getting relief when he divorced her, Lydia Child wished both to remain married to her husband, David Lee Child, and to separate their financial affairs in the wake of his multiple failures in business and professional matters.[45] In 1836, also before the first wave of statutory reform of married women's property laws, Lydia Child responded to the worsening financial troubles of her husband by telling her friend Ellis Gray Loring that her husband would sign over all of her copyrights to Loring and to her father, Convers Francis (both of whom had bailed them out of financial trouble repeatedly), in order to protect the copyrights from David Child's creditors. Repeatedly stressing that she and her husband would handle all property, including her copyrights, as "*agents* of Mr. Convers Francis," she writes to Loring: "Mr. Child will draw up a paper resigning into your hands & father's, all right and title to the copy-rights, or profits, of the Oasis, Frugal Housewife, Girl's Book, Family Library, and Philothea. From there, pay yourself and Mr. Sewall [who had financed the publication of the *Oasis*], as soon as you *can*; reserving only fathers [*sic*] yearly interest" on their debt to him of $890.[46] By distinguishing between "copy-rights" and "profits," Child demonstrates her knowledge of the precise legal status of the works listed. In one category ("profits") fell those works for which the publisher was registered copyright proprietor but still had a contractual obligation to pay royalties on sales. In this category fell the *Oasis* (an abolitionist gift book she edited and to which she contributed a substantial number of items), the *Mother's Book*, the *Girl's*

45 See two excellent modern biographies of Child for the complex bond between her and her husband: Carolyn L. Karcher, *The First Woman in the Republic: A Cultural Biography of Lydia Maria Child* (Durham: Duke University Press, 1994); and Deborah Pickman Clifford, *Crusader for Freedom: A Life of Lydia Maria Child* (Boston: Beacon, 1992).

46 Lydia Maria Child to Ellis Gray Loring, 30 Jan. 1836, in Milton Meltzer and Patricia G. Holland, eds., *Lydia Maria Child, Selected Letters, 1817–1880* (Amherst: University of Massachusetts Press, 1982), 44–5 (hereinafter *Selected Letters*).

Own Book, and the volumes of her *Family Library* series. For such works, her husband would assign *his* rights to future royalties. The other category ("copy-rights") included one book, her hugely successful *Frugal Housewife* (1829), for which her husband was the registered proprietor and could thus assign the copyright outright to her father.[47] Even if Lydia and David held advanced views on the equality of the sexes, this letter demonstrates their understanding that under the law, David owned all of his wife's property, including her copyrights, and that in their dealings with others concerning that property, David must act in his capacity as proprietor.

Her novel *Philothea* was still in manuscript when she wrote to Loring about these arrangements. Several months later, she wrote to author, editor, and publisher Park Benjamin about her previous commitment to allow him to publish the American edition of the novel, which she had also submitted to John Murray in England. "[Y]ou will please bear in mind," she writes to Benjamin, "that the copy-right belongs to my father, Mr. Convers Francis, South Natick, Mass, – It having been formally transferred to him by my husband, in part payment of money loaned to us. Therefore whatever you pay is to be intrusted [*sic*] to Ellis G. Loring, Esq. State St. Boston, as agent for my father."[48]

Although these measures provided some security for Child's literary affairs, her husband's financial affairs remained tangled, and after the U.S. Congress passed the first federal bankruptcy law in 1842 (its provisions going into effect on January 1, 1843), David Child quickly took advantage of its provisions. In 1843, Lydia confided in both Ellis Loring and Francis George Shaw about her husband's bankruptcy and her desire to separate her financial affairs from her husband's, a desire intimately tied to her decision to disassociate herself from the organized abolition movement (although not from the cause of abolition) and to devote herself to literary authorship. In a letter dated January 15, 1843, days after the bankruptcy law went into effect, she writes to Shaw seeking a loan against anticipated profits from the book publication of *Letters from New York* (a collection of columns first published in the *Anti-Slavery Standard*). She confides, "Mr. Child is now going through the

47 Lydia Maria Child, *The Frugal Housewife. Dedicated to Those Who Are Not Ashamed of Economy* (Boston: March & Capen/Carter & Hendee, 1829). According the copyright notice, David L. Child registered the copyright in the District of Massachusetts on 12 Nov. 1829.

48 Lydia Maria Child to Park Benjamin, 30 May 1836, in Holland and Meltzer, eds., *The Collected Correspondence of Lydia Maria Child, 1817–1880* (Millwood, NY: Kraus-Thomson Organization Limited, KTO Microform, 1979), 97–2 (hereinafter *Collected Correspondence*). Park Benjamin did not act as publisher for the novel, but he did, as Child directed, file for copyright registration as proprietor in the District of Massachusetts. See the copyright notice – Lydia Maria Child, *Philothea. A Romance* (Boston: Otis, Broaders & Co., 1836) – and the 13 Aug. 1836 copyright registration by Benjamin as proprietor in the District of Massachusetts. Perhaps because, as Child herself indicates in her letter, Benjamin was no longer conducting business himself as a publisher by May 1836, the book was not published under his imprint.

bankrupt process. It will not make the slightest difference with him about paying his debts, as fast as he is able; but he will be more free; and to me, it will be an inexpressible relief to be relieved from his entanglements."[49] Three months later, in her ongoing correspondence with Loring about her self-financed publication of *Letters from New York* and her recent resignation from the editorship of the *Anti-Slavery Standard*, her exultation at resigning her role in organized abolition merges with her explanation of her agreement with David about their finances: "Such powers as I have, are in their maturity now, and I feel a resolution I never felt before – to cast from me all the fetters of sand which have so miserably bound me down to unprofitable drudgery. David has agreed to part partnership, so far as *pecuniary* matters are concerned; and I *know* I can more than support *myself*."[50]

Two months later, she writes Loring again, announcing her definite resolution to "separate my pecuniary affairs entirely from David's" and to continue to reside in New York:

> Let him experiment where he will, a great load of anxiety is taken from my heart. I *do* hope he wont [*sic*] get into any more entanglements, but I feel no security about that. I mean to keep my earnings out of the way. I wish you would tell him that you approve (if you do) of my making a permanent fixture, and devoting myself earnestly to literature. I am resolved to *do* it, because it is the deliberate and calm conclusion of my mind that I *ought* not to waste any more time and energy in misdirected efforts; but I should like very much to have him satisfied and pleased with my taking such a resolution.[51]

Once again, her relief at leaving the factionalized world of organized abolition and separating physically and financially from her husband merge imperceptibly. Which "efforts" are "misdirected": her work in organized abolition or her efforts to live in full partnership with her husband? To what is she "fettered": political abolitionism or her bankrupt husband?

Loring fully supported her resolution, but her response to his support reveals her anxiety about her plans for disrupting her marital unity with David as both a legal fiction and a lived reality. Unlike Mary Gove, she did not seek absolute liberty and freedom for herself (or would not admit to it); she sought to better fulfill her duties to her husband:

> I hope you do not think because I talk of separating my pecuniary affairs from my husband's that I am seized with a selfish or monopolizing spirit. After much reflection, I have felt that this step was absolutely necessary in order to make my earnings of any use to *him* as well as myself. If I can be undisturbed in my plans, I will make a nest in N. York, where a warm corner will always be

49 Lydia Maria Child to Frances George Shaw, 15 Jan. 1843, in *Selected Letters*, 185.

50 Lydia Maria Child to Ellis Gray Loring, 21 Mar. [1843], in *Collected Correspondence*, 470–2.

51 Lydia Maria Child to Ellis Gray Loring, 12 June [1843], in *Collected Correspondence*, 498–3–4.

> ready for him. If I float about much longer, I feel that I shall become indifferent to everything, and lose my capacity for business. To pump water into a sieve for fourteen years is enough to break down the most energetic spirit.[52]

Whatever the precise nature of the equitable, contractual arrangements worked out between the Childs and one or more third parties in 1843, their negotiations predate statutory reform of married women's property law in both New York and Massachusetts. Patricia Holland describes the legal maneuvers implied in Child's correspondence with Loring as "a revolutionary step" through which she "legally separated her financial affairs from her husband's in order to protect her earnings from his creditors."[53] Although the precise nature of the legal arrangements she made is not clear, it *is* clear that, legally speaking, she was not a party to such arrangements but a passive beneficiary of them. As Child's biographer Deborah Pickman Clifford notes, "In New York, equity law permitted postnuptial agreements protecting a wife's property from her husband's creditors," but "the approval of a man was needed before she could exercise any legal authority."[54] If, indeed, their financial separation entailed the creation of a trust, Lydia was the beneficiary of a trust into which David Child conveyed "his" copyrights in her works, with another man serving as trustee for her benefit.

Furthermore, in her letter to Loring, Child demonstrates the relatively conservative logic that drove much early married women's property legislation. In the volatile economic climate of the 1840s as produced by the Panic of 1837, the federal government and the states moved to protect all sorts of family assets from creditors. The federal government enacted the first federal bankruptcy law (from which David Child benefited), and states, among other reforms, passed laws making married women's property exempt from their husbands' debts. Such exemptions provided, as legal historian Richard H. Chused notes, "another body of exempt assets [for the benefit of families] when the [economic] risk taking went sour. . . . While these acts may also be justified because they preserved inherited property from rapacious husbands or provided married women with some independent means of support,

52 Lydia Maria Child to Ellis Gray Loring, 16 June 1843, in *Collected Correspondence*, 499–1.

53 Patricia G. Holland, "Lydia Maria Child as a Nineteenth-Century Professional Author," *Studies in the American Renaissance*, 1981, 160.

54 Clifford, *Crusader for Freedom*, 179. Although I agree with Clifford's analysis of the legal situation, I do not agree with her contention that "she turned over to Ellis Loring the control of her earnings and the rights to some of her books," both because, as I explained earlier, *David* had to turn over that control and because Child's letters nowhere state explicitly or implicitly that Loring would take that role as he clearly did in 1836. Furthermore, both the 1836 and 1842 legal maneuvers might have been voided by courts of law if challenged by David Child's creditors, who could have claimed that David Child had illegally transferred "his" assets (a.k.a. Lydia's copyrights) to a third party (in the first instance, Lydia's father, and in the second instance, the trust for Lydia) to avoid rightful claims on those assets.

they also provided some husbands and families with continued access to assets despite bad economic times."[55] Working without the benefit of such statutes, Lydia Child nevertheless follows their logic by using her protected assets for the benefit of her hapless husband rather than as a basis for self-assertion and independence.

Child's marital situation was legally and emotionally complex, but despite several long periods of separation, she and her husband remained committed to their marriage, and he acquiesced in her attempts at legal and financial self-protection. E. D. E. N. (Emma) Southworth faced far greater difficulties as her estranged husband, in the fashion of the fictional Phemie's husband, attempted to appropriate her literary properties and royalties. While Mary Gove deserted her husband, E. D. E. N. Southworth's husband, Frederick Hamilton Southworth, deserted her and their children. In the 1890s, writing to her granddaughter Rose Lawrence, encouraging her in her decision not to seek a divorce from the husband from whom she had recently separated, Emma opines that divorce is a "sacrilege" against the "Divine institution" of marriage. She claims, providing seemingly authentic details, "Although while I was in England, Congress gave the courts of the District the power to grant divorces under a bill brought in by Senator Dixon of Connecticut entitled 'A Bill for the Relief of Emma Southworth,' and it was passed and became a law – much to my regret – I never availed myself of it."[56] She further claims that Robert Bonner, her editor and publisher at the *New York Ledger*, was the moving force behind the bill. The specificity and detail of her recollection have persuaded many scholars to accept her account as authentic, but the account is, in many respects, pure fabrication, with fragments of memories of the 1850s and 1860s shaped by her desire to present her own history in a light that would serve her purpose in the

55 Chused, "Married Women's Property Law: 1800–1850," 1403.

56 Emma D. E. N. Southworth to Rose Lawrence, 2 June 1895, Emma Dorothy Eliza (Nevitte) Southworth Papers, Family Correspondence, Library of Congress. Large gaps in the primary source record, confused ideas about both copyright law and married women's property law, and a willingness to take Southworth's late-life recollections about these events as accurate have caused Southworth's twentieth-century interpreters to construct very different accounts of these events from what I relate here. Regis Louise Boyle first directed the attention of scholars to Frederick Southworth's registrations of his wife's works, but the information she presents is radically incomplete (she cites only three registrations), and her interpretation of the significance of the registrations is implausible. *Mrs. E. D. E. N. Southworth, Novelist* (Washington, DC: Catholic University of America Press, 1939), 7. Among the scholarly accounts to which the additional facts I have uncovered serve as a corrective are: Kelley, *Private Woman*, 238, 262–3; Bardes and Gossett, *Declarations of Independence*, 98; Susan Coultrap-McQuin, *Doing Literary Business: American Women Writers in the Nineteenth Century* (Chapel Hill: University of North Carolina Press, 1990), 54–5; Joanne Dobson, Introduction to *The Hidden Hand* by E. D. E. N. Southworth (New Brunswick: Rutgers University Press, 1988), xix; Amy Elizabeth Hudock, "No Mere Mercenary: The Early Life and Fiction of E. D. E. N. Southworth," PhD diss., University of South Carolina, 1993, 202–9; Clara Maria Bouricius, "'A Happier Ending than Is Warranted by the Facts'; Or, How E. D. E. N. Southworth Created Sentimental Capitalism, 1849–1886," PhD diss., Harvard University, 1997, chap. 4.

1890s – persuading her granddaughter not to divorce her husband. The surviving evidence reveals that Emma Southworth was not a woman who, as she described herself to Rose, passively "suffered much" rather than seek legal redress against her husband. Instead, she actively sought a divorce early in her career (years before she met Robert Bonner); and, even if she did not succeed in that attempt or later renew it, she did her best through other means to actively repulse her husband's attempts to appropriate her literary properties and profits.

After Frederick deserted her, Emma initially taught school in her hometown, Washington, DC, but the pay was insufficient to support her family. In 1846, she began publishing fiction in weekly newspapers, first in the Baltimore *Sunday Visitor*, and then in the *National Era*, a weekly abolitionist paper edited by Gamaliel Bailey in Washington. Emboldened by her success at the *Era*, by Harper & Brothers' publication of her previously serialized novel *Retribution* (1849), and by an arrangement to serialize her works in the *Saturday Evening Post* as well as the *Era*, Emma began gathering the evidence she would need to secure a divorce from Frederick. She enlisted in her cause Henry A. Wise, who had served as congressional representative from Virginia from 1833 to 1844 and as U.S. Minister to Brazil from 1844 to 1847.[57] In Brazil, Wise had come into contact with Frederick, who was living and working there as an expatriate. She wrote to Wise in March 1850, "I have not received one line, word, message from F. H. Southworth since your return from Rio de Janeiro. I am about to petition Congress for a divorce and need all the proof of my husband's desertion that I can procure."[58] While Congress did not legislate marriage law for the states, the District of Columbia represented a significant exception to the federal nonregulation of marriage. Because she was a resident of the Washington County portion of the District of Columbia in 1850, Congress was, indeed, Emma's only avenue for a "divorce a vinculo," a divorce from the "chains" of matrimony (an absolute divorce) as opposed to a "divorce a mensa et thoro," a divorce "from bed and board" (a "partial" divorce that separated a husband and wife's legal affairs but did not allow either party to remarry – District residents could obtain a bed and board divorce from the courts).[59] In the remainder

57 For the years of Wise's career relevant to Southworth's contact with him, see Craig M. Simpson, *A Good Southerner: The Life of Henry A. Wise of Virginia* (Chapel Hill: University of North Carolina Press, 1985), chaps. 1–6. However, Simpson does not document his contact with Frederick Southworth.

58 Emma Southworth to Henry A. Wise, March 1850, E. D. E. N. Southworth Collection, Haverford College Library, Haverford, PA.

59 Although nineteenth-century American divorce law has received a great deal of scholarly attention, the District of Columbia and the peculiar legal situation of its residents seeking to end marriages has not. Both Martin Schultz, "Divorce in the South Atlantic States: Origins, Historical Patterns, and Recent Trends," *International Journal of Sociology of the Family* 16 (1986): 225–50, and Donna M. Young, "Divorce in Nineteenth Century Washington County, District of Columbia," Gender and Legal History Papers, Richard H. Chused and Wendy Webster Williams, Georgetown University

of her letter to Wise, she asks his assistance in securing the support of the Virginia congressional delegation for her petition and describes her plans for seeking support of the Mississippi delegation through her uncle, "a leading publisher in his own state."

For reasons that are not clear from the surviving evidence, she did not file her planned petition to Congress for a divorce in 1850. A decade later, however, when she was living and writing in England, Frederick Southworth attempted to gain legal control over her literary properties and earnings in the United States by registering copyrights in her published works in his own name. As Emma acknowledged publicly several times, she moved to England in order to secure copyright protection for and financial benefit from the publication of her works there.[60] Even though she remained an American citizen, she could claim copyright in England on the basis of her residence in England at the time of publication, as long as her works were published in England *first*.[61] She could *also* still claim U.S. copyright protection on the basis of her U.S. citizenship even though she resided abroad. As she did *not* publicly admit, however, she also moved to England to stave off her husband's claims to any works she wrote and published while residing there. The 1857 Matrimonial Causes Act (which applied to *all* of the United Kingdom, unlike U.S. marriage and property law, which varied from state to state) granted wives separated from their husbands feme sole status.[62] By residing in England, Emma Southworth thus doubled her proprietary interests by subverting the effects of both coverture and the absence of an international copyright agreement between the United States and the United Kingdom.[63] That is, the Matrimonial Causes Act allowed her

Law Center, Washington, DC, 1985, explain the law as it applied to residents of the Washington County portion of the District of Columbia (which included Georgetown, Southworth's residence) and report finding no petitions to Congress. However, I have located a number of such petitions by searching recently digitized congressional documents. To some extent, Maryland state law applied to Washington County residents. See Richard H. Chused, *Private Acts in Public Places: A Social History of Divorce in the Formative Era of American Family Law* (Philadelphia: University of Pennsylvania Press, 1994), an in-depth study of the transition from legislative divorce to statutory divorce in Maryland in the years just before Southworth first sought to divorce her husband.

60 Boyle, *E. D. E. N. Southworth*, 13–15.

61 Walter Arthur Copinger, *The Law of Copyright* (London: Stevens & Haynes, 1870), 112–25, offers an exhaustive discussion of the residency requirement in British copyright law.

62 Mary Poovey, *Uneven Developments: The Ideological Work of Gender in Mid-Victorian England* (Chicago: University of Chicago Press), 84. As Poovey also argues, this statute was also conservative, only slightly modifying coverture rather than overturning it. Still, it served Southworth's purposes.

63 Her letters to Bonner only indirectly, and sometimes confusedly, refer to these matters through comments about the priority of publication between English and American serializations, comments sometimes adjacent to remarks about her husband. See, e.g., 12 July 1860, 18 Feb. 1861, 15 Mar. 1861, E. D. E. N. Southworth Papers, Duke University; and 17 May 1861, Beinecke Library, Yale University. Bonner and Southworth seem to have known that some of their arrangements were subject to challenge because U.S. publication preceded the British, although they disguised such lapses by using different titles. For example, *Eudora* in the *Ledger* preceded *Até the Avenger* in the

to own her own copyrights, and British copyright practice allowed her to claim copyrights in her works in both the United Kingdom and the United States.

It is not clear whether a court in either nation would have applied the law as Emma seems to have hoped it would, and her husband was certainly undeterred, repeatedly asserting what he believed to be his undisturbed possession of his wife's literary properties. In January 1860, Frederick registered U.S. copyrights in two of his wife's works as they had been re-titled for publication in the *London Journal*, suggesting that he learned of his wife's literary successes through European channels. In February and April of the same year, apparently after he (or someone acting on his behalf) had scoured bookstores in the United States for all of Emma's books in print, he registered copyrights in all of her works as published in book form by T. B. Peterson, as well as in *The Hidden Hand* (Robert Bonner serialized *The Hidden Hand* in the *New York Ledger* in 1859, just before Emma departed for England, but Bonner and Emma would not release her most popular serial novel for book publication until decades later[64]). The validity of Frederick's copyright registrations is questionable – a copyright registration was only legally effective if filed *before* the work was first published, and all of the titles that Frederick registered were already published and protected by copyright registrations filed by Emma's publishers.[65] However, the fact that these registrations were defective did not in any way cancel out Frederick's legal right to his wife's literary properties. In fact, Emma's copyrights in her works published during the 1840s and 1850s while she resided in the United States

London Journal in 1861, while *Rose Elmer* in the *Ledger* preceded *Laura Etheridge* in the *Journal* in 1861. Boyle, *E. D. E. N. Southworth*, 40–1.

64 All of Frederick Southworth's registrations appear in the register books for the Southern District of New York. He registered the titles *Kathleen Vernon* and *The Fatal Marriage* on 21 Jan. 1860; *The Haunted Homestead* on 27 Feb. 1860; and *The Lady of the Isle, The Discarded Daughter, The Deserted Wife, The Curse of Clifton, Retribution, The Missing Bride, India, Vivia, The Three Beauties, The Two Sisters, Brandon of Brandon, The Bride of an Evening, The Island Princess, The Doom of Deville, The Hidden Hand*, and *The Lady of the Isle* on 7 Apr. 1860. *The Fatal Marriage* was the British title of *The Doom of Deville* (Boyle, 4). *Brandon of Brandon* was actually a retitled, lightly revised version of *The Curse of Clifton* (Boyle, 39), and "Kathleen Vernon" the name of the novel's heroine. Thus F. H. Southworth appears to have registered essentially the same novel under three different titles. Southworth and Bonner did not merely pass over the possibility of book publication of *The Hidden Hand* until 1888 – they actively resisted it. See Amy M. Thomas and Alison M. Scott, "The Hidden History of *The Hidden Hand*: A Case Study of 19th-Century American Conceptions of Authorship, Literature, and Publication," unpublished paper.

65 This statement necessarily oversimplifies – Emma filed for at least one copyright in her own name; the various periodical publishers for whom she wrote over the years did not all fully and properly copyright the contents of their periodicals, and her book publisher T. B. Peterson often reregistered copyrights in her serials when he published them as books. I do not have space to document this tangle of registrations here, but my primary point nevertheless stands – that a copyright registration filed as if for a new, unpublished work that was actually claiming protection for a work that had already been published was legally meaningless.

had always been, legally speaking, her husband's property, whether or not her works produced in England were.

Shortly after Frederick registered a group of copyrights in Emma's works in April, the Committee on the District of Columbia of the U.S. House of Representatives reported a new "Bill to Authorize Divorces in the District of Columbia," and Congress passed the bill into law on June 19, 1860.[66] (Contrary to Emma's claim in her letter to her granddaughter thirty-five years later, Congress never considered or passed a divorce bill entitled "A Bill for the Relief of Emma Southworth"). This statute was relatively conservative, allowing absolute divorce (divorce *a vinculo*) only on the grounds that one party was married, a lunatic, or impotent at the time the marriage was contracted, or that either party had committed adultery during the marriage. Congress authorized courts to grant partial divorces (divorce *a mensa et thoro*) on the grounds of cruelty, abuse endangering life or health, or desertion or abandonment for a period of three years. In addition, the statute contained a provision allowing deserted wives to apply to the court "for an order to protect any money or other property, real or personal, of which she may have become possessed after such desertion, against her husband or his creditors" and for status as a feme sole trader. Thus while Emma had been prepared to seek a legislative absolute divorce in 1850, with the passage of the 1860 statute, Frederick's desertion would have only entitled her to seek a partial divorce, with no right to remarry.[67]

A letter from Emma to Robert Bonner in July 1860 (his letters to her do not survive) implies that Frederick had attempted to use the copyright registrations in Emma's works he filed in January, February, and April to pressure Bonner and T. B. Peterson to pay the royalties on sales of these works to him rather than to her (and, indeed, he, like the fictional Phemie's husband, was legally entitled to claim those royalties). "I hardly think," she wrote to Bonner, "in view of the Divorce Act that F will venture to trouble you."[68] A year later, the possibility that Frederick might make yet another attempt to interfere with her literary proprietorship still haunted her. "I do not believe that there is one chance in a million of Southworth's annoying you any more," she wrote to Bonner on May 17, 1861, "but still I would not risk that millionth chance where the Ledger is concerned. I fancy his next descent, if he has life enough left to make one, will be upon my London

66 House Committee for the District of Columbia, *A Bill to Authorize Divorces in the District of Columbia, and for Other Purposes*, 36th Cong., 1st sess., 17 Apr. 1860, H. Rep. 663. As a statute, 12 Stat. 158 (1860). The bill issued from the committee with no report, and the "bill folder" in the Congressional Records at the National Archives contains no clues as to the origins of the bill or the committee's deliberations. Nor is *Senator* Dixon of Connecticut implicated in the drafting of this *House* bill.

67 Joanne Dobson's inference that Emma rejected the prospect of divorce and a subsequent marriage to Henry Hardy, a "fellow Washingtonian" to whom she had "a tender attachment" ("Introduction," xix) seems problematic in light of the provisions of the 1860 statute.

68 Emma Southworth to Robert Bonner, 20 July 1860, Duke University.

publisher; – and if he does Mr Bonner – if he does – it will be the last time he ever troubles any body in this world. And that you may take my word for."[69] Court records show no evidence that Emma ever attempted to secure a partial divorce from Frederick under the 1860 Divorce Act or that she ever sought a court order protecting her property and earnings from him,[70] but the mere threat of such legal action seems to have been a sufficient deterrent. Furthermore, Frederick's death, which seems to have occurred before the end of the Civil War in 1865, may have definitively established Emma's legal status as a feme sole without the benefit of a court order.

"America sells the bodies of blacks, and steals the brains of the whites": Authorship in the absence of international copyright

Southworth's legal situation, like that of her fictional counterpart, Phemie Hart, demonstrates that the wife-as-slave trope could come close to being a lived reality for married women authors whose estranged husbands could claim their wives' labors and properties created through those labors if they chose to exercise their legal prerogatives. When criticizing coverture's effects on the ability of creative women to control and receive full financial benefit from the products of their intellectual labors, Mary Virginia Terhune and Mary Gove Nichols rely on the implicit assumption that male authors, full legal subjects who did not become things or "disappear" when they married, could exercise such control. However, in the absence of international copyright, even male authors might have the products of their mental labors appropriated, if not by husbands, then by publishers and the reading public. Their title to their literary property fell short of the perfection to which they felt entitled as free white male citizens of the American republic. As a satirist writing in the British humor magazine *Punch* observed in 1847 of the practices of American publishers in relation to works of British authors, "An English writer is treated by America as America treats her negroes: he is turned into ready money for the benefit of the smart dealer who robs him. His brains are taken to market, and knocked down to the highest bidder.... America sells the bodies of blacks, and steals the brains of the whites."[71] In his indignation, this satirist fails to take note of the traffic in reverse, the English booksellers who "knocked down the brains"

69 Emma Southworth to Robert Bonner, 17 May 1861, Beinecke Rare Book and Manuscript Library, Yale University. This portion is also quoted in Robert Gallup, "More Letters of American Writers," *Yale University Library Gazette* 37, no. 1 (1962): 32.

70 The National Archives holds the divorce docket for the Federal District Court for the District of Columbia. The indices for divorce proceedings from the 1850s and 1860s list neither Southworth as a party.

71 "English Authors – American Booksellers," *Punch*, 24 Apr. 1847, 178.

of American authors (and before *Uncle Tom's Cabin* became an enormous popular success in Britain, there were few examples of American authors whose works were as widely circulated in Britain as those of Walter Scott and Charles Dickens in America).

Not surprisingly, before emancipation, American advocates of international copyright seldom exploited the author-slave analogy, an analogy that relied for its force on the idea that American chattel slavery was barbarous and unjust. Elizabeth Clark has observed that feminist reformers more frequently exploited the wife-slave analogy after the Civil War because "anti-slavery rhetoric was a more powerful political tool after the war precisely because of [slavery's] new legal status" as a crime rather than a sin.[72] Copyright advocates similarly shifted their rhetoric, deploying the author-slave analogy more frequently after the war. Despite the risk of backlash from antiabolitionists, the author-slave analogy occasionally surfaced in the antebellum era. In the *New-York Mirror* in 1837, an anonymous magazinist praised the efforts of the group of British authors who had just petitioned the U.S. Congress seeking copyright reform and condemned his own nation: "England has moved first in the abolition of the intellectual slave-trade – this most contemptible kind of 'man-stealing'.... As the law of copyright now exists in this country, we are the licensed robbers of the property of others – the inhospitable plunderers of stranger minds – the sponges and Jeremy Diddlers of other people's intellects. By 'We,' we mean 'the universal Yankee nation.'"[73] A copyright gives its owner the right to both control and withhold publication of a work. The writer in the *Mirror* presents the outcome of the lack of international copyright protection in the United States as producing a mirror image of Mary Gove's situation in relation to Hiram Gove: while Hiram Gove "owned" his wife's brains and refused to consent to the publication of the products of her brain, American publishers "plundered" the minds of British authors and published the contents of those minds without their consent.

In his pamphlet *On International Copyright* (1840), Francis Lieber features the author-slave analogy with a slightly different emphasis. He predicts that "civilized" nations will soon recognize literary property rights of foreigners, much as nations had progressed from allowing plunder from foreign ships to the protection of all property: "In an analogous manner we see, that the more the barbarous idea vanishes, that the author is little better than a slave, who owns his property from no inherent right, but merely at the gracious pleasure of his own government, the more vanishes likewise the gross barbarous idea that his property may be forcibly taken from him,

72 Elizabeth B. Clark, "Matrimonial Bonds: Slavery and Divorce in Nineteenth-Century America," *Law and History Review* 8, no. 1 (1990): 31.

73 "International Copyright," *New-York Mirror,* 30 Dec. 1837, 215.

wherever we can lay hold on it in foreign parts."[74] Like many copyright advocates, Lieber presents copyright as a property right arising under natural law, and nations that refuse to recognize such rights arising under natural law thus demonstrate their "barbaric" status. Again, relying implicitly on the Lockean narrative, he claims that laws created by civil government thus do not *grant* a property right to authors but instead merely provide means for an author to enforce his natural rights. Authors, he argues, should not have their labors appropriated as if they were slaves any more than merchants should have their merchandise appropriated by force merely because that property has crossed a political boundary between nations.

Despite the relative rarity of the explicit author-slave analogy, as I discuss at more length in Chapter 2, advocates of copyright reform in antebellum America used many other analogies to express essentially the same idea expressed by *Punch*, the *Mirror*, and Lieber in their analogies between authors and slaves – the powerlessness and dispossession of authors. After the war and the abolition of slavery, the author-slave analogy took center stage in reorganized and reinvigorated efforts on behalf of international copyright. One of the leaders of the new International Copyright Association, S. Irenaeus Prime, writes in *Putnam's Monthly* in 1868 about the place of copyright reform in the postemancipation nation:

> The slave trade, once regarded as a moral and respectable traffic, was prosecuted by the best men in the Church and the world. . . . Now the slave trade is justly published as piracy. . . . But the slave trade [is] . . . now no more in reality offensive to good morals than [it was] when [it] flourished under the wing of Church and State. The public conscience having been enlightened and quickened, it is now a subject for wonder that honest and honorable men were ever engaged in [it]. . . . When the public conscience is awakened to the right of authors in their works, the Carey [anti-copyright] theory will be looked upon by all conscientious persons as flagitious and immoral as Proudhon's doctrine [that all property is robbery] or the Newport trade in rum and negroes.[75]

Prime draws a parallel between the slave trade, in which traders "stole" people from Africa and transported them to Europe and the Americas, where they were forced to work without compensation, and international literary piracy, in which the authors' properties produced by their labors, rather than the authors' bodies, are transported across national boundaries and "put to work" for the financial benefit of piratical publishers.

74 Francis Lieber, *On International Copyright, in a Letter to the Hon. William C. Preston, Senator of the United States* (New York: Wiley and Putnam, 1840), 46.

75 "The Right of Copyright," *Putnam's Monthly Magazine*, May 1868, 636–7. For Henry Carey's anti-copyright theory, see chap. 3.

Prime's confidence that the public conscience would soon be awakened proved premature. In 1882, the *Century* magazine continued protesting in the same vein, arguing against a compromise with publishers and the printing trades as a means to the end of international copyright:

> Now we hold it to be self-evident that, in a question of absolute right, there can be no compromise that will last. The history of slavery in this country is a proof of this; and we do not hesitate to say that it was easier to frame a plausible justification from the Bible itself, than it is to justify the theft of literary property allowed under our laws, and justified by our law-makers.[76]

Here, the analogy between author and slave is implicit – slavery *was* a wrong against the black man, and literary piracy *still* is a wrong against the author. The *Century* implies that both practices are moral evils a "civilized" society should not tolerate. By echoing the language of the Declaration of Independence ("Now, we hold it to be self-evident" for "We hold these truths to be self-evident"), the writer also implies that authorial independence as well as authorial property rights are at stake – reader-tyrants should not "enslave" authors as the British crown "enslaved" the American colonists. Despite this argument against compromise, compromise was, indeed, the means by which international copyright was enacted in 1891, leaving copyright advocates another decade during which to continue to rail against the spectacle of authors not being treated as equals with other laborers "worthy of their hire."[77]

"[E]ven that which I earned by literature was subject to the claim of my husband, as the manual labour of the slave was subject to the claim of his master": Narrating married women's literary proprietorship in England

With abused and dispossessed male authors figuring so prominently in American copyright advocacy, the absence of dispossessed women (as

76 "Topics of the Times: Authors' Rights," *Century Magazine*, Mar. 1882, 779.

77 For other invocations of slavery and abolition in copyright advocacy in the postwar years, see American Copyright League, *What American Authors Think About International Copyright* (New York: American Copyright League, 1888), 7; Edward Eggleston, "The Blessings of Piracy," *Century Magazine*, Apr. 1882, 945; BM, "Open Letter: Another Side of the Copyright Question," *Century Magazine*, July 1885, 489; E. L. Godkin, "Law and Theft," *Nation*, 12 Feb. 1891, 130–1; and other instances discussed in chapters 3 and 4. For the related invocation of the biblical injunction that "the laborer is worthy of his hire," adopted and adapted to copyright from antebellum abolitionism, see "Speech of Samuel Osgood," 25, and "Speech of Philip Schaff," 27, in *International Copyright. Meeting of Authors and Publishers, at the Rooms of the New York Historical Society, April 9, 1868, and Organization of the International Copyright Association* (New York: International Copyright Association, 1868); and Brander Matthews, *American Authors and British Pirates* (New York: The American Copyright League, 1889), 7.

authors rather than widows of authors) in these obsessively reiterated scenes of the miseries of authors is striking. In her analysis of American novelist Elizabeth Stoddard's theorizing of an alternative economy of authorship in her story "Collected by a Valetudinarian," Ellen Weinauer contrasts Stoddard's strategies to what one might expect from women writers in the face of their dispossession: "In the context of women's exclusion from the proprietary mechanisms of the capitalist economy and the discourse of possessive individualism, and of women's increasing participation – despite these exclusions – in the literary marketplace, we can expect to find a woman writer insisting quite urgently on the importance of proprietary control."[78] While Weinauer imagines such insistence as the norm and Stoddard's alternative theorizing as a departure from that norm, the imagined norm is largely absent – at least in public discourse. The scene of a woman author's dispossession through coverture remained largely unnarratable in a culture accustomed to both narratives of authorial dispossession of their labors and property through an allegedly inadequate copyright law and narratives of wifely dispossession of other forms of property and labor through coverture.

The situation of British women authors, in many ways parallel to that of American women but also significantly different, sheds light on the gendered possibilities of constructing narratives of authorship under different legal regimes and market conditions. In the early years of statutory copyright in eighteenth-century England, the position of authors was tenuous at best, despite the fact that the law granted authors a new legal status as proprietors. Before statutory copyright, only publishers (members of the Stationers Company) could protect their exclusive right to publish a work by entering the title into the Stationers Register. Authors were the persons granted copyright by the first British copyright statute, but they had to alienate that property immediately in order to publish at all – that is, customary trade practices forced them to transfer their copyrights to publishers for a relatively small one-time payment unless they had the financial resources to self-publish. In *Nobody's Story*, Catherine Gallagher argues that poet Charlotte Lennox served as a representative author in eighteenth-century England because the law and trade practices combined to place British authors in essentially the same situation as coverture placed married women. The inability of Lennox's husband to support himself and his wife through his own endeavors was widely known in literary circles, and Lennox's literary labors supported them both. Because of coverture, however, writes Gallagher, "Charlotte Lennox's [literary] properties would technically have been her husband's anyway."[79] Because she was a married

78 Ellen Weinauer, "Alternative Economies," 169.

79 Catherine Gallagher, *Nobody's Story: The Vanishing Acts of Women Writers in the Marketplace, 1670–1820* (Berkeley: University of California Press, 1994), 198–9.

woman, coverture effectively dispossessed her of literary property, but customary trade practices that forced all authors to alienate their property in order to publish also dispossessed her. In Gallagher's reading of Lennox's situation, Lennox, as an author "doubly dispossessed" of her literary property, served "as a hyperbolic instance of authorial suffering" in literary circles because all eighteenth-century British authors, male or female, were in a "'feminized' position" in relation to the literary market.[80]

By the nineteenth century, the position of British authors had changed. Authors had more market power and were more likely to hold on to their own copyrights and be paid royalties based on the number of their books sold rather than be forced to accept a more modest one-time payment. Furthermore, the politics of copyright reform in Parliament present a mirror image to that in the U.S. Congress, which resisted international copyright as an imposition on readers' rights. According to historian of the British copyright law John Feather, international copyright measures moved easily through Parliament, where they were "presented as a matter of patriotic pride and duty rather than a restraint of trade, and as a means of preventing the exploitation of British genius by two recent ex-enemies, the United States and France."[81] Certainly, British authors sharply criticized the appropriation of their literary properties by American publishers and readers, but their relative position in their own market was much stronger: they had greater legal leverage in their arrangements with British publishers, and their proprietary interests, both domestically and internationally, received support in Parliament. In light of this shift from the eighteenth to the nineteenth century, a married British woman author no longer stood in the same relation to her copyrights as her male peers. For much of the nineteenth century, male authors could become strong proprietors and earn great profits from sales of their works, but married women remained in the same position in relation to their literary properties as Charlotte Lennox in the previous century – dispossessed of their literary property and profits through coverture. (Of course, married women authors' *husbands* were not dispossessed of the value of their wives' literary properties by publishers to the extent that they had been in the previous century.)

The spectacularly public failure of British poet Lady Caroline Norton's marriage and her subsequent advocacy for reform of coverture in England present a striking contrast to the positions of both Charlotte Lennox in

80 Ibid., 196.

81 John Feather, *Publishing, Piracy and Politics: An Historical Study of Copyright in Britain* (London: Mansell, 1994), 155. Which is not to say that the British Parliament saw no threat of monopoly or a threat to readers' interests in the expansion of copyright. As Feather also documents, attempts at domestic reform (mostly proposals for term extension) met with stiff opposition from antimonopolists and those concerned about book prices and the rights of readers.

eighteenth-century England and married women authors in nineteenth-century America. Making her own marital troubles the center of her writings on behalf of reform, Norton represents not "a hyperbolic instance of the sufferings of all authors" but the specifically female suffering of the author-wife. That specifically female suffering enabled her to align herself (noblewoman that she was) with the figure of the suffering American slave, while implying that such an alignment did not apply to her female author peers across the Atlantic. In 1854, in the wake of Harriet Beecher Stowe's tour of England, Norton published a pamphlet on *English Laws for Women in the Nineteenth Century*, arguing for reform of the laws affecting married women in England, including the laws of divorce and separation, child custody, and property.[82] Searching for a proper analogy to convey to her readers the status of married women under the law of England, Norton specifically refers to Stowe's tour and the increased English interest in the abolition of American slavery as a result. In this context, she notes an item from a Cincinnati newspaper (reprinted in the London *Times*) about a slave who contracted with his master for self-purchase and the court decision rendering that contract null and void because of the slave's legal nonexistence. Drawing a parallel between herself and this slave from Kentucky (not coincidentally the state from which the hero of *Uncle Tom's Cabin* is sold further South despite his master's promise to grant him his freedom at some unspecified future date as a reward for his exemplary behavior), Norton writes, "I find, in the slave law of Kentucky, an exact parallel of the law of England for its married women; and in this passage in the life of the poor slave Sam Norris, an exact counterpart of what has lately occurred in my own."[83] Norton recounts the (already widely known) story of her own infamously unhappy marriage and her long struggles, spread out over decades, with her separated husband over both child custody and financial matters.

82 This pamphlet was "printed for private circulation," but Norton's marital troubles were notoriously public, and the British press commented widely on both Norton's situation and her arguments for reform. For the notoriety and publicity of Norton's legal conflicts with her husband in the 1830s, see Karen Chase and Michael H. Levenson, *The Spectacle of Intimacy: A Public Life for the Victorian Family* (Princeton: Princeton University Press, 2000), 21–45. Scholarly accounts of married women's status in Victorian England routinely recount Norton's legal difficulties in both the 1830s and the 1850s. See, e.g., Mary Lyndon Shanley, *Feminism, Marriage, and the Law in Victorian England* (Princeton: Princeton University Press, 1989), chap. 1; Lee Holcombe, *Wives and Property: Reform of the Married Women's Property Law in Nineteenth-Century England* (Toronto: University of Toronto Press, 1983), chap. 4; Joan Perkin, *Women and Marriage in Nineteenth-Century England* (Chicago: Lyceum, 1989), chap. 1; and Poovey, *Uneven Developments*,chap. 3. Tellingly, no American woman author occupies a similarly central position in the scholarship on the legal status of nineteenth-century American married women.

83 Caroline Norton, *English Laws for Women in the Nineteenth Century* (London, 1854), 19. Facsimile reprint in *Selected Writings of Caroline Norton*, ed. James O. Hoge and Jane Marcus (New York: Scholars' Facsimiles & Reprints, 1978). Hereinafter cited in the text.

Most notable in this context is a contract between her and her husband settling their financial disputes – a contract the courts refused to enforce when her husband ceased to perform his obligations under that contract. Driving home the parallel between herself and Sam Norris, she writes, "Even that which I earned by literature was subject to the claim of my husband, as the manual labour of the slave was subject to the claim of his master–, because a married woman is, by the code of England (as Sam Norris by the code of Kentucky) *non-existent* in law" (p. 20).

Norton, while deploring chattel slavery in the United States, apparently believed that married American women authors did not suffer the same legal injustices with regard to their literary properties as did she and her British sisters. Looking at the United States from across the Atlantic, Norton and other British reformers imagined that they saw a rosy picture of progress against which to measure the absence of progress in England.[84] In her pamphlet, Norton positions Stowe as the culminating figure in a series of male British social reformers who used their power and authority on behalf of the oppressed (prisoners, the insane, poor children, etc.), thus implying that Stowe enjoyed the same degree of power and autonomy as did her British male predecessors and peers in the arena of reform.[85] Norton regrets her own absence from England at the time of Stowe's tour because she wishes she could have seen "one whose genius glorified that solemn and gloomy argument [against slavery], and sent it among us clothed in light. . . . I desire heartily for her that her name may hereafter be remembered with a blessing, among the names of those who were early labourers in a day now dawning, that shall bring help to the helpless. I hold her to be a holy one, and slavery an accursed thing" (p. 16). Norton assigns Stowe the role of a quasi divinity dispensing her blessings on others rather than of an object of a husband's tyrannical will as Norton herself is.[86] Pointing to British indignation at the unjust legal systems of other countries (slavery in America, abuse of political prisoners in Italy, religious intolerance in Portugal, and treatment of women in Austria), Norton insists that England subject itself to the same scrutiny with regards to married women (p. 21).

Norton occasionally references the sufferings of other women under the English law, but she focuses largely on her own sufferings and, at every turn, presents her husband's violation of her authorial property rights as a central outrage, second only to or on par with the law's and her husband's

84 See, e.g., Caroline Francis Cornwallis prodding her British audience to accept reform by pointing to the example of the United States. "The Property of Married Women," *Westminster Review* 10, no. 2 (1856): 351–3.

85 Mary Poovey puts a slightly different spin on Norton's positioning of herself through this genealogy of reformers. *Uneven Developments*, 65.

86 Although Norton effectively used Stowe and American abolitionist rhetoric to position herself as being as powerless as Stowe was powerful, Stowe's legal status as a married woman author differed little from Norton's. See chap. 4.

violation of her maternal rights in her children. Norton represents her labors as an author as intellectual and spiritual, and her husband and the law courts thus conspire not only to interfere with her ability to support herself and her children financially but to obliterate her very identity. Referring to her husband's subpoena of her publisher's accounts during one of their many disputes over finances, she protests, "If the absurd anomalies in the law which regulate claims on the husband did not exist, Mr Norton could not have subpoenaed my publishers in the County Court, to annul my right even to my own soul and brains" (p. 146).

Norton thus pointedly and repeatedly frames the question of reform of coverture as a particular necessity for women who are authors. This public linking of coverture and copyright through Norton's own life and in organized efforts for reform in subsequent years set the British public discussion about reform of coverture apart from the parallel situation in the United States. When British feminists presented their first petition to Parliament in 1856 seeking reform of coverture, the concerns of creative women appeared front and center. The second sentence of the petition advises Parliament that although the law of coverture "might once have been deemed for the middle and upper ranks, a comparatively theoretical question . . . it is no longer, since married women of education are entering on every side the fields of literature and art, in order to increase the family income by such exertions."[87] A few brief paragraphs later, the petition delicately acknowledges Caroline Norton ("That it is proved by well known cases of hardship suffered by women of station, and also by professional women earning large incomes by pursuit of the arts, how real is the injury inflicted"). Drawing to a conclusion, the petition resorts to the wife-slave analogy, asking that "legal protection be thrown over the produce of [married women's] labour, and that in entering the state of marriage, they no longer pass from freedom into the condition of a slave, all whose earnings belong to his master and not to himself."

Elizabeth Barrett Browning, among other women authors, publicly supported reform of coverture by signing this 1856 petition to Parliament. Cheri Larsen Hoeckley argues that Barrett Browning's famously happy marriage to Robert Browning made her prominent signature on the 1856 petition to Parliament in favor of reform of coverture a strategically desirable counterweight to the image of the "writing wife . . . as disastrously married" produced by the earlier public spectacle of Caroline Norton.[88] Both Norton's trials and the 1856 petition campaign, argues Hoeckley, worked against reform efforts by "allowing opponents to claim that coverture harmed only 'a few literary ladies whose peculiar talents had helped to place them in

87 Cornwallis's article reproduced the petition in a footnote. "Property of Married Women," 336–8.

88 Cheri Larsen Hoeckley, "Anomalous Ownership: Copyright, Coverture, and *Aurora Leigh*," *Victorian Poetry* 36, no. 2 (1998): 146. Hereinafter cited in the text.

a rather anomalous position'" (p. 144). Analyzing Barrett Browning's representation of women's authorship in her verse novel *Aurora Leigh* in light of her support of reform, Hoeckley finds the intersection of coverture and copyright to be the key to a narrative puzzle of the novel-length poem – why does Barrett Browning seem incapable of representing the eponymous heroine's eventual marriage? Throughout much of the poem, according to Hoeckley, "Aurora's literary property allows her the independence to replicate middle-class domestic respectability without its understood foundation of male economic prosperity and controlled female procreation and property" (p. 153). Aurora finally consents to marry Romney, but their marriage is only promised, not narrated, as Aurora "settles into the wife's role – legally, civilly, and psychologically covered by her husband" (p. 154). As Hoeckley makes clear, even in the earlier parts of the poem, Barrett Browning finds narrating Aurora's proprietorship difficult because profit potentially threatens her status as a disinterested genius and thus her moral and artistic integrity. Nevertheless, Aurora's literary career and the uses to which she puts her profits occupy most of the verse novel, while her life as a married woman poet is a promise, not a reality. Thus Barrett Browning finds unnarratable Aurora's transformation from feme sole in full possession of her literary property to marital cipher possessed by a husband.

Phemie's Temptation and the unnarratability of women's authorial possession in the United States

In a different national and legal context, Mary Virginia Terhune faced an inverted narrative dilemma in *Phemie's Temptation*. Terhune has no difficulty representing Phemie's authorship under coverture when her literary property is never fully her own. Instead, Terhune cannot narrate her postdivorce status as a feme sole author. In fact, the "temptation" of the novel's title is divorce. Once Phemie finally succumbs to this temptation (that Terhune clearly both abhors on principle and makes a justifiable necessity in response to extreme realities), the novel ends abruptly. What does Mary Virginia Terhune's imaginative evocation of this actual legal dilemma, very much like the one faced by her peer E. D. E. N. Southworth several years earlier, suggest about how the intersection between coverture and copyright shaped the production and consumption of female authorship in nineteenth-century America? Before concluding my discussion of Terhune's novel, I want to return briefly to the broader questions of the legal status of authors and the legal status of wives in American culture, or, rather, the sense that both classes of persons had no status that the law would recognize. An anonymous 1835 article in favor of copyright reform in the *Knickerbocker* indignantly proclaims that the copyright law left "genius . . . in a state of outlawry, and for no reason that we know, except that men may prey upon it."[89] An anonymous article in the *North American Review* in 1839 repeats and embellishes the figure of author-as-outlaw. In America, claims the anonymous magazinist, the author is an exception to the rule that society will protect the property of its members, so that the author "joins society, not as a party to the general bond, but as an outlaw, who is among us, but not of us. . . . He is a man of too much glory to mind hunger; and so we take away his bread, he himself protesting all the while, that, maugre the glory, he, and his children too, must needs eat."[90] It is precisely this image of the author as the powerless patriarch unable to feed his children that returns in Grace Greenwood's copyright parodies and that earlier underwrote the "widows and orphans" provision of the 1831 copyright act.

In 1845 in the *Democratic Review*, the author of "Wives and Slaves; a Bone for Abolitionists to Pick" (who signed the article only as "WJF") similarly laments the status of wives as outside the sphere of a law that grants them neither rights nor protection. WJF uses the slave-wife analogy to pointed effect to dramatize the sufferings of white women in the North, drawing a long list of equivalences between the legal status of the Southern slave and the Northern wife before ultimately proclaiming that the abandoned wife suffers more under the law of coverture than the slave under slave law. WJF elaborates at length through the concrete example of an abandoned wife who sets up a boarding house as a means of supporting herself and her children, outfitting it with furnishings purchased by the proceeds of the business. Despite her admirable enterprise and her maternal motivations for that enterprise, her husband can, perfectly legally, return to the home he abandoned, lay claim to all of the possessions his wife has purchased with the proceeds of her labor, and then leave, forcing her to begin again, with no security (or her husband's creditors can similarly take possession of "his" assets to satisfy his debts). "To the peculiar hardships of the deserted wife's condition," writes WJF, "that of the slave supplies no parallel, unless we can imagine such a thing as a *masterless* slave. As to the protection which society affords others in the acquisition and preservation of property, she is absolutely an outlaw; having no rights in the earnings of her own hands, or the savings of her own prudence."[91] The article demonstrates with painful clarity the politically problematic nature of WJF's underlying analogy – WJF uses the call for reform of coverture primarily as a stick with which to beat

89 "Community of Copy-Right between the United States and Great Britain," *Knickerbocker*, Oct. 1835, 285.

90 "Art. VI. *Remarks on Literary Property*. By Philip H. Nicklin," *North American Review*, Jan. 1839, 257. The index identifies the author as Willard Phillips.

91 WJF, "Wives and Slaves; a Bone for the Abolitionists to Pick," *United States Democratic Review*, Oct. 1845, 270.

abolitionists, who threaten the union with their attacks on the South, rather than genuinely pleading on behalf of women for their empowerment. In the end, WJF's rhetoric subverts the claims of both slaves and wives to an amelioration of their legal condition.

The article also, however, illuminates the tangled situation of the author-heroine in *Phemie's Temptation* and the ways that her situation speaks to the broader dispossession of authors in nineteenth-century America. Despite Terhune's obvious indignation at Hart's appropriation of his wife's literary profits, the novel does not wholeheartedly embrace the possibility of market-driven, proprietary authorship for women. Like many author-heroines in novels and stories of the period, Phemie's motivations for authorship are never purely economic. Although she first begins to write before her marriage to Hart because her family relies almost entirely on her for financial support, she takes up authorship again after marriage for much "higher" reasons. As she tells her husband when she is about to present him with a special inscribed copy of her book, she writes to avoid "living for my selfish gratification." God has given her strength, courage, and knowledge, and through her books she seeks to "help the weak," "cheer the desponding," and enlighten the "ignorant" (p. 178). Hart reacts violently to her authorship as a sign of her desire to separate her identity from his and to prove her own superiority. In an attempt to bring her down, he claims that he as a publisher knows the truth about women writers and that they are all money-grubbing hacks hiding behind claims of high moral purpose (p. 186). The narrator clearly intends us to understand that Hart is wrong and that Phemie truly does write only to serve others. When his desertion forces her to take up writing again for financial reasons, even that financial purpose is an unselfish one – she needs to feed, clothe, and house her daughter. Throughout, then, Phemie never labors on her own account. While Terhune puts strong, feminist words about woman's emancipation and independence in the mouth of Miss Darcy, Phemie's willing submission to dispossession undercuts the force of Miss Darcy's politics. Phemie's repeated and willing submission and dispossession, both as author and as wife, occupy much of the novel.

In the incident described at the beginning of this chapter, Hart has recently abandoned Phemie, and in the absence of her husband, she cannot sue her publisher for royalties owed to her for the sales of her book written and published before her husband's desertion of her. Three years after Hart's desertion of Phemie and his daughter, when Phemie has become (relatively) financially independent through her authorial labors, her husband reappears to spend six months in her new household, a household shared with Miss Darcy. Phemie dutifully submits to Hart's "lawful claim" to her person and her services, allowing him to live off the proceeds of her literary labors while she waits on him hand and foot. At the end of those six months, Phemie visits her publisher's office to collect the $300 in her "half-yearly copyright account," only to find that "Mr. Hart had drawn every dollar due me a week since – my publisher supposed, by my directions. I have nothing to say against this. A husband has unlimited control over his wife's wages" (p. 303). When her brother in law suggests that she leave orders with her publishers not to disburse funds to her husband, she responds, "it would do no good Joe. . . . I am powerless. All women are, I think" (p. 304).

Shortly thereafter, Phemie finally throws her husband out when he physically abuses their daughter and insists that Phemie must eject Miss Darcy from the household. Her self-assertion, however, her proclamation that "I promised to be a wife – not a slave" (p. 307), does not remove her legal disabilities under coverture. Lawyers advise her that her six-month voluntary residence with Hart would make it difficult for her to secure a divorce. Furthermore, Hart threatens to sue for custody of their child, and with this threat hanging over her head, Phemie is powerless to prevent him from continuing to appropriate her royalties:

> Three times, during this period, her husband wrote to her for money, which was forwarded to him with terrified punctuality; twice she was informed by her men of business that they had honored Mr. Hart's drafts upon them to the amount of several hundred dollars – each time, just after the publication of a new volume from her pen – a circumstance which showed how vigilant was his watch upon her, and intensified her apprehension of his sudden descent upon her folded lamb [her daughter]. The aforesaid men of business had "not thought it expedient to refuse to pay the money to the claimant, lest they should become involved in a law-suit," in which even they were sagacious enough to understand that the chances were as a hundred to one against the nominal owner of the copyright. (p. 309)

Phemie, who labors with her pen to support her daughter and whose copyrights and the income from them are part of her ongoing business enterprise of her authorship, finds herself in precisely the same position as the abandoned wife keeping a boarding house in "Wives and Slaves." Her copyrights, like the furnishings of the boarding house, are hers in name only. Without a divorce, she is a "masterless slave," whose master may reassert his claims at any time, leaving her with no security or protection, "absolutely an outlaw."

A mere page after Terhune describes Phemie's continuing vulnerability to her absent husband's claims, Phemie finally succeeds in divorcing Hart (an incident merely stated as fact rather than narrated), and the novel is over. The novel thus ends with Phemie's divorce from Hart, and that end comes very abruptly, as if Terhune doesn't know what to do with her heroine once she becomes a feme sole again and can exercise complete control over her literary property. It is the struggle and the dispossession that are the focus of Terhune's narrative energies, not secure possession.

Ultimately, Phemie as a figure of the conditions of female authorship suggests not Barrett Browning's heroine in *Aurora Leigh* but Caroline Norton. Even more than was the case for Norton, whose dispossession came solely at the hands of her husband, Phemie's situation, with her doubled dispossession through a man who is both her husband and her publisher, suggests the earlier situation of Charlotte Lennox, who was dispossessed of her literary property by both the literary market and marriage. Like American authors in the absence of international copyright, Phemie is stranded outside the sphere of the law while others appropriate her property in the market. As an author, a wife, and (metaphorically speaking) a slave, Phemie's entire dispossession for most of the novel suggests her representative status at a time when all authors, like Phemie, were in a "feminized" position in relation to the market. Despite that dispossession, neither Phemie (the abandoned author-wife, whose situation gave the lie to the legal fiction of marital unity) nor Terhune (the happily married author-wife, whose functional marriage insulated her from the law's potentially ludicrous logic) stopped writing. In fact, their legal status outside the law only motivated them to write more, and from that position on the law's margins, both the fictional character and her creator wrote their way into the center of popular literary culture and the American literary market.

Chapter 2

"Suited to the Market": Catharine Sedgwick, Female Authorship, and the Literary Property Debates, 1822–1842

In 1838, Catharine Maria Sedgwick signed a petition to Congress in favor of the passage of an international copyright law. At the heart of this petition that proclaims its signers to be "Citizens of New York" is an extravagant, masculine-gendered metaphor of American-author-as-soldier:

> Our policy, different and even adverse, to the principles prevalent throughout Europe, render us a shining mark for the envenomed arrows of jealousy and misrepresentation. Many have been the shafts already sped, and the quiver is by no means exhausted. It behooves us to avail ourselves of all means of just defence. That protection may be found in the fearless and able exertions of our native writers. Induced by every motive of patriotism to defend our institutions, they will hardly rest satisfied with remaining on the defensive. They will base their hopes of fame, and their claims to future remembrance, on the bold and manly promulgation of liberal sentiments. They will thus not only become the guardians of our country's fame, but the benefactors of our race.[1]

In the terms of the petition's extended metaphor, American authors take up arms to defend America's democratic institutions from foreign attack, implying, perhaps, a repeat of the War of 1812. By signing the petition, Sedgwick figuratively joined this authorial militia, asking Congress for support in its mission of defending America from the "envenomed arrows of jealousy and misrepresentation" fired at America from other countries. Or, following the military metaphor as it progresses from defensive to offensive military action, she represents herself as one of those who "will hardly rest satisfied with remaining on the defensive," and will instead take up the offense through "the bold and manly promulgation of liberal sentiments."

As a signer of this petition, Catharine Sedgwick placed herself in distinguished (and exclusively masculine) company. Although most of the 136 signers left no mark on history, a number of the signers were powerful men in politics, the arts, journalism, law, and education, or were young men who were on the verge of becoming powerful public figures (in the latter category, I would include Catharine Sedgwick's nephew Theodore Sedgwick, the third of that name, a young attorney, an active partisan of the

1 Senate Committee on Patents, *Memorial of a Number Citizens of New York, Praying the Passage of an International Copyright Law*, 25th Cong., 2nd sess., 24 Apr. 1838, S. Doc. 399, 1–2.

Democratic Party, and an occasional contributor to the *New York Evening Post* under the signature "Veto").[2] Although the petition Sedgwick signed is, in many ways, typical of petitions to Congress in favor of international copyright, Sedgwick's presence as a female signer is not. Harriet Martineau played a central role in organizing an 1837 British author's petition to the U.S. Congress. She first collected signatures from fifty-six British authors, including twelve women (Maria Edgeworth among them), and then sent the petition to members of the House and the Senate. However, Sedgwick was the only American woman author to sign a petition to Congress on the subject of international copyright before the Civil War.[3]

Sedgwick's decision to sign such a petition violated expectations of the proper relationship of American women to the state. Catharine Beecher explains why women should not petition the U.S. Congress in her *Essay on Slavery and Abolitionism, with Reference of Females* (published in 1837 in response to an upswing in abolitionist agitation by women, including a

2 Among the signers were: James Nack, "deaf and dumb poet" and New York celebrity; George Pope Morris, poet, playwright, and editor and proprietor of the literary magazine the *New-York Weekly Mirror*; several young men associated with the *American Monthly Magazine* (Park Benjamin, coeditor, and contributors W. A. Jones and Cornelius Mathews); W. A. Duer, President of Columbia; John Augustine Smith, president of the College of Physicians; James Brooks, proprietor of the *New York Express*; David Hale, editor and proprietor of the *New York Journal of Commerce*; John Osborne Sargent, associate editor of the *Courier and Enquirer*; Charles Anthon and James Renwick, professors at Columbia; John Torrey, professor at the College of Physicians; William Dunlap, professor at the National Academy of Design; George Folsom, librarian of the New York Historical Society; Charles Edwards, author of legal treatises and standing counsel to the British consulate; Ralph Ingersoll Lockwood, lawyer and legal treatise writer; Henry Cruse Murphy, Brooklyn City Attorney; and Samuel Swartout, Collector of the Port of New York. All these signers except Mathews may be found in Dumas Malone, ed., *Dictionary of American Biography* (New York: Scriber's, 1935). Cornelius Mathews, part of the "Young America" group of the 1840s, can be found in Perry Miller, *The Raven and the Whale: The War of Words and Wits in the Era of Poe and Melville* (New York: Harcourt Brace, 1956) and Edward L. Widmer, *Young America: The Flowering of Democracy in New York City* (New York: Oxford University Press, 2000). There were three Theodore Sedgwicks in Catharine Sedgwick's family: her father (long dead in 1838), her brother, and her brother's son. Because her nephew lived in New York City and had close ties to William Cullen Bryant and "Young America" (see Widmer), I believe he was the signer.

3 The British memorial aligns the signers' names with their works. Senate, *Address of Certain Authors of Great Britain to the Senate of the United States in Congress,* 24th Cong., 2nd sess., 1837, S. Doc. 134. House, *Authors of Great Britain,* 24th Cong., 2nd sess., 13 Feb. 1837, H. Doc. 162. For Martineau's role in organizing the British petition drive, see James J. Barnes, *Authors, Publishers, and Politicians: The Quest for an Anglo-American Copyright Agreement 1815–1854* (Columbus: Ohio State University Press, 1974), chap. 3 (I also rely on Barnes for a general history of copyright during the years covered by this chapter). Elizabeth Peabody signed an 1843 petition circulated by her nephew publisher George Palmer Putnam. Ezra Greenspan, *George Palmer Putnam: Representative American Publisher* (University Park: Pennsylvania State University Press, 2000), 100n. However, she signed as a "Publisher of Boston." House, *Copyrights. Memorial of Citizens of the United States for an International Copyright Treaty,* 28th Cong., 1st sess., 16 Dec. 1843, H. Doc. 10, 2. For a bibliography of all petitions on the subject of copyright submitted to Congress, see Thorvald Solberg, *Copyright in Congress 1789–1904: A Bibliography, and Chronological Record of All Proceeding in Congress in Relation to Copyright from April 15, 1789, to April 28, 1904* (Washington, DC: Government Printing Office, 1905).

flood of women's petitions to Congress demanding the abolition of slavery in the District of Columbia):

> In this country, petitions to congress, in reference to the official duties of legislators, seem, IN ALL CASES, to fall entirely without the sphere of female duty. Men are the proper persons to make appeals to the rulers whom they appoint, and if their female friends, by arguments and persuasions, can induce them to petition, all the good that can be done by such measures will be secured. But if females cannot influence their nearest friends, to urge forward a public measure in this way, they surely are out of their place, in attempting to do it themselves.[4]

According to Beecher's philosophy, if Sedgwick had persuaded her nephew as her "nearest friend" to sign the petition, she would have done all that she, as a woman, was entitled to do. By signing the petition herself, she stepped out of her proper sphere of influence in her family and into the proscribed scene of governmental power.[5] Even though the abolitionist women who signed petitions suffered criticism from Beecher and others for their unwomanly political actions, they nevertheless could justify their petitions as "prayers" for moral reform on behalf of others; Sedgwick more baldly petitioned in support of her own personal and financial interests and concerning a more clearly political issue. In the context of the petition, she presumed to demand action from Congress when she could not vote; and she presumed to demand an expansion of property rights when, as a woman, her relationship to the law of property was, at best, ambiguous.

Sedgwick's presumption, however, is not as great as it first appears. Despite the legal disabilities suffered even by free white women such as those who signed abolitionist petitions to Congress, they had far more public power and authority than the slave men and women on whose behalf they petitioned. In contrast, the authors who signed the "Citizens of New York" copyright petition argued on their own behalf from a position of powerlessness. The petition attempts to map out a powerful role for American authorship, but in

4 Catharine E. Beecher, *An Essay on Slavery and Abolitionism, with Reference to the Duty of American Females* (Philadelphia: Henry Perkins, 1837), 104–5. Sedgwick expresses views similar to Beecher's in *Means and Ends; or, Self-Training* (Boston: Marsh, Capen, Lyon & Webb, 1839), 253.

5 Beecher earlier violated her own advice by participating in a women's petition drive against Indian removal. Mary Hershberger, "Mobilizing Women, Anticipating Abolition: The Struggle against Indian Removal in the 1830s," *Journal of American History* 86, no. 1 (1999): 15–40; Lori D. Ginzberg, *Women and the Work of Benevolence: Morality, Politics, and Class in the Nineteenth-Century United States* (New Haven: Yale University Press, 1990), 67. On women's abolitionist petition drives, see Gerda Lerner, "The Political Activities of Antislavery Women," in *The Majority Finds Its Past* (New York: Oxford University Press, 1979), 112–28; Ginzberg, *Women and the Work of Benevolence*, chap. 3; Deborah Bingham Van Broekhoven, "'Let Your Names Be Enrolled': Method and Ideology in Women's Antislavery Petitioning," in *The Abolitionist Sisterhood: Women's Political Culture in Antebellum America*, eds. Jean Fagan Yellin and John C. Van Horne (Ithaca: Cornell University Press, 1994), 179–99; and Yellin, *Women and Sisters: The Antislavery Feminists in American Culture* (New Haven: Yale University Press, 1989), chap. 2 (specifically on Angelina Grimke, to whom Beecher was responding).

so doing, it draws attention to the dispossession of authors under the existing law. The petition explicitly claims the status of "citizens" for its signers (they are identified as both "Citizens of New York" and "American citizens"). Furthermore, the petition ascribes to authors all of the characteristics that Nancy Isenberg has identified in *Sex and Citizenship* as establishing citizenship in antebellum America (and as establishing citizenship as an exclusively male prerogative). With the end of primogeniture and property-based qualifications for suffrage in America, the American (white) "common man" established his consent to and investment in the social contract by demonstrating the masculine virtues of "force, aggression, risk, and self-defense."[6] As Isenberg notes, Thomas Jefferson suggested that militia enrollment be substituted for property ownership as evidence of the civic capacity required for suffrage.[7] By describing American authors as "bold" and "manly" militia members, the "Citizens of New York" sought to establish the civic capacity and thus full citizenship of American authors and their right to protection of their literary property by the state. However, their attempt reveals not the established centrality of American authors to the union but their marginality. Other (nonslave) laborers and traders receive state protection for their property rights, but authors, despite joining the cultural militia, receive no such recognition or protection. As Isenberg argues, even free white single women like Catharine Sedgwick were "ciphers on the boundaries of the social compact" in antebellum America. Sedgwick's signature on the "Citizens of New York" petition thus reveals the alignment of women and authors as "ciphers" in the American union.[8]

Mary Kelley's influential analysis of Sedgwick's career in *Private Woman, Public Stage* focuses on the gulf between Sedgwick's public life as a producer of literary culture and her private domestic life, and the sense of dislocation and confusion that this gulf caused.[9] Kelley's reading of Sedgwick's authorial

6 Nancy Isenberg, *Sex and Citizenship in Antebellum America* (Chapel Hill: University of North Carolina Press, 1998), 105.

7 Ibid., 25–6.

8 Ibid., 105. On militia service and citizenship, see also Linda K. Kerber, "'May All Our Citizens Be Soldiers, and All Our Soldiers Citizens': The Ambiguities of Female Citizenship in the New Nation," in *Arms at Rest: Peacemaking and Peacekeeping in American History*, ed. Joan R. Challinor and Robert L. Beisner (New York: Greenwood Press, 1987), 4–5. The question of whether or not free white women were citizens in the nineteenth century is a vexed one, particularly when women were denied access to suffrage. See also Kerber, "The Paradox of Women's Citizenship in the Early Republic: The Case of *Martin vs. Massachusetts*, 1805," *American Historical Review* 97, no. 3 (1992): 349–78; and scholarship cited in note 5.

9 Mary Kelley, *Private Woman, Public Stage: Literary Domesticity in Nineteenth-Century America* (New York: Oxford University Press, 1984). Since *Private Woman*, Kelley has shifted her focus in her work on Sedgwick to concentrate more on Sedgwick's agency as an author. *The Power of Her Sympathy: The Autobiography and Journal of Catharine Maria Sedgwick*, ed. Mary Kelley (Boston: Massachusetts Historical Society/Northeastern University Press, 1993), 36. See also Melissa J. Homestead, "Behind the Veil? Catharine Sedgwick and Anonymous Publication," in *Catharine Maria Sedgwick: Critical Perspectives*,

situation rests on the assumption that male American authors had access to cultural power and status by virtue of their literary labors and that there was a significant difference between the power and authority available to authors in public and the relatively powerless position of women in the privacy of the home. However, during the years of Sedgwick's career, writers on both sides of the copyright debate described authors, even male authors, as irrelevant, disempowered, or dispossessed. Copyright opponents dismissed American authorship as irrelevant or unnecessary, a superfluity in a market that could easily be supplied with British works. Copyright advocates, in turn, claimed authors were triply dispossessed in the American market: because of the difficulties American authors encountered in finding an audience and a market in America, because of the author's dispossession of his property in England, and because the author's property ceased to be property at the expiration of the copyright term. Placing Sedgwick's career in the context of the obsessively repeated narratives of authorial dispossession so widely circulated in the international copyright debates, I suggest that even her occasional expressions of anxiety about assuming the role of author were qualifications for, rather than impediments to, assuming that role in her historical moment. The law of coverture did not prevent Sedgwick from owning and exploiting her own literary property. Still, her status as an unmarried, childless woman left her standing outside the narratives of patrimony and descent used by copyright advocates to justify the expansion of authors' property rights. Furthermore, as Nancy Cott argues, the status of married women under coverture led to the "fixing [of] all women, not only wives, in a position of minimal citizenship."[10]

Meredith McGill has identified the theory of copyright that prevailed in antebellum America as "republican" in its privileging of the public interest and promotion of the free circulation of print and its concomitant circumscription or outright denial of private property rights for authors.[11] Although McGill ultimately seeks to de-center authorship in American literary history, I propose that Sedgwick's mode of authorship worked within the constraints of a controlling republican theory of copyright in the United States. As an author who continued to publish and whose popular success in both the United States and England grew in the absence of international copyright, her mode of authorship served as a testament to her *dis*posession as well as

ed. Lucinda Damon-Bach and Victoria Clements (Boston: Northeastern University Press, 2003), 19–35, and Kelley's response to my critique in the foreword to the volume (xiii).

10 Nancy Cott, "Marriage and Women's Citizenship in the United States, 1830–1934," *American Historical Review* 10, no. 5 (1998): 1453.

11 Meredith L. McGill, *American Literature and the Culture of Reprinting, 1834–1853* (Philadelphia: University of Pennsylvania Press, 2003), chap. 1. Grantland Rice, analyzing some of the same materials and seeing a persistence of the same rhetoric in England, labels this legal approach more broadly "utilitarian." *The Transformation of Authorship in America* (Chicago: University of Chicago Press, 1997), 76–8.

to her power and authority – the more her works circulated, the greater her losses – and positioned her in the literary field as a model republican author.[12] Who better to acquire literary property and exploit the limited possibilities of literary proprietorship in early nineteenth-century America without appearing to threaten the free circulation of print and the public interest than women authors, whose relation to property of all kinds was profoundly ambiguous?

Sedgwick's signature on the 1838 petition was not her only appearance in the context of the copyright debates. She was also the subject of a toast at an 1831 public dinner commemorating the passage of an amendment to the copyright statute extending the term of copyright protection, was praised as a model American author in published copyright advocacy, and attended an 1842 dinner in honor of Charles Dickens at which several speakers, including Dickens, spoke in favor of international copyright and at which Sedgwick was the subject of another toast. Following Sedgwick's career chronologically, this chapter rereads and resituates Sedgwick's public and private constructions of herself as an author in the context of the copyright debates, particularly the visions of American authorship and proper author-reader relations articulated in the debates. I begin with her construction of an authorial persona through her early novels (published from 1822 to 1830) and the relation of these novels to the literary nationalism that preceded the copyright debates of the 1830s and then developed coterminously with the copyright debates. I then move forward to the copyright

12 The relationship of Sedgwick and her works to American republicanism and democracy has become a critical obsession in the past decade. See, e.g., Philip Gould, "Catharine Sedgwick's 'Recital' of the Pequot War," *American Literature* 66, no. 4 (1994): 641–62 (*Hope Leslie*); Elizabeth Barnes, *States of Sympathy: Seduction and Democracy in the American Novel* (New York: Columbia University Press, 1997), chap. 4 (*A New-England Tale*); Judith Fetterley, "'My Sister! My Sister!': The Rhetoric of Catharine Sedgwick's *Hope Leslie*," *American Literature* 70, no. 3 (1998): 491–516; Maria Karafilis, "Catharine Sedgwick's *Hope Leslie*: The Crisis between Ethical Political Action and U.S. Literary Nationalism in the New Republic," *American Transcendental Quarterly* 12, no. 4 (1998): 327–44; Gustavus Stadler, "Magawisca's Body of Knowledge: Nation-Building in *Hope Leslie*," *Yale Journal of Criticism* 12, no. 1 (1999): 41–56; Sarah Robbins, "'The Future Good and Great of Our Land': Republican Mothers, Female Authors, and Domesticated Literacy in Antebellum New England," *New England Quarterly* 75, no. 4 (2002): 562–91 (didactics); Quentin Miller, "'A Tyranically Democratic Force': The Symbolic and Cultural Function of Clothing in Catharine Maria Sedgwick's *Hope Leslie*," *Legacy* 19, no. 2 (2002): 121–36; Deborah Gussman, "'Equal to Either Fortune': Sedgwick's *Married or Single?* and Feminism," in *Catharine Maria Sedgwick: Critical Perspectives*, 252–67; Susan K. Harris, "The Limits of Authority: Catharine Maria Sedgwick and the Politics of Resistance," in *Catharine Maria Sedgwick: Critical Perspectives*, 272–85; Harris, "Introduction," *A New-England Tale* (New York: Penguin, 2004), vii–xxii. "Republican" and "democratic" were highly contested terms in Sedgwick's day, and they remain highly contested terms in current theoretical and historical scholarship. I use the term "republican" primarily with reference to McGill's definition in the copyright context, but I also apply both terms in the same flexible and contradictory ways that Sedgwick's contemporaries applied them to her and her works.

debates of the 1830s, focusing on people, places, and events closely linked to Sedgwick (articles in magazines in which Sedgwick published or in which her works were reviewed, writings about copyright by her close personal and professional associates in New York, especially William Cullen Bryant, and writings by some of the men who signed the "Citizens of New York" petition with her). I also read Sedgwick's comments on authors and readers in her private writings and her didactic novellas of the mid- to late 1830s in the context of these debates, arguing that Sedgwick helped to construct and then embraced a particular vision of republican authorship in sync with the logic of the existing law rather than in opposition to it. Finally, I close with Charles Dickens's 1842 American tour, analyzing Sedgwick's position as a republican author serving readers at a time when the emerging proprietary author was under attack. What emerges from recontextualizing Sedgwick's writings and the changes in her writings from the 1820s through the 1840s is, above all, Sedgwick's canny, nuanced, and shifting responses to the sometimes conflicting discourses of literary nationalism and republican citizenship, shifts that allowed her to remain salable and relevant in a literary market that disenfranchised authors. From the beginning of her career, Sedgwick occupied a middle ground that placed her and her works between the positions articulated by the extremes of the procopyright position (copyright should be boundless, lasting eternally and recognized and protected in all countries no matter what the citizenship or residence of the author) and the anticopyright position (*all* copyright protection was an illegitimate imposition on the public interest). Patricia Larson Kalayjian argues that Sedgwick's novel *Clarence* (1830) critiques the excesses of capitalism, consumerism, and commodification in American culture in the 1820s and that Sedgwick advances her critique by promoting a revised and democratized notion of "disinterestedness," which, in classical republicanism, was a moral virtue accessible only to economically independent elites.[13] Shifting the focus to Sedgwick's circulation in the very market her fiction ostensibly critiques, I argue that Sedgwick's disinterested authorial persona had a market function. Locating herself at a point of equipoise between the two extremes of commercially interested proprietary authorship and authorial oblivion, her disinterestedness seemingly detached her from the market while simultaneously powerfully positioning her within it.[14]

13 Patricia Larson Kalayjian, "Disinterest as Moral Corrective in *Clarence's* Cultural Critique," in *Catharine Maria Sedgwick: Critical Perspectives*, 104–17.

14 Sedgwick's example would seem to bear out Sandra Tomc's speculation about how women performed "leisure" differently than did one of Sedgwick's male contemporaries, N. P. Willis: "I would venture to speculate that the woman author's very abstraction from the market might be related to her success within it." "An Idle Industry: Nathaniel Parker Willis and the Workings of Literary Leisure," *American Quarterly* 49, no. 4 (1997): 805n. However, Sedgwick's persona suggests not "leisured domesticity" but disinterested, unpaid domestic labor.

On the throne: Sedgwick's authorial debut through *A New-England Tale*

Catharine Sedgwick began writing professionally in 1822, more than a decade before the beginning of the international copyright debates. In the early Republic, copyright advocates successfully lobbied state legislatures to enact state copyright statutes, and then after the 1787 Federal Constitution reserved copyright law as a federal power, advocates successfully lobbied Congress for the enactment of the first federal copyright statute in 1790. International copyright and the possible rewards of such a reform for American authors seem to have been beyond the wildest imaginings of authors confronting a decentralized, relatively undeveloped market for literature. Under such circumstances, authorship was necessarily a modest affair, with many authors, including Catharine Sedgwick, focusing their energies on calls for a "national literature" using "native materials."

From the very beginning of her career as an author, Sedgwick carefully positioned herself in the literary field as a producer responding to readers' needs and desires rather than as an autonomous artist. Her own accounts of her motivations and contemporary biographical accounts represent her as an unwilling producer who appeared in the public world of print only because by so doing she could "do good" for her readers. In a letter Sedgwick wrote to her friend Susan Higginson Channing (sister-in-law to the well-known Unitarian minister William Ellery Channing) in 1822, for instance, describing the genesis of her first novel, *A New-England Tale*, in the same year, she claims that she began the novel as a Unitarian religious tract criticizing Calvinism and that she expanded it into a novel and published it only at the urging of her brothers.[15] However, this "private" account of her insecurities also circulated as a public account of her authorship during her lifetime. For instance, an 1834 biographical sketch in the *National Portrait Gallery of Distinguished Americans* describes the novel's origin as a tract and approvingly reports, "Such was her distrust of her abilities, and so great her reluctance to appear before the public in a work of this magnitude, that her consent to its publication was finally extorted rather than given."[16]

Sedgwick's private reluctance to publish was thus part of the public understanding of her as an author and of her position in the literary field. The heroine of the novel she reluctantly published, Jane Elton, contributed to this public construction of Sedgwick as a modest republican author. Fittingly, Jane Elton is the most modest and self-effacing of heroines, an orphan who takes years of abuse from her aunt and cousins with no resistance

15 Catharine Maria Sedgwick to Susan Higginson Channing, [May/June] 1822, in Mary P. Dewey, ed., *Life and Letters of Catharine M. Sedgwick* (New York: Harper, 1871), 153–4.

16 James Herring, James B. Longacre, and American Academy of the Fine Arts, eds., *The National Portrait Gallery of Distinguished Americans*, vol. 1 (New York: Monson Bancroft, 1834).

or comment. However, her quiet moral courage ultimately wins out, and she gets exactly what she wants: a husband as morally upstanding and self-effacing as she is and a home over which she can exercise her feminine moral influence. Her cousins, despite her aunt's insistently Calvinistic mothering of them, end up dead or exiled under difficult circumstances.

Before Jane's ascension and her cousins' falls, when the moral forces of the novel are still in equilibrium, Sedgwick stages a literary competition between Jane and her cousin Elvira. The competition serves as a parable of authorship and a map for understanding Sedgwick's own positioning of herself in the market with the anonymous publication of her first novel. Both Jane and Elvira have studied for a year at the newly created local seminary, and Jane takes most of the academic prizes ("meekly," of course). The school awards all of the prizes (except the composition prize, the most coveted of them all) during the first day of festivities. The second day, when the composition prize is to be awarded, features an "exhibition" (really a theatrical performance, but if it were called a theatrical performance, the church members in town would object). As the narrator tells us, the exhibition is designed for "the young men and boys . . . to display those powers that were developing for the pulpit, and the bar, and the political harangue."[17] Female students, the narrator tells us, "were with obvious and singular propriety" excluded, *except* for the composition prize winner, whose identity is to be kept secret until curtains are withdrawn to show the winner seated on a "throne" (p. 51). To the surprise of most of the members of the audience, Elvira, not Jane, is seated on the throne. Elvira makes the most of the opportunity to be on public display, tricking herself out in a befuddled array of borrowed finery meant to suggest European refinement ("a bright scarlet Canton crape frock, a white sarsenet scarf, fantastically thrown over her shoulder"), with her hair dressed in a "confusion of classical and pastoral orders" (p. 53). Her manner of performance is as extravagant as her dress, as she "spouts" her composition "with all the airs and graces of a sentimentalist of the beau monde" (p. 53).

Elvira's plagiaristic performance suggestively echoes Washington Irving's *Sketch Book* story "The Art of Bookmaking." In the story, Irving describes a dream in which he observes modern authors "manufacturing" books by pilfering the works of classic writers, and, literalizing the metaphor of language as clothing, dressing themselves up in this borrowed finery.[18] Sedgwick leaves the actual subject of Elvira's composition a mystery, however; clearly, for Elvira, both language and clothing are for display, not practical use. And, as it turns out, Elvira's words are "borrowed plumes," just as her costume

17 Catharine Maria Sedgwick, *A New-England Tale; or Sketches of New-England Character and Manners*, ed. Victoria Clements (New York: Oxford University Press, 1995), 51 (hereinafter cited in the text).

18 For a stimulating reading of "The Art of Bookmaking" and Irving's "The Mutability of Literature" as paired meditations on the nature of literary property, see Rice, *Transformation of Authorship*, 70–80.

and her manner are (p. 54). A member of the audience recognizes her composition as an essay published in a Boston newspaper many years earlier. Once Elvira's fraud is discovered, the curtain opens again to reveal Jane "seated on the throne, looking like the 'meek usurper,' reluctant to receive the honour that was forced upon her" (p. 54). Both her dress (a "plain" frock and only simple flowers in her hair) and her composition (on the subject of "gratitude") are functional and unadorned. She wrote her composition on gratitude as an expression of gratitude to Mr. Lloyd, the man who paid the school fees that enabled her to attend the school when her aunt refused to pay.

Elvira, the "bad" author of Sedgwick's parable, in her befuddled imitation of European models in her dress and her lack of originality in her composition, only puts on a show of being an author and originator. She is a showy queen on the throne, ruling over her audience or subjects in order to get the promised reward (the prize) and public fame for her "talents." She, however, like "bad" American authors later lamented by copyright advocates, fails to take up the labor of adding to the stock of truly "American" literature made from native materials or of serving her audience's moral and intellectual needs as citizens of a democratic republic. In fact, even the essay that she plagiarizes from an American newspaper may itself have been plagiarized from an even earlier English source: British periodical essays on general, nonpolitical subjects of the variety we might imagine Elvira to have selected, circulated and recirculated for years in American newspapers, often without attribution.

Jane, in contrast to Elvira, manages to appear on the throne, revealed by the withdrawing of a stage curtain, without performing and without claiming power and authority over her audience (and without plagiarizing – she writes her original essay from the heart in response to local circumstances). Crucially and ironically, her obvious reluctance and lack of staging give her the moral authority over her audience that she purportedly refuses to seek. As Sedgwick repeatedly reminds us in her descriptions of the preparation for the festivities, they take place in the "meeting house" of an orthodox Calvinist congregation. When those curtains withdraw to reveal a reluctant Jane, they figuratively expose Jane within the holy of holies inside the temple, the place where only the high priests and no woman can enter. Her absence of performance and pretension and her unwillingness to claim the prize as her property after Elvira's exposure make her a nonauthor author. Her role as "good" author is revealed only because her nonperformance performance follows Elvira's bad author drama. Jane, like Sedgwick, her self-effacing and anonymous creator, gets the prize and the power because she has no power and professes not to seek it.[19]

19 See Victoria Clements on "the novel's elevation of authorship," with Jane's reading of the prize essay as one example of how the novel unleashes a potentially radical threat to the gendered social order

Jane's ascent to the modest and morally instructive throne of authorship marks a turning point in the story. Although Jane continues to suffer silently for some time before her ascent to the throne of marriage and ready-made maternity (Mr. Lloyd's young daughter Rebecca is the "happy mistress of ceremonies" at the wedding [p. 164]), the Wilson family begins to crumble as each child, in turn, falls to personal wrack and ruin. Martha, married to a tavern keeper, beats her children and dies young from the effects of excessive drinking. David becomes a rake who seduces, impregnates, and abandons a young girl. To support his financial extravagance, he takes to forgery and highway robbery, ending up an exile after escaping from prison. Elvira finally elopes with a French dancing master, and although Sedgwick does not tell us of her ultimate fate, Elvira last appears in the novel with her new husband, running to escape New England town bullies who threaten to tar and feather him for bad debts.

Sedgwick clearly assigns the blame for the fate of the Wilson children to Mrs. Wilson. She endows them with the evil light of her Calvinist imagination, and as the "*author* of their existence" (emphasis added), as Sedgwick calls her, the misdeeds of her children "will convey a reproach and reflect dishonour" on her (p. 46).[20] In a world in which grace is all and good works are futile, Mrs. Wilson perversely claims the moral transgressions of her children as signs of grace: "There is more hope . . . of an open, outrageous transgressor, than of one of a moral life" (p. 148). But, as her son David writes in his parting letter to her, ". . . you have destroyed me. You . . . taught me . . . that there was no difference between doing right and doing wrong, in the sight of the God you worship. . . . If you taught me truly, I have only acted out the nature totally depraved, (your own words,) that he gave to me" (p. 155). Mrs. Wilson sets in motion the tragedy of her family, and when Jane finally makes her understand the invidious moral effects of the life narrative in which she schooled her children, she almost loses her powers of speech to a stroke. Sedgwick, behind the tale, provides instrumental instruction, a tract to warn others against the dangers of imagining their lives and moral choices as meaningless. However, she also provides a positive, as well as a negative, example: Jane, the self-effacing doer of good deeds, serves as a model for true Christian living and as a stand-in for Sedgwick, *her* mother-author.

by allowing a woman to occupy the position of authorial subject. *New-England Tale*, xx, xxiii. Like Kelley, however, Clements overstates the supposed power available to those taking up authorship in America in 1822.

20 For a nuanced reading of Sedgwick's Unitarian critique of Calvinism in *A New-England Tale*, see Daniel P. Buchanan, "Tares in the Wheat: Puritan Violence and Puritan Families in the Nineteenth-Century Liberal Imagination," *Religion and American Culture* 8, no. 2 (1998): 205–36. See also Harris, "Introduction." For the faults of Mrs. Wilson's theology and child rearing, see Barnes, *States of Sympathy*, 80–2. On the novel's dual address to unjust parents like Mrs. Wilson and virtuous daughters trying to distinguish between just and unjust exercise of authority, see Susan K. Harris, *19th-Century American Women's Novels: Interpretive Strategies* (New York: Cambridge, 1990), chap. 1.

Jane's good deeds thus reflect well on Sedgwick, who authored her as a character.

Sedgwick's strategic deployment of anonymity in the publication of this and subsequent works (which, as I have argued elsewhere, was never true anonymity, and which she decisively abandoned when writing for magazines and annuals in the 1840s)[21] contributed to her power and authority. *A New-England Tale* carried no name on the title page, but the dedication "to Maria Edgeworth, as a slight expression of the writer's sense of her eminent services in the great cause of human virtue and improvement" signals the author's alliance with a clearly defined authorial persona. A brief notice of the book in the *North American Review* reinforces this connection, saying, "If rumor has rightly attributed this excellent production to a female pen, we may with far greater confidence boast of a *religious* Edgeworth in our land, than a wonder-working Scott."[22] Throughout Sedgwick's career, reviewers recurred to this analogy to Edgeworth to define both Sedgwick and her works, sometimes finding Sedgwick artistically inferior to Edgeworth but also finding her morally superior because of the more religious tone of her writings.[23] In the first review to identify Sedgwick by name (an 1828 review of *Hope Leslie*), the reviewer notes approvingly, "She appears to move onward, with a becoming modesty; and if her track is not distinguished by the splendor, which belongs to some among her predecessors and contemporaries, it will at least lead no one astray."[24] That very lack of splendor, the lack of obvious attempts at self-aggrandizement (including her "anonymous" publication), conferred on Sedgwick moral authority and the right to true fame in the American market. Such a construction of Sedgwick as an author was not the only or an inevitable outcome, but the product of design and careful staging. Sedgwick staged for herself the same sort of first appearance in public that she staged for Jane Elton. At the beginning of the age of self-promotion and publicity, Sedgwick appeared in public without appearing to seek publicity. In Sedgwick's second novel, *Redwood* (1824), Grace Campbell, a headstrong young society woman, tells Ellen Bruce, the modest, countrified heroine, "The days are past when one might 'do good by stealth, and blush to find it fame' – this is the age of display – of publication."[25] Nevertheless, both

21 Homestead, "Behind the Veil?"

22 Review of *The Spy* in *North American Review*, July 1822, 279. This very brief notice is appended as a footnote to a review of James Fenimore Cooper's second novel.

23 See, e.g., James Fenimore Cooper's unsigned review of *A New-England Tale* in *The Literary and Scientific Repository*, May 1822, 340. Attributed and reprinted in *Early Critical Essays, 1820–1822*, ed. James F. Beard, Jr. (Gainesville, FL: Scholars' Facsimiles and Reprints, 1955). See also review of *Redwood* in *Atlantic Magazine*, July 1824, 236; review of *The Travellers* in *New York Review & Athenaeum Magazine*, June 1825, 34–5; review of *Hope Leslie* in *Western Monthly Review*, Sept. 1827, 289; and review of *The Linwoods* in *North American Review*, Jan. 1836, 194.

24 Review of *Hope Leslie* in *Western Monthly*, 290.

25 Catharine Maria Sedgwick, *Redwood* (New York: E. Bliss & E. White, 1824), 2:152.

Sedgwick and many of her heroines manage to "do good by stealth" and thus achieve fame without appearing to seek it.

In her third novel, *Clarence* (1830), Sedgwick again successfully negotiated her public authority through a virtuous, self-effacing heroine (Gertrude Clarence) who performs a series of heroic and selfless good deeds on behalf of others while withholding her name. Just as Sedgwick pairs Jane Elton with Elvira, she pairs Gertrude Clarence with Mrs. Layton, and through this pairing, Sedgwick consolidates her role as an Americanized version of Maria Edgeworth. Sedgwick insistently links Mrs. Layton to Madame de Stäel and particularly to de Stäel's poet-heroine Corinne, while she links Gertrude Clarence with Maria Edgeworth, the author to whom reviewers, at Sedgwick's prompting, insistently linked Sedgwick. Like Elvira in *A New-England Tale*, Mrs. Layton functions both as a figure of a corrupt foreign authorship and a figure of the American reader ensnared by the corrupt values of the foreign literature flooding the American market. Mrs. Layton's library is as elaborately decorated as her person, "filled," says the narrator, "with the flowers of foreign literature, and the popular productions of the day."[26] In an extended comparison of Gertrude's and Mrs. Layton's tastes in literature, the narrator tells us, "Mrs. Layton preferred [poetry] which addressed the passions; Gertrude, that which touched the affections. . . . Mrs. Layton revelled in the sibylline revelations of Mad. de Stäel. Gertrude's soul was thrilled by them, but she preferred Miss Edgeworth – preferred the beneficent genius who has made the actual social world better and happier, to her who by a motion of her wand could create an imaginative world, and disclose a possible, but unattainable beauty" (2:146–7). Mrs. Layton feeds her "passions" and learns all of her devious strategies for manipulation and self-aggrandizement through her uncritical consumption of foreign literature and the adoption of that literature's values. In modeling herself after Edgeworth, Gertrude (and behind her, Sedgwick) does not merely ape inappropriate foreign values as Mrs. Layton does in her imitation of de Stäel and Corinne because Gertrude responds to the "actual social world" around her in a way designed to make that world "better and happier."[27]

Copyright advocates often argued in the 1830s and 40s that American authors needed to write more books reflecting American values so that America would not be filled with women (or men) like Mrs. Layton. As William Cullen Bryant, a close Sedgwick family friend and consistent public

26 Catharine Maria Sedgwick, *Clarence; or, a Tale of Our Times* (Philadelphia: Carey & Lea, 1830), 2:45 (hereinafter cited in the text).

27 Elements of the plot of the second half of the novel and the focus on women's reading owe much to Edgeworth's novel *Belinda*. On reading in *Belinda*, see Heather MacFayden, "Lady Delacour's Library: Maria Edgeworth's *Belinda* and Fashionable Reading," *Nineteenth-Century Literature* 48, no. 4 (1994): 423–39. Sedgwick's resolution of the plot and her literary points of reference are, however, distinct from Edgeworth's.

advocate of international copyright, argues in his 1843 *Address to the People of the United States in Behalf of the American Copyright Club,* bringing foreign literature into the home was like "open[ing] a fresh vial of poison upon [the] hearthstone."[28] With the good and the bad literature promiscuously mingled in the market, wonders Bryant, how can readers rightly choose the literature the reading of which will be morally beneficial?: "Readers have multiplied to an extraordinary extent...but we venture to suggest, that wise men and wise women have not grown up quite in proportion; that the intermixture of good and evil has been so skillfully managed, that it would require a very wise man, and a very wise woman, to choose between the two" (p. 12). Clearly, Mrs. Layton is not a wise enough woman to make such moral distinctions, and even Gertrude Clarence temporarily falls under the sway of Mrs. Layton's beautiful but corrupt performance. The narrator also draws attention to the ways in which other characters in the novel fall under foreign sway through reading. As the narrator remarks with irony of the villain Pedrillo's ability to fascinate and flummox most Americans with what turns out to be his faux-Spanishness, "It must be confessed there is a charm to our republican society, in a foreign name and aristocratic pretensions, like the fascinations of a fairy tale to children" (1:214). A number of times in the novel, characters express an absolute faith in foreign judgment, a worshipping of foreign print authority. Miss Patty believes Americans have "degenerated" because "the English travellers and English reviews all say so" (2:153), and another lady remarks, "I never read *American* novels, there's no high life in them" (1:155). The novel clearly aims to educate readers to be able to distinguish between good and bad, the properly American and republican and the improperly European and aristocratic, both in person and in print, while providing a piece of the good American and republican literature called for, literature which, in Bryant's words, would function for the reader like a ballad sung "in the mother tongue always, and sounding of the father-land, their own fields, their own firesides, their own homes" (p. 13).

Reviews of *Clarence* and other Sedgwick novels use exactly the same terms to praise Sedgwick that Bryant and other copyright advocates would use several years later to set out a program for the future of American authorship protected by copyright. For instance, the *Ladies Magazine and Literary Gazette*

28 William Cullen Bryant, *An Address to the People of the United States in Behalf of the American Copyright Club, Adopted at New-York, October 18, 1843* (New York: American Copyright Club, 1843), 11 (hereinafter cited in the text). The authorship of the pamphlet is in dispute. George Goodspeed casts doubt on Bryant's sole authorship. "The Home Library," *Papers of the Bibliographical Society of America,* 42, no. 2 (1948): 111–12. The editors of Bryant's letters attribute it to Bryant. *Letters of William Cullen Bryant, Vol II: 1836–1849,* ed. William Cullen Bryant II and Thomas G. Voss (New York: Fordham University Press, 1977), 246–7. In any event, the prominent placement of Bryant's name on the pamphlet and his editorializing in the *Evening Post* in favor of international copyright would have led readers in the 1840s to assume that Bryant was at least coauthor.

praises "the author of 'Clarence' as the first and best of American novelists" and her work as "a public benefaction . . . doing honor to her country and her sex. It is not a trifling good she has effected to prove, by her own success, that American characters, scenes, and circumstances of being, may be wrought into a romance, which shall be intensely interesting, and yet not foreign to our habits of life, or dangerously exciting to the passions. Novels will be read by our people, and the only way to prevent the re-publication of the vapid trash, or worse, the licentious overflowings of the English press, is to support generously, with national pride, the efforts of our own talented writers."[29] This reviewer does *not* go as far as international copyright advocates would in a few years, demanding that the law be reformed so as "to prevent the republication" of English novels unsuited to American readers and circumstances. However, the same argumentative structure that would be used more than a decade in the future to explicitly link Sedgwick and the cause of international copyright is already in place in 1830 – literary nationalists praise Sedgwick's works as a bulwark against "the licentious overflowings of the English press."

"The most efficient agents of perpetuating our liberties and our union": Arguments for and against the expansion of copyright in the 1830s and 1840s

By the late 1820s, James Fenimore Cooper, whose works, like Sedgwick's, were widely read in England, was grumbling privately about the lack of international copyright protection. In 1826, Gulian Verplanck, a man of letters, newly elected Congressman, and Cooper's fellow Bread and Cheese Club member, tried to induce Congress to consider international copyright, but his initiative failed to gain support, and Congress would not turn to the matter for another decade.[30] In the same year, Cooper scolded Philadelphia publishers Carey, Lea and Carey for promoting what he believed to be an inadequate proposal to reform copyright: "You will never have a National Literature until you put the Native writers on a level with the English by giving some rights to the latter."[31]

Cooper's interest in international copyright remained exceptional in the 1820s, however. The attention of authors and the general public began to

29 Review of *Clarence* in *Ladies' Magazine and Literary Gazette*, July 1830, 320.

30 *Letters and Journals of James Fenimore Cooper*, ed. James Franklin Beard (Cambridge: Belknap, 1960), 1:136.

31 James Fenimore Cooper to Carey, Lea and Carey, 11 Mar. 1828, ibid., 1:259. Martin Buinicki ably traces Cooper's engagements with the international copyright issue over the course of his career, although he overstates Cooper's priority in such engagements. "Negotiating Copyright: Authorship and the Discourse of Literary Property Rights in Nineteenth-Century America," PhD diss., University of Iowa, 2003, chap. 1.

shift toward copyright reform when Noah Webster succeeded in his efforts to lengthen the term of copyright protection in 1831. On February 3, 1831, Congress extended the first term of copyright protection from fourteen to twenty-eight years, and also allowed "widows and orphans" of authors rather than only authors themselves to renew copyright registrations for a second fourteen-year term, thus extending the maximum possible term from twenty-eight to forty-two years. Literary New York feted Verplanck (who shepherded the legislation through Congress) at a public dinner for his successful "exertions in Congress to place literary property on a secure and permanent footing." William Cullen Bryant both helped to organize the dinner and reported on it at length in the *New York Evening Post.*[32] Among the other organizers of the dinner were poet Charles Fenno Hoffman, Judge John Irving (brother of Washington Irving, who was living and working in London at the time as secretary to the United States legation), painter Charles Ingham (who later painted the portrait of Catharine Sedgwick that became the most widely distributed image of her), Chancellor James Kent, author James Kirke Paulding, and last, but not least, Catharine's brother Robert Sedgwick, a New York lawyer in whose home Catharine resided much of the year.

Despite the celebratory tone of the dinner, the speeches just as often comment on the difficulties of American authorship and the perceived inadequacies of the statutory law of literary property. The subject of international copyright per se, as opposed to copyright term extension, is mentioned only once, in a brief toast: "*An international Copy-right Law* – The only link required to complete the chain of reciprocity between nations" (perhaps potential international copyright advocates restrained themselves so as not to antagonize "our most enterprising booksellers and printers," who were in attendance). However, the speeches touch on themes that appear repeatedly in later years in international copyright advocacy. Noah Webster had originally sought in 1828 "that the existing laws respecting copyrights may be so amended as to give to authors and their heirs the *exclusive* and *perpetual* property in their works."[33] Judge Irving, the master of ceremonies and primary speaker, focuses on the continuing gulf between protection for other forms of property and the transitory protection granted to literary

32 "Dinner to the Hon. Gulian C. Verplanck," *New York Evening Post*, 30 Apr. 1831, [2]. All subsequent quotations are from this account. For the relationship between Bryant and various Sedgwick family members, see his memoir in Dewey, *Life and Letters*, 437; Richard D. Birdsall, "William Cullen Bryant and Catherine [*sic*] Sedgwick – Their Debt to the Berkshire," *New England Quarterly* 28, no. 3 (1955): 349–71; and Widmer, *Young America*. The most complete account of Bryant's involvement with and writings on international copyright is Robert B. Sargent, "Anglo-American Encounter: William Cullen Bryant, Dickens, and Others," in *William Cullen Bryant and His America: Centennial Conference Proceedings 1878–1978*, ed. Stanley Brodwin and Michael D'Innocenzo (New York: AMS Press, 1983), 179–96.

33 Quoted in Solberg, *Copyright in Congress*, 136.

property: "[T]he noblest efforts of the mind, which have consumed hours of thought and have employed the strongest energies of our nature, when once embodied should be considered as common property, and be appropriated often to the use of those who not only have not the power to invent, but often not the capacity to appreciate them, except for mere mercenary purposes." Telling a story of the miseries of authorship that appears repeatedly in the writings of copyright advocates (and which copyright opponents just as often refuted), Irving proclaims, "The history of genius" is a "history of privation." Literary authors inevitably end their days in "penury" and leave no estates, Irving argues, because of the short term of copyright protection.

Gulian Verplanck, focusing on the positive rather than negative lessons of history, praises the wisdom of the founding fathers for including a copyright clause in the Constitution: "They knew that the best security of national union and national power, was to be sought in the influences of national literature, science, arts and education. They saw clearly that their own legislation, and that of those who were destined to administer the government they had reared, would be but feeble and temporary without the aid of that more potent and lasting, although secret and silent legislation, which acts on the mind and the affection." Echoing the preamble to the Constitution, he expresses a wish that national literature, science, art, and education, "as the most efficient agents in perpetuating our liberties and our union," will "continue for ages to shed their blessings upon our posterity." Such efforts need not be high or grand, Verplanck opines, because this beneficial influence "is exerted not less in the humblest literary efforts to instruct the infant mind, than in the labours of the teacher of high science, or those of the philosophical historian, or in the glorious inspiration of the orator, the painter or the poet."

Although Catharine Sedgwick was not present at this exclusively male (and heavy-drinking) public dinner, she nevertheless makes an appearance as the subject of a slightly obscure, unattributed toast that plays on her reputation as "the American Edgeworth": "the Name – which delicacy forbids us to breathe – which reminds us of the grace of Sevigne, and the invention of Edgeworth." In the *Post*, Bryant obligingly removes any possible obscurity by prefacing the toast with a note: "[Our readers will have no difficulty in perceiving that the following toast alludes to the accomplished author of Redwood and Hope Leslie]." In a sense, the figure of Sedgwick, and female authorship more generally, hangs suspended over this dinner and its sometimes contradictory claims for American authorship. In Judge Irving's estimation, literary genius ignores the pecuniary aspects of literary production while looking to higher motives, but it is "our" role, Judge Irving tells his audience, "to regard and protect its [genius's] interests." While sympathizing with (implicitly male) authors who want to leave estates for their children, Judge Irving comes perilously close to portraying the typical author as a child incapable of handling his own affairs and requiring parental guardianship, or as an adult woman attending to the emotional and spiritual needs of a family while her husband handles the public and financial affairs of the family. Authors, like women and children, require an intermediary to stand between them and the commercial public. Standing doubly ambiguously in relation to property as a woman author, Sedgwick is even more vulnerable than Judge Irving's literary genius, the fruits of whose labors become common property appropriated by mercenaries. Unable to claim full political rights, she takes up the work that Verplanck claims the founding fathers designed for American authorship, legislating over the mind and the affections. Central and yet peripheral, powerful and yet disempowered, Sedgwick is an unnamable contradiction standing both in and outside the program for American authorship advocated by the speakers at the dinner.

Despite their strenuous praise of copyright, the speakers at the 1831 dinner are obviously struggling against a strong and cohesive argument *against* copyright. Although the protracted public debates about international copyright had not yet begun, those debates would begin soon; and, for most of the century, copyright opponents would carry the day. As Meredith McGill persuasively argues in her analysis of anti-international copyright petitions to Congress, copyright opponents succeeded because they located republican and nationalistic values in the manufacturing of books rather than in their content and the production of that content by American authors. Casting international copyright as a threat to American industry and "locating national identity in the process of production, they make the powerful claim that manufacturing, and not literature, is America's true cultural product."[34] Even though personal economic interests clearly motivated the political efforts of copyright opponents (many of whom were men who owned printing houses and other book-manufacturing concerns or who were skilled laborers employed in them), these men often framed their arguments in terms of the interests of average readers and of the wage laborers working in paper, printing, and binding factories. That is, they successfully portrayed the struggle over international copyright as a struggle of average Americans to maintain their rights in the face of overreaching demands by greedy and power-hungry authors. As Trevor Ross argues in his analysis of the copyright debate in eighteenth-century England, such arguments that set the interests of authors against those of readers have the potential to alienate authors from their audience.[35]

Two exchanges in Bryant's *Evening Post* illustrate the typical argumentative strategies of copyright opponents. In 1836, Bryant gave space in the *Post* to a pseudonymous article by "Eleuthera," who attacked the idea of international copyright. Even though Bryant made his own opposition to Eleuthera's

34 McGill, *American Literature,* 95.

35 Trevor Ross, "Copyright and the Invention of Tradition," *Eighteenth-Century Studies* 26, no. 1 (1992): 14–15.

position clear, Eleuthera makes a persuasive appeal to the interests of the *Post*'s readers. He warns them that "the effects of [an international copyright law] would be to exclude foreign books almost entirely from our market, by limiting their circulation to the wealthy" and "to close the thousands of establishments engaged in their manufacture, thereby producing distress and ruin."[36] Inverting Verplanck's claim that American authorship is the foundation of republican government, Eleuthera locates republican values in the unrestricted circulation of *foreign* books, the restriction of which would "sap the very foundation of our government by shutting up the avenues of popular intelligence on which the glorious superstructure has been reared, and by a scrupulous regard to which alone it can be perpetuated." American authors of real merit and genius, he claims, do not write only for "lucre," but for "esteem and respect." In fact, he implies, any author who argues for international copyright essentially proves that he has no real talent. Do not, he warns the *Post*'s readers, allow "the great mass of mankind – the toiling million – [to be plunged] into a state of ignorance, poverty, and misery" for the sake a few money-grubbing authors.

A year later, Bryant gave space in the *Post* to New York publisher Theodore Foster, so that he could respond to allegations published in the *Post* by Frederick Saunders of the British publishing house of Saunders & Otley that Foster's American reprinting of a Saunders & Otley title was "dishonourable."[37] Foster tells the *Post's* readers not to be fooled by Saunders's verbal sleight of hand, which turns Foster's perfectly legal business practices into a badge of dishonor. "[T]he illustrious men who have hitherto managed our national concerns," he tells readers, "have been of the opinion that it was the most conducive to the welfare of the community to leave the republication of foreign works entirely free from all restrictions." Thus his republication of a British book in America is entirely permissible and even laudable. Noting attempts under way to change the copyright law, he warns "the publick" not be fooled: "Should the publick . . . coincide in the opinion to allow themselves to be left unprotected to the rapacity of English Booksellers, I as a publisher, have little objection." Readers will be, he assures them, "the chief sufferers" under the "monopoly" power of British publishers.

In their arguments against international copyright, copyright opponents thus present a mirror image of the arguments of copyright advocates: focusing on the "diffusion of knowledge" among "the people," they declare authors irrelevant or even identify them as impediments to that diffusion.[38]

36 Eleuthera, "International Copyright Law," *New York Evening Post*, 25 Aug. 1836, [2].

37 Theodore Foster, "To the Publick," *New York Evening Post*, 31 Jan. 1837, [2]. On Saunders & Otley's U.S. publishing ventures and connections to Bryant, see James J. Barnes, *Authors, Publishers, and Politicians*, 56–60.

38 For one of the most spectacular instances of this line of argument, see Senate, *Memorial of a Number of Persons Concerned in Printing and Publishing, Praying an Alteration in the Mode of Levying Duties on*

According to the logic of copyright opponents, by asserting proprietary claims, American authors proved themselves to be unrepublican and un-American. In the map of the field of literary production drawn by copyright opponents, the American book trade (encompassing both the capitalists who invested in it and the laborers in its factories) was the primary originator or author of books, even if those books were "English works." In its 1838 report recommending against international copyright, the Senate Committee on Patents complains that an Anglo-American copyright law would "enable [British publishers and authors] to monopolize the publication here as well as in England, of all English works for the supply of the American market!"[39] According to this economic logic, "English works" are a product category that any American manufacturer is entitled to produce in response to consumer demand, as if books were fabric, and as if British manufacturers should not be allowed to hold a monopoly over the production of calicos. Whereas copyright advocates claimed that America's dispersed population required a true American literature to create and maintain a republican national identity, copyright opponents opposed all barriers to the widest diffusion of print across dispersed communities, even if those barriers were authors. The 1838 Committee on Patents report thus argues that while English readers, clustered in cities and industrial towns, might borrow expensive books from lending libraries, the isolated American farmer has to purchase his books and cannot afford to pay much for them. The less expensive the books, the committee argues, the more thoroughly knowledge can be diffused. Compensation to authors and resulting higher prices will impede this diffusion: "The multiplication of cheap editions of useful books, brought within the reach of all classes, serves to promote that general diffusion of knowledge and intelligence, on which depends so essentially the preservation and support of our free institutions."[40] The Senate Committee promulgates a vision of the market for book that figuratively erases the author as producer by installing all classes of readers at the top of the market hierarchy, controlling the multiplication and circulation of books without authors.

This decentering and dismissal of authors by copyright opponents enraged many copyright advocates, especially those who most stressed the "sacred rights of authors" as the primary rationale for copyright law. They harken back to a mythical era of perpetual common law copyright in England, before the first English copyright statute in 1710 or before the House of Lords' decision in *Donaldson v. Beckett* in 1774, which held that there never

Certain Books, and Remonstrating Against the Enactment of an International Copy-right Law, 27th Cong., 2nd sess., 13 June 1842, S. Doc. 323. McGill discusses this and similar petitions in greater detail. *American Literature*, chap. 1.

39 Senate Committee on Patents, *Report to accompany Senate Bill No. 32*, 25th Cong., 2nd sess., 25 June 1838, S. Doc. 494, 3.

40 Ibid., 5.

had been a perpetual common law of copyright in England *or* that the limited term of protection specified in the 1710 Statute superseded the common law. In his 1838 pamphlet *A Plea for Authors, and the Rights of Literary Property, by an American*, Grenville Sackett (an attorney and a signer with Sedgwick of the 1838 "Citizens of New York" petition) laments the "unheard of stretch of legislative tyranny *and* injustice" by which "an author was compelled, for the protection of a few years interest in what was then acknowledged to be his property, to sacrifice the far greater, and it might be the more valuable portion of it."[41] Complaining that the limited term of copyright discourages men who would be the best authors from taking up authorship, he asks rhetorically whether perpetual copyright "would . . . not be a noble inducement for truth and intelligence to step forward and aid in the permanent progress of social improvement? Would it not excite the genius to be told that 'not only your sons but your son's sons shall rejoin in your honest efforts to add to the happiness of man, not as dependants or beggars, but as the heirs of the high inheritance derived from your elevated exertions?'"[42] From Sackett's perspective (a perspective shared by many copyright advocates), statutory copyright was an inferior, beggarly sort of property not worth acquiring, an insult to its creator and possessor; any man who wants to provide for his wife and children during his lifetime and after his death must turn his intellectual energies elsewhere. In a similar vein, Cornelius Mathews (another signer of the 1838 petition with Sedgwick) complains hyperbolically of the disrespect America shows to its authors. In an 1843 lecture delivered during his tenure as the secretary of the American Copyright Club, he claims that in the natural order of things, an author produces his works in quiet deliberation and then serious readers reverentially consume them and engage the author's ideas. America, however, has reversed this natural order: "Here an author is an anomaly; a needless excrescence of nature; a make-trouble and mar-plot, a mere impertinence. A book is supposed to grow up by some sort of spontaneous process beyond the seas, and to be imported into this country with Rootabaga [*sic*] and Yellow Hop."[43]

41 Grenville A. Sackett, *Plea for Authors, and the Rights of Literary Property. By an American* (New York: Adlard & Saunders, 1838), 18. Grantland Rice (*Transformation* 90, 192n.) and Michael Newbury (*Figuring Authorship in Antebellum American* [Stanford: Stanford University Press, 1997], 225n.) note that this pamphlet is sometimes attributed to Washington Irving. Rice claims at least coauthorship for Irving, or even that Sackett did not exist. On Sackett (a real person), see his obituary ("Deaths," *New York Evening Post*, 9 Mar. 1858) and a contemporary notice of his copyright writings ("Editor's Table," *Knickerbocker*, Aug. 1840, 187). Note also that the American Antiquarian Society copy is inscribed "To the Hon. John Davis with the respect of the author Grenville A Sackett."

42 Sackett, *Plea*, 25.

43 Cornelius Mathews, *The Better Interests of the Country, in Connexion with International Copy-right* (New York: Wiley & Putnam, 1843), 12. McGill rightly emphasizes the increasingly conservative and elitist

Central to the copyright debates, then, was the question of just who "manufactured" books. Authors in their garrets? Or papermakers, typesetters, pressmen, binders, and the capitalists financing their work? In an 1837 *North American Review* article, H. R. Cleveland chastises copyright opponents for their logical "mistake" about precisely this question: "It is the writers who are to be regarded as the manufacturers, not the publishers. The American publishers, who reprint English works, are the importers and venders of foreign manufactures."[44] Such a claim was not self-evident, however. Copyright advocates needed to create a theory of literary property that supported this claim of authorial manufacture, and they, like British advocates of copyright before them, found this narrative in John Locke's theories of the origins of property (see Chapter 1), in which a man acquires property out of the state of nature by mixing his labor with it. In an 1836 *Post* editorial, for instance, Bryant shows his indebtedness to Lockean theory in his response to editorials from other newspapers claiming that copyright was a monopoly. Bryant, staunch Democrat that he was, could not leave such an imputation unchallenged. "A copyright law," he protests, "confers no new privilege or immunity" to authors in the marketplace, but instead, because of the time limits imposed on copyrights, "absolutely takes away a portion of an author's right of property in a work of his own creation, and renders no equivalent, except the mere guarding the remainder with some special provision."[45] Bryant justifies his claim of a preexisting, "natural" property right by telling a parable about an American Indian who makes a bow from the branch of a tree in a common hunting ground. "Even the Indians," Bryant protests, "respect each other's exclusive claim to the creations of their own efforts, to that species of property which owes its value to individual labour and skill."[46] Were it not for the limits of the copyright statute, imposed "to promote the benefit of the mass" at the expense of the individual, claims Bryant, an American author's literary property would be "of the same enduring character, as the mechanic's to the results of his skill, or the farmer's to the product of his industry."[47]

In 1837, in a *Post* editorial published in the wake of the British Authors Memorial, Bryant repeats the same story of the Indian and his bow. Although he still maintains that the analogy supports copyright, using the language of

impulses behind Matthews's literary nationalistic pronouncements in the 1840s in her analysis of Poe's relationship to literary nationalism. *American Literature,* chap. 5. I am more interested, however, in the continuities in copyright advocacy from the 1830s and the early 1840s.

44 H. R. Cleveland, "My Prisons; Memoirs of Silvio Pellico of Saluzzo," *North American Review,* Jan. 1837, 134.

45 27 Sep. 1836, *New Evening York Post,* reprinted in William Cullen Bryant II, ed., *Power for Sanity: Selected Editorials of William Cullen Bryant, 1829–1861* (New York: Fordham University Press, 1994), 57.

46 Ibid. 47 Ibid., 58.

Romanticism, he also distinguishes artistic creation as a higher and ultimately less material form of making. By applying his labor to the common stock of language, writes Bryant, the author "has filled the mass of lifeless words with the light of his own reason, the energy of his own feeling, the glow of his own imagination; he has breathed into it the breath of life, infused into it a portion of his own mind. We give it a name which signifies how peculiarly it is his; we call it his 'work,' his 'production'; if in verse, we call it his 'poem,' which is derived from a Greek word signifying a making or creation."[48] The product of this godlike act of creation (*poesis*), fashioned by the immaterial labors of mind and spirit rather than muscular labors of the arm and hand, is "even more exclusively" the author's because it does not take anything away from the common stock, Bryant argues. The Indian removes a sapling from the forest, but "the author leaves the treasury of language as full as ever."[49]

"Suited to the Market": Catharine Sedgwick as a model republican author

Throughout the debates over international copyright, the materiality or immateriality of the author's labor and his literary property was a vexed question, but the arguments claiming materiality are the most relevant for understanding Catharine Sedgwick's authorial positioning contemporaneously with these debates and the concrete possibilities (rather than the Romantic imaginings) of authorship in the antebellum years.[50] As Nicholas Bromell persuasively argues in *By the Sweat of the Brow: Literature and Labor in Antebellum America*, the hierarchical relationships between mental and manual labor and between body and mind were in flux in the 1830s and 1840s, with manual labor and the body not yet subordinated to mental labor and the mind.[51] That is, Bryant's and other copyright advocates' claims that an author's labors were immaterial and thus of a higher status would not necessarily have been authoritative or persuasive when set against claims for the value of the physical labors of those engaged in book manufacturing. Thus many copyright advocates seeking to justify authorial proprietorship logically did so by describing writing as embodied labor. In the words of the

48 27 Mar. 1837, *New Evening York Post*, reprinted in Ibid., 66. 49 Ibid.

50 For materiality versus immateriality in the copyright debates, see Newbury, *Figuring Authorship*, chap. 4. Although Newbury focuses on the *failure* of copyright advocates to establish a claim of materiality for authorial labors and property, Sedgwick's descriptions of the nature of her labors suggest that even though such claims may have failed in the courts and the Congress, authorial claims of materiality still could underwrite power and authority.

51 Nicholas Knowles Bromell, *By the Sweat of the Brow: Literature and Labor in Antebellum America* (Chicago: University of Chicago Press, 1993).

1830 House of Representatives report recommending the passage of the 1831 copyright revision act, "Though the nature of literary property is peculiar, it is not the less real and valuable. . . . [T]he literary man . . . writes and labors assiduously as does the mechanic or husbandsman. The scholar who secludes himself, and wastes his life, and often his property, to enlighten the world, has the best right to the profits of those labors: the planter, the mechanic, and the professional man, cannot prefer a better title to what is admitted to be his own."[52] Although the author's labors are intellectual and might seem insubstantial and abstract, the author toils in his garret, expending his physical strength, like others who acquire property through their labor by tilling a field or building a house.[53]

In addition to the analogies to farm and craft production deployed in this report and by others to describe the nature of the author's labors, copyright advocates also insisted on the materiality of the author's property by analogizing it to trade goods, a form of property not clearly attached to the trader by his labor. Most insistently, copyright advocates analogized literary property to a "bale of merchandise." If the U.S. government protected the property rights of a British merchant in his cargo, so the argument went, why should American publishers and readers be free to appropriate a British author's *book* and vice versa?[54] In even more modest and homely analogies likening literary property to material objects subject to ownership and consumption, some copyright advocates analogized literary property to food, decrying British literature as food inappropriate to the tastes and health of American readers/eaters. In the words of Grenville Sackett, "From feeding on aliments, such as which was not prepared for us, but suited to the palates of a widely different people, we have spoiled our taste for the more wholesome Spartan broth that befits our condition. The plainness of our republican institutions grows vulgar beside the gorgeous vanities of aristocratic pomp."[55]

For American authors, these conflicting demands represented a difficult challenge and a seemingly impossible balancing act: how could authors establish authority in the market without readers seeing them as merely impediments to the "free flow" of desperately needed information and

52 House Committee on the Judiciary, *Copy-right*, 21st Cong., 2nd sess., 17 Dec. 1830, H. Rep. 3, 2.

53 For extended versions of the farming analogy, deployed in support of an argument for perpetual copyright, see Sackett, *Plea*, 2; and Francis Lieber, *On International Copyright, in a Letter to the Hon William C. Preston, Senator of the United States* (New York: Wiley & Putnam, 1840), 44.

54 For examples of the "bale of merchandise" analogies used in the 1830s and '40s, see, e.g., Senate, *Report with Senate Bill 223*, 24th Cong., 2nd sess, 16 Feb. 1837, S. Doc. 179, 1; Lieber, *International*, 44; Bryant, *Address*, 6; House, *Memorial of Nahum Capen, of Boston, Massachusetts, on the Subject of International Copyright*, 28th Cong., 1st sess, 15 Jan. 1844, H. Doc. 61, 5.

55 Sackett, *Plea*, 30. For other uses of the books-food analogy in the 1830s and '40s, see, e.g., "International Copyright," *New-York Mirror*, 11 Feb. 1837, 263; "International Copyright," *New-York Mirror*, 30 Dec. 1837, 215; and Lieber, *International Copyright*, 59.

instruction? How could authors serve the national interest and give readers appropriate "American" books while also claiming proprietary rights and their attendant financial rewards? Catharine Sedgwick emerges as a singularly successful author at precisely this juncture between two conflicting sets of demands, as a supremely self-effacing and disinterested author who was, nevertheless, professionally successful precisely because she produced the "right" books for American readers while making modest proprietary claims suited to the American cultural climate.

Twice in the span of about a year between early 1836 and early 1837 (the year that led up to the beginning of organized efforts on behalf of and against international copyright), Sedgwick used the phrase "suited to the market" in letters to her family to describe the works she was then producing, namely her didactic novellas. Her uses of this phrase demonstrate how Sedgwick positioned herself in the field in relation to the available discourses of authorship, readership, and property. In early 1836, she wrote to her brother Charles about plans for marketing her second didactic novella, *The Poor Rich Man and the Rich Poor Man*. Despite her established popular and critical success as one of America's truly "national" writers,[56] she begins the letter to her brother by striking a classic self-effacing pose. She chides him for his excessive "confidence in another's ability and success," which makes him "put [her] up to making money out of [her] poor brains." "Depend on it," she tells him; this goal "is a dream."[57] However, she quickly shifts her focus away from her professed intellectual inadequacy to the workings of the market and her place in that market in the absence of international copyright. She focuses her attention in particular on cheap editions of a novel by Edward Bulwer (later Sir Edward Bulwer-Lytton). Bulwer's novels were the most often decried by literary nationalistic copyright advocates and were among the most widely reprinted in the cheap pamphlet editions that flooded the American market in the late 1830s and early 1840s, a period characterized by a volatile boom and bust economy. Sedgwick complains, "I may go on as I have, if my life and health continue, earning a few hundred dollars a year, and precious few too; but, while such a novel as Rienzi can be sold here for fifty cents, as both editions are, I can not hope, even if I could call to my aid the 'cutest stock-jobbers of Wall Street, to continue, by any play upon the gullible species, to make much out of my handicraft."[58]

56 On Sedgwick's reputation as a "national author" classed with Irving, Bryant, Paulding, Cooper, and Hawthorne, see "The New Copyright Law," *American Monthly Magazine*, Feb. 1838, 107–8.

57 Catharine Maria Sedgwick to Charles Sedgwick, 4 Feb. 1836, in Dewey, *Life*, 252.

58 Ibid. See also Catharine Maria Sedgwick to Charles Sedgwick, 17 Mar. 1830, ibid., 204–5, on *Clarence*'s competition with British reprints. For a contemporary published procopyright complaint about Bulwer in almost exactly the same vein, see "Copy-Right. No. 1. To the Writers of America," *American Monthly Magazine*, Feb. 1837, 157. Note also that opposing herself to Bulwer was not the only possible option for gaining a foothold in the American market. N. P. Willis established his place in the market by fashioning himself as the "American Pelham." Thomas N. Baker, *Sentiment and*

Despite the difficulties of competing on such unequal terms with English novels, Sedgwick tells her brother, "I am as eager to make money as you are – to make it for me," and she outlines her attempts to secure some financial benefit from English and French publication of her works in the absence of international copyright. Finally, while denigrating the quality of *The Poor Rich Man*, she still claims, "There are good notions, suited to the American market, in it."

A year later, on March 8, 1837, she wrote to Charles's adolescent daughter Kate, explaining the "secret" of the recent success of *The Poor Rich Man* by analogizing the book to simple food or particular varieties of coarse, strong everyday cloth U.S. textile mills produced with American cotton for the American market (most U.S. cotton was shipped abroad to British textile mills, which then sold manufactured cotton cloth back to American consumers): "It is, like bread-stuff, or like satinets and negro-cloths, to be a little more modest in my comparison, suited to the market, the thing wanted."[59] She goes on to discuss a number of shorter pieces she was in the process of composing, each tailored to its particular market niche: a "religious article," several pieces for the "souvenirs" or gift books, which, she comments, require "as thin potations as a *hôpital des malades*."[60] In short, why make yourself a fancy dress and cook an elaborate banquet when the market calls for coarse work clothes and some gruel? In the context of the metaphors of author-reader relations used by copyright advocates at about the time Sedgwick wrote this letter, her likening of her books to simple food demonstrates her willingness to provide the simple "aliment" American readers needed, the "Spartan broth" called for by Grenville Sackett. By describing her own works as "thin potations" to feed to invalids, Sedgwick deprecates the purely aesthetic qualities of her works, but she also figures them as necessary and nurturing to the health and well-being of her republican readers/patients.[61] In her public and private constructions of her authorial identity, Sedgwick never claims to be a supremely self-confident artistic creator in the Romantic mode, a person essentially detached from reader desires or expecting readers to conform themselves to the author's vision. Instead, she presents herself, as she does in her letter to her niece, as a craftsperson working with local raw

Celebrity: Nathaniel Parker Willis and the Trials of Literary Fame (New York: Oxford University Press, 1999), chap. 3. See also Tomc, "Idle Industry," on Willis's performance of authorship as leisure.

59 Catharine Maria Sedgwick to Kate Sedgwick, 8 Mar. 1837, in Dewey, *Life*, 260.

60 Ibid., 261.

61 My conclusions concerning Sedgwick's mode of authorship resemble Bromell's. I agree that Sedgwick believed authorship "[requires] self-abnegation" rather than "self-expression" and that fulfilling an immediate social need rather than "producing great works of lasting appeal" was her goal. *Sweat of the Brow*, 142–3. However, I disagree with his contention that Sedgwick aligned moral influence and literary labor with incorporeality. My reading of Sedgwick's letters suggests that she imagined her moral influence as an author as being produced by materialized, domestic labors (sewing, cooking, etc).

materials (grains and cotton) to fashion the goods (bread stuff, negro-cloth, and satinets) that reader-consumers need to lead their lives comfortably and appropriately.

In the context of the copyright debates, even Sedgwick's repeated private renunciations of literary ambition serve to position her powerfully *within* the literary market rather than remove her *from* it. Sedgwick begins an 1837 letter to her friend and frequent correspondent the Reverend William Ellery Channing with a statement that seems to be a renunciation of authorial ambition: "I thank Heaven that I am not now working for the poor and perishing rewards of literary ambition."[62] The nature and the character of this statement in context, however, are complex and contradictory. Although she expresses a belief that the rewards of literary ambition may be "unattainable" for her (leaving unstated a presumption that her gender may make those rewards unattainable), she turns this very unattainability into an asset, into proof of her service to the *proper* object of literary endeavors: service to the moral growth of the nation through her writing of didactic novellas (the letter is a response to a letter from Channing in which he praises *The Poor Rich Man*). As she claims in her letter to Channing, "I think the time has gone by, or, perhaps, has not come to our country, when they [the rewards of literary ambition] are legitimate objects. With the great physical world subdued to the wants of the human family, there is an immense moral field opening, demanding laborers of every class, of every kind and degree of talent. Neither pride nor humility should withhold us from the work to which we were clearly 'sent.'"[63] Although she here describes her divinely appointed "mission" as an author in the language of moral guardianship rather than in the language of military service used in the copyright petition she signed a year later, she nevertheless sees authors, including herself, as crucial to the integrity of the American nation. In addition to the military metaphor, the "Citizens of New York" petition also links land and literary labor through the image of a moving Western frontier: "Rapidly increasing in territory and population, it has *now* become our duty to provide ourselves with a literature which shall explain, defend, and disseminate our principles throughout our borders, which shall cement more strongly our Union, and urge our people forward on their onward career."[64] In her letter to Channing, she argues that because the work of settlement and subduing the physical world is coming to a close, energies once directed at those aims must now be directed to the work of building a nation on moral principles that will best serve the people who inhabit that tamed land. She writes not for the sake of "art" and the rewards of aesthetics; she writes instead to serve the moral development of American readers and the American nation those readers constitute.

62 Catharine Maria Sedgwick to William Ellery Channing, 24 Aug. 1837, in Dewey, *Life*, 271.

63 Ibid. 64 Senate, *Memorial of a Number of Citizens of New York*, 1.

Sedgwick deprecates herself with many of these statements about her own authorship and authorship in general, and she aligns herself with certain models of proper womanly behavior. Because of such statements, modern critics have tended to describe her decision to shift from producing novels proper to writing didactic novellas as a disappointing retreat for literary ambition.[65] However, Sedgwick's self-deprecating statements also reveal her alignment with a powerful model for American authorship, not just her estrangement from a center of power. By emphasizing the materiality of her labors, she, like copyright advocates in their articles, pamphlets, and petitions, puts herself on par with ordinary laborers. This strategy does not, however, simply deny her authorial power; it also aligns her with the discourse of property used to justify authorial property claims in the copyright debates. If she engages in material manufacture, her claim to property in her works is clear and obvious. By mixing her labor with common materials, she becomes entitled to claim the transformed substance as her property. By figuring her work as modest home manufacture rather than the great work of capital, like the monumental work that publishers claimed for themselves in anticopyright rhetoric, she puts herself in a properly subservient relation to readers and publishers. She "owns" her books, and others cannot appropriate and sell them in violation of her rights (at least in America), but *readers*, those who will purchase and consume her books, are ultimately the most powerful figures. If she does not produce and offer appropriate wares, her "rights" are for naught. In her authorial self-fashioning through images of home-based manufacturing, Sedgwick thus walked a fine line between claiming proprietary power as an author and abjuring a claim that she would secure at the expense of readers' (and publishers') interests.

Reviews of Sedgwick's didactic novellas provide evidence that readers understood and approved of Sedgwick's authorial positioning with her shift to didacticism precisely as she intended them to. Reviewers praised her five novels (*A New-England Tale*, *Redwood*, *Hope Leslie*, *Clarence*, and *The Linwoods*) as a "public benefaction," but such praise markedly increased with her generic shift. A review of *Home* and *The Linwoods* (both published in 1835) in the *American Monthly Magazine*, for instance, praises her shift to didacticism in *Home* in language that echoes Gulian Verplanck's claims for the importance of American authorship in creating and maintaining the American republic: "Miss Sedgwick's works begin to claim a higher place than that of elegant literature. She is evidently a republican writer, in a

65 See, e.g., Judith Fetterleys' description of Sedgwick's turn to didacticism: "[S]uch works fit more comfortably into Sedgwick's definition of appropriately feminine behavior than did success as a major novelist." *Provisions: A Reader from 19th-Century American Women* (Bloomington: Indiana University Press, 1985), 44. Patricia Larsen Kalayjian recognizes that Sedgwick's contemporaries "did not... automatically relegate didacticism to a position of inferiority," but she still finds her shift disappointing. "Her 'Classic Pen': Critical Politics and the Reputation of Catharine Maria Sedgwick," PhD diss., Duke University, 1991, 63, 79–80.

department which has hitherto been devoted to glorifying the spirit of feudalism and its consequent false views; and which certainly has never before been made a refracting atmosphere to diffuse the light of our institutions over the whole surface of our society, though so admirably adapted to this purpose."[66] The reviewer praises Sedgwick for the moral benefits conferred by all of her works, but especially *Home*, through which, the reviewer opines, Sedgwick shows "the marks of a true genius for commencing a literature for the mass of the American people which shall bring up their moral tone to the spirit of their institutions."[67] Like many reviewers, including Harriet Martineau in the *London and Westminster Review*, the reviewer recognizes Sedgwick's shift to a "lower" form of literature as an embrace of a *higher* ambition for her literary works, an ambition exactly suited to the condition of American society. As Martineau argues, by seemingly reducing the ambition and complexity of her fiction, Sedgwick shows that she "apprehends the principles which are the life of good fiction, – that its interest lies in the revelation of the human spirit which it affords; that this revelation can be better made, as in real life, through the medium of small incidents than of great events. . . . She rises from imitation and conventionalism into originality and nature."[68] To return to *A New-England Tale* and Jane Elton's appearance on the stage to recite her prize composition, Elvira's elaborate and imitative appearance preceding Jane's magnifies the effect of Jane's simplicity by way of contrast. In a sense, Sedgwick served as her own Elvira, writing several more elaborately wrought and conventional novels after *A New-England Tale*, imitating plot and character devices developed by her English predecessors. By leaving these devices behind, she set the stage for her own appearance as plain Jane, the plain author of didactic novellas, presenting functional and unadorned narratives, and her performance as Jane gained luster from its contrast with the more Elvira-like performances that preceded it.[69]

Referring to a saying invoked by several other reviewers, an 1837 review of *The Poor Rich Man* in the *Christian Examiner* remarks, "If we dared to allude to so trite a saying as that which sets ballad-making above law-making, we would say that the writer of works like this, and its twin-sister, 'HOME,' has the character and the fortunes of this nation more at her disposal than any

66 "The Novels of Miss Sedgwick," *American Monthly Magazine*, Jan. 1836, 20.

67 Ibid., 21.

68 Harriet Martineau, "Art. III," *London and Westminster Review* (American edition), Oct. 1837, 46.

69 Sedgwick's chosen form in her didactic novellas is not, of course, sui generis. When the Reverend Henry Ware asked her to write the book that became *Home*, he suggested Harriet Martineau's *Illustrations of Political Economy* as a model. Henry Ware to Catharine Maria Sedgwick, 31 Jan. 1845, in Dewey, *Life*, 239. Still, both Sedgwick herself and her reviewers understood the difference from her earlier works and from novels and romances generally to be particularly "American" (and, strangely enough, even Martineau praises the "originality" of fictional strategies Sedgwick arguably appropriated from Martineau).

ambitious politician in the land."[70] Assigning ballad-making to Sedgwick as an appropriate activity rather than lawmaking is clearly a gendered maneuver. As the *American Monthly Magazine* argues, literature is particularly suited to "feminine genius" as opposed to the implicitly masculine genius of "pure reasoning from first principles" required of Josiah Quincy, Daniel Webster, and other writers of laws, constitutions, and political treatises.[71] Such categorizing clearly set limits for the types of writing for which women writers would be praised,[72] but those limits coincided, in significant respects, with the limits American law and culture set for American authorship. Reviewers clearly placed Sedgwick *at the center* of a national literary project, and they recognized this literary project as being equally or even *more* important to the young nation than the more overtly political projects of writing laws and political treatises. Reviewers argued that the masses lacked the knowledge and training they needed to govern themselves, and a "feminine genius" like Sedgwick, using her own novel adaptation of the novel form, could "apply principle to domestic and social action, and, like spring and summer, to breathe beauty into and over the sublime but wintry outline of the political system drawn over masculine power," thus creating "a work of... far-reaching beneficence."[73] Her literary labors may have been as important as the writing of laws, but neither form of authorship granted proprietorship and financial rewards. In making the analogy between laws and literary texts, her reviewers imply that both the Constitution and Sedgwick's didactic tales "belonged" to the public more than they did to their authors (*Wheaton v. Peters*, the first copyright case decided by the Supreme Court in 1834, established that the law, including judicial opinions, was public property that could not be claimed as private property under the copyright statute).[74]

Sedgwick's generic shift to didactic novellas was broadly important as a gesture of disinterested republican authorship, but her specific commentary in these novellas on the importance of books and reading contributed more directly to her continuing construction of her own authorship in relation to American readers. Sarah Robbins has suggested that by portraying scenes of domestic literacy instruction in her didactic works, Sedgwick participated in a larger project of expanding the definition of Republican Motherhood by portraying American mothers as "essential cultural agents" engaged in "meaningful public acts."[75] Looking more broadly at Sedgwick's

70 Review of *The Poor Rich Man*in *Christian Examiner*, Jan. 1837, 398.

71 "Novels of Miss Sedgwick," 24.

72 Nina Baym documents how reviewers during the period applied different standards to women authors than to men. *Novels, Readers, and Reviewers: Responses to Fiction in Antebellum America* (Ithaca: Cornell University Press, 1984), chap. 5.

73 "Novels of Miss Sedgwick," 25.

74 On the logic of *Wheaton v. Peters*, see McGill, *American Literature*, chap. 1.

75 Sarah Robbins, "Future Good," 567, 581. See also Robbins on the generic status of Sedgwick's didactics and the ways that these literacy narratives seek to both empower and contain the lower

representations of books, readers, and authors in her didactic works, we find Sedgwick strategically effacing her authorial agency even as she constructs a powerful role for all of the readers in the family circle. In her first didactic novella, *Home* (1835), Sedgwick creates a model republican family, the Barclays, who are defined by their roles as both consumers and producers of print. Mr. Barclay, a printer, manufactures books for a living, and the consumption of books is central to the family's functioning. As Richard Brodhead notes of the plotting of family life in *Home*, Sedgwick's "first chapter narrates the assembling of ingredients by which the home is constituted in the first place – and in this account the family's books (made visible in its conspicuous bookcase) are listed with its first priorities."[76] When Mr. Barclay and his new wife move into their exceedingly modest, small, and plain first home in New York City, his wife is delighted and surprised to pull back the curtain of a bookcase unexpectedly filled with books – several volumes of history of England and America, classic works of English literature from the preceding centuries (Shakespeare, Milton, Pope, etc.), works of moral and religious philosophy, and a host of dictionaries and reference books (the Bible is *not* on the bookshelf, but only because Mr. Barclay has placed it on a parlor table for easier daily use by the family).[77] By repeating this scene in two other didactic tales, Sedgwick makes the plenitude of print central to her definition of American republican home life. In *Live and Let Live, or, Domestic Service Illustrated* (1837), the full bookshelf in the serving maid's room exemplifies the "realizing sense" of the model mistress of the full humanity of her servants and the permeability of class boundaries in America.[78] In *The Poor Rich Man and the Rich Poor Man* (1836), it is the family of the "rich poor man" that stocks its own bookshelf and then later has another bookshelf stocked for it by a model landlord.[79]

In *Home*, when Mrs. Barclay inquires how the small sum of money given to them by her father could have bought so many books, Mr. Barclay explains, "Since I have earned more than I was obliged to spend, I have made a yearly investment in books, as the stock which would yield the best income.... Instead of twenty-five dollars' worth of glass and gilding, we have some of the best productions of the best minds. Instead of the poor gratification of our vanity, or at best our eyes, we have a productive capital

classes. "Periodizing Authorship, Characterizing Genre: Catharine Maria Sedgwick's Benevolent Literacy Narratives," *American Literature* 76, no. 1 (2004): 1–29.

76 Richard Brodhead, *Cultures of Letters: Scenes of Reading and Writing in Nineteenth-Century America* (Chicago: Chicago University Press, 1993), 45.

77 Catharine Maria Sedgwick, *Home, or Scenes and Characters Illustrating Christian Truth* (Boston and Cambridge: James Munroe & Co., 1835), 8–9 (hereinafter cited in the text).

78 Catharine Maria Sedgwick, *Live and Let Live; or, Domestic Service Illustrated* (New York: Harper & Brothers, 1837), 190.

79 Catharine Maria Sedgwick, *The Poor Rich Man and the Rich Poor Man* (New York: Harper & Brothers, 1836), 105, 174–5.

from which we may derive exhaustless pleasure, which hundreds may share, and which those who come after us may enjoy. O, who can estimate the value of a book!" (pp. 9–10). When Mr. Barclay's panegyric to books climaxes with a claim that books are like the ancient's household gods, but better because "mine have living and immortal souls," the narrator interrupts to comment, "Mr. Barclay was a printer and might magnify his art; but what honor is not due to that art, which makes the spirits of the departed, our familiar companions and instructors, – which realizes the doctrine of metempsychosis, and transfuses the souls of the departed into the living" (pp. 10–11). In these passages in *Home*, and in similar passages in her other didactic novellas, Sedgwick promulgates a vision of consumption of print that simultaneously centers and decenters the author. She celebrates authors as immortal souls, but the skill and labor of printers in each age is the key to circulation of those souls, and the "profit" made from circulation of literary "stock" belongs to readers, not to authors. In her reading of *Home* in *Sentimental Materialism*, Lori Merish characterizes the Barclay's books, along with other material objects furnishing the Barclay household, as "sentimental property," the possession and proper care of which constitute the Barclays and other antebellum Americans as middle-class subjects.[80] And, indeed, characters and the narrator explicitly label books as property; significantly, however, readers, not authors, are the proprietors. Many of the books on the Barclay's bookshelf are by authors long dead, their works by definition public property and thus financially accessible even for a barely middle-class family like the Barclays, a family that in a democratic republic must be educated through reading to exercise its power intelligently. (Sedgwick does not seek a direct role for Mrs. Barclay in that democracy – her participation is as a republican mother who educates her male children for full citizenship and exerts a beneficent moral influence on Mr. Barclay, who "represents" her in the polis). In order to educate themselves for responsible participation in a democracy, members of the model republican family do not read cheap contemporary British trash. Instead, they read classics that enrich the mind and life stories that provide models of republican lives (Marshall's *Life of Washington* is on the bookshelf, and Mr. Barclay later reads Benjamin Franklin's life aloud to his children "to impress its valuable instruction" on them [p. 88]). "Hundreds," Mr. Barclay advises, may enjoy a book, which may circulate in multiple copies again and again, and readers may incorporate authors' ideas into their lives. The proprietary author does not interfere and, indeed, has no power to interfere with or control the *reader's* "property" in the *author's* ideas.

80 Lori Merish, *Sentimental Materialism: Gender, Commodity Culture, and Nineteenth-Century American Literature* (Durham: Duke University Press, 2000), 127. Merish arrives at this interesting reading of *Home*, however, through an inaccurate biographical characterization of Sedgwick (119).

In *Means and Ends; or, Self-Training* (1839), Sedgwick speaks directly as a didact to young people rather than through fictional narratives, but she reinforces and elaborates the message of her didactic novellas in an entire chapter on "What to Read, and How to Read." Oscillating again between the poles of centering and decentering the author, she claims extraordinary powers for authors while putting the readers in control. She thus constructs a powerful position for herself as an author while instructing readers in how to subvert her authority for republican ends. "What is a book, my young friends?" she asks. Claiming a godlike creative power for authors derived from their years of intellectual labor, and claiming again the powers of metempsychosis for print, she continues, "Is [a book] not a cabinet which contains the most interesting creation of God, the mind of a human being, a portion of the Divine mind? From this mind you may have been separated by intervening ages, oceans may have divided you. But here it has come to your home, to dwell with you, to impart to you its best thoughts, to communicate to you its observations and experience, and to share with you the treasures of knowledge acquired by days, and nights, and years of laborious study."[81] Although her claims here echo those of copyright advocates (recall the editorial in which Bryant both tells the parable of the Indian's labor of making his bow from common materials and claims that authorial labors are *poesis*, an act of original making; or Verplanck's scene of the author's years of laborious study in his garret), she quickly shifts away from any possible claim of the author's property to describe the reader's property. Recalling past ages when books were luxury items, she celebrates the present in America, where books "abound in the humblest of homes" (p. 222). Metonymically substituting authors for their books, she tells her readers that historians, travelers, biographers, and poets can personally visit their homes, and although she opines that "such friends deserve respect, honor, and all observance" (p. 223), she does not ask that readers respect or honor their "friends'" proprietary rights. Instead, the property again resides in the reader: "[I]n his book, the treasures of his mind are given to you; you have not merely a glimpse of them – they abide with you. They wait your leisure and convenience" (p. 223).

In her estimation, books are the "best property" of all classes of readers, rich and poor (p. 224), but a property that readers must select carefully. While analogizing the pleasures of reading to the pleasure of social intercourse with a person, Sedgwick nevertheless tells her young readers, "[B]ooks have an obvious advantage over society. You cannot always choose your company, you may choose your books; at least you may reject those that are worthless and unimproving" (p. 226). As she remarks in the preface to her account

81 Catharine Maria Sedgwick, *Means and Ends: Or, Self-Training* (Boston: Marsh, Capen, Lyon & Webb, 1839), 222 (hereinafter cited in the text).

of her European travels, *Letters from Abroad* (1841), "An apology for a book implies that the public are obliged to read it"; but there *is* no such obligation because it "would reverse the order of nature – transfer the power from the strong to the weak."[82] In Sedgwick's estimation, the author is weak because the reader can choose whether or not to read the author's book.

In her didactic novellas and essays, Sedgwick emphasizes the reader's agency and the reader's property in texts over authorial claims to literary property; paradoxically, however, these books proved to be her most valuable literary properties. Whereas *Clarence* was issued in only one edition, *Home* went through twenty.[83] By turning to didacticism, she embraced both new work to be done and more channels of distribution. Her didactic texts, rather than simply being published and separately marketed as books, were republished in school and Sunday school "libraries." *Home* first appeared as the third publication in the Reverend Henry Ware's *Scenes and Characters Illustrating Christian Truth*, a Unitarian tract series. She describes to her brother Charles her ideas for building up new channels of distribution in small New England towns for *The Poor Rich Man*, telling him that the publisher should "[let] it be known to their correspondents in the New England country towns what sort of a thing it is, intended for popular consumption, that it may at once be for sale in the country towns. If I should continue the series, this may be important."[84] Sedgwick revised *Morals of Manners* (1846) so that "ten or twelve hundred" could be distributed by the New York School Committee to families of public school children.[85] One correspondent, a Dr. Cummings, even wrote to her to report that he intended to "devote the remainder of [his] life to the diffusion of [her] books among [his] fellow mortals," and that he had persuaded his Unitarian minister "to give a copy of 'Home' to every couple he marries."[86] Religious and educational publishing were two areas of the market in which American-authored texts were preferred and predominated and through which American authors could gain access to an American mass market. As one copyright advocate noted in the *American Monthly Magazine* in 1837, only Americans could produce hymnbooks suitable for use in American churches and schoolbooks suitable for American schools, but these American-authored books still sold cheaply. Copyright opponents claimed that international copyright would create many such American "monopolies" in the market, causing the prices

82 Catharine Maria Sedgwick, *Letters from Abroad to Kindred at Home* (New York: Harper & Brothers, 1841), ix.

83 Damon-Bach, Allison J. Roepsch, and Homestead, "Chronological Bibliography of the Works of Catharine Maria Sedgwick," in *Catharine Maria Sedgwick: Critical Perspectives*,297–8. This bibliography also documents the appearances of Sedgwick's didactic works in libraries and series.

84 Catharine Maria Sedgwick to Charles Sedgwick, 22 July 1836, in Dewey, *Life*, 254.

85 Catharine Maria Sedgwick to Kate Sedgwick Minot, 6 Dec. 1846, ibid., 300.

86 Dr. Cummings to Catharine Maria Sedgwick, Aug. 1851, ibid, 222.

of both American- and British-authored books to rise; so why did the school- and hymnbook "monopolies" not produce high prices? Because educational and religious books "are intended for the multitude, as the greatest portion of the books printed in the United States must be, and they must therefore be sold cheap, or not at all. . . . They *must* be sold cheap; for the readers of our country, as a class, *must* and will have them so; and if the publishers refuse to sell them so, the authors will do it themselves."[87] Sedgwick's didactic texts found a mass-market audience that her novels did not because they were appropriate for distribution through such religious and educational channels.[88] By "retreating" from "literary" ambition, she thus secured a better position for herself in the market for American-authored books.

"Works in this tone . . . will go further than any parchment Bill of Rights to perpetuate our political blessings": Catharine Sedgwick as model republican author in the wake of Charles Dickens's 1842 American tour

Sedgwick's shift to didacticism just preceded the heated barrage of debate in print over the international copyright issue. She was ripe for appropriation as a figure of republican authorship in these debates precisely because of this shift. Congress declined to pass international copyright legislation in 1838, and public comment on the subject somewhat subsided until 1842, when Charles Dickens first toured America and the American press widely criticized him for his remarks in favor of international copyright. Once again, Sedgwick became an important figure in debates about the place of American authors in the copyright law and American culture, a paradoxical figure who simultaneously embodied the power of authorship in a democratic republic and the dispossession of authors by the law.

In the wake of Dickens's tour, the *North American Review* published several articles in favor of the passage of an international copyright law, including one by J. G. Palfrey, editor of the *Review* (like all other articles in the *Review* published during the 1830s and 1840s, no author's name was attached to

87 H.C., "Copyright Law. No. 3," *American Monthly Magazine*, Oct. 1837, 376.

88 For the mass-market innovations of religious publishing during this period, see David Paul Nord, "The Evangelical Origins of the Mass Media in America, 1815–1835," *Journalism Monographs* 88 (1984): 1–31. Nord's primary example is the American Tract Society, which Evangelicals controlled and thus was not accessible to Sedgwick and others in Unitarian circles. Nevertheless, Nord's analysis suggests the stunning scope and power of religious publishing during the period. Noah Webster's Blue Back Speller was the most notable success in educational publishing, the one that may have inspired H.C.'s comments in the *American Monthly Magazine* on schoolbooks. See E. Jennifer Monaghan, *A Common Heritage: Noah Webster's Blue-Back Speller* (Hamden, CT: Archon Books, 1983).

the article in print).[89] Palfrey's article is a fairly typical piece copyright advocacy, which trots out well-worn tropes to support its argument. He claims that a law giving American authors a fair chance will spur authors to produce higher quality works better serving the interests of American readers than foreign-authored novels. Elaborating the basic bale of merchandise analogy and adding names and concrete details, Palfrey describes the market for literature in the absence of international copyright as one in which bales of merchandise shipped by the Rothschilds and Barings to American ports "are no more property . . . as is that property, belonging to Edgeworth and Southey by right of creation, which, the moment it touches our shores, is turned over to uncontrolled plunder."[90] Responding to claims that American readers *prefer* to get books cheap rather than paying authors for them, Palfrey turns to the literature-food analogy, reasoning that the statement cannot be true, or if it is true, that it is a disgrace to American readers: "Not many of our countrymen would bring a good relish to the stalled ox served up *gratis* from their helpless neighbor's herd; we do not know them, if they prefer intellectual food they so relish should be seasoned with the thought of making no return to the producer" (p. 252).

Although much of his article is typical, he departs from the norm in one striking respect: Palfrey singles out one American author, "Miss Sedgwick," for her "service to patriotism" through her authorial labors. Arguing that the English novels flooding the American market in the absence of an international copyright law fill the heads of impressionable young American readers (the "merchant's daughter and the farmer's boy") with fevered dreams of the lives of English nobility, he identifies Sedgwick's didactic novellas as the only suitable antidotes available:

> In our opinion there is scarcely a better service of patriotism than is to be rendered by the multiplication of works . . . in the tone of some of those, in which the upright genius of Miss Sedgwick has kindled the sympathy of readers in the virtues that benefit the American citizen, and awakened their veneration and love for that essential dignity and charm, which every man and woman in this nation may aspire to wear. We do think, that whoever has been reading "Woodstock" [a novel by Sir Walter Scott, subtitled *The Cavalier: A Tale of the Year Sixteen Hundred and Fifty-one*], with a genuine surrender of himself to the artist's power, is in such a peril of finding himself inoculated with the subtile virus of that man-worship, namely *loyalty*, that he

89 William Cushing's 1878 index identifies Palfrey as author, and Palfrey also obliquely acknowledged his authorship many years later in a published letter to the International Copyright Association. International Copyright Association, *International Copyright: Meeting of Authors and Publishers* (New York: International Copyright Association, 1868), 9.

90 J. G. Palfrey, "Petition of Certain Legal Voters of Boston and Its Vicinity to the Honorable Senate and House of Representatives in Congress Assembled, Praying for the Passage of an International Copyright Law," *North American Review*, July 1842, 246 (hereinafter cited in the text).

> will do well presently to apply "Live and Let Live," or some such generous febrifuge, to restore a republican sanity to his distempered blood. Works in this tone, – more abundant and more highly wrought the better, – instructing the common mind of this nation to appreciate its privileges, – forming it to discharge, and winning it to love, the duties of its position, – will go further than any parchment Bill of Rights to perpetuate our political blessings. They must be written in America; they can be produced nowhere else. And when rulers come a little to their sense of their own duty, they will take care to provide some encouragement for the production of such works. If on every shelf in the American States, where now lies a copy of "Pelham" [a novel by Edward Bulwer, subtitled *Adventures of a Gentleman*], we could substitute one of "Home," or of "The Poor Rich Man and Rich Poor Man," we hesitate not at all to say, that there would forthwith be a most substantial effect produced on the respectability of the national character, and the stability of national institutions. Works of a similar character, in much greater number, – and, for aught we know, of much higher order, – there will be, when the grave and reverend guardians of the nation's welfare, in Congress assembled, shall be disposed to attend to their duty in the premises. Readers cordially greet such work, but authors must live while they write them; and this they will have no security for doing, till legislators shall have made that easy provision, which depends on them, for the encouragement of a literature instinct with the spirit of republican virtue. (pp. 261–2)

Just as Sedgwick privately described some of her writings as food to feed the ill and bemoaned the cheap copies of Bulwer's novels being hawked on the streets of New York, Palfrey publicly proclaims that consuming Sedgwick's didactic novellas will cure the brain fever induced by reading representations of British aristocratic life in the fictions of Bulwer and others. In merging copyright advocacy with an extended positive review of Sedgwick's didactic novellas, however, Palfrey paradoxically demonstrates the success of Sedgwick positioning of herself in the market in the *absence* of international copyright. By both praising Sedgwick and asking Congress to reform the law, Palfrey ultimately argues that Congress should reform the law so that more American writers will be able to embrace the patriotic literary ambition that Sedgwick (apparently alone in Palfrey's estimation, or at least most praiseworthily) has embraced despite the obstacles posed by the law.

Despite his resort to proprietary logic in his analogy between a farmer who owns an ox and an author who owns a book, Palfrey's argument for copyright does not ultimately rest on the injury done to the owner of the ox (the author) – the welfare of the ox-eaters (readers) concerns him more. Like many American copyright advocates, even some of those who most strenuously stressed the author's "sacred rights of property" and called the most loudly for "justice to authors," Palfrey claims that recognizing authors' rights will benefit the reading public and the American nation. Palfrey's promotion of Sedgwick as a model republican author thus occurs in the context of a public interest–based argument in favor of copyright, and he carefully frames his argument as a response to and critique of a very different pro-copyright argument, one based on the self-interest of authors and publishers. Like most article writers for the *North American Review*, Palfrey responds to a book or article published elsewhere. In this case, he responds to a "Petition of Certain Legal Voters of Boston and its Vicinity to the Honorable Senate and House of Representatives in Congress assembled, praying for the Passage of an International Copyright Law," a petition published in the *Boston Daily Advertiser*.[91] The *Daily Advertiser* petition responds to yet another petition, an anticopyright petition claiming to represent the interests of "publishers, booksellers, writers, editors, printers, papermakers, and other persons interested in the sale of books" in Boston.[92] Charles Dickens's visit to Boston spurred both Boston petitions because during his visit, he spoke in favor of international copyright at one of the events honoring him as an author. The *Daily Advertiser* petition makes no claim that an international copyright law will serve the reading public, but instead maps out how a change will promote the "interests" of authors and others in the book trades by giving them access to the British market and better standing in the American market. Palfrey, in response, claims in his opening paragraph, "It is not . . . for the prosperity of the writers, that we care . . . but we do care for the character of our country" (p. 246). Later, in his praise of Sedgwick, he decries the incompatibility of the values embodied in English literature with republican virtues, calling for a truly American literature that will kindle "the sympathy of readers in the virtues that benefit the American citizen" (p. 261). The *Daily Advertiser* petition to which Palfrey responds is titled so as to emphasize the status of its signers as voters, who may thus exercise their electoral power to reinforce their economic interests – if Congress does not enact international copyright, the "voters" who have signed the petition will elect new Congressmen who will. In response, Palfrey offers up Catharine Sedgwick, an author who, as a woman, cannot vote at all and who continues to serve her country through her writing even though the current legal system fails to serve her interests. Palfrey thus offers Sedgwick up as an example of supreme authorial *dis*interestedness in order to counter the interested petitioning of both copyright advocates and opponents.

91 "International Copyright," *Boston Daily Advertiser*, 4 June 1842, [1]. Either this petition was not ultimately submitted to Congress or Congress did not print it.

92 The petition printed in the *Advertiser* identifies the petition to which it is responding only through this descriptive phrase, but the referent is clear – Senate, *Memorial of a Number of Persons Concerned in Printing and Publishing, Praying an Alteration in the Mode of Levying Duties on Certain Books, and Remonstrating Against the Enactment of an International Copy-right Law*, 27th Cong., 2nd sess, 13 June 1842, S. Doc. 323.

The military metaphor deployed in the "Citizens of New York" petition that Sedgwick signed similarly places an emphasis on the public good (the "onward career" of "our people" in a reading republic) as opposed to private pecuniary interest. Many pieces of copyright advocacy, including both the 1838 petition and Palfrey's article, thus make the same argument that Gulian Verplanck claimed the founding fathers made by including a copyright clause in the Constitution: that the wide circulation of American literature would create and define the American union. As long as American publishers were, in the words of the "Citizens of New York," "but mere re-publishers of foreign books," America would continue to be "deluged with a flood of ephemeral [British] literature, that has been anything but favorable to our moral and republican notions."[93]

Dickens's works, of course, represented a substantial current in that "flood" of reprinted British literature deluging the American market. When he proceeded from New England to New York on his 1842 American tour, Catharine Sedgwick made another telling appearance as an American bulwark against that flood. More than a decade after the 1831 dinner honoring Verplanck for his efforts on behalf of the act extending the copyright term, he was one of the masters of ceremony at a New York dinner honoring Dickens. The press had already roundly criticized Dickens for his public remarks in favor of international copyright at dinners in Hartford and Boston, and stung by the criticism, he in his New York speech approaches the question so tentatively and obliquely that his remarks take the form of a justification of his right to have spoken in the past rather than of an actual argument in favor of international copyright: "As I came here, and am here, without the least admixture of one hundredth part of one grain of base alloy, without one feeling of unworthy reference to self in any respect, I claim in reference to the past for the last time, my right in reason, in truth and in justice, to approach, as I have on two former occasions, a question of literary interest. I claim that justice be done, and I prefer that claim as one who has a right to speak and be heard."[94] Turning from himself and his

93 "Citizens of New York," 2. In his taxonomy of the copyright debates, Rice describes the anticopyright position as "utilitarian" and as valuing circulation, while he labels the procopyright position as Lockean and valuing rights and possession. *Transformation of Authorship*, 76. Such a dichotomy, which Rice himself admits to be oversimplified (186n.), fails to account for this position, which argues for authors' rights based on a utilitarian rationale.

94 William Glyde Wilkins, *Charles Dickens in America* (London: Chapman & Hall, 1911), 127. Modern scholars have differed greatly in their interpretations of Dickens's actions and motivations with respect to the copyright issue on his tour. See, e.g., Sidney P. Moss, *Charles Dickens' Quarrel with America* (Troy, NY: Whitson, 1984); Jerome Meckier, *Innocent Abroad: Charles Dickens's American Engagements* (Lexington: University Press of Kentucky, 1990); Alexander Welsh, *From Copyright to Copperfield: The Identity of Dickens* (Cambridge: Harvard University Press, 1987); and McGill, *American Literature*, chap. 3. What is most important for understanding Sedgwick's relationship to theses event is not Dickens's actual motivations but the widely publicized critique of Dickens as greedy and self-interested.

own interests to Washington Irving (Verplanck's co-master of ceremonies), the rest of Dickens's speech vigorously displays disinterested praise of the talents of another. He concludes with a toast: "I am sure, in the presence of such writers as Bryant, Halleck and – But I suppose I must not mention the ladies here – *The Literature of America* – she well knows how to do honour to her own literature, and to that of other lands, when she chooses Washington Irving for her representative in the country of Cervantes." While praising American literature, Dickens's toast also draws attention to one of the most (in)famous instances of the supposed impossibility of sustained American authorial success in the period – Irving succeeded spectacularly early in his career with *The Sketch Book* and gained a reputation as the best American writer of fiction. However, his later works never equaled that early commercial and critical success, and he received diplomatic appointments as a form of patronage enabling him to research and write histories.[95] Washington Irving was absent from the 1831 dinner because of a diplomatic appointment to England, and in 1842 he was in the United States but was about to depart for a new appointment to Spain, "the country of Cervantes."

Further submerged in Dickens's toast, however, is Catharine Sedgwick, one of the "ladies" whom Dickens cannot name but whose name he would have otherwise recited in the toast, a writer who continued to write in the face of the lack of international copyright. Just as her brother Robert helped to organize the 1831 dinner in honor of Verplanck, her nephew Theodore Sedgwick, her fellow signer of the 1838 petition, helped to organize the 1842 New York Dickens dinner. Although the company at the 1831 dinner, like that at many such public dinners, was exclusively male, as Philip Hone, another organizer of the 1842 dinner, recounts in his diary: "An unusual feature of this festivity was the presence of a coterie of charming women, who were first stowed away in a small room adjoining the upper part of the hall, and who, with a laudable and irrepressible curiosity to hear me, and others equally instructive and agreeable, at the lower end, edged by degrees into the room, and finally got possession of the stage behind the president [Irving], to the discomfiture of certain pleasant old bachelors and ungallant dignitaries, but to the great delight of us who profess to have better taste in such matters."[96] Among the group that he describes as a "flying squadron" is "Miss Sedgwick," the "lady" most qualified to be mentioned in the same breath as William Cullen Bryant, FitzGreene Halleck, and Washington

95 Of course, Irving never married, so his relationship to the narratives of patrimony and descent used to justify the expansion of copyright is far from simple. For a provocative reading of the bachelor as a figure of authorship, see Bryce Traister, "The Wandering Bachelor: Irving, Masculinity, and Authorship," *American Literature* 74, no. 1 (2002): 111–37.

96 Wilkins, *Charles Dickens*, 149.

Irving, but whom Dickens "supposes he must not mention."[97] As at the 1831 dinner, she hovers above the fray, an unnamable contradiction, a writer who continues to write and serve even when the laws of commerce advise against it.

In a letter to Unitarian minister Orville Dewey describing Dickens's "royal progress" through the United States and the warm outpouring of emotions from "all classes," Catharine Sedgwick modestly describes her own presence at the dinner. Avoiding the issue of copyright, she praises Dickens for his disinterested praise of Irving: "It was beautiful to see, at his dinner here – of which I, with about fifty other of womankind, had the good fortune to be spectator – the heartiness with which he [Dickens] took the laurels from his own loaded brow and covered Irving's, so that for a moment we all forgot, as he meant we should, that it was somewhat faded and shorn of its earlier glory."[98] By mentioning the traditional laurels as a sign of respect for literary achievement, Sedgwick indirectly refers to Irving's own toast at the dinner, to "*International Copyright* – It is but fair that those who have laurels for their brows should be permitted to *browse* on their laurels."[99] This toast in turn elicited from Cornelius Mathews (a signer of the 1838 petition with Catharine Sedgwick and in 1842 the editor of a short-lived literary magazine, *Arcturus*) a long-winded, accusatory speech vilifying American publishers, readers, and Congress for their participation in and support of literary theft. Sedgwick, like most of the press, including even the strongly procopyright *Evening Post*, declined to mention Matthews's speech. She and Bryant apparently found its tone and emphasis on commercial matters in poor taste at such a function. Once again, within the range of arguments deployed by copyright advocates, we find Sedgwick aligned with public interest–based arguments, closer to the republican rhetoric of copyright advocates privileging circulation of print for the benefit of readers than to the indignant author-centered rhetoric of Cornelius Mathews.

Although Dickens felt constrained against mentioning a "lady's" name at a public dinner and Sedgwick herself remained the soul of modesty about her own importance, literary history and the history of authorship remain incomplete if scholars fail to mention Sedgwick's name and presence at this dinner and her clear importance to literary culture in the estimation of her contemporaries. Judged according to the ideology of authorship that came to predominate in the late nineteenth and early twentieth

97 The other names Hone lists, in a list that does not account for all 50 women present, are Mrs. Davis, Mrs. Colden, Miss Wilkes, Mrs. Dickens, Miss Wadsworth, the Misses Ward, Mrs. Parrish, and Miss Anna Brigden. Other than Dickens's wife, the other women elude definitive identification, but none of them seems to have been a well-known author in 1842.

98 Catharine Maria Sedgwick to Orville Dewey, 26 Feb. 1842, in Dewey, *Life*, 280–1.

99 Wilkins, *Charles Dickens*, 139.

centuries, Sedgwick appears entirely marginal (and, indeed, the first histories of American literature written at the turn from the nineteenth to the twentieth century easily dismiss her).[100] Judged according to the standards of her own historical moment, a moment at which the law privileged readers' access to literature over authors' property rights, Sedgwick's importance and the means through which she achieved that importance become legible. Expectations concerning proper behavior for a "lady" constrained Sedgwick, but these constraints mirrored constraints placed on authorship by the law and enabled Sedgwick (and her female successors) to exploit the full potential of the American literary market structured by the law. Both central (the peer of Bryant, Halleck, and Irving) and liminal (unnamed, silent, and claiming an unauthorized position behind the podium), both powerful and dispossessed, Sedgwick at the dinner figures precisely the situation of American authorship in her historical moment and the ways that a woman was particularly well qualified to inhabit that position.

100 Kalayjian, "Classic Pen," chap. 3.

Chapter 3

"*When I Can Read My Title Clear*": *Harriet Beecher Stowe and the* Stowe v. Thomas *Copyright Infringement Case (1853)*

In 1853, Harriet Beecher Stowe filed a copyright suit against F. W. Thomas, a Philadelphia publisher who had published an unauthorized German translation of *Uncle Tom's Cabin* in his newspaper, *Die Freie Presse*. Stowe brought suit in the federal circuit court in Philadelphia, thus ironically placing her claim in the hands of Justice Robert Grier, a notable enforcer of slave-owners' interests under the Fugitive Slave Law. Grier found that Stowe's property rights in her novelistic plea for resistance to the Fugitive Slave Law were very narrow and that she could not prevent Thomas from publishing a translation without her authorization. In the conclusion to the court's opinion, Grier writes:

> By the publication of Mrs. Stowe's book, the creations of the genius and imagination of the author have become as much public property as those of Homer or Cervantes. Uncle Tom and Topsy are as much publici juris [public property] as Don Quixote and Sancho Panza. All her conceptions and inventions may be used and abused by imitators, play-rights and poetasters. They are no longer her own – those who have purchased her book, may clothe them in English doggerel, in German or Chinese prose. Her absolute dominion and property in the creations of her genius and imagination have been voluntarily relinquished. All that now remains is the copyright of her book; the exclusive right to print, reprint and vend it, and those only can be called infringers of her rights, or pirates of her property, who are guilty of printing, publishing, importing or vending without her license "copies of her book." A translation may, in loose phraseology, be called a transcript or copy of her thoughts or conceptions, but in no correct sense can it be called a copy of her book.[1]

1 Throughout, I quote from and cite to the version of the case collected in the *Federal Cases* at the end of the century (23 Fed. Cas. 201, Case No. 13,514), 208. John William Wallace, the reporter for the Third Circuit, originally reported the case (12 Wall. Jr. 547). The case was also reported in the *American Law Register* without the arguments of counsel (2 Am. Law Reg. 210). In the *American Law Register* and in the manuscript, the last sentence begins, "In tropical, but not very precise phraseology. . . ." The Copyright Office's compilation of all American copyright decisions does not reproduce the arguments of counsel found in Wallace's report and the *Federal Cases* compilation. Wilma S. Davis, ed., *Decisions of the United States Courts Involving Copyright and Literary Property 1789–1909* (Washington, DC: United States Copyright Office, 1980), 2482–6. Thomas's translation was not the only unauthorized German

Not surprisingly, copyright and history of the book scholars often quote this conclusion, with its startling and puzzling image of Tom and Topsy ludicrously dressed in the "clothes" of German and Chinese language; but they also quickly dismiss the court's holding as an inexplicable aberration or as an example of the immaturity of the copyright law in 1853.[2]

This chapter analyzes the case in depth from a number of perspectives, taking *Stowe v. Thomas* seriously as a source of historical knowledge about copyright, authorship, Harriet Beecher Stowe, and her novel that might otherwise remain inaccessible. What can the case tell us about authorship and the copyright law in 1853? How did the law allocate power between authors and readers? What exactly was the nature of the author's property right under the copyright law? And how did these issues come to be resolved in a legal opinion that metaphorized these questions as a dispute over the right to control the exploitation of slave bodies?

As I argue in Chapter 2, in the 1820s and 1830s, Catharine Sedgwick fashioned a modest authority for herself as the producer of literary material objects that she encouraged readers to appropriate as their "best property." Turning from the context of debates about reprinting in the absence of international copyright to the law of infringement, we nevertheless find the same potential friction between authors and readers over the control of literary property, with Stowe, at least momentarily, claiming a public, strongly proprietary authorial role that put her interests at odds with readers. In the context of *Stowe v. Thomas*, Stowe asserted rights to her work as an immaterial product of mental labor, and this claim to an immaterial literary property could have, if successful, given Stowe greater power and authority as an author and proprietor. Not only could others not appropriate her words as they appeared on the physical pages of her book, argued

translation. Lewis N. Dembitz also published a serialized German translation in the *Beobachter am Ohio*, a Louisville, Kentucky, paper. John J. Weisert, "Lewis N. Dembitz and *Onkel Tom's Hütte*," *German American Review* 19, no. 3 (1953): 7–8. It is not clear whether Stowe never discovered this publication or whether she discovered it and forced the newspaper to stop, because only a single issue of the newspaper (14 Feb. 1853) survives.

2 Benjamin Kaplan, *An Unhurried View of Copyright* (New York: Columbia University Press, 1967), 29–31. Lyman Ray Patterson, *Copyright in Historical Perspective* (Nashville: Vanderbilt University Press, 1968), 214. Patterson and Stanley Lindberg, *The Nature of Copyright: A Law of Users' Rights* (Athens: University of Georgia Press, 1991), 76–7. Alice Schreyer, "Copyright and Books in Nineteenth-Century America," in *Getting the Books Out: Papers of the Chicago Conference on the Book in 19th-Century America*, ed. Michael Hackenberg (Washington, DC: Center for the Book, Library of Congress, 1987), 127–8. Peter Jaszi, "Toward a Theory of Copyright: The Metamorphoses of 'Authorship'," *Duke Law Journal*, 1991, 477. Martha Woodmansee and Peter Jaszi, "The Law of Texts: Copyright in the Academy," *College English* 57, no. 7 (1995): 772. Paul Goldstein, *Copyright's Highway: From Gutenberg to the Celestial Jukebox* (New York: Hill & Wang, 1994), 57. Lawrence Venuti, *The Scandals of Translation: Towards an Ethics of Difference* (London: Routledge, 1998), 57–8. For Meredith McGill's, Michael Newbury's, and Robert Cazden's analyses of the case, see paragraphs that follow. Stephen Best's extensive analysis of the case appeared too late to be incorporated into mine. *The Fugitive's Properties: Law and the Poetics of Possession* (Chicago: University of Chicago Press, 2004), chap. 2.

Stowe, they also could not adapt the immaterial, incorporeal essence of her work by dressing it in new material forms. The case proved to be a legal dead-end – the court denied Stowe the expansive proprietary rights she sought, and no other author seems to have had the cause, desire, and means to pursue a similar claim before the U.S. Congress amended the copyright statute in 1870 to give copyright owners the right to control translations of their works.[3] Stowe's failure is nevertheless revealing and instructive. By filing suit, Stowe attempted to enlarge dramatically the legal domain of the author in American copyright law, giving authors more powerful proprietary rights and the possibility of greater profits at the expense of readers. I focus throughout on the central paradox of Stowe's situation laid bare by Grier's legal opinion – that Stowe, a woman who often presented herself and her authorship in self-effacing, maternal terms, is revealed in the context of *Stowe v. Thomas* to be an agent in the literary marketplace attempting to assert and police a property claim in her literary characters (figuratively, the children of her brain). If, as she is reported to have said, "God wrote the book,"[4] what was she doing in court defending *her* absolute right to sell Tom and Topsy?

Before analyzing the legal opinion and the factual circumstances surrounding the case, I first explore debates concerning copyright and authorship contemporary to the case. Later in the chapter, in addition to considering how the law regulated the circulation and consumption of Stowe's literary text, I link these concerns "outside" of Stowe's novel to her production of the "inside" of the novel, suggesting that we might understand Stowe's ruminations on the property status of slaves in *Uncle Tom's Cabin* as, in part, encoding anxieties about the relationship between an antebellum woman author and her literary property. Stowe's legal status as a married woman plays an important, although not central, role in this chapter. Rather, her situation sheds light on the ways that the question of an author's title in her *or* his work potentially converged with the discourses of slavery and abolition. Still, coverture ultimately haunts and constrains Stowe. Although

3 Thorvald Solberg, ed., *Copyright Enactments of the United States, 1783–1906* (Washington, DC: Government Printing Office, 1906), 46–7. As I make clear later, the case was also a dead-end in that it received very little publicity in the English-speaking American community and thus, to my knowledge, did not outrage other authors. Siva Vaidhyanathan thus misrepresents my reconstruction of the case and its significance on this point. *Copyrights and Copywrongs: The Rise of Intellectual Property and How It Threatens Creativity* (New York: New York University Press, 2001), 49–50.

4 I have found no reliable source attributing this precise statement to Stowe. However, she clearly did often describe her authorial labor as subsidiary to God's agency in the composition of the novel. See, for instance, her son's statement in his biography of her that she "repeatedly said . . . 'I could not control the story; it wrote itself;' or 'I the author of 'Uncle Tom's Cabin'? No, indeed. The Lord himself wrote it, and I was but the humblest of instruments in his hand. To Him alone should be given all the praise'." Charles Edward Stowe, *Life of Harriet Beecher Stowe Compiled from Her Letters and Journals* (Boston: Houghton Mifflin, 1889), 156. In any event, in the popular imagination, the statement captured a perceived truth about Stowe as an author.

she attempted to map out a role for herself as masterful proprietor of her literary children, in the end, both the copyright law and her status as a married woman made such desires unrealizable fantasy.

"Authorship . . . is not all the world of letters": Stowe and the situation of the American author under the copyright law in the 1850s

Catharine Sedgwick achieved popular success as an author during her years of highest productivity (the 1820s and 1830s as the author of books, and also during the 1840s as an author of short works for magazines). However, not until the 1850s did an American author's copyright become a truly valuable property. The United States of the 1850s represented the largest potential literary market ever up to that time, with more literate adults than in any other country. The large number of potential consumers, combined with advances in book manufacturing technologies (steam printing presses, stereotype plates, case-binding) and the advent of steam railroads to transport books quickly and inexpensively throughout the country, made the true national "bestseller" possible for the first time. Whereas at the peak of Sedgwick's career a "good" sale of a novel was several thousands, in the 1850s the standard for success became tens of thousands. The U.S. sales of *Uncle Tom's Cabin*, generally conceded to be at least 300,000 during the first year after its publication, far outstripped its closest competitors.[5]

Stowe received royalties from her publisher for the sale of those 300,000 volumes,[6] but did her copyright give her the right to benefit financially from other uses of her plot and characters? In the context of the international copyright debates, copyright advocates focused their energies on securing for American authors in England and English authors in America the right to print and sell copies of an entire work. Such wholesale reprinting required no further literary labor, but instead required the labor of those involved in manufacturing copies of the book (typesetters, press operators, binders). If an

5 See Susan Geary for the shift of scale in sales in the 1850s. "The Domestic Novel as a Commercial Commodity: Making a Best Seller in the 1850s," *Papers of the Bibliographical Society of America* 70 (1976): 365–93. Michael Winship has recently debunked widespread claims of the novel's continuing high sales in subsequent years. "'The Greatest Book of Its Kind': A Publishing History of 'Uncle Tom's Cabin'," *Proceedings of the American Antiquarian Society* 109, no. 2 (1999): 309–32. For my purposes, the truly phenomenal first year sales are the proper point of reference.

6 See Susan Geary, "Harriet Beecher Stowe, John P. Jewett, and Author-Publisher Relations in 1853," *Studies in the American Renaissance* (1977): 345–67, and Susan Coultrap-McQuin, *Doing Literary Business: American Women Writers in the Nineteenth Century* (Chapel Hill: University of North Carolina Press, 1990), chap. 4, for Stowe's after-the-fact dispute with her publisher over royalty rates. Whether or not one believes that Jewett really did give Stowe lower than the customary royalty rate, thus depriving her of her fare share of the profits, the aggregate amount of money Stowe received still put her in a class by herself.

author has legally secured the right to make and distribute copies of a work, another person who simply makes and distributes more or less exact copies clearly violates the copyright holder's right; but what about others who somehow reshape or alter the work (as was the situation in *Stowe v. Thomas*), translating it into another language, abridging it, or adapting it from one form to another, from novel into play, or poem into novel, before making and distributing copies? And what if someone uses the work, but neither makes nor distributes physical copies of the copyrighted work (that is, what if someone reads or performs it or an adaptation of it before an audience)?[7] Should the author derive the benefit from these uses? How wide should the domain of the author under copyright law be?[8]

The extraordinary popularity of *Uncle Tom's Cabin* put Harriet Beecher Stowe in a position to raise exactly these questions. After *Uncle Tom's Cabin* sold more copies in England than in America, and probably sold more copies in England than any *English* novel ever had, no one could respond to pleas for Anglo-American copyright by asking, as Sydney Smith famously did in the *Edinburgh Review* in 1820, "Who in the four quarters of the globe reads an American book?"[9] As Eaton Drone remarks in his highly regarded 1879 *Treatise on the Law of Property in Intellectual Productions* in his analysis of *Stowe v. Thomas*, the copyright in *Uncle Tom's Cabin* was "one of the most valuable American copyrights."[10] Although Michael Winship has recently proved that widely reported claims of sales of a million or more copies in the United States in the 1850s, '60s, and '70s, were wildly exaggerated,

7 Others profited greatly from performances of dramatic adaptations of *Uncle Tom's Cabin*, but the law gave Stowe no right to control such adaptations and performances, and she showed little interest in claiming or exploiting such rights. In 1856, Congress amended the law to give the owner of a copyright in a play the exclusive right to control public performances, but Congress did not give the owner of the copyright in a novel the exclusive right to adapt that novel into a play until 1870. Solberg, *Copyright Enactments*, 43, 46–7. Eva Hemmungs Wirtén, focusing on Victor Hugo's role in calling for international copyright, finds the issues of translation and the internationalization of literary property to be ineluctably linked, but the drive for Anglo-American copyright (in which translation was not an issue) and the internal American market for translation discussed in this chapter complicate such a claim. *No Trespassing: Authorship: Intellectual Property Rights, and the Boundaries of Globalization* (Toronto: University of Toronto Press, 2004), 38–41.

8 The author is the legally defined person in copyright law to whom property rights accrue, but the author may, and often does, assign those rights to another, commonly the publisher. Thus in practical terms, as Patterson and Lindberg note, expanding the rights of the "author" in copyright law often actually expands the domain of the publisher, not the author. *Nature of Copyright*, 77. However, Stowe did not assign her copyright in *Uncle Tom's Cabin*, and the question of copyright was, and is, still widely perceived as a question of "author's rights."

9 Review of Adam Seybert, *Statistical Annals of the United States of America*, *Edinburgh Review* 33 (Jan.–May 1820): 79–80. On the English popularity of *Uncle Tom's Cabin*, see Audrey Fisch, "Uncle Tom and Harriet Beecher Stowe in England," in *The Cambridge Companion to Harriet Beecher Stowe*, ed. Cindy Weinstein (New York: Cambridge University Press, 2004), 96–112.

10 Eaton Drone, *Treatise on the Law of Property in Intellectual Productions in Great Britain and the United States* (Boston: Little Brown, 1879), 455.

many authors, publishers, and readers around the world *believed* that more people in the world had read *Uncle Tom's Cabin* than any other fictional work previously published. In the words of the (admittedly partial) *National Era* at about the time Stowe filed suit against Thomas, *Uncle Tom* was "the book of the age – a work which has gone through more editions and translations, been more widely circulated, and has created more sensation and discussion than any work issued during the present century."[11] Thus in the popular understanding, Stowe had more to gain than any other author by exercising her copyright and more to lose when the copyright law did not offer her protection (Eaton Drone was particularly indignant that *Stowe v. Thomas* "made worthless" a particularly valuable copyright).[12] Stowe thus became an important figure through which the country debated the perceived successes and failures of the copyright law in serving the interests of American authors, readers, and publishers. Her spectacular success explains, in part, why she became the plaintiff in one of the very few nineteenth-century American copyright cases concerning a work of fiction – Stowe had a much more valuable interest to protect than most of her author peers.

But what exactly was the copyright law supposed to do for American authors like Stowe? Did authors have an inherent natural right that the law recognized? Or was the law a government grant of privilege designed to spur production for the benefit of readers? Did authors create something new and valuable that had never existed before? Or did they merely collect odd bits and pieces of preexisting material? In 1853, when Stowe filed suit, the American press continued to frequently and hotly debate these questions as they had earlier in the 1830s and '40s. In the late 1840s, yet another attempt to pass legislation reforming the copyright law to grant authors greater proprietary rights through reciprocal copyright with other nations (particularly England) failed. In the early 1850s, copyright advocates briefly shifted their efforts to negotiating such reciprocal relations by treaty.[13] Public debates over the expansion of authors' proprietary rights spurred by these attempts at reform are thus a crucial context for understanding the significance of Stowe's claim in *Stowe v. Thomas*.

In 1843, writing anonymously as the president of the American Copyright Club, William Cullen Bryant decried the failure of the American law to accord literary property (in the form of foreign-authored works) the same

11 "Uncle Tom Abroad," *National Era*, 24 Mar. 1853, 46. In a similar vein later in the century, see Frances Willard, "Harriet Beecher Stowe at Home," *Chautauquan*, Feb. 1888, 287.

12 Drone, *Treatise*, 455. In fact, Drone comments at length on the absurdity of the decision (454–5), even though its holding as to translation had been superseded by statute, and he frames the entire treatise with an extended protest against the position taken by Grier that copyright protects only the specific material manifestation of an author's work in print (p. 6).

13 James J. Barnes describes the efforts to bring about a treaty, including attempted bribery of Congressmen, in detail. *Authors, Publishers and Politicians: The Quest for an Anglo-American Copyright Agreement, 1815–1854* (Columbus: Ohio State University Press, 1974), chap. 9–12.

protection as it did other forms of property: "Word and thought – the very elements of a diviner life – made sacred, it remains for this country to say that the issues of the head shall have an acknowledgment when they come to us in the shape of books, at least equal to the fabrics created by the hand."[14] Although Stowe's thoughts about some of the specific copyright issues raised by the *Stowe v. Thomas* case have not survived,[15] she did publicly take a stand on the international copyright issue. Like Bryant, she asked why the law did not accord her literary property the same protection as it did more material forms of property. After receiving a letter from an English publisher offering to pay her a royalty for every copy sold of his edition of *Uncle Tom's Cabin* in return for her approval of designating his edition the "author's edition," Stowe forwarded the publisher's letter to Horace Greeley of the *New York Tribune* with her own letter, asking, "Might a man *honorably and justly* seize on another's estate, because some legal imperfection in the title allowed him to do so? and is it any better to seize on the avails of his talents?"[16] Although Bryant, Stowe, and others I discuss in Chapter 2 argued for stronger protection of literary property rights on the basis of analogies to material property, a recognition that literary property is both like *and* unlike material property qualified and complicated such procopyright claims. Copyright advocates argued that the author's property should receive the same legal recognition *as* property as did a piece of fabric or a landed estate, but they also argued that the author's property was immaterial, and thus both a more elusive and a "higher" form of property. In Bryant's words, the "issues of the head" are "elements of a diviner life."

Scholars studying the history of European copyright law in England and Germany have linked the emergence of the author as proprietor in the law with the rise of Romanticism and its claims for the special status of the author as original genius.[17] Their analyses of this dynamic illuminate the tension also confronted by American authors, including Stowe, as they sought to define the nature of literary property and their legal status as creators and proprietors. As Martha Woodmansee argues in her essay "The Genius and the Copyright," in eighteenth-century Germany, authors seeking to ground

14 William Cullen Bryant, Francis L. Hawks, and Cornelius Mathews, *An Address to the People of the United States in Behalf of the American Copyright Club* (New York: American Copyright Club, 1843), 6–7. On disputes over the authorship of this pamphlet, see chap. 2, note 28.

15 E. Bruce Kirkham (e-mail to the author), who has collected copies of all known Stowe correspondence and who is preparing an edition of Stowe's letters, has reported to me that his database of letters includes no correspondence concerning the suit.

16 "Copyright and Natural Right – Letter from Harriet Beecher Stowe," *New York Daily Tribune*, 16 Sep. 1852, 4.

17 France's copyright law has a very different genealogy, which I will not treat here. See Carla Hesse, "Enlightenment Epistemology and the Laws of Authorship in Revolutionary France, 1777–1793," *Representations* 30 (Spring 1990): 109–37; and Molly Nesbit, "What Was an Author?" in *Authorship: From Plato to the Postmodern, a Reader*, ed, Sean Burke, 247–62 (Edinburgh: Edinburgh University Press, 1995).

their claims of ownership in their works found it "necessary to show that this work transcends its physical foundation . . . to show that [the work] is an emanation of [the author's] intellect – an intentional as opposed to a merely physical object." In short, they argued that a "writer" is an "author," an originator, founder, or creator, a singular genius rather than a mere craftsman who is only one of many contributing his labors to the manufacture of a book.[18] In addition to supplanting the notion of the author as one of many craftsmen, the Romantics sought to supplant the other available neoclassical model of authorship, that of the author as "inspired – by some muse, or even by God." As Woodmansee argues, rather than seeing themselves as vehicles or instruments of some "higher, external agency," they "internalized the source of that inspiration. That is, inspiration came to be regarded as emanating not from outside or above, but from within the writer himself."[19]

Mark Rose traces a different trajectory in England, where copyright emerged earlier than in Germany as a regulatory scheme for the protection of printer–publishers' interests (the Stationer's Company in seventeenth–century England registered the exclusive rights of printers – not authors – in "copies," that is, authors' manuscripts). According to Rose, after the publisher–sponsored passage of the first English copyright statute in 1710 (the Statute of Anne), a new class of professional authors, such as Alexander Pope, began to use the copyright law for their own benefit. As a result, a theory of literary property as immaterial developed alongside a notion of the work as material property like any other property. As Rose notes, the analogy between literary property and a landed estate (precisely the analogy Stowe deployed in her demand for international copyright) "provided a comforting sense of weight and tangibility" to literary property. However, the discourse of literary property simultaneously "was moving away from its old foundation in the materiality in the manuscript as object."[20] In the case of *Pope v. Curll* (concerning the unauthorized publication of Alexander Pope's manuscript letters), "the notion of the essentially immaterial nature of the object of copyright was born."[21] Through the process of litigation and further legislation, inquiries concerning the nature of literary property

18 Martha Woodmansee, "The Genius and the Copyright: Economic and Legal Conditions of the Emergence of the 'Author'," *Eighteenth-Century Studies* 17, no. 4 (1984): 443, 429.

19 Ibid. 429. For the cross-cultural and ancient origins of the supplanted idea that God, rather than individuals, created and thus owned all ideas and words, see Carla Hesse, "The Rise of Intellectual Property, 700 B.C.–A.D. 2000: An Idea in the Balance," *Daedalus: Journal of the American Academy of Arts and Sciences* 131 no. 2 (2002): 26–45.

20 Mark Rose, *Authors and Owners: The Invention of Copyright* (Cambridge: Harvard University Press, 1993), 58. More recently, Joseph Loewenstein has traced the Renaissance prehistory of the possessive authorship without renaturalizing authors' rights in copyright as based in nature. *The Author's Due: Printing and the Prehistory of Copyright* (Chicago: University of Chicago Press, 2002). *Ben Jonson and Possessive Authorship* (Cambridge: Cambridge University Press, 2002).

21 Rose, *Authors*, 60.

came to center "on the same pair of terms, the author and the work, a person and a thing. The complex social process of literary production – relations between writers and patrons, writers and booksellers, booksellers and readers – became peripheral," thus "[a]bstracting the author and the work from the social fabric."[22] The English Romantics claimed a similar model of authorship, and William Wordsworth called upon such arguments in his petitions to the British Parliament in the early nineteenth century asking Parliament to extend the term of copyright in England.[23]

However, as Meredith McGill has persuasively argued in her examination of America's first Supreme Court copyright decision, *Wheaton v. Peters* (an 1834 case concerning an abridged edition of the official compilation of U.S. Supreme Court decisions), the American law did not "inherit" unaltered the English law's "concern with individual rights in texts." Instead, the American law saw private property claims to printed texts as an encroachment on the *public's* right of unrestricted access to all printed texts: "*Wheaton v. Peters* established going-into-print as the moment when individual rights give way to the demands of the social and defines the private ownership of a printed text as the temporary alienation of public property. It is with the circumscription of individual rights and not with their extension that nineteenth-century American copyright law is primarily concerned."[24] As the many petitions to Congress, Congressional reports, and periodical articles and editorials concerning the subject of international copyright amply demonstrate, authors and their interests were not central to American copyright law in nineteenth-century America, and attempts to reshape the American law to make authors' proprietary rights central were met with well-organized resistance. Throughout most of the century, the object of the

22 Ibid., 88. Rose's analysis stops short of a full consideration of English Romanticism and its convergence with the copyright law, although he sees Romanticism as providing "codified answers" to questions about the nature of property (p. 132). For the convergence of "authorship" in the law with the ideology of Romanticism and the consequences for American copyright jurisprudence in the nineteenth and twentieth centuries, see Peter Jaszi, "The Author Effect" (esp. 466–71); and Peter Jaszi and Martha Woodmansee, "The Ethical Reaches of Authorship," *South Atlantic Quarterly* 95, no. 4 (1996): 947–77. Taking a slightly different route, Catherine Gallagher also emphasizes the birth of originality and immateriality as characteristics of literary property in the eighteenth century, but she characterizes it as a result of the detachment of the author from the mass circulation of printed books as objects. *Nobody's Story: The Vanishing Acts of Women Writers in the Marketplace, 1670–1820* (Berkeley: University of California Press, 1994), 63.

23 Martha Woodmansee and Peter Jaszi, eds., *The Construction of Authorship: Textual Appropriation in Law and Literature* (Durham: Duke University Press, 1994), 4–5. Martha Woodmansee, "The Cultural Work of Copyright: Legislating Authorship in Britain 1837–1842," in *Law in the Domains of Culture*, ed. Austin Sarat and Thomas R. Kearns (Ann Arbor: University of Michigan Press, 2000), 65–96. Susan Eilenberg also documents Wordsworth's lobbying but finds copyright to be a "materialization" rather than an immaterial abstraction. "'Mortal Pages': Wordsworth and the Reform of Copyright," *English Literary History* 56 (1989): 351–74.

24 Meredith L. McGill, *American Literature and the Culture of Reprinting*, 1834–1853 (Philadelphia: University of Pennsylvania Press, 2003), 45–6.

law remained protection of the interests of American manufacturers who reprinted English books (usually without permission and without paying royalties) and the preservation of resulting low book prices, so that American readers could purchase and consume those American-manufactured (although not American-authored) books. As late as 1873, the U.S. Senate easily dismissed the importance of authors in the business of making books. In a report recommending against the passage of an international copyright bill, the Joint Committee on the Library reasons,

> Authorship, standing by itself, although the essential element, still, it is not all the world of letters, and cannot in any measure, having at heart the interests of literature, be considered as standing independent by itself. If it be conceded to be the soul of science, it is essential that its productions should be embodied in books, and these involve the varied skill, industries, and cunning workmanship of many hands, and at last, and not the least important agency, the enterprise, capital, and address of the publisher through whom these books are to be introduced to the reading public.[25]

In Woodmansee's and Rose's narratives of the development of copyright in Europe, the proprietary author of copyright supplanted just such definitions of the book as a material object created by many, rather than an intentional object dependent for its existence solely on the author.[26] However, in nineteenth-century America, the author had not ascended to the peak of Romantic agency, presiding over and rationalizing the functions of all other actors in the production, circulation, and consumption of literary works. Stowe and other American authors trying to negotiate their own symbolic and legal authority thus found themselves contending with conflicting and contradictory discourses of authorship: their arguments in favor of the expansion of copyright demonstrate that they knew the limits of their position under the American law, but they also gestured toward the more expansive symbolic powers and the legal proprietary rights for authors potentially underwritten by the Romantic ideology of authorship.

Arguments over which mode of authorship should prevail in the American law, the author as subsidiary and unimportant or the author as transcendent and all-encompassing, most often arose in the international copyright debates. However, at least one copyright opponent, Henry Carey, understood Stowe's claim in her suit against F. W. Thomas to raise exactly these issues. Carey was the heir to a prominent Philadelphia publishing house, but he retired from the everyday business of running the firm to become a

25 Senate Join Committee on the Library, *Report*, 42nd Cong., 3rd sess., 7 Feb. 1873, S. Rpt. 409, 4.

26 Indeed, the Senate report description of how books are made sounds very much like a 1753 German dictionary definition of "book" quoted by Woodmansee as an example of the understanding the Romantics sought to supersede. "The Genius and the Copyright," 425.

political economist. In 1847, he became a staunch protectionist and advocate of the tariff. In the 1850s, he lent his voice and his protectionist economic theories to an influential group of men involved in the Philadelphia book trades who opposed international copyright.[27] In 1853, just before Grier issued his decision in *Stowe v. Thomas*, Carey published *Letters on International Copyright*, which became a touchstone of the anticopyright position until the 1880s, when copyright advocates and opponents entered into a collaboration that enabled the passage of the 1891 International Copyright Act. In *Letters*, Carey specifically takes note of the *Stowe v. Thomas* case without directly naming Stowe: "In this country, the only attempt that has yet been made to restrict the right of translation is in a suit now before the courts, for compensation for the privilege of converting into German a work that has yielded the largest compensation that the world has yet known for the same quantity of literary labor."[28] In consonance with his overall argument, Carey sees the "right" of translation as belonging to the public rather than to Stowe, and he thus sees Stowe's suit as an attempt to "restrict" that right. He implies that Stowe had already been more than adequately compensated for her labor and that she should not be able to prevent others from producing their own translations, in effect asking for *more* compensation even though she would not labor for that additional compensation. In Carey's view, the only justification for the grant of copyright to authors is to give incentive for authorial production that will benefit the public. An author who labors little, produces a bad product, or whose work does not truly benefit the public should thus not be granted a copyright at all.

In fact, in Carey's view, almost all fiction writing falls into this category of labor not entitled to compensation. Referring to the works of Walter Scott, Washington Irving, and Charles Dickens, Carey claims that they all made "no contribution to knowledge" (p. 24), that a literary author merely "collect[s] a great number of facts that he has dressed up in different forms" (p. 25). Those facts and ideas, says Carey, belong in the first instance to the

27 For a recent treatment of Carey's economic theories (but not his application of those theories to copyright), see Andrew Dawson, "Reassessing Henry Carey (1793–1879): The Problem of Writing Political Economy in Nineteenth-Century America," *Journal of American Studies* 34, no. 3 (2000): 465–85. See also A. D. H. Kaplan, *Henry Charles Carey: A Study in Economic Thought* (Baltimore: Johns Hopkins University Press, 1931), and George Winston Smith, *Henry C. Carey and American Sectional Conflict* (Albuquerque: University of New Mexico Press, 1951). Smith describes Carey's treatise *Slave Trade, Domestic and Foreign: Why It Exists, and How It May Be Extinguished* (Philadelphia: A. Hart, 1853) as "in a sense a response to Uncle Tom's Cabin," "the greatest of all propaganda novels against slavery" (p. 35).

28 *Henry C. Carey, Letters on International Copyright*, 2nd ed. (New York: Hurd & Houghton, 1868), 37 (hereinafter cited in the text). Page references are from this 1868 edition, which includes a lengthy preface that I will take note of later. However, the main text of the 1853 edition remains intact in the 1868 edition.

public, and an author who writes a book is like a man who creates a bouquet from flowers in someone else's garden:

> The owner of the garden would naturally say to him: "The flowers are mine, but the arrangement is yours. You cannot keep the bouquet, but you may smell it, or show it for your own profit, for an hour or two, but then it must come to me. If you prefer it, I am willing to pay you for your services, giving you a fair compensation for your time and taste." This is exactly what society says to Mr. Dickens, who makes such beautiful literary bouquets. . . . Nevertheless, the author objects to this, insisting that he is the owner of the bouquet itself, although he has paid no wages to the man who raised the flowers. (p. 25)

Only great scientific and philosophical men who *create* new ideas and new knowledge, argues Carey, actually grow new flowers, and copyright does not protect those ideas.

Carey's main target is a proposed copyright treaty with England, a method of effecting copyright reform that he finds particularly objectionable because it attempts to bypass the people's representatives in Congress in favor of the presidential power of treaty-making. However, he goes much further than attacking treaty-making as undemocratic – he implies that *all* copyright is an illegitimate imposition on the rights of the reading public. In light of this imbalance between the rights of authors and readers caused by copyright, Carey predicts a time in the future when the public will no longer tolerate a monopoly given to bouquet gatherers who perform only the slightest labor in return for that monopoly. Scornfully addressing authors, Carey asks, "Can it be supposed that when, but a few years hence, our population shall have attained a height of fifty millions, with a demand for books probably ten times greater than at present, the community will be willing to continue to you a monopoly, during forty-two years, of the right of presenting a body that is common property, as compensation for putting it in a new suit of clothing?" (p. 32). According to Carey, the forty-two-year monopoly on the right to print and sell copies of a work that copyright granted an author in 1853 (a twenty-eight-year first term, and the right to renew the copyright for a fourteen-year second term) was too much compensation. The public owed a fiction writer little or no compensation for these trivial (and implicitly feminized) activities of arranging thoughts into bouquets or dressing those thoughts in "clothing" of language. In examining the specifics of the literary field in 1853, Carey pointedly cites Stowe as an example of the principle that "the whole tendency of the existing system is to give the largest reward to those whose labors are the lightest" (p. 36). Rather than forty-two years of monopoly, says Carey, Stowe and writers like her deserved only a year's worth of copyright for their labors.

"A change of linguistic dress": *Stowe v. Thomas* and the law of copyright infringement

Stowe's attempt to enforce her copyright in her lawsuit against F. W. Thomas, the Philadelphia publisher of the German American newspaper *Die Freie Presse*, is remarkable in a number of ways.[29] Stowe's often domestic, self-effacing authorial persona, particularly her widely publicized self-description of the composition of *Uncle Tom's Cabin*, makes her an unlikely plaintiff. Stowe claimed both that "God wrote" *Uncle Tom's Cabin* and that she wrote the novel in response to a vision, which came to her while she was receiving communion, of Tom's flogging death at the hands of Simon Legree.[30] Both of these origin stories align her with a pre-Romantic mode of authorship through external inspiration, deemphasizing her role as originator and instead emphasizing the mimetic nature of the novel, both in the sense that the novel is meant to represent reality accurately and in the sense that she was merely a copyist, transcribing a vision that

29 Forrest Wilson, the only Stowe biographer to make more than passing note of the *Stowe v. Thomas* decision, garbles the facts in a number of ways. *Crusader in Crinoline: The Life of Harriet Beecher Stowe* (Philadelphia: Lippincott, 1941), 331. Stowe filed suit on 11 Mar. 1853, two-and-a-half months after Thomas began serial publication on 1 Jan. 1853, and obtained a preliminary injunction against Thomas on 22 Mar. 1853, several days after Thomas completed newspaper and pamphlet part serial publication but apparently before publication of his book edition. Adolf Strodtmann's translator's afterward to the Thomas edition is dated 16 Mar. 1853 and does not mention Stowe's suit – in fact, Strodtmann writes of his plan's to translate Stowe's "next work." *Onkel Tom's Hütte, Oder: Leben Unter Den Verstossnen* (Philadelphia: F. W. Thomas, 1853). The case was heard on 27–8 Oct. 1853, when the court was in session, and Grier rendered his decision on 24 Dec. 1853. Thomas subsequently issued a complete translation in book form, which went through several editions. Robert E. Cazden, *A Social History of the German Book Trade in America to the Civil War* (Columbia, SC: Camden House, 1984), 370n. Under an act passed by Congress in 1819 and still in effect in 1853, the federal circuit courts, which were normally appellate courts, had original jurisdiction over copyright cases. Solberg, *Copyright Enactments*, 36. For the case chronology and facts, see the manuscript case file, *Die Freie Presse*, and reports in the *Cummings' Evening Telegraphic Bulletin*, which covered most fully the federal courts sitting in Philadelphia.

30 For Stowe's accounts of the composition of the novel, see E. Bruce Kirkham, *Building Uncle Tom's Cabin* (Knoxville: University of Tennessee Press, 1977), chap. 4. The most complete account of the communion table vision origin story appears in her preface to the 1879 edition of the novel, which makes Stowe a close analogue to the unwilling Mary of the Annunciation, impregnated by an all-powerful God at the moment of inspiration, and which figures her subsequent creative labor as the involuntary labor of childbirth. *Uncle Tom's Cabin* (Boston: Houghton, Osgood & Co., 1879). See also her comments reported by J. C. Derby that "[c]reating a story is like bearing a child, and it leaves me in as weak and helpless a state as when my baby was born." *Fifty Years among Authors, Books and Publishers* (New York: G. W. Carleton & Co., 1884), 521. For domestic scenes of production, see, e.g., James Parton, *Daughters of Genius: A Series of Sketches of Authors, Artists, Reformers, and Heroines, Queens, Princesses, and Women of Society, Women Eccentric and Peculiar* (Philadelphia: Hubbard Brothers, 1888), 76–7; "[When Mrs. Stowe Was Composing Uncle Tom's Cabin]," *The Woman's Journal*, 15 Jan. 1870, 16; and E. P. Parker, "Harriet Beecher Stowe," in *Eminent Women of the Age*, ed. James Parton (Hartford: S. M. Betts & Co., 1868), 312.

did not originate within her. Her accounts of the material labors of writing also consistently represent her writing as a form of domestic production (done in the kitchen in stolen moments between other domestic tasks), with her children as her first audience. In these domestic and maternal scenes, Stowe's authorial labors resemble Catharine Sedgwick's self-representation of her authorial labors as cooking or weaving done to meet the needs of readers. In these self-representations, Stowe is not the Romantic author and agent creating and originating the novel from within herself. Instead, in another sense of the word *agent*, Stowe describes herself as merely an agent of some force beyond her control rather than as a subject acting independently. As she wrote to the Earl of Shaftesbury while she was compiling the *Key to Uncle Tom's Cabin*, "If they call the fiction dreadful, what will they say of the fact, where I cannot deny, suppress, or color? But it is God's will that it must be told, and I am the unwilling agent."[31]

Copyright law, however, grants property rights as a reward for creative labor, and if she was a pre-Romantic author who was "inspired" rather than a Romantic author who was herself a godlike creator, then what happened to her legal authority? In the 1907 edition of *Christian Science*, Mark Twain ridiculed Mary Baker Eddy for her claim that God wrote *her* book *Science and Health*, the scripture of the Christian Science movement. Eddy reported in her autobiography that she had sued to protect the copyright in the book, and in his critique, Twain wonders how, if she was "merely an amanuensis, and furnished neither the language of *Science and Health* nor the ideas," she could claim copyright in the book. Concludes Twain, "The Deity was the Author of the whole book, and Mrs. Eddy merely His telephone and stenographer."[32]

Also remarkable is the fact that Stowe had a legally valid copyright in *Uncle Tom's Cabin* to even attempt to enforce through litigation. Stowe often described herself as a literary ingenue before the book publication of *Uncle Tom*. In a letter to Eliza Follen (an American writer of children's verse and a member of prominent Boston abolitionist family), written at the height of her popularity in both America and England, Stowe describes her naïveté when arranging for the book publication of *Uncle Tom*: "Having been poor all my life and expecting to be poor the rest of it, the idea of making money by a book which I wrote just because I could not help it never occurred to me. It was therefore an agreeable surprise to receive ten thousand dollars as the first-fruits of three months' sale." Even as Stowe emphasizes her helplessness and passivity in this letter, she immediately contradicts herself and reveals her shrewd knowledge of the marketplace and copyright. In the

31 Charles Stowe, *Life of Harriet Beecher Stowe*, 174.

32 Mark Twain, *Christian Science* (New York: Harper, 1907), 143–4. Thanks to Siva Vaidhyanathan for drawing my attention to this reference.

next sentences in her letter to Follen, she notes that one of the English publishers who pirated her work intended to offer her an interest on the sales of his British edition (the same publisher whose action prompted her to write to Horace Greeley about international copyright): "I am very glad of it, both on account of the value of what they offer, and the value of the example they set in this matter, wherein I think justice has been too little regarded."[33]

In direct contradiction to her representations of herself as a literary ingenue, Stowe's actions immediately prior to publication reveal her sophisticated and aggressive management of her career and her protection of her own interests. While claiming not to plan for the novel's success (or, indeed, even for separate publication of the novel after its serialization in the *National Era*), she took the prescient and somewhat unusual step of registering the copyright in the novel in her own name before serialization began.[34] Without this piece of legal forethought and planning, Stowe would not have been in a position to file suit because registration of a copyright before publication was an essential precondition to legal recognition of her literary property rights. In the international copyright debates, copyright advocates often argued for the materiality of the literary work because basic legal recognition of literary property *as* property when it crossed national boundaries was the primary issue. Even in many nineteenth-century copyright cases before *Stowe v. Thomas* (including *Wheaton v. Peters*), however, the legal disposition of competing claims often rested on an initial determination of whether the plaintiff possessed a property that the law was bound to protect at all (in *Wheaton v. Peters*, the court held that the plaintiff had failed to fulfill all of the requirements for registration, and thus the question of whether the defendant's abridgment was an infringement was irrelevant).[35] Because Stowe had registered her copyright and thus possessed a property that the law was obliged to protect, the court hearing *Stowe v. Thomas* had to define the nature of that property and rule on whether Thomas's translation infringed her property rights under statutory copyright.

33 Harriet Beecher Stowe to Eliza Follen, 16 Feb. [1853], in Annie Fields, ed., *Life and Letters of Harriet Beecher Stowe* (Boston: Houghton Mifflin, 1897), 176.

34 She registered the copyright in the District of Maine federal court on 12 May 1851, depositing a copy of the entire novel on 1 Apr. 1852. See Chapter 4 for a discussion of the periodical copyright situation. See also Kirkham's speculative reconstruction of Stowe's motivations for registering the copyright. *Building of Uncle Tom's Cabin*, 70.

35 See McGill, *American Literature*, 69, for the incredibly technical and seemingly ludicrous logic of this determination. Michael Newbury describes the court's rejection of Stowe's claim as being of a piece with the failure of efforts on behalf of international copyright: "Once again . . . the rights of literary ownership and the sense of the text as an ownable commodity were drastically circumscribed when they might equally well have been strengthened by the courts." *Figuring Authorship in Antebellum America* (Stanford: Stanford University Press, 1997), 183. However, as I make clear, the court did recognize Stowe's text as a material "ownable commodity" like other ownable commodities. If the court had recognized its immaterial nature, Stowe's claim would have succeeded.

Even though Stowe's copyright registration put her in a position to file suit, the question of copyright and translation was by no means a settled point of law in 1853. Stowe thus could not have assumed that the outcome of her suit was a foregone conclusion. In the only extensive commentary on the case in the English-language press, an anonymous article in the weekly *New-York Tribune* in April 1853 (shortly after Stowe filed suit) both supports Stowe's claim on principle and acknowledges that her case under the American statute was weak: "As for the absolute moral right, we see nothing in the nature of things to limit the ownership of the author. It is his [*sic*] work and ought to be the essential *right* of the case, – which is legitimately subject only to such limitations and conditions as Society, acting for the general welfare, may see fit to establish."[36] Nevertheless, the reporter concedes, "[I]t is far from certain that our legislation is such as Mrs. Stowe's complaint against Mr. Thomas would seem to suppose . . . [T]he case is not directly foreseen or provided for by the statute; and unless Mrs. Stowe's position can be established inferentially from its spirit, or from the construction of some hitherto unnoticed phrase in its language, the Court will have to decide against her." Foreseeing this outcome, the author calls for a revision of the copyright statute so that it would conform to moral principle.[37]

As the *Tribune* had predicted, Justice Robert Grier construed the statute narrowly and followed the most conservative school of thought in his ruling. Quoting the famous English copyright case *Millar v. Taylor*,[38] Grier asserts that the whole right of the author in his work "rests upon the foundation of the property in the copy." Elaborating on the meaning of "copy," Grier states, "A 'copy' of a book must, therefore, be a transcript of the language in which the conceptions of the author are clothed; of something printed and embodied in a tangible shape. The same conceptions clothed in another language cannot constitute the same composition; nor can it be called a transcript or 'copy' of the same 'book'" (p. 207). That is, copyright restricted the author's right in a work to the words on the page; copyright does not protect elements of plot and characterization, which another might appropriate and then describe in words other than those the author chose. To expand on Grier's use of this common copyright metaphor of language as "clothing" ideas (a metaphor Carey also uses in his critique of copyright), the

36 "'Uncle Tom' at Law," *New-York Weekly Tribune*, 16 Apr. 1853, 3. Like Grier in his opinion, this reporter uses the masculine pronoun to refer to "the author" in discussions of general legal principles, using "she" only when the referent is specifically Stowe.

37 More briefly, the *National Anti-Slavery Standard* reported on the filing of the suit almost simultaneously with the *Tribune*, framing the report with an ironic comment about a Northern minister's threat to sue Stowe for libel because of her naming him as a slavery apologist in the first edition of the novel. "Uncle Tom in the Courts of Law," *National Anti-Slavery Standard*, 14 Apr. 1853, 187.

38 For accounts of the circumstances of this case, see Mark Rose, *Authors and Owners*, 78–82; Patterson, *Copyright in Historical Perspective*, 168–72; and Kaplan, *An Unhurried View of Copyright*, 12–15.

nature of the work protected by copyright is merely material, like clothing; literature is a linguistic article of manufacture, and the author has the right to control exact reproduction of those linguistic clothes in the form of words printed on the page. Although there is a body under this clothing, which the author may have created or conceived, the body becomes common property once the author displays it to the public dressed in language. If another person dresses this body in new linguistic clothes, he becomes an "author" in his own right.

Grier thus directly contravenes the arguments advanced by Stowe's lawyers, Samuel H. and Samuel C. Perkins, a father-son team of Philadelphia lawyers,[39] and the opinions of the author of America's first copyright treatise, lawyer George Ticknor Curtis. In their arguments on her behalf, Stowe's attorneys claim, "An author is the 'creator,' the 'efficient cause of a thing.'[40] In respect to a book, he is the creator of the ideas – the thought – the plan – the arrangement – the figures – the illustrations – the argument – the style of expression. The exclusive right to sell these is what is secured by copyright. The right is original, inherent; a right founded on nature, acknowledged, we think, at common law; a right which stands on better ground and is more deeply rooted than the right to any other property whatever. Now, a translation is an infringement of this right" [citations omitted] (p. 202). As authority, Stowe's lawyers cite Curtis's 1847 *A Treatise on the Law of Copyright*. Curtis, who was a published author of several legal and political treatises in addition to his copyright treatise, strongly advocates an expansion of authors' rights under copyright.[41] In particular, he expresses a strong opinion in favor of international copyright, and he takes on the then current state of the law with respect to abridgments, which he considers "contrary to principle."[42] Briefly, abridgements of books were considered

39 Samuel H. Perkins was admitted to the bar in July 1851 after studying law in his father Samuel C. Perkins's office. Samuel H. also earned an LLB from the University of Pennsylvania in 1852. Charles Robson, ed., *The Biographical Encyclopedia of Pennsylvania of the Nineteenth Century* (Philadelphia: Galaxy Publishing Company, 1874), 51. Forrest Wilson erroneously claims that Stowe's family lawyer and relation from Hartford T. C. Perkins handled the case. *Crusader in Crinoline*, 331. Unfortunately, no legal correspondence from 1853 survives in the papers Samuel H. Perkins deposited with the Historical Society of Pennsylvania, but the Philadelphia Perkinses were clearly the lawyers representing Stowe.

40 The Perkinses are quoting Noah Webster's *Dictionary*, which defines an author as "one who produces, creates, or brings into being; the beginner, former, or first mover of any thing; hence the efficient cause of a thing. It is appropriately applied to one who composes or writes a book." *An American Dictionary of the English Language* (Springfield: George & Charles Merriam, 1852), 87.

41 Grantland Rice seemingly confuses George Ticknor Curtis with his publisher cousin, George William Curtis, and characterizes his treatise as a "defense of utilitarian rights." *The Transformation of Authorship in America* (Chicago: University of Chicago Press, 1997), 86. Although Curtis does concede some of the tenets of the utilitarian position, overall, he argues for an expansion of the author's individual rights under copyright and for the fundamental immateriality of the author's work as a basis for the expansion of those rights.

42 George Ticknor Curtis, *A Treatise on the Law of Copyright* (Boston: Charles C. Little & James Brown, 1847), vii (hereinafter cited in the text).

to be new works "authored" by the abridger. The original author thus could not sue successfully for copyright infringement unless the abridgement was so inconsequential that it preserved most of the original work. Consonant with the Romantic view of the author as creating an intentional object and owning that object in its immaterial form, Curtis sees literary property not as material, but as "incorporeal": "When we consider the incorporeal nature of literary property, it will be apparent that no writer can make and publish an abridgment, without taking to himself profits of literary matter which belong to another" (pp. 275–6). He further sees the right to abridge a work to be part of the author's right "to avail himself of the profits to be reaped from all classes of readers, both those who would purchase his production in a cheap and condensed form, and those who would purchase it in its more extended and costly shape" (p. 278). That is, the author has property rights in his incorporeal creation, and these rights include the right to give that incorporeal, immaterial creation different material shapes by changing its linguistic dress.

Curtis extends the same logic of the author's Romantic agency that he uses in his critique of the law on abridgments to his critique of the law on translation. He notes that there had been no American cases on translation and that the English decisions all involved translations of works that were in the public domain. The original works were in the public domain either because they were very old (i.e., works of classical antiquity in Greek or Latin) or because they were new works by non-English authors not entitled to copyright protection in England.[43] According to Curtis, these cases "merely tend to show that the act of translation, by giving a new dress to the work, incorporates with it the pains and labor and learning of the translator" (p. 291), thereby giving the translator a copyright in the translation. In 1847 no cases presenting facts analogous to the *Stowe v. Thomas* case had yet arisen, but Curtis opines as to what he believes should be the reasoning used to decide such a case: "The new language in which [the author's] composition is clothed by translation affords only a different medium of communicating that in which he has an exclusive property; and to attribute to such a new medium the effect of entire originality, is to declare that a change of dress alone annihilates the most important subject of his right of property. It reduces his right to the narrow limits of an exclusive privilege of publishing in that idiom alone in which he first publishes" (p. 293). The

43 In arguments of counsel, both sides take note of one British case that falls outside of these categories, *Burnett v. Chetwood*, 2 Mer. 441. Burnett, an Englishman, wrote a treatise in Latin and sued Chetwood for copyright infringement for publishing a translation of his modern Latin into English. However, although Burnett sued under the copyright law, Lord Chancellor Parker enjoined publication in English because the translation made the heretical ideas obscured by the Latin language more broadly accessible. Parker's ruling follows the same judicial logic that denied copyright protection to obscene works. Venuti also discusses this case in juxtaposition with *Stowe v. Thomas*, but misunderstands and misrepresents both the law and facts of both cases. *Scandals of Translation*, 57.

only issue decided in *Stowe v. Thomas* was whether the translation Thomas published infringed Stowe's copyright. That is, Thomas did not deny that he had published a translation, nor did he assert that Stowe did not have a valid copyright in *Uncle Tom's Cabin*. In fact, Thomas's attorneys cheerfully concede in their argument that Thomas and his translator, Adolf Strodtmann, appropriated Stowe's entire work: "We have confessedly taken not a part, but the whole. We concede and we boast that we have taken every syllable, comma and i-dot of the original" (p. 205). The question before the court, they claim, "cannot be how much we have taken, for we have taken all; nor how much we have added, for we have added nothing: but only how have we taken, and what have we done with it?" (p. 205).

What they had done with it was translate it into German, and that translation, so they argued, did not infringe Stowe's right to multiply her copy. Judge Grier accepted this view. Although he conceded (as Henry Carey did not) that Stowe did create the novel's "conceptions and inventions," he found that her conceptions and inventions had no status as property once she published her book. Because they had no status as property, she could not prevent others from selling them as long as those others contributed their own labor in dressing her immaterial conceptions in new, concrete linguistic dress. Tom and Topsy were "the creation of the genius and the imagination of the author" – out of her imagination, in a godlike act of creation, she had brought new souls into the world – but she had property rights only in the words ("the language in which the conceptions of the author are clothed") that she used to describe those "souls." Clearly, if Grier had accepted Stowe's arguments and followed Curtis's lead, giving her property rights in the incorporeal "souls" of her novel, Stowe would have prevailed and Thomas would have been permanently enjoined from publishing the German translation and forced to surrender his profits to Stowe.

Stowe was not concerned, however, with stopping publication of the Thomas translation merely to protect an abstract or symbolic right, or even to collect the (probably small) profits Thomas had accrued from serial publication before the preliminary injunction. Instead, she sought to protect the market for her *own* translation. In 1852, Stowe, uniquely positioned to exploit such an opportunity because of Calvin Stowe's strong German language skills and connections to German academic culture, commissioned her own *authorized* German translation of *Uncle Tom's Cabin*, for which she registered a copyright in her own name.[44] By early 1853, her publisher, John P. Jewett, was advertising that the translation would be available in February

44 Joan D. Hedrick documents Calvin Stowe's book-buying trips to Germany on behalf of academic libraries. *Harriet Beecher Stowe: A Life* (New York: Oxford University Press, 1994), 99–101. As documented by Stowe's affidavit filed in *Stowe v. Thomas*, Calvin Stowe even assisted von Hutten with the translation. Affidavit of Harriet Beecher Stowe (3 Mar. 1853), 5, Third Circuit Court of Appeals records, Mid-Atlantic Branch of the National Archives, Philadelphia, PA. (Her claims in this affidavit are the basis for the German-language press's accusations of "false swearing"). The affidavit

of 1853. The first installment of Strodtmann's translation appeared in *Die Freie Presse* on January 1, 1853. As Stowe's affidavit filed with the complaint in *Stowe v. Thomas* explains, she was "in hopes and reasonably expected to receive large profits from the sale" of the authorized translation and stood to be "greatly injured" in respect of what she saw as her "sole right" to exploit the market for translations for sale in America.[45] In addition to the German translation, Stowe had already authorized a Welsh translation, which was published by Robert Everett for the "100,000 Welsh emigrants in this country."[46] To return to George Ticknor Curtis's analysis of copyright in translations, although the author's property may be incorporeal, legal title to this incorporeal property grants power in the marketplace; the person who holds title to this incorporeal property has the sole right to multiply material "copies," which can be sold on the market as commodities. As her attorneys noted at the beginning of their arguments, the question of translation had been made the subject of legislation in continental Europe, but the question was actually much more pressing in America, where the copyright statute made no special provisions: "The question is more important in America than elsewhere, owing to the originally mixed character of our people, and to the constant emigration of foreigners to our country, most of whom become our citizens long before they can read our language. This influx from the continent of Europe is greatly increasing. It will go far to change the nature of our population. There is no doubt that the question is of deeper importance in this country than it ever has been in this or any other country, at any time before" (p. 201). Strong abolitionist sentiments in the German American community and the large number of German-language speakers, both recent immigrants and more established immigrants who continued to speak, read, and write German, made German the most obvious and profitable target for a translation of an English-language, American-authored

of John P. Jewett, Stowe's publisher, adds more details concerning publication of the authorized translation and documentation of the copyright. See also Jewett's advertisement in the 18 Feb. 1853 *Liberator* advertising a Feb. 15 publication date, and advertisements of two German bookstores (Schäfer & Koradi and Weis & Wick) in the 2 Mar. 1853 *Philadelphier Demokrat* announcing the authorized translation as available. The authorized translation was clearly available on 2 Mar., if not 15 Feb., so for a period of several weeks, Stowe's authorized translation competed directly with the continuing serialization in *Die Freie Presse*. Beginning in Feb. 1853, Jewett also advertised that a German translation of *A Key to Uncle Tom's Cabin* was being prepared. The German-language press claimed to have access to portions of this translation and harshly criticized it (Cazden, *Social History*, 351), but in the absence of surviving copies, I assume that Jewett decided not to issue it. Clearly, however, Stowe's commercial interests in the translation market at the time she filed suit were great.

45 Affidavit of Harriet Beecher Stowe, 5–6.

46 Wilson, *Crusader in Crinoline*, 331. The complaint and Stowe's and Jewett's affidavits also make note of the existence of this translation, although they provide no details. I have examined a copy of what is apparently the "authorized" Everett Welsh translation, and, interestingly, it bears no copyright notice and may be a reprint of a Welsh translation first published in London the previous year. *Caban F'ewyrth Twm* (Remsen, NY: J. R. Everett, 1854).

text to be marketed within the United States, and both Thomas and Stowe sought to exploit this economic potential.[47] At stake in *Stowe v. Thomas* was the right to exploit fully all sectors of the market, and Stowe, living in a large, highly literate, multilingual country, attempted to do just that: to expand the legal concept of authorship far enough to give her, as an author, the right to exploit *all* segments of the (American) market, whether or not they were English speaking.

With the exception of the *Tribune* article, the English-language press, unlike the German-language press, took only cursory note of the suit and Grier's opinion. To the English-language newspapers in Philadelphia, the case was a piece of legal arcana that even Stowe's celebrity status could not make of interest to the general public. In a formulaic brief report copied almost verbatim to several other Philadelphia papers, the *Cummings' Evening Telegraphic Bulletin* reported the outcome of *Stowe v. Thomas* in a few sentences on Saturday, December 24, 1853, the day that Grier read the opinion in court:

> The case of Harriet Beecher Stowe against F W Thomas, the German publisher in this city, who was charged with an infringement of the plaintiff's copyright of "Uncle Tom's Cabin," by publishing a German translation of that work, was decided this morning by Judge Grier, who gave a very learned and elaborate opinion on the subject. The Court decided, that a translation was not an infringement of the plaintiff's copyright. It is the first decision upon this question either in Europe or America, and as the books are all silent upon the subject, the legal ability of counsel was greatly tested. The arguments of counsel displayed a vast variety of learning, and necessarily the case was ably argued. S H and S C Perkins, appeared for the pltff; and Benj H Brewster and Charles Goepp, for the defendant.[48]

Several papers also printed the decision in its entirety, but with only a brief introduction noting the case's novelty.[49] The failure of the English-language

47 For German support of abolitionism, see Bruce Levine, "Immigrants, Class, and Politics: German-American Working People and the Fight against Slavery," in *The German Forty-Eighters in the United States*, ed. Charlotte L. Brancaforte (New York: Peter Lang, 1989), 119–40; Levine, "Immigrant Workers, 'Equal Rights,' and Anti-Slavery: The Germans of Newark, New Jersey," *Labor History* 25, no. 1 (1984): 26–52; and Levine, "Free Soil, Free Labor, Freimänner: German Chicago in the Civil War Era," in *German Workers in Industrial Chicago, 1850–1910, A Comparative Perspective*, ed. Hartmut Keil and John B. Jentz (DeKalb: Northern Illinois University Press, 1983), 163–82.

48 "Courts," *Cummings' Evening Telegraphic Bulletin*, 24 Dec. 1853, [6].

49 See the *Daily News*, 26 Dec. 1853; *North American and United States Gazette*, 26 Dec. 1853; *Sunday Dispatch*, 25 Dec. 1853; *Pennsylvania Freeman*, 29 Dec. 1853; and *Pennsylvanian*, 26 Dec. 1853. *The New York Times* copied the case report from the *Pennsylvanian* on 27 Dec. 1853. The contemporary newspaper reports include the sentences later omitted in Wallace's official report. Because of the extremely low survival rate of German newspapers (I was able to locate only a handful of German–language newspapers from 1853, even though hundreds are know to have been published at that time), my claim about the prominence given to the case in such venues is necessarily speculative.

Philadelphia press to give serious attention to the case certainly did not arise from a belief that the copyright law had no relevance or interest for its readers. For instance, after failing to report the decision even in its coverage of the local courts, the *Public Ledger* prominently featured an anti-international copyright editorial on December 27, 1853, denouncing proponents of the copyright treaty between England and America being considered by Congress for failing to consider the public interest: "The State has invariably denied the literary man's right *per se*, by stepping in to determine what rights society, for its own good, could concede him. Here, in fact, lies the *gist* of the question. The public, as well as the author, has rights in this matter."[50] In short, the English-language press could not see that *Stowe v. Thomas* had important public policy implications because it did not *directly* involve the English-speaking and English-reading public's interests. (Even the exceptional *New-York Tribune* article treats the question as a relatively arcane one of legal interpretation rather than as a likely focus of popular public interest).

The German-language press, however, recognized that Stowe's claim against Thomas represented an attempt to expand the private property rights of authors to the possible detriment of *German* readers. The German American press was outraged that Stowe claimed the right to make *her* translation the *only* one available, or to prevent the publication of a translation altogether.[51] That is, they recognized that copyright law gives the copyright owner both the right to control the multiplication and distribution of copies of the copyrighted work *and* the right to *refuse* to allow the work to be multiplied and distributed. The *New-Yorker Staats-Zeitung*, one of the most widely distributed German newspapers in America,[52] indicated the potential popular interest in the case by giving a pair of articles on the suit the space on the front page of its Sunday edition normally devoted to popular

However, the prominence and vehemence of the articles discussed below are strong evidence of a much stronger interest and concern than shown by the English-language press. Thomas's German-language rival in Philadelphia, the *Philadelphier Demokrat*, did not cover the case, but this omission is not surprising considering the paper's opposite political stance to *Die Freie Presse*. On the political rivalry of the papers, see Ken Fones-Wolf and Elliott Shore, "The German Press and Working-Class Politics in Gilded-Age Philadelphia," in *The German-American Radical Press: The Shaping of a Left Political Culture, 1850–1940*, ed. Elliott Shore, Ken Fones-Wolf and James P. Danky (Urbana: University of Illinois Press, 1992), 64–5.

50 "A Copy-Right Treaty," *Philadelphia Public Ledger*, 27 Dec. 1853.

51 The most interesting press account would be Thomas's own in *Die Freie Presse*, but he only mentions the court hearing briefly on 28 Oct. 1853, and then on 26 Dec. 1853, he offered some "short remarks" on Grier's opinion and promised to comment on the case in more detail later. I have examined the most complete run of *Die Freie Presse* at the German Society of Pennsylvania, and his longer remarks likely appeared in the missing 2 Jan. 1854 issue. On 7 Jan. 1854, the *Cincinnati Volks-Blatt* reprinted a German translation of Grier's opinion, crediting it to *Die Freie Presse*, so at the very least, Thomas must have run a translation of the opinion on 2 Jan. 1854.

52 Levine, "Free Soil," 171.

serial novels. Otto Reventlow describes the case as "not only important for book dealers, but also more or less important to all 'Germans'" because a win by Stowe would give American authors too much power over German American readers:

> Should it depend on the arbitrary whim of a perhaps narrow-minded, nativistically inclined author or publisher, whether works of American literature in good or indeed in any kind of translation should be permitted to reach a non-English speaking public? The Anglo-American bookseller, who possesses a ready-made public in all parts of the United States, has the right to reprint the whole of European literature, German, English, French, etc.; – should only the German-American bookseller, whose public . . . must be collected and established, not be granted the right to make Anglo-American literature available to his compatriots through good-quality translations?[53]

The question of the quality of competing translations is central to Reventlow's analysis because he believed that Stowe was attempting to force a bad translation on German readers. Cataloging what he considered to be the horrors of Stowe's translation ("entirely un-German expressions, grave language mistakes, or other irrefutable flaws" on "every page"[54]), Reventlow argues that the law should allow translations to compete on the market so that readers can choose according to their own tastes. As Thomas's lawyers later conceded in court, the sale of Stowe's own translation *was* "impaired" by Thomas's publication of the Strodtmann translation, but only because "her translation has less genius than ours" (p. 206). Readers had been given a choice, and they had chosen to purchase the translation published by Thomas, not that authorized by Stowe.

The *New-York Tribune* reported with mild approbation that Stowe had refused a settlement proposed by Thomas (the terms undefined), suggesting that her refusal resulted from a wish to establish a legal principle. Reventlow and other German Americans, however, gave this refusal central emphasis in their attacks on Stowe's character.[55] Reventlow, reporting details not

53 [Otto Reventlow], "'Onkel Tom's Hütte in' Deutschamerika," *Atlantische Studien* no. 2 (1853): 204–6. Robert Cazden's work has been an invaluable guide in my research into the German-language press's response to this case. He identifies the authors of the articles discussed here, identified only as "R" and "B" in their bylines, as Otto Reventlow and August Becker. *Social History*, 370n. Like Cazden, I cite the *Atlantische Studien* appearance of these articles because of the greater legibility of the type and the division into pages, but the *Atlantische Studien* appearance is a reprint of two separate articles originally published in the *New-Yorker Staats-Zeitung* on 6 Apr. 1853 under two separate titles, Reventlow's "Ist Uebersetzung Nachdruck?" and Becker's "Mrs. Harriet Beecher Stowe und Onkel Tom's Hütte, Ein Beitrag zur Christlichen Moral." All translations from the original German are mine, produced in collaboration with Clinton Stevens.

54 Reventlow, "Onkel Tom's Hütte," 207–8.

55 August Becker concludes his piece with a criticism of Stowe's failure to settle: "She seems to have thought only of making money, otherwise she wouldn't have insisted on suppressing the Strodtmann translation. This is made even more obvious by the fact that an arrangement with Mr. Thomas could

included in the *Tribune* article, claims, "Mr. Thomas offered (merely in order to avoid the scandal of such a lawsuit) an extremely favorable settlement to Mrs. Stowe, in which he offered her the publication rights of his translation as a gift, if she were to abstain from the lawsuit." "What light," he asks the "public," does her insistence on continuing the lawsuit "shed on the character of the 'pious' and 'Christian' Mrs. Stowe?"[56] In a pointed attack on Stowe's piety, Reventlow quotes extensively from Stowe's affidavit in the case, in which she "swears" to the high quality of the translation, and accuses her of false swearing. "Either Mrs. Stowe understands absolutely no German," he writes sarcastically, "in which case she gave an oath very frivolously on a subject, where she knowingly was in no condition to be a judge, or she understands German, in which case she gave an oath even more frivolously false."[57]

To Reventlow and his German-speaking brethren, F. W. Thomas and Adolf Strodtmann (his translator) were not faceless figures notable only because they incurred Stowe's wrath. They were important agents of German language and culture in America – agents whose ability to do this important work could be destroyed if Stowe's claim succeeded. As the New York correspondent of *Atlantis*, a monthly German-language magazine published in Detroit, complained sarcastically, "Madame Stowe, bathed in tears and with her eyes turned towards heaven, indeed *swears* that this translation is *good*, and this the world must believe, and Herr Thomas is perhaps headed for ruin if he must pay thousands of dollars to the courageous, heroic author who promotes the universal rights of man."[58] The *Atlantis* transforms the disinterested woman who used the power of emotion and tears to convert American readers to abolition into a woman using meretricious tears to veil the commercially interested motives behind her attack on F. W. Thomas.

have easily been made" (p. 214). Most of Becker's article actually argues against the existence of a German-language market for Stowe's novel because of the weak national and cultural identity of the immigrant community, their debased tastes in literature, and the lateness of the publication of the translations. As Cazden notes, however, the fact that after winning the suit, Thomas printed several editions of the Strodtmann translation, the last in 1874, strongly suggests that there was a market for the book. *Social History*, 370n. Thomas's 1864 edition includes a preface linking the novel to the Civil War and to the recent Emancipation Proclamation. *Onkel Tom's Hütte, Oder, Leben Unter Den Verstossnen* (Philadelphia: Verlag von F. W. Thomas, 1864).

56 Reventlow, "Onkel Tom's Hütte," 206.

57 Ibid., 209.

58 Letter from New York correspondent (dated 23 Apr. 1853), *Atlantis* 1, no. 10 (1853): 159. In his years in the United States (1852–56), Strodtmann co-owned a bookstore, published translations, and in 1853 edited and published a short-lived humor magazine *Die Lokomotiv*. Cazden, *Social History*, 173–6, 184n. William Frederic Kamman, *Socialism in German American Literature* (Philadelphia: Germanica Press, 1917), 40. Strodtmann's own voice is missing from the public record of comment on the case. Although Kamman quotes from an issue of *Die Lokomotiv*, I have located no copies in American libraries.

Mrs. Stowe selling Tom and Topsy: The peculiar role of abolitionist politics in *Stowe v. Thomas*

My discussion of the case thus far has focused squarely on the copyright issues at stake in the case, but other factors may have weighed heavily in the outcome. Stowe's authorial agency with respect to *Uncle Tom's Cabin* was, of course, intimately tied to the abolitionist message of her novel, and her commercial interest in the exploitation of her characters potentially conflicted with her abolitionist critique of capitalist market economics. The *Atlantis* correspondent's parting shot in his invective against Stowe brings this conflict into sharp focus: "Thus does an American abolitionist propagate her teachings. Will we in Europe finally realize that this abolitionism, at least the whining, pietistical abolition of Mrs. Stowe, is a humbug and a money business, like Barnum's Sea Tiger or Tom Thumb?"[59] That is, Stowe, like P. T. Barnum, made a business of selling "characters" to the public, and despite her claims to moral and ethical purity of purpose, she ruthlessly attempted to harm her German American competitor. Rather than incidentally using the sale of her book to promote abolitionism, claim her German American critics, Stowe used abolitionism purely to sell her book.

The attack on Stowe in the German American press presents the strange spectacle of abolitionists attacking the world's most famous advocate of abolition. Both Otto Reventlow and August Becker, who wrote a companion piece attacking Stowe's suit that appeared alongside Reventlow's in the *Staats-Zeitung*, were, like many intellectuals who fled the failed revolutions of 1848 in Germany, staunch abolitionists dedicated to the ideology of "free labor and free men."[60] The editor of the *Atlantis*, Christian Esselen, was also a radical Forty-Eighter,[61] and the anonymous article on *Stowe v. Thomas* published in the *Atlantis* is careful to attack not all abolition but only the "whining and pietistical sort" practiced by Stowe. F. W. Thomas emigrated from Germany in 1837 and thus missed the revolutions of 1848, but his abolitionist politics were similar (his decision to publish a translation of *Uncle Tom* in his paper to make it accessible to German Americans clearly demonstrates his abolitionist sympathies). Soon after 1853, Thomas officially affiliated *Die Freie Presse* with the new national Republican Party.[62] In contrast, the *Staats-Zeitung*, supported by older established commercial interests in the New

59 Ibid., 159.

60 A. E. Zucker, *The Forty-Eighters: Political Refugees of the German Revolution of 1848* (New York: Columbia University Press, 1950), 276, 230. Carl Wittke, *Refugees of Revolution: The German Forty-Eighters in America* (Philadelphia: University of Pennsylvania Press, 1952), 268–9.

61 Zucker, *Forty-Eighters*, 292. Wittke, *Refugees of Revolution*, 68–9.

62 Fones-Wolf and Shore, "The German Press," 64–5; Carl Wittke, *The German-Language Press in America* (Lexington: University of Kentucky Press, 1957), 40–1, 84, 141.

York German community, was conservative and antiabolitionist.[63] Nevertheless, abolitionist and antiabolitionist forces within the German American community, even if they did not agree on the abolitionist message of Stowe's novel, joined forces to attack her abolitionism as meretricious and her lawsuit as a commercially motivated assault on the rights of German American readers. The remarks of the German press brings us back to the extraordinary image in Justice Grier's opinion of Tom and Topsy being "abused" by "those who have purchased [Stowe's] book." What Grier's opinion implies the German press makes explicit – that Stowe, the abolitionist author, had profited by "selling" her slave characters to the public. However, as Grier held, once she *had* sold them, they and their labors no longer "belonged" to her. They "belonged" to the public at large, which could do with them as it pleased.

What are we to make of Grier's metaphorizing that part of the work that Stowe does *not* own as her slave characters? On the strictly abstract level of legal analysis, the metaphor reveals a serious flaw in the copyright metaphor of language as clothing. The metaphor both implies and denies a body underneath the linguistic clothing. It implies a body because clothing by definition covers bodies, but the purported logic of the analogy also denies the presence of a body because language is supposed to be material or corporeal, and the ideas, conceptions, and inventions, which are "clothed" by language, are supposed to be *incorporeal*. In a visually stunning but wholly illogical metaphor, then, Grier makes the naked circulating *bodies* of Stowe's characters represent Stowe's *incorporeal* creations. Whatever the logic (or illogic) of making the bodies of Stowe's characters stand in for her "conceptions" and "inventions," Grier crucially asserts that Stowe cannot control their circulation after she publishes her book: "All her conceptions and inventions may be used and abused by imitators, play-rights and poetasters. They are no longer her own – those who have purchased her book, may clothe them in English doggerel, in German or Chinese prose."

To some extent, Grier simply describes here the actual result of Stowe's limited control under the copyright law over the appropriation by others of her fictional characters: Uncle Tom and Topsy *were* used and abused by poetasters, who wrote bad verses about them, and particularly by playwrights, who produced many dramatic adaptations of the novel that made Tom and Topsy the objects of comic scorn rather than Christian compassion (although, as Jim O'Loughlin persuasively argues, at least in the case of Topsy, "the minstrel element" was already there in the novel for "later adapters to re-articulate . . . back into the tradition from which she had

63 Levine, "Free Soil," 171; Wittke, *German Press*, 79–82; Stanley Nadel, "The Forty-Eighters and the Politics of Class in New York City," in *German Forty-Eighters*, ed. Brancaforte, 51–66.

partially 'grow'd'").[64] Those same playwrights and poetasters also commercially exploited Little Eva, Stowe's saintly white child heroine (playwrights particularly delighted in having Eva physically ascend to heaven before the eyes of playgoers), but Grier does not make Eva a character in his legal drama in miniature. In its focus on the abuse of slave bodies, one might identify Grier's dramatic tableau as an accurate depiction of what Saidiya Hartman calls a "scene of subjection" fundamental to chattel slavery in the United States. As Hartman argues, legal prohibitions against the black slave's self-defense against white abuse encoded "the submission of the slave to all whites. . . . Since the subjection of the slave to all whites defined his condition in civil society, effectively this made the enslaved an object of property to be used and abused by all whites."[65] Further, as Hortense Spillers argues, the passage of the Fugitive Slave Law made the slave "as much the 'property' of the collusive state as he or she was the personal property of the slaveholder."[66]

Still, legal logic and analysis simply cannot persuasively account for Grier's extremely peculiar invocation of Tom and Topsy in the opinion. However, the manuscript version of Grier's opinion reveals a telling earlier version of a key sentence, and this deleted sentence suggests a possible extralegal logic driving Grier's choice of the metaphor and even his ultimate holding against Stowe in the case. In the manuscript, in place of the published sentence that begins "All her conceptions and inventions may be used and abused," Grier first wrote the beginning of a different sentence that he crossed out and chose not to continue: "They may be made the heroes of poems." Grier seems to have decided that use and abuse were more appropriate to Tom and Topsy than heroism, despite the fact that Tom is clearly Stowe's intended hero (she even identifies him as "the hero of our story" in the novel's first description of him).[67] Even though Stowe created Tom and Topsy, the court will not step in to prevent the abuse of them. Instead, "those who purchase her book"

64 Jim O'Loughlin, "Articulating Uncle Tom's Cabin," *New Literary History* 31, no. 3 (2000), 581. On the stage adaptations, see Thomas F. Gossett, *Uncle Tom's Cabin and American Culture* (Dallas: Southern Methodist University Press, 1985), chap. 14.

65 Saidiya V. Hartman, *Scenes of Subjection: Terror, Slavery, and Self-Making in Nineteenth-Century America* (New York: Oxford University Press, 1997), 24. In his analysis of Stowe as a juridical thinker, Gregg D. Crane emphasizes the "iconic power of her higher law images" as she "place[s] a fugitive at the door of every reader." *Race, Citizenship, and the Law in American Literature* (New York: Cambridge University Press, 2002), 60. Thus Grier also subverts Stowe's strategy for reconfiguring jurisprudence through images by creating his own iconic tableau of Tom and Topsy.

66 Hortense Spillers, "Changing the Letter: The Yokes, the Jokes of Discourse, or Mrs. Stowe, Mr. Reed," in *Uncle Tom's Cabin*, Norton critical edition, ed. Elizabeth Ammons (New York: Norton, 1994), 545.

67 "At this table was seated Uncle Tom, Mr. Shelby's best hand, who, as he is to be the hero of our story, we must daguerreotype for our readers." *Uncle Tom's Cabin, or, Life Among the Lowly* (New York: Penguin, 1981), 68 (hereinafter cited in the text).

may dress Tom and Topsy in new linguistic clothes, even if those clothes are absurdly inappropriate and transform Stowe's characters into soulless and grotesque parodic figures divorced from her abolitionist intentions. Even though Stowe "created" Tom and Topsy, her intention to make them heroic is irrelevant because the "public" now owns them. Thus in another peculiar turn of logic, Grier transforms Stowe's slave characters, persons whom, by definition, a particular free person claims title to as private property, into an emblem of *public* property, property that belongs to everyone and thus to no one person in particular.[68] Despite the legal reality of the broader public ownership and subjection of all slaves to all whites noted by Hartman and Spillers, as Hartman also notes, "The few restrictions placed upon the uses of the slave property concerned only the master's rights of property."[69] It is precisely Stowe's property rights as "master" of her characters that Grier's scene insists on erasing and denying with his claim that she is no longer master because she has "sold" them.

Why would Grier choose this extraordinary metaphor to conclude an opinion that was essentially complete without it? Indeed, several versions of the opinion published in 1853 and 1854 exclude the sentences about Tom and Topsy, and Grier's legal reasoning remains clear and coherent without them. The existence of versions of the opinion excluding the Tom and Topsy metaphor underlines the metaphor's status as excess.[70] Although intention is necessarily difficult to determine (and although judges are supposed to apply the law as it is to the facts before them, whatever the circumstances or personal feelings external to that determination), Grier and his court had good reason to want to undermine Harriet Beecher Stowe's authority. Indeed, Grier's opinion in *Stowe v. Thomas* may have been written with that goal in mind, whatever the merits of the copyright issues raised by the case. At the time of the *Stowe v. Thomas* decision, Grier's position on the abolition question was crystal clear. Congress appointed Grier as the Supreme Court justice for the Third Circuit in 1847 in part because he held the "approved" sentiments toward the responsibility of the courts for the return of fugitive

68 See also Meredith McGill's analysis of the Grier's use of slave characters as public property, reading those figures as a means through which Grier intends to suture over sectional conflict and create a new national unity. *American Literature*, 74.

69 Hartman, *Scenes of Subjection*, 25.

70 Although the manuscript of the opinion includes these sentences, John William Wallace, the Third Circuit reporter, omitted them in his published report, perhaps because in the context of a volume consisting entirely of Grier's opinions, with a substantial number of them being Fugitive Slave Law cases, Grier's venom against Stowe was too obvious. See note 1. The three sentences omitted from Wallace's report but included in the *Federal Cases* (derived from the *American Law Register*) and the newspaper reports are "Uncle Tom and Topsy are as much publici juris as Don Quixote and Sancho Panza" and "They are no longer her own – those who have purchased her book, may clothe them in English doggerel, in German or Chinese prose. Her absolute dominion and property in the creations of her genius and imagination have been voluntarily relinquished."

slaves under the 1793 Fugitive Slave Law.[71] After the enactment of the 1850 law, Grier was one of the first circuit justices to be called upon to enforce the law. Although other circuit courts were active in enforcement, Grier's assignment to the Third Circuit made him one of the most active and vociferous judges in the enforcement of the law because of Philadelphia's role as one of the first Northern stopping places for fugitives and because of anti–Fugitive Slaw Law agitation and resistance centered in the city. In late 1850, Grier asked President Fillmore for a general order authorizing the deployment of federal troops to preserve order, and Grier used his published charges to juries in Fugitive Slave Law cases to pontificate on the importance of enforcement of the law to the preservation of the union.

Not surprisingly, such behavior did not endear him to abolitionists, particularly those who counseled resistance to the Fugitive Slave Law. As William Lloyd Garrison fumed in a late 1852 editorial in the *Liberator* concerning the so-called Wilkes-Barre Slave Case prosecuted against Northern white men who assisted a fugitive, "Of Judge Grier we know nothing, except as he has revealed himself on the bench since the passage of that most infernal of enactments, the Fugitive Slave Bill. That seems to have operated upon him as the Ithuriel spear did upon the toad, transforming him into a palpable devil. . . . Mark how, with a venom of pro-slavery oozing out of every pore of his body, he affects the greatest impartiality towards the noble men on trial for a Christ-like deed of mercy!"[72] Several days before Grier heard the arguments of counsel for *Stowe v. Thomas* in October 1853, the *Liberator* protested again against Grier's role in another Fugitive Slave Law case, saying, "Judge Grier, of the Supreme Court of the United States, has eminently distinguished himself among the tribe of subservient magistrates" anxious to enforce the law.[73] Later, in his capacity as a Supreme Court justice, Grier was in the majority on the infamous *Dred Scott* decision, which denied Dred Scott, an escaped slave, status as a citizen and thus the standing to sue for his freedom in federal court.

71 For brief biographies of Grier, the least studied Taney Court justice, see Carl B. Swisher, *History of the Supreme Court of the United States, Vol. 5: The Taney Period 1836–64* (New York: Macmillan, 1974), 572; and Frank Otto Gatell, "Robert C. Grier," in *The Justices of the United States Supreme Court, Their Lives and Major Opinions*, ed. Leon Friedman and Fred L. Israel (New York: Chelsea House, 1969), 2:873–83. Under the Circuit Court Act of 1802, each federal circuit was presided over by a supreme court justice, who rode the circuit from venue to venue, sitting as part of a two-judge panel, with the second judge being the local federal district court judge. Robert A. Carp and Ronald Stidham, *The Federal Courts*, 3rd ed. (Washington, DC: CQ Press, 1998), 16–17. The circuit court panel for *Stowe v. Thomas* consisted of Grier and Eastern District of Pennsylvania's Judge John Kintzing Kane, who was equally unbeloved by abolitionists. Grier's only surviving papers are a few letters to Kane concerning fugitive slave cases that are part of Kane's papers at the American Philosophical Society in Philadelphia. There are no letters concerning *Stowe v. Thomas*, although Kane's notes on the attorneys' arguments survive.

72 "Charge of Judge Grier," *Liberator*, 19 Nov. 1852, 2.

73 "Judge Grier's Decision," *Liberator*, 21 Oct. 1853, 166.

Paradoxically, then, Justice Grier, a notable enforcer of the Fugitive Slaw Law, sat in judgment of Stowe's claim for enforcement of her copyright in a novel that is essentially a six-hundred-page plea for public resistance to the Fugitive Slave Law, a novel that in its serialized form ran concurrently in the *National Era* with detailed reports on Grier's handling of the so-called Christiana Riots case, yet another case against white men who assisted fugitive slaves.[74] Readers residing in the Third Circuit who took Stowe's novel to heart by imitating the actions of the members of the Byrd family (who self-consciously choose to violate state and federal law to assist fugitives Eliza and Harry in their escape) could have found themselves subject to prosecution in Grier's court. Thus although German Americans may have used the press to attack Stowe while not undermining the larger abolitionist cause, Grier had clear motivation to use his opinion in the case to undermine both Stowe and the cause promoted by her novel.

A copyright suit filed by Stowe as plaintiff presented no straightforward opportunity for Grier to turn the suit against Stowe and her novel, however. The abolitionist message of Stowe's novel caused Grier to confront a choice much like that presented to nineteenth-century judges presented with a suit for copyright infringement of an obscene work. Well-established common law principles obliged a judge to deny property rights to producers of pornography seeking suppression of unauthorized reproductions of their works. However, by denying injunctive relief to the proprietor of an obscene work, a judge might allow wider circulation of that work (that is, because two editions would remain on the market, more and probably cheaper copies would be available for readers to purchase).[75] Similarly, if Grier had enforced Stowe's property rights in her characters by granting a permanent injunction against Thomas's translation, he might have restricted the circulation of Stowe's novel, but he also might have enabled Stowe to earn more profits. Instead, he found in favor of Thomas, effectively declaring Stowe's characters to be free for all to appropriate. His decision thus promoted wider circulation and greater public access to Stowe's "conceptions and inventions" and the abolitionist message they carried.

At precisely the time that Grier was writing his opinion in *Stowe v. Thomas*, one Philadelphia newspaper recognized the threat that wide circulation of Stowe's slave characters presented to Grier's authority as an enforcer of the Fugitive Slave Law. The *Pennsylvania Freeman* reprinted a satiric item from a Pittsburgh newspaper, a "report" that an application for an injunction against

74 On the Christiana Riots case, see Paul Finkelman, *An Imperfect Union: Slavery, Federalism, and Comity* (Chapel Hill: University of North Carolina Press, 1981), 251–5. Coverage of the case ran in the Nov. and Dec. 1851 *National Era*.

75 For an explanation of the dilemma faced by judges who, under Anglo-American common law practice, did not grant injunctions under the copyright law to owners of copyrights in obscene works, see Joseph Story, *Commentaries on Equity Jurisprudence*, vol. 2. (Boston: Hilliard, Gray & Co., 1836), II:213.

the performance of a theatrical version of *Uncle Tom's Cabin* had been made to Grier on the grounds that the play fostered abolitionist sentiment and encouraged violations of the Fugitive Slave Law.[76] The report reads, in part:

> Those who desire to see the play of "Uncle Tom's Cabin," now performed nightly at our Theatre, should attend to it at once, or they may be too late – as a report was current last week that an application would be made to Judge GRIER, of the United States Court (in session in this city,) for an injunction to stop it, on the following among other grounds: First it is calculated to bring into disrepute the institution of slavery, and the various acts of congress passed to sustain it, by showing that the very best Christians are liable (when slaves) to be sold in the shambles, religion and all, and whipped to death for adhering to their faith. Second: It is calculated to increase the number of abolitionists and "fanatics," and put "kinks" in people's heads – thus disqualifying them as jurors in Judge GRIER'S Court, and directly interfering with the administration of justice according to the law.... Fifth: Its whole tendency is to encourage slaves to run away from their masters contrary to Scripture and the Fugitive Slave Law – and to incite men to a breach of the peace and to a resistance of the laws of their country; thus encouraging "treason," and striking a deadly blow at the "integrity of the Union."

If, as this report suggests, Grier had cause to suppress performances of *Uncle Tom's Cabin* as a play because audience members became treasonous abolitionists as a result of watching it, Grier certainly had motivation to keep the novel out of the hands of some readers by granting Stowe an injunction against Thomas. Instead, Grier, the legal guardian of the interests of slave owners, encouraged the wider circulation of Stowe's abolitionist ideas by refusing to grant her an injunction.

Although the decision against Stowe allowed for greater dissemination of Stowe's ideas, Grier's opinion also potentially undercut Stowe's moral authority by exposing an uncomfortable truth about Stowe's relation as an author to her work and to her literary characters – a relationship that is both protectively maternal and economically exploitive. By making Tom and Topsy the emblems of Stowe's "creations" and "conceptions," Grier brings to mind the classic trope of the (male) author's book as his child – a child produced out of his brain rather than from a woman's womb. Although in one sense the novel as a whole is the author's child, Grier's

76 "From the Pittsburgh Despatch: Judge Grier and Uncle Tom," *Pennsylvania Freeman*, 15 Dec. 1853. As a federal circuit justice, Grier would have traveled throughout his circuit territory, which included Pittsburgh as well as Philadelphia, on a regular schedule (see note 71). Despite modern skepticism that the stage versions of *Uncle Tom's Cabin* were genuinely abolitionist, as Eric Lott (and this news report) documents, nineteenth-century critics clearly believed that the theatrical versions of the novel did promote abolitionist sentiment. *Love and Theft: Blackface Minstrelsy and the American Working Class* (New York: Oxford University Press, 1993), chap. 8.

use of the metaphor slides into a metonymic substitution of Tom and Topsy as characters for the work as a whole as her brainchild. He thus figuratively transforms Uncle Tom and Topsy into Stowe's children, and Stowe, their "mother," has willingly subjected those children to abuse by selling them.[77]

As a number of critics have noted, *Uncle Tom's Cabin* proposes maternity – a sphere of influence uncorrupted by commercial interests – as an antidote to the market and trade.[78] As Gillian Brown argues, Stowe's families operate according to an economic model, even if that model is not a market model. White women assimilate slaves into the human community by owning them in the same way that they "own" their own white children: "Stowe replaces the master-slave relation with the benign proprietorship of mother-child, transferring the ownership of slaves to the mothers of America. . . . [S]laves are synonymous with children because they lack title to themselves and need abolitionist guardianship – which is to say, maternal aid. . . . By imitating God's parental economy, mothers approximate heaven in their homes.[79] As Brown also makes clear, however, mothers may "own" the fugitive slaves under their care and their own white children, but this proprietorship is stripped of the moral taint of slave ownership because it is not commercially interested. The mothers of America will not sell their "children," white or black. Grier's opinion in *Stowe v. Thomas* cleverly uses the scene of Tom and Topsy's abuse to suggest that Stowe has violated the values so passionately promoted in her own novel – she has "sold" Tom and Topsy, her brainchildren, depriving them of her maternal guardianship and exposing them to use and abuse. By incorporating the characters of the novel into his opinion,

77 As Rose notes in *Authors and Owners*, procopyright forces in the eighteenth-century British copyright debates used the copyright paternity trope to justify the creation of copyright, arguing that a man has the same right in the children of his brain (his literary creations) as he has in his children, raising the uncomfortable specter of fathers freely selling their children in the marketplace (pp. 38–9). For a detailed theoretical discussion of the copyright paternity trope in the eighteenth century in England, see Richard G. Swartz, "Patrimony and the Figuration of Authorship in the Eighteenth-Century Literary Property Debates," *Works and Days* 7, no. 2 (1989): 29–54. *Stowe v. Thomas* thus does not inaugurate an entirely new copyright trope, but considering Stowe's authorial persona and the values promulgated by her texts, the shock value of the image is certainly more striking. For a suggestive discussion of the implications of the metaphor for the modern law governing reproductive technology, see Mark Rose, "Mothers and Authors: *Johnson v. Calvert* and the New Children of Our Imaginations," *Critical Inquiry* 22, no. 4 (1996): 613–33. See also Wirtén on Victor Hugo's masculinist rhetoric in an 1878 speech in favor of international copyright. *No Trespassing*, 5, 19.

78 See Elizabeth Ammons, "Heroines in Uncle Tom's Cabin," *American Literature* 49, no. 2 (1977): 161–79; Jane P. Tompkins, *Sensational Designs: The Cultural Work of American Fiction, 1790–1860* (New York: Oxford University Press, 1985), chap. 5; and Gillian Brown, *Domestic Individualism: Imagining Self in Nineteenth Century America* (Berkeley: University of California Press, 1992), chap. 1. But see also Lori Merish, "Sentimental Consumption: Harriet Beecher Stowe and the Aesthetics of Middle-Class Ownership," *American Literary History* 8, no. 1 (1996): 1–33; and Ann Douglas, *The Feminization of American Culture* (New York: Knopf, 1977), 3–5 (both contend that Stowe's sentimentality is always deeply complicit in commodity capitalism).

79 Brown, *Domestic Individualism*, 32.

Grier, an apologist for slavery, thus effectively turns Stowe's own characters and her novel's moral critique against her. His opinion encourages public "use and abuse" of Tom and Topsy, while suggesting that Stowe herself is responsible for this abuse of "slaves" because of her own commercial interests in and exploitation of them in the marketplace.

Who has "Title" to Tom? *Uncle Tom's Cabin* as a parable of literary property

Grier's "reading" of Stowe's authorial situation does not merely expose a scene external to the novel and contradicting the novel's values; instead, it also uncovers concerns deeply embedded in the novel's narrative. Concerns about her conflicting roles and about the limits and possibilities of authorial property rights were part of Stowe's "scene of writing."[80] I have argued that Grier metaphorized literary property as slave bodies to accomplish his antiabolitionist ends. However, even apart from the context of Grier and Stowe's conflict over the enforcement of the Fugitive Slave Law in 1853, Grier's opinion suggests that we might fruitfully read Stowe's slave characters as particularly appropriate figures through which the author imagines her relationship to her literary work. As Lori Merish argues in *Sentimental Materialism*, "Stowe's sentimental inscriptions of slaves as objects of white maternal care (a care partly performed through writing) both invest black bodies with forms of 'white' (feminine, middle-class) emotion, and define black subjects as objects of 'legitimate' (white) proprietary authority."[81] Slave bodies, appropriated by Stowe through writing and made into what Merish calls "sentimental possessions," are peculiarly appropriate emblems of an author's work understood as literary property – the work is a person, the child to which the author gave birth and which seems to take on a human, emotional life of its own; but the work is also a thing, more particularly a property, which the author owns and can sell and which others may "steal." Stowe's original subtitle for the novel, *The Man That Was a Thing* (a title advertised in the *National Era* but not used on any of the serialized installments), suggests just this combination of properties that make Tom peculiarly suitable as a figure of Stowe's authorial property.[82] This peculiar

80 I use this phrase in the sense that Richard Brodhead defines it in *Cultures of Letters: Scenes of Reading and Writing in Nineteenth-Century America* (Chicago: University of Chicago Press, 1993), 8. See Introduction.

81 Lori Merish, *Sentimental Materialism: Gender, Commodity Culture, and Nineteenth-Century American Literature* (Durham: Duke University Press, 2000), 154.

82 As Susan Belasco Smith notes, this original subtitle "tends to focus our attention on one central character," a focus more appropriate to Stowe's early plans for a much shorter work focusing exclusively on Tom, while the published subtitle, *Life Among the Lowly*, is more suited to the sprawling, multicharacter work she actually produced. "Serialization and the Nature of *Uncle Tom's Cabin*," in *Periodical Literature in Nineteenth-Century America*, ed. Kenneth M. Price and Susan Belasco Smith

relation of authors to their works, which are both things and persons, is memorialized in the etymology of the word *plagiarism*, which is derived from the Latin word *plagiarus*, one who abducts the child or slave of another. As Grier's opinion suggests, the author is both mother and proprietor of her work.

Stowe's actions prior to the publication of *Uncle Tom's Cabin* show her keen awareness that her "child" was vulnerable to "abduction." Not only did she take care to register the copyright in the novel in her own name before serialization began, she also retained ownership of the copyright during its initial book publication, rather than transferring the copyright outright to the book publisher, as many authors did. She also knew that her own work was, as most literary works are, derived from others. She had herself "stolen" characters and plots from other works of fiction, from the minstrel tradition, from abolition tracts, and especially from slave narratives (and, notoriously, after the novel's publication, Stowe peremptorily declined Harriet Jacobs's request that Stowe coauthor a book about Jacobs's life in and escape from slavery, instead attempting to appropriate Jacobs's life story as an element of her *Key to Uncle Tom's Cabin*, a work designed to document the veracity of the novel's representations of slavery).[83] She originally wrote the novel for the *National Era,* a political antislavery newspaper that juxtaposed extensive coverage of Fugitive Slave Law cases and other news items concerning the legal and political aspects of the slavery controversy with fictional stories and tales (some about slavery, but many simply sentimental or humorous works designed for general family reading).[84] The *National Era* was thus full of accounts of slaves who had, in a sense, "stolen" themselves from their owners, becoming fugitive property that Southern slave owners asked the

(Charlottesville: University Press of Virginia, 1995), 73–4. As an index to Stowe's concerns and state of mind as she began writing the novel, however, the original subtitle is still illuminating.

83 For Stowe's indebtedness to abolition tracts and slave narratives, see Kirkham, *Building of Uncle Tom's Cabin*, chap. 4; Hedrick, *Harriet Beecher Stowe*, chap. 18; and Robert B. Stepto, "Sharing the Thunder: The Literary Exchanges of Harriet Beecher Stowe, Henry Bibb, and Frederick Douglass," in *New Essays on Uncle Tom's Cabin*, ed. Eric Sundquist (New York: Cambridge University Press, 1986), 135–53. For her divergence from the slave narrative tradition, see Sundquist's introduction to *New Essays on Uncle Tom's Cabin* (pp. 16–17). For Stowe's attempt to appropriate Jacobs's story for the *Key*, see *Incidents in the Life of a Slave Girl*, ed. Jean Fagan Yellin (Cambridge: Harvard University Press, 1987), 234–5. For Stowe's indebtedness to blackface minstrelsy, see Hartman, *Scenes of Subjection*, 26–9; Lott, *Love and Theft*, 33, 222; and O'Loughlin, "Articulating *Uncle Tom's Cabin*."

84 On the importance of the mixed-genre nature of the *Era* and its mixed-gender audience to Stowe's literary strategies, see Susan Belasco Smith, "Serialization," and Sarah Robbins, "Gendering the History of the Antislavery Narrative: Juxtaposing *Uncle Tom's Cabin* and *Benito Cereno, Beloved* and *Middle Passage*," *American Quarterly* 49, no. 3 (1997): 531–73. For the importance of the *Era*'s free soil politics to a proper reading of the political valence of Stowe's appeals to and rehabilitation of emotional engagement in her novel, see David Grant, "*Uncle Tom's Cabin* and the Triumph of Republican Rhetoric," *New England Quarterly* 71, no. 3 (1998): 429–48.

courts to return to them. Such cases suggestively foreshadow Stowe's attempt in *Stowe v. Thomas* to have the courts return her fugitive literary property to her.

The novel's anxiety about the status of slaves as property and the vicissitudes and abuses to which slave property is subjected reflects, in part, Stowe's anxiety about authorship and about her own role as a proprietor of her literary work. What was to be the fate of her own work and her literary characters? Could she prevent others from "abducting" them? What were the possibilities and limitations of literary proprietorship under the copyright law in America in the early 1850s? The central issue of Grier's opinion – who has "title" to Tom? – is also the central issue of the novel. Through its exploration of Tom's status as both person and property and particularly through its examination of Tom's relationships to his various owners, both human and divine, the novel explores Stowe's anxious questions about the possible appropriation and exploitation of her slave characters, as well as the conflicts between Stowe's maternal values and her authorial proprietorship. If we read Tom as a figure of literary property, then each of his owners represents a possible model of authorial proprietorship. Although the novel attempts to construct a positive model of proprietorship in accord with the novel's maternal critique of the marketplace, the novel just as often exposes the limitations and liabilities of authorship and Stowe's participation in market economics.

The novel begins, of course, with Tom's status as private property foregrounded as Mr. Shelby transfers Tom's title to the slave trader Haley in satisfaction of a debt. As Meredith McGill notes, on one level Grier's opinion implicitly analogizes Stowe's relation to her novel to *Mrs.* Shelby's relation to Tom at the opening of the novel – both Stowe and Mrs. Shelby are "helpless in the face of a slave transaction."[85] Mrs. Shelby wants to prevent the sale of her family's slaves, but her husband holds the legal and economic right to do so, and Mrs. Shelby, like Stowe, cannot prevent the use and abuse of Tom after he is sold. While secretly disapproving of slavery and of her family's role as slave owners, Mrs. Shelby has nevertheless tried to make slavery and her family's commercial interest in Tom and the other slaves disappear by treating them just like her children, as human creatures with souls. As she tells Eliza before she finds out that Mr. Shelby does indeed plan to sell Uncle Tom and Eliza's son, Harry, "I would as soon have one of my own children sold" (p. 52) (and, perhaps, Stowe expects her readers to know that Mrs. Shelby's assurance that she had absolute power to keep "one of her own [white] children" under her own care is misplaced – under coverture, *Mr.* Shelby was the custodial parent, and he had the legal authority to remove them from their mother's care, even if he could not *sell* them as he could sell

85 McGill, *American Literature*, 74.

his slaves).[86] After she learns the truth about her husband's transaction with the slave trader, Mrs. Shelby realizes that her earlier efforts to humanize her slaves were futile, and she says, "I was a fool to think I could make anything good out of such deadly evil" (p. 84). As the slave trader Haley tells Mr. Shelby, Tom's religious sentiments are a "valeyable thing in a nigger, when it's the genuine article" (p. 42). By exercising a maternal and benevolent moral guardianship over her slaves, she has actually made them *more* valuable as property, suggesting also the paradox of Stowe's authorial position – the better she "raises" her characters, the more likely others are to want to appropriate them. As Walter Benn Michaels notes, however, the problem with the Shelby family's ownership of slaves is not primarily the status of their slaves as property, but the fact that property is, by definition, alienable and that slaves are subject to sale, seizure, and foreclosure like other property.[87] If Mr. Shelby has a legally "perfect" title to Tom, then Tom is a perfectly alienable property, which Mr. Shelby can transfer to another at his will (or which can be taken from him against his will if he pledged his property to secure a debt and he cannot repay the debt).

Mrs. Shelby mothers the slaves under her care, but she does not give birth to them. Stowe, as an author, both "mothers" her characters and brings them into being; she is their creator and God as well as their guardian. Tellingly, the novel insists that we understand the relation between God and Tom as a sort of extraordinary property relation, thus encoding Stowe's fantasy of a truly perfect and *inalienable* title to her literary creations. Although Mrs. Shelby's maternal proprietorship fails, God's "ownership" of Tom does not fail. At many important junctures, the novel objects to Tom's commodification, the cruel irony of a man being turned into a thing subject to ownership and trade. For instance, the narrator expresses appropriate outrage at the objectification of Tom as he sits shackled among bales of cotton on his trip downriver to Legree's plantation ("for even a legal enactment that he shall be 'taken, reputed, adjudged in law, to be a chattel personal,' cannot blot out his soul, with its own private little world of memories, hopes, loves, fears, and desires") (p. 481). However, once Tom reaches the plantation, his ultimate defense against Legree is not that his soul is free, but that God owns his soul. When Legree claims that he owns Tom "body and soul," Tom answers, "No! no! no! my soul an't yours, Masr! You haven't bought it, – ye can't buy it! It's been bought and paid for by one that is able to

86 Clearly, by the time she wrote for *Hearth & Home*, Stowe knew the child custody provisions under coverture. See Chapter 1. The fact that the law permits white fathers to disperse even their white families complicates Arthur Riss's contention that the novel represents racially homogeneous families as "real" and offering "real protection," while plantation patriarchy offers a "pseudo" family offering only "fictional protection" to its members. "Racial Essentialism and Family Values in 'Uncle Tom's Cabin,'" *American Quarterly* 46, no. 4 (1994): 513–44, 530.

87 Walter Benn Michaels, *The Gold Standard and the Logic of Naturalism* (Berkeley: University of California Press, 1987), 104.

keep it" (p. 508). Tom here draws on the image of Christ in his role of the "Redeemer" who "bought" eternal life for mortal sinners with his blood shed on the cross. That is, Christ has purchased Tom's soul and freed him from bondage to sin and death (thus Stowe's title "The Victory" for the chapter in which Tom triumphs over despair and feels assured of his soul's salvation, his ultimate victory over sin and death).

Tom celebrates his "victory" by singing an Isaac Watts hymn that begins, "When I can read my title clear/To mansions in the skies" (p. 557). That is, Tom's victory over sin and death in Christ assures him a place in the house of his Father (God) in heaven. Watts's hymn draws on Christ's words in John 14 the night before his crucifixion, the same words that Tom reads from his Bible as he begins his first steamboat journey downriver: "Let not your heart be troubled; ye believe in God, believe also in me. In my Father's house are many mansions. . . . I go to prepare a place for you" (p. 229).[88] Watts's hymn also draws on the Biblical image of the Judgment Day as a time when all will read in God's book whether they have been saved or damned, but Watts conflates this image with the secular image of a title register, a book in which the ownership and transfer of real property are recorded. Watts's compound image suggests that each person will be able to read in God's book whether or not he has been reserved a place in God's house in heaven. On the Judgment Day, then, Tom's ownership of his place in God's house will be revealed – it will be revealed that he has "clear title." In singing the hymn, Tom looks forward to the victory over sin and death and his place in God's house that Christ's death has "bought" for him; but in another sense, Tom does not gain true ownership or self-possession.[89] He merely trades a place in one master's house for a place in the house of The Master, a place that he will keep forever because God holds the title to him permanently and will never transfer it to another. It is this message that Tom takes to the weary and oppressed slaves who are his fellow captives, not a message of freedom but of a new and better master, a "compassionate Redeemer and a heavenly home" (p. 559). If Stowe's relation to Tom is like that of God to Tom, then authorship allows Stowe "perfect" ownership and eternal possession of her characters. Then again, God's ownership of Tom is not truly perfect except in heaven. God can only own Tom's soul, not his body. In fact, Tom's soul victory only drives Legree to further abuse Tom's body, thus hastening Tom's death. Tom's *body* remains subject to sale and subject to "use and abuse" by whoever owns his body as property. Only when Tom dies and reunites with his creator in heaven, leaving his body behind on earth, is he completely saved from being alienable property.

88 When Stowe puts the verses in Tom's mouth, she omits the clause beginning "ye believe."

89 Michaels reads the hymn as evidence of Tom's inability to own property and himself, but misses the question of divine "ownership." *Gold Standard*, 102. Tom can't own himself, but God can own his soul. See also Riss, "Racial Essentialism," 531–2.

In some respects, then, God's relationship to Tom represents a far-reaching fantasy of Stowe's authorial power – as "God" to her work and her characters, her title to them is both perfect and eternal. However, the dichotomy of body and soul also potentially undermines this power and perfect possession. Even if Stowe is God to Uncle Tom and her book, she has godlike possession only until she publishes her book. If she absolutely "owns" Tom's "soul" in some spiritual sense, she can have, as Grier's decision makes clear, no *property* rights in that soul. Once she reveals that soul to others by clothing it in language, once she "publishes her book," Tom's immaterial part becomes public property, which is to say *no one's* property. As Grier opines in *Stowe v. Thomas*,

> An author may be said to be the creator or inventor, both of the ideas contained in his book, and the combination of words to represent them. Before publication he has the exclusive possession of his invention. His dominion is perfect. But when he has published his book, and given his thoughts, sentiments, knowledge, or discoveries to the world, he can have no longer claim an exclusive possession of them. . . . The author's conceptions have become the common property of his readers, who cannot be deprived of the use of them, nor their right to communicate them to the world, clothed in their own language. (p. 206)

To retranslate these concepts back into the novel's terms, Tom's earthly body, his material part equivalent to the material "clothing" of Stowe's ideas in language, belongs to Stowe, and only she has a right to make and sell copies of Tom's "body." However, others may appropriate Tom's "soul" (the immaterial thoughts, sentiments, and ideas constituting his character, which Stowe communicated to readers through language) and clothe it in a new earthly body, even figuratively applying the lash to Tom's body until he is horribly disfigured. With multiple Toms circulating in the market (Stowe's authorized Tom and the disfigured Toms who resemble him), how are readers to know which Tom is the real Tom? How are they supposed to see through his mutilated body to his divinely created "soul" (that is, Stowe's ideas)? In the world of the literary marketplace, as Grier's opinion recognizes and even encourages, even Tom's "soul" is in danger of being disfigured and corrupted as a result of the proliferation of disfigured Tom bodies.

The novel illuminates not only Stowe's authorial conflict with the market and her only partially successful attempts to make over property relations in the image of the divine maternal author, but also Stowe's inevitable participation in market relations as a proprietary author. I want to return to and complicate the notion of Stowe's position in *Stowe v. Thomas* as analogous to that of Mrs. Shelby in *Uncle Tom's Cabin*. Although Mrs. Shelby takes a maternal role with the slaves on her husband's plantation, she is not the woman who gave birth to them or "made" them. Stowe, as an author-mother, gives birth to her literary children and also raises them. In some respects, then, Stowe's role as an author-mother is analogous to that of the many slave mothers she portrays in the novel, including Cassy, who have their children sold away from them. However, as the white "mother" of black "children," Stowe as an author-mother more closely resembles her white male slave-owning characters, such as Cassy's father and Cassy's "husband"-owners, who are both biological fathers of and owners of some of their slaves. In an 1856 letter, Stowe's childhood friend Georgiana May plays on just this implied relation of Stowe as an author to her characters. May reports that she is in the midst of reading Stowe's second novel, *Dred*, and she remarks of one of the primary slave characters in the novel: "I have made 'Old Tiff's' acquaintance. *He* is a verity, – will stand up with Uncle Tom and Topsy, pieces of negro property you will be guilty of holding after you are dead. Very likely your children may be selling them."[90]

As May's remarks make clear, both Stowe's owning and selling of Uncle Tom and her other slave characters are peculiar economic and legal phenomena. Just as slavery was America's "peculiar" institution and slaves a peculiar form of property, "things" under the law that were also thinking, feeling human beings, so also copyright ownership is a peculiar form of ownership. Stowe both holds *and* sells her "negro property," and her children may do the same after her death. As Francis Lieber argues in his 1840 treatise in favor of international copyright, unlike real estate the primary value of copyright as property does not lie in the thing itself. Instead, "[I]ts value consists chiefly in the right of multiplying the work."[91] *Stowe v. Thomas* ultimately reveals that Stowe's structural relation to the marketplace is not like Mrs. Shelby's or even like that of a slave trader like Haley. She does not sell her "negro property" downriver once, her property forever escaping her control unless she buys that property back. Instead, she can multiply her characters, "dressed" in language and clothed in the paper of copies of her books, thus selling them again and again. This is both the magic and the horror of copyright – Stowe as an author can sell her "children" over and over again (at least until the term of her copyright expires – another limitation on her claims to absolute and eternal possession). In fact, although copyright also gives her the authority *not* to sell her children and to prevent others from selling them, her right has economic value only if she sells them and prevents others from selling them without her permission. To be an author under the copyright law is by definition to sell one's literary children in the market, whether an

90 Georgiana May to Harriet Beecher Stowe, 26 July 1865, in Charles Stowe, *Life*, 269. For the record, both *Dred* and *Uncle Tom's Cabin* were in the public domain by the time of Stowe's death in 1896, both their twenty-eight-year original terms and fourteen-year renewal terms having expired.

91 Francis Lieber, *On International Copyright, in a Letter to the Hon William C. Preston, Senator of the United States* (New York: Wiley & Putnam, 1840), 21.

author sells those children once to a publisher by transferring the copyright outright or retains title in order to directly control their repeated sale.

Stowe, Carey, authors, and slaves in 1868

Even in the face of her defeat in *Stowe v. Thomas*, Stowe quietly continued on the same course of expanding her proprietary reach to include the non-English-speaking market, even though, there being no legal recognition of her right to control exclusively translation of her works for sale in America, she could not ask a court to uphold her property rights. Stowe published a German translation of her second antislavery novel, *Dred, A Tale of the Great Dismal Swamp*, in 1856, again registering the copyright in her own name and this time not publicizing the name of her translator. Her career as a public figure in the copyright debates was not yet over, however. In 1868, Henry Carey reprinted his 1853 *Letters on International Copyright*, adding an extended preface placing the issues he originally considered before the Civil War in a postwar, Reconstruction context. Describing the copyright question as a "trial," with copyright advocates as "plaintiffs" and readers as "defendants," he decries efforts to extend in "space" and "time" the "monopoly privileges" of authors (p. 3). Looking at the pre–Civil War conflict in regional terms, he describes a peculiar marriage of convenience between North and South, between a region that produced most American literature and a region dominated by an aristocratic class that preferred to restrict the access to print to members of its own class: "Northern and Eastern advocates, representing districts in which schools and colleges abounded, insisted that perpetuity and universality of privilege must result in giving the defendants cheaper books. Southern counsel, on the contrary, representing districts in which schools were rare, and students few in number, insisted that extension of privilege would have the effect of giving to planters handsome editions of the works they needed, while preventing the publication of 'cheap and nasty' editions, fitted for the 'mudsills' of the Northern States" (p. 4). From Carey's perspective, the failure of the 1853 copyright treaty with Great Britain was a triumph for readers and democracy. He scoffs at efforts to revive an organized movement in favor of international copyright, describing an article in the *Atlantic Monthly* advocating international copyright as "a labored effort at reducing the literary profession to a level with those of the grocer and the tallow-chander," as both demeaning to authors and inaccurate because authors are already wealthy and not entitled to more (p. 5).

As he did in 1853, Carey heaps scorn on Stowe without printing her name, coyly describing her as "a lady writer who, by means of a sensational novel of great merit and admirably adapted to the modes of thought of the hour, had been able to earn in a single year, the large sum of $40,000, though still deprived of two hundred other thousands she is here [in the

Atlantic Monthly article] said to have fairly earned" (p. 5). He groups together Stowe, Washington Irving, and Noah Webster, asking readers to consider the value of their labors in comparison to the value of the labors of Union political leaders during the war. Referring to John A. Andrew (the governor of Massachusetts during the entire war, noted for raising the first black regiment, and who died of a stroke in 1867), he writes: "The late Governor Andrew's services were surely worth as much, per hour, as those of the authoress of 'Uncle Tom's Cabin,' yet did he give five years of his life, and perhaps his life itself, for far less than half of what she had received for the labors of a single one" (p. 6). He also compares Abraham Lincoln's salary as the President to Irving's royalties from sales of *The Sketch Book*, but he does not limit himself to underpaid statesmen. "Studying the lists of the honored dead," he writes, "we find therein the names of men of high renown whose widows and children are now starving on pensions whose annual amount is less than the monthly receipt of any one of the authors above referred to" (pp. 6–7). How, he asks bitterly, can the country resist establishing a pension fund for war widows and orphans at a time when Congress was willing to consider "taxing" the people for "pensions" for authors? (p. 7). He does not repeat the truism that Stowe was "the little lady who started this great big war," but the implication is clear: international copyright would allow Stowe to profit at the expense of war widows, women left helpless because their husbands served in a war she precipitated.

But Carey does not end his attack on Stowe with suffering white women and children. He also holds Stowe and copyright advocates responsible for the effects that international copyright might have on freed slaves striving for literacy. Before the war, he writes, some in the North claimed that international copyright would lead to a cheapening of books, but they now promote the virtues of the finer books (and higher prices) that will result from reform:

> [T]he argument of to-day, coming from the North, [is] an almost exact repetition of that which, twenty years since, came from the South – from the mouths of men who rejoiced in the fact that no newspapers were published in their districts, and who well *knew* that the way towards preventing the dissemination of knowledge lay in the direction of granting the monopoly privileges that had been asked. The anti-slavery men of the present thus repeat the argument of the pro-slavery men of the past, extremes being thus brought close together. . . . The wealthy Carolinian, anxious that books might be high in price, and knowing well that monopoly privileges were opposed to freedom, gladly cooperated with Eastern authors and publisher, anti-slavery as they professed to be. The enfranchised black, on the contrary, desires that books may be cheap, and to that end he and his representatives will be found in all the future co-operating with the people of the Centre and the West in maintaining the doctrine that literary *privileges* exist in virtue of grants from

> the people who own the materials out of which books are made; that those privileges have been perhaps already too far extended; that there exists not even a shadow of reason for any further extension; and that to grant what now is asked would be a positive wrong to the many millions of consumers, as well as an obstacle to be now placed in the road towards civilization. (pp. 9–10, 13)

He predicts that expansion of copyright will result in further concentration of economic power in the East, where all authors and publishers will reside, while most readers will reside in the western and central regions of the country. On the basis of such regional antagonism, he predicts a second civil war: "On the one side, there will be found a few thousand persons interested in maintaining the monopolies that had been granted to authors and publishers, foreign and domestic. On the other, sixty or eighty millions, tired of taxation and determined that books shall be more cheaply furnished. War will then come" (p. 14). Naturally, he does not put himself on the side conspiring against the interests of the masses. Instead, he claims for himself the status of a truly disinterested party, a rare author who does not object to the reprinting of his book. Writing of himself in the third person, he claims, "[H]is sole reason for writing [books] having been found in a desire for strengthening the many against the few by whom the former have so long, to a greater or lesser extent, been enslaved. To that end it is that he now writes, fully believing that the *right* is on the side of the consumer of books, and not with their producers, whether authors or publishers" (p. 14). *He* has no desire to "enslave" readers, but, by implication, a certain lady author who traffics in representations of slaves is among those who would turn readers into *their* slaves.

It is important to note, however, that Carey describes Stowe's proprietary aims, not her achieved status – with a revision of the law, she *would* become the slave master of readers, but such reforms were twenty-three years in the future. The tide was very slowly *beginning* to turn toward international copyright, but in the absence of international copyright, Stowe occupied a very different place in the national imaginary than Carey believed she should. Although the press (and particularly the Southern press) occasionally castigated Stowe for her commercial motivations, and although many reported and commented on Stowe's profits from the record-breaking sales of *Uncle Tom's Cabin*, Stowe maintained a public persona of commercial disinterestedness. This authorial persona was produced, in part, by copyright advocates, whose use of her as their victim-heroine made her just as famous for how much money she *lost* to English sales of the novel (for which she received no royalties) as she was for her American profits. Indeed, Carey's critique of Stowe is a pointed response to James Parton, then involved in efforts to found what would become the International Copyright Association (and who was the husband of Stowe's former Hartford Female Seminary student, Fanny

Fern). In the opening sentence of the late 1867 *Atlantic Monthly* article in favor of international copyright referred to scornfully by Carey in his 1868 preface, Parton proclaims, "There is an American lady living at Hartford, in Connecticut, whom the United States has permitted to be robbed by foreigners of $200,000. Her name is Harriet Beecher Stowe."[92] If slavery had, as Stowe claimed in *Uncle Tom's Cabin*, robbed slaves of their very selves, copyright advocates in post–Civil War America implicitly aligned Stowe with the slave, rather than the slave owner: she was a woman unjustly robbed of the products of her labor.

As slavery as a present reality receded, copyright advocates became more explicit in their invocations of this analogy between the American or the English author disempowered by the lack of Anglo-American copyright and the slave unprotected by the law in antebellum America (an analogy I discuss in more depth in Chapter 1). Argued David McGregor Means in the *Independent* in 1886,

> No one can imagine a more sacred right of property than the right which every man has to sell the labor of his hands. But twenty-five years ago this right was not recognized in some portions of our country. Every argument that can be advanced against copyright could have been urged against emancipation. It is true that an author cannot be compelled to write by the lash, as a slave was compelled to work; but if, under pressure of necessity, a foreign author does write, and is unfortunate enough to write anything that the American public cares for, that public can take it from him without recompense – without even the recompense of his daily bread, which the master allowed his slave.[93]

Stowe's situation as author of *Uncle Tom's Cabin* as represented to the American public by copyright advocates was exactly analogous to the situation described by Means, with gender and national polarities reversed – under the "pressure of necessity" as the wife of a poorly paid theologian, she wrote with high moral aims and low economic expectations, and the British public "took without recompense," while British publishers made enormous profits.

When Stowe entered the realm of copyright, then, she was both empowered and disempowered. The law offered Stowe commercial power and the chance to claim status as a divine creative figure. As *Stowe v. Thomas* reveals, however, the law also granted her only limited private property rights, favoring instead the reading public's right of access; and in the absence of international copyright, she could not be a proprietor abroad at all. By asserting her claim in *Stowe v. Thomas*, she attempted to push the boundaries of the American law's concept of authorship, but this concept of authorship was also inextricably bound up with the economic rights to

92 James Parton, "International Copyright," *Atlantic Monthly*, Oct. 1867, 430.

93 David McGregor Means, "The Nature of Copyright," *Independent*, 25 Feb. 1886, 229.

be enjoyed by the owner of a copyright; and the extension of the author's economic rights potentially diminished readers' opportunities for access and use. While she claimed to be a mere passive scribe and domestic producer of material objects, she also attempted to assert property rights in her immaterial, incorporeal work as an author invested with full Romantic agency. Some, like George Ticknor Curtis, maintained that the law failed to recognize the true nature of the author's property in his creations and asked that the law recognize the author's true power. However, such arguments for "recognizing" the author's power were also attempts to *create* new power through the agency of the law. If the law did not grant this power so that the author could exercise it in the marketplace, the author's supposed power was illusory. When Congress greatly expanded the rights of the author under copyright by passing the International Copyright Act in 1891 (and earlier and on a smaller scale in 1870, when Congress gave copyright owners the ability to reserve and control dramatization and translation rights), the law shifted the allocation of power between author and reader, no longer finding its primary rationale in serving readers' needs for access, but instead looking to expand and reinforce continually the growing proprietary domain of the author.

If readers enslaved authors by taking their labors and property from them without compensation, who better to occupy the position of author than a woman, especially a married woman, whose claims to her own labor and property were already tenuous? When Stowe wrote her scathing critique of the common law of coverture in 1869 (see Chapter 1) analogizing the status of married women under the law to that of American slaves before the Civil War, she wrote from personal experience of the limits the law placed on her legal agency. While she, like Mary Virginia Terhune, was married to a man who supported her literary career and happily took direction from his wife, Harriet Beecher Stowe necessarily relied on Calvin Stowe's continuing renunciation of his potential power as a husband. Furthermore, she repeatedly confronted his status as the single legal subject of their marriage in public negotiations with others whether or not he exercised his power in private negotiations between them as husband and wife. Even in the context of *Stowe v. Thomas*, Stowe could only attempt to recover her property with the cooperation and consent of her husband. Although she registered the copyright in the novel in her own name, the property thus acquired immediately became his property. *Calvin* Stowe signed the publishing contract with John P. Jewett, and *Calvin* Stowe was the primary plaintiff in the suit against Thomas. As the first paragraph of the complaint in the suit announced, "Calvin E. Stowe, of Andover Massachusetts, a citizen of the State of Massachusetts, and Harriet Beecher Stowe his Wife, bring this their bill against F. W. Thomas, of Philadelphia in the district aforesaid, Printer."[94]

94 Complainants Bill (dated 3 Mar. 1853, filed 11 Mar. 1853), *Stowe v. Thomas* manuscript case file.

Although they brought the suit jointly and relied on Harriet's rights as proprietor of the copyright in *Uncle Tom's Cabin*, Calvin was the sole legal subject of the marriage and thus the "citizen" with access to the courts. Her status and even her state of residence (recited in the complaint because it is a crucial element determining jurisdiction and venue for a lawsuit) depended entirely on his. While the law placed clear limits on the power of the author, those limits did not prevent Stowe and her female peers, whose legal identities the law of coverture also effaced, from succeeding commercially on an unprecedented scale. Indeed, those limits enabled the success of Stowe and her peers by allowing them to appear both to be powerless and self-effacing *and* to exploit fully the circumscribed possibilities of the market.

Chapter 4

"Every body sees the theft": Fanny Fern and Periodical Reprinting in the 1850s

At a pivotal moment in her autobiographical novel *Ruth Hall* (1854), Fanny Fern stages the eponymous heroine's triumph over a threat of unauthorized book publication of her popular newspaper sketches. Ruth has stopped writing for the weekly newspaper the *Pilgrim* because she is being paid more for her sketches by the *Household Messenger* and because she is anticipating income from the publication of a book collecting her earlier newspaper writing. The disgruntled editor of the *Pilgrim*, Mr. Tibbets, threatens to "immediately get out a cheap edition of your articles, and spoil the sale of your book."[1] Ruth, who initially allowed herself to be Tibbets's doormat when she was desperate to gain entrée into writing as a profession, uses this opportunity to assert her independence as an author. She tells Tibbets that she will not be "frightened, or threatened, or *insulted*": "Even had I not myself the spirit to defy you . . . you could not accomplish your threat; for think you my publishers will tamely fold their arms, and see *their* rights infringed? No, sir, you have mistaken both them and me" (p. 157).

Ruth's self-assertion here paradoxically takes the form of an assertion of her *publishers'* rights to her book. They have invested capital in the enterprise of publishing her book, says Ruth the businesswoman, and the rights of capital will not be infringed. However, Ruth's claim is not entirely economic. She also employs implicitly gendered langue of propriety, claiming the right to be protected from insult by the "gentlemen" who will be escorting her and her book in public/ation. At about the same time, and less ambiguously, Ruth decides to forego a one-time fee of $800 from the publisher for the right to publish the book (her "copyright") in favor of a royalty per copy sold. This shrewd decision concerning her literary property leads directly to her final moment of triumph when her editor and friend John Walter presents her with a $10,000 bank stock certificate representing her earnings from that book.

This chain of events in the novel has led Michael Newbury to claim, "[C]opyright functioned as a kind of hero in both Fern's novel and her life

1 Fanny Fern, *Ruth Hall and Other Writings*, ed. Joyce Warren (New Brunswick: Rutgers University Press, 1986), 157 (hereinafter cited in the text). Throughout, I normally refer to the author of Ruth Hall as "Fanny Fern" or "Fern." I depart from this practice when discussing a particularly satiric sub-persona, whom I designate "Fanny" (in quotations), and when discussing legal matters to which her shifting legal identity and name are central, I specify her legal name.

by guaranteeing both her and her heroine an otherwise unattainable wealth and independence while protecting them from exploitation. Fern's literary life and her depiction of it in *Ruth Hall* feature an unabashed celebration of the literary as property created by a statute sufficiently strong to protect that writer's economic interests."[2] Although copyright clearly does function as a sort of heroic "character" in *Ruth Hall*, this chapter argues that the relationship between Fern's career and her novel and Fern's relationship to the regimes of literary property are more complex than Newbury's formulation suggests. Newbury's reading reinscribes gender hierarchies of value by reading Fern and her works as unimaginative and uncritical celebrations of commodity capitalism and the literary market, while reading Nathaniel Hawthorne and Edgar Allan Poe as engaging these structures subtly and critically. Such a reading ignores both gender's crucial effects on property relations and the complex interplay between fact and fiction in *Ruth Hall* and Fern's sketches.

An examination of the circulation of Fern's sketches in periodicals, especially early in her career, reveals not, as Newbury would have it, security and stability guaranteed by statutory copyright, but a constant oscillation between authorial possession and dispossession, between the appearance and disappearance of literary property and proprietorship.[3] In her early career, Fanny Fern proved to be an astute player at the game of so-called exchange publication (described in more detail later), an informal network of periodical circulation largely unregulated by the copyright statute. Rather than engage in the typical "feminine" strategies of authorial self-effacement, like Catharine Sedgwick or Harriet Beecher Stowe, however, Fern repeatedly drew attention to her popularity and played with the dangers of literary proprietorship. She exposed how writers in the newspaper she "wrote for" as

2 Michael Newbury, *Figuring Authorship in Antebellum America* (Stanford: Stanford University Press, 1997), 194. I will not take note of all of Newbury's errors of fact and interpretation in his reading of both Fern's life and works, but attentive readers will see them. This chapter also implicitly critiques two other influential readings of Fern as a triumphant capitalist. Richard Brodhead, *Cultures of Letters: Scenes of Reading and Writing in Nineteenth-Century America* (Chicago: University of Chicago Press, 1993), chap. 2. Ann Douglas Wood, "The 'Scribbling Women' and Fanny Fern: Why Women Wrote," *American Quarterly* 23, no. 1 (1971): 3–24.

3 Fern's *New York Ledger* columns in their original periodical context have received some scholarly attention. Nicole Tonkovitch, *Domesticity with a Difference: The Nonfiction of Catharine Beecher, Sarah J. Hale, Fanny Fern, and Margaret Fuller* (Jackson: University Press of Mississippi, 1997), chap. 3. Joyce W. Warren, "Uncommon Discourse: Fanny Fern and the New York Ledger," in *Periodical Literature in Nineteenth-Century America*, ed. Kenneth M. Price and Susan Belasco Smith (Charlottesville: University Press of Virginia, 1995), 51–68. Laura Laffrado, "'I Thought from the Way You Writ, That You Were a Great Six-Footer of a Woman': Gender and the Public Voice in Fanny Fern's Newspaper Essays," in *In Her Own Voice: Nineteenth-Century American Women Essayists*, ed. Sherry Lee Linkon (New York: Garland, 1997), 81–96. Claire C. Pettengill, "Against Novels: Fanny Fern's Newspaper Fictions and the Reform of Print Culture," *American Periodicals* 6 (1996): 61–91. Her *Olive Branch, Musical World & Times*, and *True Flag* columns (i.e., those published before her fictionalization of that portion of her career in *Ruth Hall*) remain largely unexamined.

well as those reprinting her sketches poached on what she considered to be her "property," not just copyrights, but her "literary property" broadly and sometimes fancifully construed, including her persona and style of writing. These "violations" of her self and her property, figured by both her and those who wrote about her in explicitly gendered and sexually charged terms, marked her status as a hot commodity.

One clear example of the instability of Fern's literary proprietorship emerges if we set *Ruth Hall's* fictionalization of Fern's career against an infamous response to Fern and to *Ruth Hall*. In the context of *Ruth Hall*, "Ruth" vanquishes "Tibbets," the editor of *The Pilgrim*; but by February 1855, readers of *Ruth Hall* might have known of Fanny Fern's inability to vanquish her own disgruntled former editor, William Moulton of the *True Flag*. In February, New York publishers H. Long & Brother issued *The Life and Beauties of Fanny Fern*, an anonymously edited, unauthorized collection of Fern's newspaper sketches. Satirically following the convention of other "life and beauties" volumes, the anonymous editor intersperses the sketches (the "beauties" of Fanny Fern) with critical commentary on the sketches and on *Ruth Hall* and with vignettes constituting a scandalous biography of their author (the "life" of Fanny Fern). Despite Ruth Hall's implied claim of a legally enforceable right to foreclose Tibbetts's threatened publication, the compiler of *Life and Beauties*, almost certainly William Moulton,[4] faced no such prohibitions. In the preface to the volume, the editor carefully (and for the most part correctly) explains the legality of his actions: "The lives of distinguished men or women have always been accounted public property, and, in narrating that of Fanny Fern, we have confined ourselves to simple facts, leaving fancy-pictures to be filled up by others. In giving selections from her 'Beauties,' we present the reader with a bouquet of 'Ferns,' all freshly gathered. In so doing, we have infringed no one's copy-right; the sketches having been copied, in every instance, from the papers to which they were originally contributed."[5] He indeed "infringed no one's copy-right" by reprinting Fern's sketches in book form because the editors of the weekly papers from which he reprints her sketches, the *True Flag* and the *Olive Branch*, like many editors of weekly periodicals, did not take the steps necessary to secure copyright protection for the contents of their newspapers.

More telling than the presentation of the bare legal facts of the situation is the figurative language Moulton uses to describe this situation. He specifies that the "lives of distinguished men *or* women" are public property, but Fanny Fern's status as a *woman* with a public life is clearly central, making her works seem easier to appropriate and intensifying the effects on

4 My own examination of commentary published in the *True Flag* concerning *Ruth Hall* and *Life and Beauties* leads me to concur with Joyce Warren's identification of the anonymous editor as Moulton. *Fanny Fern: An Independent Woman* (New Brunswick: Rutgers University Press, 1992), 112.

5 *The Life and Beauties of Fanny Fern* (New York: H. Long & Brother, 1855), iii–iv.

her reputation of this appropriation. He conflates Fern with her "leaves," collapsing her life into her works and her body into her words. Whereas "Ruth Hall" claimed the lady's right to be protected by her gentlemanly publishers, Moulton here implies that Fanny Fern, as a lady tarnished by her own misconduct, is easy pickings. No one has the right to protect her, and she has no right to herself. Ruth Hall maintains both self-possession and privacy after the book publication of *her* sketches; but after the publication of *Ruth Hall* and because of the lack of copyright protection for her works, argues Moulton, Fanny Fern, both her life and her works, has become public property over the deployment of which she can exercise little control. The same laws and customs controlled the circulation of male writers and their works through reprinting, but, as Moulton's comments demonstrate, a woman writer's problematic relationship to publicity and property produced a different and heightened narrative account of these effects. Not all periodical authors were women in the marketplace, but, as the metaphors used to describe Fern's situation often suggest, the American author's tenuous possession of self and property made that author *like* a woman.

If Fanny Fern really did not have a legally enforceable right to prevent publication of a volume such as *Life and Beauties*, why did she attempt to stage for herself (through her character Ruth Hall) a claim to such possession? This chapter argues that *Ruth Hall* was, in part, an attempt by Fern to establish a stable authorial persona that could secure future proprietary claims (an attempt that, the publication of *Life and Beauties* reminds us, was not entirely successful in the short run). However, as I also argue, Fern created that stable proprietary self only after successfully exploiting a different mode of authorship and circulation in her early years writing for weekly periodicals. The presence in the marketplace in February 1855 of two competing representations of Fanny Fern, one authorized (*Ruth Hall*) and one unauthorized (*Life and Beauties*), serves as a reminder that *Ruth Hall* did not offer the only available construction of the early history of Fanny Fern as a print phenomenon. By offering this example, I resituate Fanny Fern in the early periodical context that enabled the publication of both books, a context in which unfettered reprinting rather than proprietary control of circulation was the norm, but a context in which Fern nevertheless thrived. Ultimately this chapter seeks to reimagine *Ruth Hall*'s function in relation to the contradictory and multiple constructions of "Fanny Fern" available to readers before the novel's publication, contradictory and multiple constructions produced in a periodical marketplace largely unregulated by copyright and thus not open to authorial proprietorship and control. For readers who had already encountered the Fanny Fern phenomenon in its multiple and unstable periodical instantiations, *Ruth Hall* constructed through "Floy" (Ruth's pseudonym) a new, more stable Fern who would author-ize future book and periodical manifestations.

However, even the relatively stable authorial persona created through *Ruth Hall* obscured prior instability produced by Fern's status as a married woman.

Further changes to her marital status in the future held the same disruptive potential. Crucially missing from Newbury's account and central to mine is the law of coverture and the complications it introduced into Fern's career in the 1850s. The legal and social consequences of her estrangement from her second husband, Samuel P. Farrington, made Fern an easy target for Moulton's attack in *Life and Beauties.* With the disruption of the marital unity between Sara and Samuel Farrington, "Fanny Fern" became a legal and social paradox, a woman with no identity separate from her husband's who lived apart from him and conducted a public career as a writer. One of the central revelations of *Life and Beauties* is the fact of her second marriage and its eventual dissolution. This revelation is a pointed response to the absence of a fictional analogue to Samuel Farrington in her novelization of her life and career in *Ruth Hall.*[6] While Fern was again, very briefly, a *feme sole* in early 1854 when she contracted with a publisher to write her autobiographical novel, unauthorized reprinting of her works made her ability to control her literary properties tenuous at best, and her third marriage, to Samuel Parton, forced her to renegotiate her literary proprietorship yet again.

"[T]o receive credit for the article whenever it is copied": The rules of exchange publication

In *Walden*, Henry David Thoreau complains of what he believed to be the provincial reading habits of his Concord neighbors: "If we will have newspapers, why not skip the gossip of Boston and take the best newspapers in the world at once? – to not be sucking the pap of 'neutral family papers,' or browsing the 'Olive Branches' here in New England."[7] Although Thoreau's own *Week on the Concord and Merrimack Rivers* failed to find a national audience, he misreads (or willfully misrepresents) the potential geographic reach of authors who published in the *Olive Branch*, the weekly paper that launched Fanny Fern's career as a national mass-cultural phenomenon. Every week in Boston in 1851 and 1852, as Thoreau labored over his revisions of *Walden* in Concord, Fanny Fern wrote short newspaper sketches in a variety of modes addressing all members of the middle-class family – short and scathing satirical sketches of social types, flirtatious "letters" addressed to her editor and her male admirers, sentimental stories of the deaths of young children, sprightly confidential chats with married women about the foibles of the typical

6 Shortly before *Life and Beauties* became publicly available, Moulton disclosed Fern's "secret" in the *True Flag*. Reprinting an item from the *Bee* and quoting the *New-York Mirror's* report of a denial that Fanny Fern is Sarah Farrington, he writes, "Fanny don't fancy the name of Farrington, and will never own up to it, if she can help it. She calls herself Mrs. Eldredge – still retaining the name of her first husband." *True Flag*, 20 Jan. 1855.

7 Henry David Thoreau, *Walden*, ed. J. Lyndon Shanley (Princeton: Princeton University Press, 1989), 109. For a provocative reading of Thoreau's figuring of authorial labors in *Walden*, see Newbury, *Figuring Authorship*, 144–150.

husband, and instructive tales directed at young readers. Once the *Olive Branch* and later the *True Flag* published her works for the consumption of Boston area subscribers, her works quickly moved beyond this localized audience through the mechanism of reprinting, finding their way into both other weekly papers (essentially, weekly literary magazines published in newspaper format) and daily newspapers across the country.

Contemporaneous with Fern's early career, English publishers legally appropriated *Uncle Tom's Cabin* and other American-authored novels (and, as discussed at length in Chapter 3, a court held that a German translation of *Uncle Tom's Cabin* for the German American market did not infringe Stowe's copyright). However, wholesale, nonadaptive reprinting of recent American-authored literary works in book form for the American market was rare. In contrast, newspapers routinely appropriated American-authored works first printed in other American newspapers or magazines. Indeed, newspapers in the 1850s could not have functioned if a strict, proprietary mechanism had controlled the circulation of texts. Under postal regulations designed to promote the free circulation of information in a democracy, editors could send copies of their papers to other newspaper editors without paying postage. Although many daily or weekly papers had some regular contributors (paid or unpaid) who "wrote for" that particular paper, editors relied on the contents of other papers received through exchange with other editors to fill out each issue. With scissors in hand, an editor would review copies of the exchange papers and select items for inclusion in his (or, more rarely, her) own, giving the typesetters clippings from other papers from which to set type. This loosely organized "system" of exchange between editors gave editors easy and inexpensive access to the contents of hundreds of other papers. The postal subsidy was essential to the system, but reserving scores, or even hundreds, of copies of each issue for exchange circulation carried its own cost. Each editor thus "purchased" the privilege of receiving free newspapers and being able to reprint their contents by sending out his or her paper in return, by giving credit to the source for any reprinted items, and by occasionally inserting favorable notices or "puffs" concerning papers from which he reprinted pieces.[8]

8 For a detailed discussion of the laws regulating postal subsidies for newspapers, see Richard B. Kielbowicz, *News in the Mail: The Press, Post Office, and Public Information, 1700–1860s* (New York: Greenwood Press, 1989), esp. chap. 8. For postal exchange's relation to democracy, see Richard R. John, *Spreading the News: The American Postal System from Franklin to Morse* (Cambridge: Harvard University Press, 1995). Charles Johanningsmeier briefly and cogently explains the place of exchange in the distribution of literary texts as a precursor to the fiction syndicates. *Fiction and the American Literary Marketplace: The Role of the Newspaper Syndicates, 1860–1900* (New York: Cambridge University Press, 1997), chap. 2. See also Meredith McGill, *American Literature and the Culture of Reprinting, 1834–1853* (Philadelphia: University of Pennsylvania Press, 2003), Introduction and chap. 4 (on Poe's negotiation of exchange reprinting), and Augusta Rohrbach, "'Truth Stronger and Stranger Than Fiction': Reexamining William Lloyd Garrison's Liberator," *American Literature* 73, no. 4 (2001): 726–55 (for Garrison's exploitation of the advertising value of exchange reprinting).

Copyright offered no protection whatsoever to much of the content of daily and weekly newspapers, in part because the administrative process required to secure protection would have been particularly burdensome to fulfill for periodicals published with such frequency. Under the laws in effect in the early 1850s, in order to secure copyright protection for a published work, the author or proprietor had to register the title with the clerk of the local federal district court *before* publication and pay a small fee to make this entry into the register (registration), include a notice of copyright registration in *each and every* published copy of the work using exactly the required statutory language (notice), and, *within three months* of publication, deposit the required number of copies of the published work with the district court to be forwarded to the Secretary of State (deposit).[9] The first Supreme Court copyright decision in 1834, *Wheaton v. Peters*, held that all of these statutory requirements were absolutely essential to perfect the title in a statutory copyright. Furthermore, held the court, if a copyright registration under the statute proved to be defective because of an error or errors in the registration process, the published work fell into the public domain and was free for all to use because the common law did not protect published works. Indeed, Wheaton, the plaintiff in the case, lost his suit against defendant Peters because Wheaton deposited a wrong number of copies of his work, and the court found that this administrative mistake invalidated his copyright.[10]

Not surprisingly, many papers did not jump through the hoops necessary to register copyrights in the contents of each individual issue. A weekly trip to a federal district court and a payment of a registration fee seems to have held scant appeal for many papers, especially considering their ability to thrive and prosper in the absence of copyright. The first two weekly papers for which Fanny Fern wrote, the *Olive Branch* and the *True Flag* (both published in Boston), did not register copyrights in their contents. That is, although each of these paper paid Fanny Fern for the right to publish her manuscript productions, once the papers printed them, all comers were legally free to reprint her sketches; and periodicals all over the country, from local country papers to the radical feminist monthly the *Una*, did just that.[11] Even later in her career, when Fern wrote for two papers that

9 In early 1850s, the registration, notice, and deposit requirements in effect derived from the 1831 Copyright Act. Thorvald Solberg, ed. *Copyright Enactments of the United States, 1783–1906* (Washington, DC: Government Printing Office, 1906), 38. A requirement of depositing additional copies with the Smithsonian Institution and the Library of Congress was added in 1851 (p. 42). With the creation of a copyright registration section within the Library of Congress in 1870, these procedures changed (p. 46). However, the onerous nature of the procedures for periodicals remained until the 1909 Act clarified the status of periodicals and created special procedures for registering "serial" publications.

10 On *Wheaton v. Peters*, see McGill, *American Literature*, chap. 1.

11 Among the publications in which I have found reprintings of Fern's sketches during the 1850s and early 1860s are *Arthur's Home Gazette*, the *Boston Daily Bee*, the *Saturday Evening Post*, the *Home*

did copyright their contents (the *Musical World & Times* and the *New York Ledger*), her sketches continued to circulate through the exchange system with the blessings of her editors, as long as exchanges that scissored Fern's columns gave the customary source credit.

Both Fern and her early editors proved to be astute players at this game of exchange publication, turning what to many modern observers appears to be a system at odds with the interests of authors and editors into a tool for building and then consolidating such interests. In the world of newspaper exchange, text was not merely reprinted and circulated without comment. Instead, authors, editors, and readers often carried on printed discussions about the mechanisms of exchange circulation. Fern and her editors cleverly used this commentary to build a market identity for Fern. Both the *True Flag* and the *Olive Branch* draw attention to original materials in their pages by heading certain items, including Fern's columns, "written for the Olive Branch" or "written for the True Flag" or "Original Tale." They also usually indicate their indebtedness to other periodicals with varying degrees of specificity, putting the name of the source of the piece at the bottom (for instance, "Godey's Lady's Book," or the name of a newspaper, or, less specifically, the notation "Exchange"). When papers reprinted "original" pieces not protected by copyright, they had no *legal* obligation to anyone to offer even that much credit. However, a clearly understood extralegal system regulated the circulation and attribution of Fanny Fern's sketches and similar reprinted pieces, a sort of "gentleman's agreement" among editors, honored as often in the breach as in the observance. Note, for instance, this fairly typical "squib" (nineteenth-century periodical argot for a brief paragraph) from an early 1853 issue of the *True Flag*, after Fern had been writing for the paper for a little more than a year:

> The editor of the Wellsville Patriot is informed that the sketch entitled "Elise de Vaux," by Fanny Fern, originally appeared in the True Flag, and was copied from our columns by the Olive Branch. The Patriot, alluding to our popular contributor, remarks "that she has gained an almost worldwide reputation in a very brief period." Certainly, every article from her pen that appears in the True Flag is copied into at least a hundred exchanges, and about two-thirds of them neglect to give the proper credit, just as you have done. Please recollect, hereafter, that the True Flag is Fanny Fern's "organ," and govern yourself accordingly.[12]

Ostensibly, the editor of the *True Flag*, William Moulton, is addressing his brother editors concerning their obligations under the exchange system.

Journal, the *Una*, the *Revolution*, the *Pennsylvania Freeman*, the *Montgomery (Ala.) Weekly Advertiser* and the *Montgomery (Ala.) Weekly Post.*

12 *True Flag*, 29 Jan. 1953. "Elise de Vaux" appeared first in the 13 Mar. 1852 *True Flag*, and was reprinted in the 8 May 1852 *Olive Branch*, which gave due credit to the *True Flag*.

They have failed to give credit for the original source of Fern's sketches (that is, the *True Flag*, not Fern) and they should, on ethical if not legal grounds, give credit where credit is due. However, despite the notice's address to a professional audience and its function as postage-free business correspondence carried within the exchanged paper copy, such notices also form part of the periodical text ordinary readers are invited to read. As the *True Flag* repeatedly reminded its readers through these notices ostensibly directed to other editors, Fanny Fern was popular, and Fanny Fern wrote original pieces for them. By drawing attention to how many times Fern's articles had been reprinted, Fern's editors drew their readers' attention to the articles as valuable and worth reading. "Look here," they say, "and be among the first to see what hundreds of editors across the country find interesting enough to reprint for *their* readers."

Although the circulation of the *True Flag* and the *Olive Branch* was largely local, they clearly saw the exchange system and Fern's wide reprinting as opportunities to attempt to build their subscription lists.[13] As part of an informal quid pro quo, editors who copied from exchange papers were expected to "puff" the papers from which they copied and to publish information on how to subscribe to them. As Fern's popularity grew, the *Olive Branch* and the *True Flag* ratcheted up the intensity of their pleas for recognition as the papers Fanny Fern "wrote for," indicating that this distinction, although it carried no legal significance, carried a value and cachet in the market. Shortly after publishing the admonition to the editor of the *Wellsville Patriot* quoted earlier, the editor of the *True Flag* reprinted a brief letter from Fern to the editor of the *Evening Transcript* correcting his assertion that she "wrote for" another Boston paper. His own commentary follows the reprinted letter:

> The above communication, which appeared in the Evening Transcript, was rendered necessary by a mean and dishonest claim made by a contemporary, and advertised in the Boston dailies, that Fanny Fern was a contributor to his paper. He steals her literary reputation, without rendering her any equivalent; although she never wrote a line for him, and he knows that she is strongly opposed to any such disreputable use of her name, in connection with his paper. A man who would deal thus basely with a *lady*, and build up his own success on her popularity, would not scruple to sell his own grandmother to a soap-maker, for five dollars.[14]

13 Both papers clearly geared their contents to readers with the Boston orbit, for instance, publishing information about marriages and deaths in the Boston area. The *Olive Branch*'s editor was a Methodist minister, and weekly reports of "Methodist Protestant affairs" are predominantly local. Information concerning their history and circulation is scant. Frank Luther Mott mentions the *True Flag* in passing as a "Boston weekly." *A History of American Magazines 1850–1865* (Cambridge: Harvard University Press, 1938), 35–6. Mary Noel very briefly describes the history of both papers and the presumed profitability for their owners, especially in the case of the long-lived *True Flag*. *Villains Galore: The Heyday of the Popular Story Weekly* (New York: Macmillan, 1954), 49–50.

14 *True Flag*, 12 Feb. 1853. It is worth noting that the *True Flag* itself became significantly less scrupulous in its reprinting of Fern's sketches once her original contributions to the paper became sporadic and

Exactly what is Fanny Fern's place in this debate between two editors, both of whom want to claim the benefit of her "reputation" and popularity for themselves? On the one hand, *her* place seems to be the most powerful and secure. Her popularity is unquestioned, while two insecure editors fight for the right to build their own popularity on a claim to enabling hers. On the other hand, repeated dishonorable encroachments on Fern's name are the primary evidence of her popularity. Her popularity is thus inseparable from a chronic crisis of authorial reputation, the type of crisis to which she, as a "lady," is particularly susceptible – the more widely her sketches are reprinted, the more frequently strange men endanger her reputation by claiming false alliances with her, making her look like a woman of easy virtue. After the moment when she transfers her manuscripts to an editor so that they can appear in print, circulation of her sketches remains largely beyond her control, and circulation always threatens to spiral out of control. As an unaccompanied lady in the marketplace, implies the editor of the *True Flag*, she can only rely on his vigilance and his efforts to protect her reputation. (Ironically, Moulton himself eventually made the most aggressive attack on that reputation by publishing *Life and Beauties* – once she was no longer under his "protection," he felt free to take advantage.)

At every point during Fern's career in the early 1850s, the risks and rewards of this out-of-control circulation are inseparable, with the risks most often linked to and intensified by her status as an unaccompanied woman in the marketplace. As I noted in Chapter 2, in debates over international copyright, the interests of authors and readers were set against each other, with those arguing against international copyright maintaining that the free circulation of British works unimpeded by copyright benefited American readers. Throwing a bone to authors, copyright opponents often claimed that unauthorized circulation of an author's works (in England for an American author or in America for an English author) redounded to the author's credit. As publisher Philip Nicklin argued in 1838 in his *Remarks on Literary Property*, "[I]f an author's reputation does not gain by the admiration of millions, the word has different meanings on the two sides of the Atlantic; and so far from injury being done to [British authors'] property, the fact is, that their American fame is echoed back across the ocean, and increases the value of their copyright at home."[15] The case of Fanny Fern illustrates how the absence of copyright in her newspaper sketches and the wide, unfettered, *domestic* circulation of those sketches through reprinting did, indeed, benefit her interests as an author.

then ceased altogether. The *True Flag* filled "Fanny Fern's Department" with uncredited reprints. See, e.g., "A Rap on Somebody's Knuckles" and "An Omnibus Ride" (*True Flag*, 25 June 1853), reprinted without credit from *Olive Branch*, 11 June 1853; and "A Sketch from Life" and "When your wife begins to scold" (*True Flag*, 17 Sep. 1853), reprinted without credit from the *Musical World & Times*, 3 Sep. 1853.

15 Philip H. Nicklin, *Remarks on Literary Property* (Philadelphia: P. H. Nicklin & T. Johnson, 1838), 15.

Her interests and threats to her interests, however, closely jostle each other at every turn. An 1853 squib in the *New York Musical World & Times* suggests how the uncontrolled and controlled circulation fed off one another:

> It will be seen on reference to our advertising columns that Messrs. Derby and Miller of Auburn have made arrangements to publish a book by that witty, sparkling, electric and original writer "Fanny Fern," whose identity is past finding out, and whose writings are now more universally read in this country than those of any other author. Our exchange list numbers over nine hundred papers and reaches to the confines of Newspaper-dom, and in all these journals "Fanny Fern's" sketches are constantly being published, and the author quoted as the most popular paragraphist of the day. *This gives her a weekly circle of at least one million friendly readers*; and we think we hazard nothing, therefore, when we affirm that FERN LEAVES FROM FANNY'S PORTFOLIO will be "A Book which will sell."[16]

The *Musical World & Times* is hardly a neutral observer: Fern's brother Richard Storrs Willis edited the journal, and shortly after her brother published this squib, Fern began writing for the journal exclusively for a period of several months. Nevertheless, the paragraph suggests a clear logic of how extensive reprinting of Fern's sketches through the exchange system built for Fern a national audience while she was writing on a piecework basis for two papers with local circulation. The presence of this readymade national audience then attracted a book publisher, who could feel assured of a market for a collection of those already widely disseminated sketches.[17] A favorable review of *Fern Leaves* in the *Home Journal* similarly credits wide exchange reprinting as the source of the book's popularity: "It is only two years ago, since she sent her first leaf to the printers, and she is now known wherever a paper in the English language penetrates. She had not to *seek* a publisher for her collected writings: most of the leading publishers sought them. And now that they are published, they sell like the smoking ears of Indian corn on a summer's eve."[18] The reviewer later opines that the "editorial fraternity" throughout the English-speaking world ought to "repay" Fanny Fern for "furnishing them with a profusion of *short* paragraphs, with which to brighten their columns" by "giving universal publicity to her volume, in the sale of which she is interested." *Fern Leaves* did, indeed, succeed spectacularly for its time. It sold nowhere near as many copies as *Uncle Tom's Cabin* (despite claims in advertisements that its initial sales exceeded the rate

16 *Musical World & Times*, 5 Mar. 1853.

17 J. C. Derby's reminiscences considerably after the fact in 1884 portray his thought process and motivations in precisely this way. *Fifty Years among Authors, Books and Publishers* (New York: G. W. Carleton & Co., 1884), 208.

18 *Home Journal*, 1 June 1853. The *Home Journal* was edited by Fern's other brother, N. P. Willis. See Warren for James Parton's publication of this review during Willis's absence and Willis's enraged reaction to this positive press for his estranged sister. *Fanny Fern*, 106.

of sales of Stowe's novel). Nevertheless, it sold 70,000 copies, putting it in a league with popular novels such as Maria Cummins's *Lamplighter*, which sold 90,000 copies. *Ruth Hall*, written exclusively for book publication and securely protected by copyright, circulated almost as widely, selling 55,000 copies.[19]

In 1853, when Derby & Miller published *Fern Leaves*, Fern wrote for the *Musical World & Times*. Very briefly in 1854, she wrote for the *Saturday Evening Post*, before giving up newspaper writing while writing *Ruth Hall*. She finally returned to newspaper writing under contract with Robert Bonner's *New York Ledger* in 1855. The *Musical World*, the *Post*, and the *Ledger* all copyrighted some or all of their contents while Fern was writing for them (the *Musical World* copyrighted each issue in its entirety, the *Post* copyrighted Fern's and Grace Greenwood's columns, and the *Ledger* copyrighted each issue in its entirety, in addition to separately securing copyright for certain pieces that it considered valuable, namely many of its serialized novels and Fanny Fern's sketches). The fundamental right protected by copyright is the right to make and sell copies of the protected work, so one might presume that Fern's editors would have used copyright law to shut down the circulation of Fern's sketches through the exchange system. However, Fern's editors made it clear through the notices to exchanges published in their papers *both* that certain contents of their publications were protected by copyright *and* that other papers were nevertheless free to reprint those contents. On the front page of every issue of the *Musical World* in which Fern's sketches appeared is this notice: "Each number of *The Musical World & Times* is copyrighted. Editors are at liberty, however, to copy from our columns if mindful of the courtesy of accrediting articles." Editorial squibs draw particular attention to the desirability of Fern's items for reprinting, and as in the papers published without copyright, these notices serve to draw attention to the value of Fern and the *Musical World* for its subscribers. For instance, an April 1853 paragraph entitled "A Luxury for Editors" in the *Musical World* draws attention to the paper's own munificence in offering up a Fern sketch for other editors to reprint: "On another page we publish an article from the brilliant pen of FANNY FERN, entitled 'The Bore of Sanctum,' the perusal of which will, we think, give any editor 'the most vindictive pleasure'. . . . We have only to add, that it will not offend us in the least to receive credit for the article whenever it is copied, as the copyright is secured."[20] Here, as elsewhere, the editor does not deploy copyright as

19 For the marketing of both *Fern Leaves* and *Ruth Hall* and sales of other works at the time, see Susan Geary, "The Domestic Novel as a Commercial Commodity: Making a Best Seller in the 1850s," *Papers of the Bibliographical Society of America* 70 (1976): 365–93.

20 *Musical World & Times*, 16 Apr. 1853. The *True Flag* obliged, both reprinting and giving credit (30 Apr. 1853). During her brief stint at the *Saturday Evening Post*, it published a very similar notice. "To the Press," 7 Jan. 1854.

a means to prevent reprinting per se or to receive payment (royalties) from other editors for the privilege of reprinting. Instead, he uses statutory copyright as leverage within the extralegal exchange system as an instrument to exert pressure on reprinting editors to give credit to the *Musical World*, and, never far behind, to "puff" the periodical and publish subscription information. To use the legal terminology that these notices never use explicitly, the *World* grants a royalty-free license for periodical reprinting to other editors, as long as the reprint gives credit to the *World*.

In at least one instance, again, prominently reported on the front page of the *Musical World* for its readers as well as its exchange editors to see, the *Musical World* reported that it had asked its lawyers to pursue legal action under the copyright law against a few exchanges who had failed to give credit for reprinted articles. In particular, the *Musical World* emphasizes that its ownership of registered copyrights gave it the power to collect money damages from offenders:

> We have handed over a few contemporaries who persist in taking articles, without giving proper credit, from the *N.Y. Musical World & Times*, to our lawyers. As it costs something to infringe upon a copyright, it is possible that the offenders may shortly come to the conclusion that honesty would have been the best policy. The articles which are most copied without credit, are the contributions of FANNY FERN. These cost us a round sum, as that writer commands higher prices, so far as we know, than any one else now writing for the press; and we *should* have the full benefit to be derived from their extensive circulation, and we *intend* to have it, if there are law and lawyers enough in the Union to get it for us. Each number of our paper is copyrighted, and *each article* copied from it must be accredited to the *N.Y. Musical World & Times*.[21]

Clearly, the "full benefit derived from extensive circulation" here is *not* to control periodical reprinting or to receive royalties from such reprintings, but to receive credit as the source, and to convert that "credit" into a financial benefit in the form of increased circulation and subscriptions. The notice to its exchanges also gives the *Musical World* an opportunity to boast to its readers concerning its payments to Fern, thus highlighting for readers the value that their subscription dollars had purchased.[22] For the *Musical World* and the *New York Ledger* (which registered copyrights) as for the *Olive Branch* and the *True Flag* (which did not), the benefit to be gained from publishing Fern's sketches was the association of Fern's name with the name of the

21 *Musical World & Times*, 11 June 1853. The *Musical World* apparently did not file suit against its unnamed exchange papers. However, the publication of the threats in the magazine demonstrates the publicity value of copyright infringement.

22 Interestingly, after Oliver Dyer left the *Musical World & Times*, leaving Richard Storrs Willis the editor and sole proprietor from 17 Dec. 1853 onward, the magazine ceased to register copyrights.

paper as an "original contributor." Copyright or no copyright, none of them expected or even desired that Fern's sketches appear "exclusively" in their papers, instead seeking the widest possible reprinting of her sketches through exchange.

"Does any but the genuine coin ever get counterfeited?": Fanny Fern dances through the periodical minefield

Fanny Fern's editors devoted much space to these comments on the reprinting of Fern's works, demonstrating their substantial interests, financial and otherwise, in the dynamics of exchange publication. Fern herself was not, however, merely a passive object in this elaborate game of reprinting and writing about reprinting. Her authorial interests, sometimes in harmony with the interests of her editors and sometimes at odds with them, were implicated in the exchange system. Although an editor presided over the copies of the exchanges from within his "sanctum," Fern clearly had access to the sanctum, finding material on which to build her sketches and participating in the project of drawing reader attention to the reprinting of her sketches. In a number of her sketches, she describes the editorial sanctum and what transpires there.[23] Many other sketches take the form of "letters" written to her editors, whether "Dear Mr. Norris" (William Norris, editor of the *Olive Branch*) or "Dear Mr. True Flag" (Moulton served anonymously as the editor of the *True Flag*), protesting their editorial action or inaction. Her sketches also often begin with a quotation from another newspaper, either clearly labeled as to source, unlabeled, or labeled as "Exchange," just as her paragraphs were labeled (or not) when reprinted in other papers.[24] As her popularity grew, this process of commenting on exchanges even doubled back on itself, with Fern responding to an exchange who had responded to her.[25] Readers often became writers, responding to and appropriating from Fern's columns. At least twice in the *True Flag*, for instance, readers wrote original sketches in the personae of characters from earlier Fanny Fern

23 See, e.g., "The Model Editor," *Olive Branch*, 22 May 1852; "Everybody is Having a Vacation Except Editors," *Olive Branch*, 21 Aug. 1852; "Editors," *True Flag*, 15 Jan. 1853; and "The Bore of Sanctum" *Musical World & Times*, 16 Apr. 1853.

24 Fanny Fern began using this strategy regularly in about April 1852. See, e.g., an untitled article in *Olive Branch*, 10 Apr. 1852, responding to an uncredited paragraph beginning, "You, young loving creature. . . . " However, she used a wide range of citation strategies, including the following examples displaying this range, all in 1852: Untitled (*Olive Branch*, 5 June) beginning with a quote attributed to *Blackwood's Magazine*; Untitled (*Olive Branch*, 14 Aug.) embedding in her own article a poem she finds "in one of the papers among the list of marriages"; "A Woman's Advice" (*True Flag*, 21 Aug.) beginning with a paragraph attributed to the *Buffalo Advertiser*, "A Lady on Money Matters" (*True Flag*, 4 Sep.) quoting the *True Flag*'s response in a previous issue to a paragraph in the *Military Argus*; and Untitled (*Olive Branch*, 25 Dec.) beginning by quoting an entire poem from "Exchange."

25 See, e.g., *True Flag*, 1 Jan. 1853.

sketches.[26] In the *Olive Branch*, some readers adopted their own pseudonyms and personae to engage Fern's satiric "Fanny" persona in discussion, competition, and particularly flirtation. In response, Fern, writing sketches and letters in her Fanny persona, comments most insistently on the periodical context in which her works circulated, protesting how others have "stolen" her "style." This persistent line of self-reflexive commentary reveals Fern's self-conscious construction and promotion of a persona in dialectic with her periodical context and her readers, a dialectic that she often figures in the gendered language of flirtation.[27] In these published letters and sketches, she makes it clear that she herself had poached on another's territory at the very beginning of her career, and that carrying out this very public policing of her newly created persona was part of her strategy for promoting her own popularity and engaging reader interest.

In early 1852, "Fanny" even responded in the *Olive Branch* to a number of published and unpublished marriage proposals from readers, always refusing but still encouraging this continuing discussion of whom she should marry or whether she should marry at all. The marriage proposals came in response to her early 1852 "letter" to Norris in the *Olive Branch*, in which she anticipates an indignant response from women readers to another of her "letters" published in the same issue. In that letter, "Fanny" rebuffs "Eva," a female reader writing seeking her friendship, by claiming that "women *never make decent friends to their own sex*." "Fanny" tells Norris that she will need male protection from female readers once they read her letter to Eva:

> *My Dear Mr. Norris* – May I venture to hope you don't wear a jacket, for I must hold on to the skirt of somebody's coat after stirring up such a hornet's nest of women. . . . Now you know how nicely I got out of that scrape with Mr. Carpet-Bag, when I meddled with his old lady Partington. He shut up my mouth with such a big sugar plum that I've never opened it since to wag my tongue or pen against her or "Ike" but these women, with their squibs and crackers, will keep peppering away at me until the millenium [*sic*], if you don't put a stop to it. See what it is to be a lone unprotected female. I shall have to get married, that's a fact.[28]

This "letter," packed with references decipherable to many *Olive Branch* readers but almost indecipherable to a modern reader, demonstrates how

26 "Look Before You Leap" (*True Flag*, 24 Apr. 1852) elicited a response from "Jemmy Jessamy" (*True Flag*, 1 May 1852). "Bachelor Housekeeping" (*True Flag*, 30 Oct. 1852) elicited a response from "An Old Bachelor" (*True Flag*, 20 Nov. 1852).

27 Warren also examines these early disputes, but takes her protestations against imitators as signs of Fern's true uniqueness. *Fanny Fern*, 113.

28 *Olive Branch*, 31 Jan. 1852. The interplay between Fern and male readers here and elsewhere during her early periodical career belies Tonkovich's claim that the "Fanny Fern" pseudonym "insists that her work be read as if written by a woman and is addressed primarily to other women." *Domesticity with a Difference*, 54.

difficult it is to extract many of Fern's early writings from their periodical context. "Mr. Carpet-Bag" was Benjamin Shillaber, a writer of humorous periodical sketches and, in January 1852, the editor of a recently established (and ultimately short-lived) weekly humor magazine, the *Carpet-Bag* (which, careful *Olive Branch* readers would have known, was published in Boston from editorial offices in the same building occupied by "Dear Mr. Norris's" newspaper).[29] Shillaber's most famous creation was "Mrs. Partington," a sort of Yankee Mrs. Malaprop, whose unintentionally humorous sayings became the fodder for reprinted "squibs" in papers throughout the country. Mrs. Partington was a widow of the departed "Corporal" Paul Partington (a member of the local militia during the War of 1812), and "Ike" Partington was her orphaned nephew and adopted son.[30]

Although "Fanny" doesn't specify exactly how she "meddled with [Shillaber's] old lady Partington," it seems likely that the subject of his ire was Fern's imitation of Mrs. Partington's style in her late 1851 sketch in the *Olive Branch*, "Aunt Charity's Advice to her Nephew on Leaving Smithville."[31] Writing in the form of a soliloquy in the voice of a rural Yankee old maid, Fern peppered the sketch with what one might call Partington-isms. "[I]f my remission had been asked," says Charity to her nephew, substituting "remission" for "permission," "you never–d ha–went" to Boston. She warns him of the "proomiskus" nature of boarding house food, and tells him what to do with boarding house "sasenges" (sausages): "es-*chew* 'em." Although Fern adopted many voices and personae in her subsequent columns, she did not bring back Aunt Charity or her distinctive (but not original) style of speaking.

Just as "Mr. Carpet-Bag" defended his turf, the style of comic expression that made "Mrs. Partington" a national newspaper byword, "Fanny" asked Norris to help defend "hers." In July of 1852, invoking again their run-in with Shillaber, "Fanny" protested imitations of "Fanny." Norris writes that she called on him in person, asking him to tell her the true identity of "Sweet Pea," a contributor whom she perceived to be poaching on her territory. When he refused to divulge Sweet Pea's identity, she wrote

29 There are other references to the *Carpet-Bag* and Mrs. Partington in the 1851 issues of the *Olive Branch* that would have given readers the information they needed to decipher these references. See "Partington Courtesies," 5 July 1851, and an untitled "puff," 27 Dec. 1851, which may have been the penalty Shillaber extracted from Norris as recompense for Fern's imitation of Mrs. Partington's style.

30 Shillaber's early Partington newspaper paragraphs are collected in *The Life and Sayings of Mrs. Partington* (1854). Mrs. Partington first appeared in the *Boston Post* in 1847. For brief accounts of Shillaber's works and career, see Clyde G. Wade, "B. P. Shillaber," in *American Humorists, 1800–1950*, part 2, ed. Stanley Trachtenberg (Detroit: Gale, 1982), 434–8 (*Dictionary of Literary Biography*, vol. 11); and Daniel G. Royot, "B. P. Shillaber," in *Encyclopedia of American Humorists*, ed. Steven A. Gale (New York: Garland, 1988).

31 *Olive Branch*, 22 Nov. 1851.

him "the following rather caustic letter," which he published in the *Olive Branch*:

> *Dear Mr. Norris*: You remember how touchy *Mr. Carpet Bag* was when I got up a *spurious Mrs. Partington*? Well, *you* said I *mustn't*, and I *didn't!* (any more;) and now just *please* strangle in the birth any embryo imitations of Miss "Fanny," *won't* you? It seems to me *just as fair in this case as the other*. I shall turn John, or Sam, or something, I *know*, if you don't! for it makes me *cross!* I *do* think you are just like all the rest of *man*kind, and *love* to *tease!* How *can* you? Do be good to me now? You don't know how *awfully* you frighten me when you look so *stern*; I don't know whether to run away or cry. Yours affectionately, FANNY.[32]

Norris concedes "Fanny's" point, charging that it is "a sort of piracy to assume the peculiar style of any popular writer. It is precisely the same as merchants or manufacturers appropriating each other's trade marks without the consent of the owner – besides, those who assume other people's style of writing, never come up to the original. . . . We shall therefore discourage our contributors from borrowing each other's styles of writing." Despite Norris's identification of Fern as an "original," the first and the higher quality thing that imitators can never hope to match in quality, his analogy to trademark infringement is telling. Legally, a company acquires rights in a word or symbol as a trademark not because the company invents something new and original, like a new machine entitled to patent protection by virtue of its truly innovative character. Instead, a company acquires trademark rights by "adopting" a word or symbol not currently used by its competitors and by establishing through exclusive use in the marketplace a connection in consumers' minds between that mark and the company as a source of a particular product. At stake in this feud over alleged misappropriations of Fanny Fern's style is not true originality, a distinctive personal quality of voice that cannot be imitated. Instead, "Fanny" seeks to "mark" a particular segment of the market as hers by excluding others from adopting "her" style of expression.

This point becomes clearer several months later when "Fanny" adopts Norris's notion of her style as a "mark" in further infighting with other *Olive Branch* contributors. Fern responds to a published letter signed "Harry Honeysuckle," an *Olive Branch* contributor who protests that *he* is not one of those scoundrels mimicking her style; indeed, he claims, *his* style has been stolen too. Not persuaded, "Fanny" accuses him of imitating her "models":

> Did you know, my dear "Honeysuckle," that plants sometimes *choke* each other? You'll die of *Fern-strangle* one of these days, if you don't leave off shooting round a corner at my *"Model" factory!* Don't you suppose I see the

32 *Olive Branch*, 3 July 1852.

> *spurious* models? Don't you suppose *every body else* sees them? and does any but the genuine coin ever get counterfeited, hey? Don't I appreciate the unintentional compliment? "Steal my thunder"? They can't do it Harry. It has "*my mark*" on it. Every body sees the theft. You'd better let me alone, "Harry," if you don't want to be a "FIXED"*![33]

By using the word "model," Fern puns on the titles of a series of sketches she published in the *Olive Branch*, each of which used the word "model" in the title as an adjective describing either the best or the worst of a class of people.[34] For instance, her negative "Model Lady" "puts her children out to nurse and tends lapdogs," and her positive "Model Boarder" "goes through the catechism to his landlady without a wry face." Fern extended this series from April through August, which implies that it was popular with both readers of the *Olive Branch* and editors of exchange papers, who found these very short sketches (most a single paragraph and no longer than three column inches) ideal targets for scissoring. By imitating her "models," Harry had thus tried to insinuate himself into a patch she had earlier cultivated and the luxuriant greenery of which she was still harvesting. Harry, in short, was not welcome to hoe the same plot.

Fern threatens to "fix" Harry for his production of "*spurious* models," using the same adjective she used to describe her own imitation of Mrs. Partington. However, she acknowledges the implicit compliment of his theft and the powerful gaze of "every body" also seeing the theft and, implicitly, the compliment. For those who have *not* seen the theft, she draws their attention to it (much as her editors draw attention to uncredited reprinting by exchanges), and thus draws attention to the desirability of her style as a "model." That is, she berates Harry Honeysuckle's production of a "spurious Fern" to promote the consumption of models properly marked by the name Fanny Fern.

As reprinting of her sketches continued and she published books of collected and newly written sketches, Fanny Fern and her editors increasingly drew attention to alleged encroachments on her name in addition to encroachments on her style, indicating that her name had become widely enough known to be a valuable commodity. Earlier, she and her editors policed her stylistic territory, building up a recognizable product identity that would encourage readers to seek that product from "Fanny Fern" rather than from other sources who circulated a similar product. Once the value

33 *Olive Branch*, 16 Oct, 1852.

34 The sketches published under the Fanny Fern signature in the *Olive Branch* in this series are "The Model Baby" (3 Apr. 1852); "The Model Gentleman," "The Model Lady," and "The Model Boarder" (24 Apr. 1852); "The Model Editor" (22 May 1852); "The Model Beau" (12 June 1852); "The Model Widow," "The Model Widower," and "The Model Doctor" (26 June 1852); "The Model Slanderer" (10 July 1852); "The Model Parvenu" and "The Model Sea Captain" (24 July 1852); "The Model Step-Mother," "The Model Grandmamma," and "The Model Grandpapa" (7 Aug. 1852).

of her sketches had been established and had made her name a recognizable commodity, that name had the power to confer value in the other direction, making any product bearing her pseudonym valuable. "What's in a name?" asks the *Musical World & Times* in a review of Fanny Fern's first juvenile book, *Little Ferns.* Reporting a delay in the publication of the book due to heavy advance demand, the *World* answers its own question: "[T]he name of FANNY FERN alone commanded this unprecedented sale. What, then, is in a name? It would seem that there are a great many thousand dollars in *some* names."[35] In addition to reports of imitations of her style of writing, at various times her editors at the *Olive Branch,* the *True Flag*, and the *Musical World & Times* reported that Fern's articles were reprinted without her name or were reprinted with the name of another affixed to them, that articles not written by her were attributed to her and then widely reprinted with that attribution, and that others were falsely reporting that Fanny Fern was writing articles under other pseudonyms.[36]

Exactly how would a reader have been able to decipher this continual slipping and shifting of authorial identity? A laudatory unsigned review of *Fern Leaves* in the May 1853 *Musical World*, most likely by its editor and Fern's brother Richard Storrs Willis, makes extravagant claims concerning the absolute distinctiveness of Fern's style and the impossibility of such confusion. Noting the large number of imitators, he claims that readers must quickly realize that it requires "genius" to pull off her style and that attempts at imitation only demonstrate just how distinctive Fern's genius is:

> Imitators are mere satellites; and, in the nature of things, they can never rise to an equality with the central luminary around which they revolve and from which they derive their twilight radiance. They are useful, however; inasmuch as their vapidness serves admirably as a foil to the excellence of the brilliant original; the contrast rendering the beauties of the model all the more apparent and enjoyable. Fanny Fern can succeed in this style, but her imitators cannot: with her it is natural; with them it is assumed. Style (as Carlyle might express it) is an objective manifestation of one's subjectivity – it is the *form of the mind*, – it must fit the thought as the skin fits the body;

35 *Musical World & Times*, 10 Dec. 1853.

36 On articles being reprinted without her name, see the "Beautiful Sentiment" incident described later. On articles being reprinted with other names, see *Musical World & Times*, 9 July 1853, accusing the *Home Journal* of passing off a Fern sketch as "Laurie Todd on Spinsters." The *Home Journal* did, indeed, print "Sunshine and Young Mothers" (*Olive Branch*, 30 July 1852) as by Grant Thornburn writing as "Laurie Todd" (25 June 1853). On attribution of articles not by her to her, see, e.g. *Musical World & Times*, 9 Apr. 1853, on the attribution of "Gentlemanly Accomplishments" to Fern (The *Olive Branch* printed "Gentlemanly Accomplishments" on 16 Apr. 1853 attributed to Fanny Fern). On claims that Fanny Fern wrote under other pseudonyms, see Fern's "letter" to the editor of the *True Flag*, 12 Mar. 1853. Similar letters to Bonner also appear in the *New York Ledger* after she began writing for him.

and it is just as ridiculous to "try on" another's style as it would be to try on another's skin.[37]

Willis's metaphor elides the instability of Fern's presence in the periodical marketplace, stabilizing and naturalizing this presence through the metaphor of body and skin. In a periodical marketplace where sketches were reprinted and reprinted again, with the inevitable accretion of errors, changes, and edits, the shape of Fern's very skin changed; and, if we follow Willis's logic, would her subjectivity also have changed? Would the reader of a tenth-generation reprint of one of her squibs have encountered the "same" Fern-y subjectivity as a reader of the squib would in its original publication context in the *World*? And exactly how could readers discern the "objective" nature of the subjectivity of a woman whose true identity was, in early 1853, still not generally known? Fern's periodical readers might be more accurately described as reading her clothing, not her skin, and as the exchanges in the *Olive Branch* make clear, imitation of her style of clothing was rampant.

Even Fanny Fern's editors, those who presumably would have been most intimately acquainted with the author and her style, fell prey to the confusion made inevitable by reprinting. In late 1853, for instance, in the *Olive Branch*, the editor printed a letter from a reader, G. L. Lane. Lane's letter asks about a sentimental sketch titled "Crushed Jewels," describing the death of young children, which appeared in a Boston daily newspaper several weeks earlier and was credited to Fanny Fern. Mr. Lane points out that the *Olive Branch* previously published the article under the name of its "original" contributor, Patience Pepper, and he asks, "Does Fanny use other people's good things, or is this the work of other hands?"[38] The editor sheepishly responds: "Our correspondent is just in time with his correction, as we need blowing up quite as much as anybody in the matter. We saw the article in question in the Herald, and supposing it one of Fanny Fern's from her book, we transferred it to the columns of the fourth page of this paper, where those who have never seen it, can admire it, and give credit where it belongs – viz: to our gifted correspondent 'Patience Pepper.' We stand pretty much in the same attitude of the newspaper–man who copied his own editorials." A reader turning to the Ladies' Department on page 4 sees, uncorrected, the text of "Crushed Jewels" attributed to Fanny Fern.[39]

37 *Musical World & Times*, 28 May 1853. 38 *Olive Branch*, 1 Oct. 1853.

39 "Crushed Jewels" did, indeed, appear originally under "Patience Pepper's" name. *Olive Branch*, 10 July 1852. Lane specifies that the misidentified reprint appeared in the "Daily Herald, for Sept. 21st," most likely the *Boston Daily Herald*. The *Olive Branch* was a four-page paper printed on a single sheet. Pages 1 and 4 would have been printed simultaneously, and, this anecdote implies, these pages were set and printed first, before pages 2 and 3, which would have been printed on the reverse of the same sheet. Norris may have been forced to leave the uncorrected item on page 4 rather than sacrifice the entire print run. As Fanny Fern no longer wrote for the *Olive Branch* in October 1853, Norris had access to Fern's work only through reprinting.

Once Fanny Fern's name has been affixed to an item by someone else, admits Norris, he is powerless to distinguish between his own contributors. Indeed, as he admits, in the shifting waves of exchanged text, editors sometimes cannot identify their *own* skins, let alone those of their contributors, and they fall prey to reprinting their own editorials as if they were by someone else.

In June of 1853, several months prior to the misattributed "Crushed Jewels" incident, Fern had stopped contributing pieces to the *Olive Branch*. By the close of 1853, when it became clear that Fern would not resume her contributions of original materials to the *Olive Branch*, the paper also stopped reprinting her sketches from other periodicals. After the publication of *Ruth Hall* at the end of 1854, which bitterly satirizes Norris and the *Olive Branch* through its depiction of Mr. Lescom and the *Standard*, the paper became actively hostile to Fern's work. By 1855, Fern was under contract to write exclusively for the *Ledger* for a high weekly salary. As the *New York Ledger* notes with smug satisfaction in an 1856 paragraph titled "Sour Grapes," "[b]y the way, one of FANNY'S articles which we published a few weeks ago, and which was extensively copied in the country papers, *without her name being attached to it*, appeared in the Olive Branch last week under the caption 'A BEAUTIFUL SENTIMENT.' The Olive Branch . . . is the most bitter enemy FANNY has in the newspaper field, and yet *it* compliments her writings when her name is not connected with them, and the editor does not suspect her to be the author."[40] Here, the presence or absence of Fern's name changes the value of the unchanged textual artifact, making it acceptable or unacceptable, worthy or unworthy of reprinting, depending on what the editor thinks of Fanny Fern. Her name, or lack thereof, thus powerfully shaped the circulation and reading of her texts.[41]

"They must purchase themselves out of bondage": *Ruth Hall*'s construction of Fanny Fern through Floy

Having established some of the complexities and ambiguities of literary proprietorship visible throughout Fanny Fern's periodical career, and most particularly and acutely in the early years of that career, I return to *Ruth Hall* and the narrative it constructs of the relation of a woman periodical writer

40 *New York Ledger*, 8 Mar. 1856. See *Olive Branch*, 8 Mar. 1856, for the uncredited printing of Fern's "Beautiful Sentiment." In a similar vein, the *Musical World* notes that the *Dayton Daily City Item* both criticizes Fanny Fern's book as fit only for the sewer and reprints her articles without her name as the author. *Musical World & Times*, 19 Mar. 1853.

41 Michele Foucault's analysis of the function of the author's name in the circulation of texts has influenced the framing of this discussion. "What Is an Author?" in *The Foucault Reader*, ed. Paul Rabinow (New York: Pantheon, 1984), 107–8.

to her literary property. About two-thirds of the way through the novel, the eponymous heroine, whose pseudonym Floy has effectively hidden her real identity, reads and sorts through an assortment of fan letters forwarded to her by Mr. Lescom, editor of the *Standard*, for which she writes a weekly column. Ruth is a widow, and she has struggled valiantly since her husband's death to support herself and her two daughters despite the difficulty of finding work and the callousness of relatives who will not support her financially. The fan letters that do not interest her, she hands to her young daughter Nettie as playthings. She hands to Nettie a letter from a Southern reader proposing marriage on the basis of his acquaintance with her through her newspaper columns. He "confessed to one hundred negroes, 'but hoped that the strength and ardor of the attachment with which the perusal of her articles had inspired him, would be deemed sufficient atonement for this in her Northern eyes. . . . Would she not smile on him? She should have a box at the opera, a carriage, and servants in livery, and the whole heart and soul of Victor Le Pont.'" (pp. 152–3). She reserves for herself and takes more seriously a letter from a book publisher offering to publish a collection of her newspaper pieces, paying her either a royalty on each copy sold *or* an $800 flat fee "for her copyright." Ruth, who has metamorphosed from an economic innocent into a shrewd businesswoman during the course of the novel, weighs the evidence of her popularity, including her fan letters, against the security of $800 in hand and decides to take a risk. She bangs her fist on the table and declares that her book "*shall!*" sell enough to repay the risk many times over (p. 153).

This scene offers a clear schematic of the choices available to Ruth: either remarry and become little more than a high-class slave to a man or maintain her economic independence and absolute self-possession through authorship. Clearly, Ruth has already made her choice and does not even consider the first option, but its presence powerfully shapes the narrative. Fern leaves no doubts about the risks to a woman's selfhood if she sells herself into marriage in order to gain financial security and social status. Before Ruth takes up authorship, she tries to support herself by sewing, and then unsuccessfully tries to get a job teaching. Ruth only finds the motivation to try authorship after witnessing the horrible fate of Mary Leon, a woman who had been her friend before the death of Harry Hall, Ruth's husband. When Ruth first meets Mary, she is married to a wealthy man, and Mary knows that her husband considers her merely an ornamental appendage to his fine establishment. As she tells Ruth, "The chain is none the less galling, because its links are golden" (p. 52). Just before taking up her pen, Ruth discovers, entirely by chance, that Mary's husband locked her up in an insane asylum because he tired of her. Ruth finds out, too late, that Mary was calling out her name as she lay dying, and Ruth and her daughter are the only mourners at Mary's graveside funeral. Mary Leon is an extreme example of the plight of the woman dispossessed through marriage: she first possesses worldly goods that are not really hers, and which instead evidence her figurative enslavement to her husband; then, when her husband strips her of all of those goods and of her identity as wife and mother, she inevitably sinks into the insanity from which she allegedly already suffered when her husband committed her to the asylum.[42]

In her review of *Ruth Hall* in the *Una*, Elizabeth Cady Stanton emphasizes just this trajectory in Ruth's story, her movement from the slavery and dependence first of marriage and then of penurious, dependent widowhood before she begins writing, to absolute self-possession through paid labor: "The great lesson taught in Ruth Hall is that God has given to woman sufficient brain and muscle to work out her own destiny unaided and alone. Her case, like ten thousand others, goes to prove the common notion that God made woman to depend on man, a romance, and not a fact of every-day life."[43] Most other reviewers, including another reviewer in the *Una*, Caroline Healy Dall, read the novel as autobiography, but they attacked Fern for her unwomanly public censure of her family through her satiric portrayals of them in the novel.[44] Stanton, however, proclaims that the narrative of Ruth's life should be read with the same respect accorded to a slave narrative. Rebuking the writer of a negative review of *Ruth Hall* in the *Anti-Slavery Standard*, Stanton instructs her readers to "read 'Ruth Hall,' as you would read the life of 'Solomon Northrup,' a Frederick Douglass, – as you would listen to the poor slaves in our anti-slavery meetings. . . . The next *mulatto slave* that comes North, and gets upon a platform, to tell of the cruelty and injustice of *father and brethren*, hiss him down, – read him the laws of the Mohammedans and Christian on 'filial reverence.'"[45] Stanton specifies a "mulatto slave" to make clear the irony of criticizing both the slave and Fern for a lack of "filial" reverence. In both cases, implies Stanton, the man vilified by the autobiographer is both oppressor and father: through her autobiographical novel, Fern criticizes her own father for his cruelty and indifference to her after she was widowed, and in a slave narrative (typically written by a man born into slavery in the South), the mulatto slave criticizes his cruel owner and master, who fathered him by raping a slave woman (as Frederick Douglass implies in his narrative). By

42 Susan K. Harris finds a similar function for the Mary Leon episode, grouping it with the extended anecdote about Mrs. Skiddy, Ruth's landlady, who, like Mary, is deserted by a husband but who, unlike Mary, triumphantly claims her economic independence. *19th-Century American Women's Novels: Interpretive Strategies* (New York: Cambridge University Press, 1990), 121–2.

43 Elizabeth Cady Stanton, "Ruth Hall," *Una*, Feb. 1855, 30.

44 For the most comprehensive account of the reception of the novel, see Warren, *Fanny Fern*, chap. 8. Linda M. Grasso explicates the terms of the debate between Stanton and Dall over the proper reading of *Ruth Hall*, focusing on the place of female anger in feminist reform rhetoric and its relationship to anger expressed in service to abolitionism. *The Artistry of Anger: Black and White Women's Literature in American, 1820–1860* (Chapel Hill: University of North Carolina Press, 2002), 136–44.

45 Stanton, "Ruth Hall," 29.

specifically referencing the narrative of Solomon Northrup, who was born free in the North and kidnapped South into slavery, Stanton drives home the slave-wife analogy from a different angle – white women are born free, and marriage "enslaves" them, taking away the freedom they enjoy before marriage.[46]

In the language of feminist reform of the 1850s, then, Fern, representing her own situation through that of her heroine, Ruth, had "purchased" herself out of bondage through her authorial labors, and she was entitled to rebuke those who had tried to keep her and other women economically "enslaved." As Paulina Wright Davis argued at an 1853 women's rights' convention in New York in a speech reprinted in the *Una*, "Who ever can *pay* for himself, and support himself, may be free. When a man's intrinsic manhood is really worth as much as he will bring in the market, he may be his own purchaser, and pass, even under the laws of slavery from the condition of bondage to that of freedom."[47] Davis urges women to recognize this truth, to "*go to work*. They must press into every avenue, every open door, that custom and law leave unguarded, aye, and themselves withdraw the bolts and bars from others still closed against them, that they may enter and take possession. They *must* purchase themselves out of bondage."[48] The final chapter of *Ruth Hall* dramatically demonstrates Ruth's own self-purchase by reproducing the certificate attesting to her ownership of $10,000 worth of bank stock shares (shares purchased with her earnings from that book collection of her newspaper sketches for which she might have been paid $800). As a woman who writes, secure possession of her literary property guarantees her self-possession.

The novel notices in passing the ways that reprinting troubles Ruth's absolute control over the circulation of her property and her self, but the threat is minimized. As her first editor, Mr. Lescom, tells her, "Your very first articles are copied . . . into many of my exchanges. . . . A good sign for you Mrs. Hall; a good test of your popularity" (p. 130). He also notes, and then regrets telling her when she asks for higher pay, that letters from readers in other states have come in asking to subscribe to his paper because her articles are to appear there regularly. In a chapter entitled "Soliloquy of a sub-editor," Horace Gates (the subeditor of the *Irving Magazine* under Ruth's brother, Hyacinth Ellet) soliloquizes about his working days, during which he assembles a substantial portion of the *Irving* magazine by scissoring articles by Fanny Fern and others. However, only we as readers hear this soliloquy on the mechanisms of reprinting – Ruth does not.

46 Northrup was held as a slave in Louisiana from 1841 to early 1853, when his freedom was secured; his *Twelve Years a Slave: Narrative of Solomon Northrup, a Citizen of New-York, Kidnapped in Washington in 1841, and Rescued in 1853*, was published in the spring of 1853 by Derby & Miller, virtually simultaneously with their publication of Fern Leaves from Fanny's Portfolio.

47 "P. W. Davis's Remarks at the Convention," *Una*, Sep. 1853, 137–8.

48 Ibid., 138.

Although Ruth understands reprinting's usefulness as a gauge of popularity, she remains aloof from the chaotic process of exchange publication that swirls around her. As discussed at the opening of this chapter, she vanquishes her second editor, Mr. Tibbetts, when he threatens to bring out an unauthorized collection of her sketches, and once that threat has been removed, her authorized collection of sketches conveniently allows her to move above and beyond the fray, finally claiming the possession of her bank stock certificate as evidence of her book's large readership. When her sketches earlier appeared in the *Standard* and the *Pilgrim*, her audience was fractured: readers encountered her work in its first publication in two newspapers under editors who wanted to exploit her but were unsympathetic to her aims. Through subsequent reprintings of her sketches in exchange papers, her audience further fractures as her sketches appeared in multiple contexts beyond her control (indeed, we might imagine that the Southern slave master who writes to propose marriage read her sketches as reprinted in a Southern paper and that the process of reprinted circulation has transformed Floy into a potential slave-wife, like Mary Leon). In contrast, the common experience of reading Ruth's book organizes her later reading audience – these readers all read a volume she organizes and authorizes and which presents her work only in the context of other pieces of her work. In Fern's fictionalization of her career, no disputes over the nature of the woman writer or her sketches even seem imaginable because by the end of the novel Ruth has claimed firm control over her self-representation. Even misinformation spread by her family and the threat of unfair reviews inevitably fall in the face of her book and its power to manage its audience.

As the publication of *Life and Beauties* shortly after the appearance of *Ruth Hall* reminds us, however, Fanny Fern's early pieces in the *Olive Branch* and the *True Flag* and subsequent exchange reprintings invited just such a dispute over the "real" nature of the woman and her sketches. Although she strategically omits such disputes from *Ruth Hall*, such disputes were inextricably bound up with the wide circulation of her sketches through exchange reprinting, and such unauthorized periodical reprinting enabled the publication of *Ruth Hall*. That is, the legitimate and illegitimate – the authorized and the unauthorized – circulations of "Fanny Fern" in print were inseparable and interdependent. As H. Long & Brother's advertisements for *Life and Beauties* suggest, the book functioned not as a replacement for *Ruth Hall* or for Fern's authorized collection of her newspaper sketches, *Fern Leaves*, but as a companion for both, a key to the life of the author and the true character of her writings. "Who is Ruth Hall?" the advertisement asks; "Is Ruth Hall Fanny Fern or somebody else? And if Fanny Fern is not Ruth Hall, who is Fanny Fern?"[49] After the teasing questions, the advertisement shifts to certainty, describing how *Life and Beauties* "presents vivid, life-like

49 *True Flag*, 24 Feb. 1855.

pictures of the charming and brilliant author of Fern Leaves and Ruth Hall, at her own fireside, in the Editor's Sanctum, in the street, at church, and everywhere, and in every position she is the same fascinating woman." Even readers who have read Fanny Fern's sketches in the newspaper or in book form or who have read *Ruth Hall* will find that the volume offers them additional materials they have not yet read and from which they will receive the same pleasure and satisfaction in reading: "In this volume, several of Fanny Fern's efforts appear for the first time in book form. The reader will find they possess the same attractive features which characterise [*sic*] all her productions."

In notices concerning *Life and Beauties* published in the *True Flag*, William Moulton characterizes the sketches anthologized as "lively and racy to a degree" and as exhibiting a "peculiar freedom of expression." In addition, he claims that Fern "suppressed" these sketches by not including them in *Fern Leaves*.[50] By publishing a selection of allegedly scandalous suppressed sketches and coupling them with the allegedly suppressed scandalous facts of Fern's biography, the compiler of *Life and Beauties* clearly aimed to damage Fern's personal reputation. However, *Life and Beauties* could not succeed in its commercial aim (that is, selling many copies of *Life and Beauties*) without Fern's success.[51] Furthermore, if *Life and Beauties* sold well, that additional circulation became part of the Fanny Fern phenomenon, even though that circulation was beyond Fern's control. A brief review of *Life and Beauties* in *Graham's Magazine* articulates this symbiotic relationship between the legitimate and illegitimate Ferns. Argues the reviewer, *Life and Beauties* may contain

> such waifs and estrays [*sic*] as the first collection did *not* embrace – such as were over spicy, a little beyond the most distant mark proposed – gathered together and commented on, it is true, by no kindly hand or heart . . . yet

50 *True Flag*, 24 Feb. 1855. Scholars have tended to take this claim at face value, but Moulton's claim that *Life and Beauties* consists largely of "suppressed" sketches is demonstrably untrue. Among the sketches that Moulton selected and that also appeared in *Fern Leaves* are "The Best of Men Have Their Failings," "A Lady on Money Matters" (retitled by Moulton as "Fanny Fern on Money Matters"), "Two in Heaven," "'Summer Days'; or, The Young Wife's Affliction" (quoted almost entirely in a biographical chapter in *Life and Beauties* titled "The Husband's Death"), "The Orphan, or the Life at Rook Farm" ("The Orphan" in *Life and Beauties*), "The Flirt," "The Invalid Wife" (in *Life and Beauties* under the title "The Wife's Devotion," a title assigned to it in *True Flag*, 16 Oct. 1852, when it was reprinted from the original untitled appearance in *Olive Branch*, 2 Oct. 1852), "The Angel Child," "I Can't," "A Night-Watch with a Dead Infant," "The Cross and the Crown," and "A Chapter on Clergymen." Note also that Moulton included items that Fern could not have included in *Fern Leaves* because they first appeared after *Fern Leaves* had already gone to press (e.g., "Don't Disturb Him!" *Olive Branch*, 9 Apr. 1853, reprinted in *True Flag*, 30 Apr. 1853).

51 My reading of this relationship thus differs from that of Lauren Berlant, who claims that *Life and Beauties*' purpose was "simultaneously to capitalize on and to undercut the vast popularity of *Ruth Hall*." "The Female Woman: Fanny Fern and the Form of Sentiment," *American Literary History* 3, no. 3 (1991): 429.

> still very interesting, indeed, indispensable to all who would study with calm analytic science that extraordinary phenomenon of Fanny Fernism which combines in merry union the most extraordinary and startling incongruities on record. If it be true that our merits are best set forth by our demerits and our successes by our failures, our great qualities by our littleness . . . then we shall like the Ferns none the worse for this collection of amusing, malicious mischief, which, whatever its object was, cannot fail to be regarded by the "wicked world" as uncommonly lively reading.[52]

Despite the alleged lower quality of the sketches, argues the reviewer, the sketches are nevertheless essential as lively reading in and of themselves, and are, even more importantly, an essential key to an understanding of the "Ferns" found in *Fern Leaves*; all devoted students of Fern must have *both* books.

As a paragraph notice in the *True Flag* notes, the *Life and Beauties* volume was sold "uniform with" *Ruth Hall*, making clear H. Long's intention to create just such an essential link between the two books. The publisher cannily imitated the practices of legitimate publishers, who sold "uniform editions" of an author's works to solidify an author's reputation and market value. Typically, a publisher bringing out a new work by a known author would bring out new editions of the author's previous works, bound "uniform with" the author's new work, thus encouraging readers to purchase the new and the old books as a uniform set. Indeed, *Life and Beauties* is the same octavo size as *Ruth Hall*, and its binding design plays off the design of the *Ruth Hall* binding. The words "Life and Beauties" on the spine of the book are in the same size and style as the lettering of the spine of *Ruth Hall* and are surrounded by the same abstract design of curved lines. However, where the *Ruth Hall* binding features a fern design below the words "Fanny Fern," the *Life and Beauties* spine substitutes a similarly sized and placed design of a snake coiled around a steel-nibbed pen. The binding signals the book's dual status as an attack on Fern (the female "snake" who wields a pen) and as a symbiotic twin of Fern's autobiographical novel, visually constructing the two volumes as items of the same authorial oeuvre.

The symbiotic bindings resituate Fanny Fern in the early periodical context that enabled the publication of both books, a context in which unfettered reprinting rather than proprietary control of circulation was the norm. Under the sign of the Fanny Fern pseudonym, Fern's early sketches offered a multiplicity of voices and identities to readers, from sentimental to satiric and all shades in between narrated in the third person, "soliloquized" in the voice of a named character, spoken by an unidentified first person, or spoken in the first person voice of "Fanny." Even within the identifiable persona

52 "Literary Notices," *Graham's*, Aug. 1857, [179]. *Graham's* apparently reviewed a later reprint of *Life and Beauties* by Philadelphia's T. B. Peterson.

of Fanny, readers would have found it difficult to locate a stable character, let alone *the* character of the unnamed writer behind the pseudonym. In an 1852 letter to "Jack Plane," one of the many readers offering "Fanny" his hand in marriage, "Fanny" warns that his attempts to get her real name out of her editor will not succeed, and that he will fail utterly if he seeks proof of Fanny Fern's identity in "her":

> Now your only hope lies in *me*, and *such* a dance as I shall lead you! I'm a regular "Will o' the Wisp"; everything by turns, and nothing long. Sometimes I'm an old maid, sometimes a wife, then a widow, now a Jack, then a Gill [*sic*], at present a "Fanny." If there's anything I abominate it's *sameness*; no article of furniture in *my* premises stands in the same spot two days in succession. If I'd born a *twin*, I should have *poisoned t'other* one; and if I was married, and my husband told me he loved me, TWICE in *the same words*, I'd take the tongs and put him out the window.[53]

Reprinting complicated even this intentional multiplicity of voices and personae, which was at least in part under Fern's control. As a writer, she could decide to change the "self" manifested in her writings from old maid to wife or from a Jack to a Jill; but *others* could also change Fanny Fern into the anonymous author of "A Beautiful Sentiment," or they could turn Patience Pepper into Fanny Fern.

It is precisely this multiplicity and instability of "Fanny" as a print phenomenon that is missing from Fern's fictionalization of that experience through "Floy." Although Ruth Hall gains full possession of herself, her identity, and her literary property, the periodical circulation of Fanny Fern's works troubled her self-possession and proprietorship and caused her identity to remain very publicly in a state of constant crisis. The symbiotic pairing of *Ruth Hall* and *Life and Beauties* also points to a peculiar void in Fern's novelization of her life: *Life and Beauties* encompasses both biography and anthology, narrating the events of Fern's life while also collecting and reprinting her sketches in all of their multiplicity and instability; in contrast, *Ruth Hall* omits "Floy's" sketches. In *Ruth Hall*, we never actually read Ruth's articles or are told precisely what they are about or what sort of style they employ. No samples or excerpts appear, and neither the narrator nor a character ever describes the subject matter of a particular article or her articles in general (with the exception, late in the novel, of an expression of surprise from an unnamed man that she can write so convincingly about "poverty" when her brother claims that the family always supported her and she was never poor [pp. 176–7]). We learn all about the *labor* of her writing, the scratching of her pen, her throbbing brow and weary fingers, and we know what she buys with her literary earnings ("bread for her children" [p. 133]); but the novel does not represent the object produced by those

53 *Olive Branch*, 3 Mar. 1852.

laboring hands and exchanged for the money with which Ruth purchases the bread.[54]

The closest we get to those absent articles are readers' reactions to them, and many of these reactions are represented through fan letters addressed to Floy, which are "quoted" in part or "reproduced" in full in the novel. Moved in some way by those powerfully absent sketches, her readers ask for a bust of Floy for a young lady's collection, ask her to write for them (everything from family histories to poems memorializing dead family dogs and celebrating infant school "jubilees" to school compositions), thank her for the personal comfort they enjoy reading her columns, or seek her hand in marriage. These are private communications, however, from person to person, whether sincere or misguided. There are no indications that "Floy," like "Fanny," explicitly solicits these marriage proposals from fans or toys with them in public. She does not seek them, and she dismisses them without comment: like Victor Le Pont's proposal, they are meaningless pieces of paper, suitable only for child's play and essentially unrelated to her labors.

In the absence of the actual sketches, the novel clearly intends that we should rely on the reader responses that Ruth values and to which she responds to understand the true nature of "Floy."[55] Although "Fanny" warned her readers in the *Olive Branch* not to seek "Fanny Fern's" true character in her sketches, *Ruth Hall* argues that readers *can* find Ruth Hall in "Floy's" sketches. She puts aside marriage proposals and requests for her professional literary services, but she consistently responds to readers who feel they can read her heart in her sketches. "Mary R.—," an invalid, writes to says that "every week your printed words come to me, in my sick chamber, like the ministrations of some gentle friend"; Ruth responds to Mary's letter by bowing her head and offering a "grateful prayer" (pp. 136–7). Ruth decides she must write a response to a letter from "Mary Andrews," the dying wife of an alcoholic husband; this Mary writes Floy to ask her to adopt her baby when she dies because Floy is "*not* a stranger, for I have read your heart in your many writings. In them I see sympathy for the poor, the sorrowing, and the dependent; I see a tender love for helpless childhood" (p. 165). A letter from a man who claims to be "a better son, a better brother, a better husband, and a better father" because of "the words you have spoken (though unintentionally) so directly to me" prompts

54 See Kristie Hamilton's excellent reading of Ruth's literary work as "labor and not avocation" through its alignment with other forms of labor in the novel, such as sewing, and implicitly with representations of women's factory labor in the larger culture. "The Politics of Survival: Sara Parton's *Ruth Hall* and the Literature of Labor," in *Redefining the Political Novel: American Women Writers, 1797–1901*, ed. Sharon M. Harris (Knoxville: University of Tennessee Press, 1995), 101–2.

55 Maria C. Sanchez reads the absence of Floy's columns and the presence of fan letters as maintaining Ruth's genteel modesty and making her a "ghostly," "silent," "displaced," and "deferred" figure rather than as the wailing and highly embodied figure I locate. "Re-possessing Individualism in Fanny Fern's *Ruth Hall*," *Arizona Quarterly* 56, no. 4 (2000): 49.

Ruth's tears of gratitude, as she feels that the letter "repay[s]" her for her hard hours of literary labor (p. 183). These readers all believe that they have found the true character of the author in her sketches, and Ruth's responses to them confirm that they truly have. In the absence of "Floy's" sketches, the novel presents us with these scenes of an embodied Ruth crying and praying, inviting us to read her body as representing the truth of those sketches.

One key reader combines this ability to read her heart and life in her sketches with commercial sense. Mr. John Walter, editor of the *Household Messenger*, sits puzzling over Floy's sketches in the *Standard* not because he seeks personal consolation, but because he recognizes that a connection between "Floy's" name and the name of his paper would have "advertising" value. He reads her sketches as collectively voicing "a wail from her inmost soul," "a whole history of wrong, and suffering, and bitter sorrow" (p. 140). He seeks her out in the flesh, wanting to confirm this truth by reading it in her face. By withholding "Floy's" sketches, the novel asks us to imagine them as this univocal, autobiographical wail, a wail uniquely distinguishable from the writing surrounding it and uniquely valuable to readers (and to the newspapers who publish it); and in "Floy's" wail, readers who read correctly find Ruth Hall body and soul. By establishing this equivalence between sketch and writer, between pseudonym and true identity (Floy and Floy's sketches = Ruth Hall and Ruth's voice), the novel also suggests that readers apply the same interpretive strategies to the clearly autobiographical novel and its author (if Floy's sketches = Ruth Hall's wail from the heart, and Ruth Hall = Fanny Fern, then Ruth's wail = Fanny Fern's sketches). The absent presence of Floy's sketches and the presence of her more fully described body substitute for and write over the material history of Fanny Fern in print, obliterating the traces of the multiple and unstable "Fanny" that enabled *Life and Beauties* by substituting the "wail from her inmost soul" and the body of a widowed woman author for this multiplicity. Fern thus used *Ruth Hall* and its fictional heroine to construct a new, more stable Fanny Fern, subject to and capable of possession, proprietorship, and control, and who would author-ize future book and periodical manifestations.

In writing over her early periodical career, Fern also wrote out another crucial element of the instability of her early career – her second husband, Samuel P. Farrington. Ruth Hall can claim that bank stock certificate representing royalties from sales of her book at the end of the novel in her own name because she is a widow and thus a feme sole. As Maria C. Sanchez observes of this moment, the bank stock certificate witnesses the "birth" of "the public persona, 'Ruth Hall' . . . as a property-owner and economic agent. . . . [A]lthough it was the death of Ruth's husband which precipitated her poverty, it was only as a widow that Ruth could have acceded to such public transaction. . . . The fact that in 1854, black women's names continuously appeared on public documents as possessions in and of (but not for) themselves lends the bank note its extraordinary nature; to own bank stock a woman must own, at the very least, her own self, and thus the bank note serves as a kind a kind of self title."[56] No husband can claim Ruth's royalties, and she requires no trustee to oversee her separate estate. She thus owns both herself and her literary properties. Like a slave with free papers, implies the novel, she now has independent passage in the world.[57]

This implicit analogy between Ruth and an emancipated slave doubly mystifies the status of Ruth and of her factual analogue and creator, however. As Lauren Berlant rightly argues, Ruth's situation is *not* exactly parallel to that of a slave with free papers. Juxtaposing the novel's celebration of the bank stock certificate with Harriet Jacobs's melancholy contemplation of the papers certifying that her New York benefactors have purchased her freedom in *Incidents in the Life of a Slave Girl*, Berlant explains, "Both women have struggled to procure these papers, but while the one [Jacobs's] denotes the minimal unit of freedom experienced by an American citizen, the other denotes a successful negotiation of the national-capitalist public sphere, a profitable commodification of female pain and heroism in an emerging industry of female cultural workers."[58] Although Berlant's correction accurately applies to an equivalence between Ruth as a fictional character and "Linda Brent" as Jacobs's autobiographical persona, the correction is not entirely accurate with respect to Fern's life history. A portion of the profits produced by Fern's commodification of female experience in the early years of her career did not legally belong to her. At the time that Fanny Fern signed the contract arranging for publication of *Fern Leaves* and at the time some months later when she received her first profits from the sales of the volume, she believed herself to be, and very well may have been in fact, legally married to a man she despised.

The woman then legally known as Sara P. Farrington began publishing in the *Olive Branch* in July 1851, five months after Samuel Farrington advertised in the Boston papers that he would not be held financially liable for her support.[59] A year and a half later, when she signed a contract with Derby & Miller for the publication of *Fern Leaves* on February 10, 1853, she was still estranged and living apart from Samuel Farrington. She was not, however, to her knowledge, legally separated or divorced from him – only a firm belief that she was still married to him could have induced her to sign the contract for publication of her first book under her legal married name,

56 Sanchez, "Re-possessing Individualism," 48.

57 See Grasso for a brief, convincing account of how Fern's novel shows a clear debt to the literary strategies of the slave narrative tradition. *Artistry of Anger*, 145–6.

58 Berlant, "Female Woman," 448.

59 Advertisement of Samuel P. Farrington, *Boston Daily Bee*, 25 Feb. 1851, [3]. Clipping in Fanny Fern and Ethel Parton Papers, Sophia Smith Collection, Smith College Libraries (hereinafter Fanny Fern Papers).

"Sara P. Farrington." In May of the same year, she signed an amended contract with respect to *Fern Leaves* under the same name.[60] The book hit the stores on June 1, 1853, and if Derby's advertisements are to be believed, it had sold nearly 40,000 copies by September.[61] On September 4, 1853, J. C. Derby's lawyer, Samuel P. Blatchford, wrote to a lawyer in Chicago asking him to verify that Samuel Farrington had divorced Sara in Illinois. On September 8, while awaiting confirmation, a woman now signing her name "Sara P. Eldredge" entered into a new contract with Derby & Miller. The new contract specifies terms for the continuing publication of *Fern Leaves* and declares, "All former contracts in relation to [*Fern Leaves*] . . . are hereby revoked and declared null & void."[62]

Shortly thereafter, Derby received a letter from his attorney enclosing a certified copy of an Illinois divorce decree severing the marital ties between Samuel and Sara Farrington on the ground that Sara had deserted Samuel.[63] He also forwarded to Derby a letter from Chicago lawyer James H. Collins, reporting on his investigation. Without having been told that Sara Farrington was Fanny Fern, Collins had deduced her identity, and the notion that he was (at least indirectly) writing to "Fanny" turned Collins's head. He begins his letter with a businesslike report of the facts and the application of the law to the facts, but the knowledge of Fern's identity causes him to veer off course, first into joking comments on the loose divorce laws and practices of neighboring states Kentucky and Indiana (in the 1850s, Indiana was a notorious migratory divorce haven),[64] and second into flirtatious commentary on the consequences of "Fanny's" new status as a "free" woman:

> I Enclose a certified Decree in the case of Farrington v. Farrington as you request. . . . Also a copy of the First & Third Section of the Divorce Act of this State – These sections declare the causes for which a Divorce a vinculo may be had & the condition of the partners. . . . Although the act does not declare that both parties may marry again, yet such is the construction after law – There

60 Contract between Derby & Miller and Sara P. Farrington, 2 May 1853, Fanny Fern Papers. The February contract does not survive but is clearly referenced in the amended contract.

61 Geary, "Domestic Novel," 382.

62 Contract between Derby & Miller and Sara P. Eldredge, 8 Sep. 1853, Fanny Fern Papers. See also Contract between Derby & Miller and Sara P. Eldredge, 6 Sep. 1835, with respect to *Fern Leaves Second Series* and *Little Ferns* – two days earlier, she believed herself to be divorced.

63 Samuel P. Blatchford to J. C. Derby, 17 Sep. 1853, Fanny Fern Papers. Derby's letters to Blatchford and Blatchford's to James H. Collins are not present, but the chronology and the content of these letters can be reconstructed through the extant letters.

64 States became "migratory divorce havens" by passing relatively liberal divorce laws and by not looking too closely into whether or not a complainant had met residency requirements. In the early 1850s, Indiana was the most (in)famous migratory divorce haven. Nelson Manfred Blake, *The Road to Reno: A History of Divorce in the United States* (New York: Macmillan, 1962), chap. 9. Glenda Riley, *Divorce: An American Tradition* (New York: Oxford University Press, 1991), chap. 4.

> is no inhibition upon either party – The Decree is not as full or formal as I always draw up in such cases, but it is, I think, sufficient, and compared to our loose Kentucky, or *Hoosier* practices – You may therefore advise "Fanny Fern" (for it is understood here that the Divorced lady is Fanny herself) that she is a *free* woman and no longer subject to her late lord Samuel – That she is absolutely divorced and the bands dissolved, & she free from all marriage obligations and at liberty to contract matrimony when & with whom she likes.[65]

Indeed, after the dry preliminaries, Collins's letter could pass for a letter in the *Olive Branch* from one of "Fanny's" admirers proposing marriage.[66] Like "Jack Plane," who believed he could read the truth of "Fanny" in her newspaper columns, Collins's letter implies that he had read the truth about Sara Farrington in Fanny Fern's columns, and the truth he found was that Sara/Fanny was a flirt anxious to get back into sexual circulation, not a shrewd author looking to secure her literary properties.

In forwarding Collins's letter to Derby, Samuel Blatchford repeats, in an entirely formal mode, his correspondent's advice, adding that Samuel Farrington "can never question the legality of his divorce, or set up at any time hereafter any rights as husband of the defendant either in her person or property."[67] Unfortunately, the copy of the divorce decree Collins procured bears only the date of the copy's certification, not the date that the divorce became effective. Furthermore, as Fern's biographer Joyce Warren notes, the original court records were destroyed in the Great Chicago Fire. Still, considering that the divorce law of Illinois required one year's residence prior to obtaining a divorce on the part of the complainant and required that the period of desertion by the absent spouse claimed as a ground for divorce be at least two years in length,[68] it seems likely that Fern was, indeed, still Mrs. Samuel Farrington when she entered into her original contract with Derby & Miller in February 1853. The cancellation of the original contract and entering into a new contract in September thus had a dual purpose – to distinguish postdivorce from predivorce profits from sales of the volume and to properly bind Sarah Eldredge as a feme sole to the terms of her agreement with Derby & Miller. Although Samuel Farrington had no legal claim to the literary properties Fern created after he divorced her, the profits

65 Jas. H. Collins to Saml. Blatchford, 8 Sep. 1853, Fanny Fern Papers.

66 Interpreting this same sequence of events and documents, Warren focuses exclusively on the advice about property in these letters and surmises that Derby and Fern specifically asked about the status of her property in order to fend off an illegitimate attempt by Farrington to claim Sara's literary earnings. *Fanny Fern* 202–3. However, as my analysis makes clear, Farrington very well may have had a legally legitimate (if unjust) claim to the royalties from *Fern Leaves*.

67 Samuel P. Blatchford to J. C. Derby, 17 Sep. 1853, Fanny Fern Papers.

68 The enclosure to Collins's letter is absent in the Fanny Fern papers, but Farrington clearly sued for and obtained the divorce under the 1845 Illinois divorce statute. *Revised Statutes of the State of Illinois* (Springfield: Walters & Weber, 1845), chap 33, sec. 1 and 3.

from the sale of *Fern Leaves* may have lawfully belonged to him. Elizabeth Cady Stanton's assessment of the significance of the narrative presented in *Ruth Hall* was more accurate than she realized: Fanny Fern *had* "purchased herself out of bondage" to Samuel Farrington, a man whose existence she does not acknowledge in the novel and refused to acknowledge for the rest of her life. Or, more accurately, Fanny Fern, who had "escaped" from the conjugal home and had been living her life as if she were actually a free woman, had been "emancipated" by her marital master without her knowledge or consent. A few months later, *Life and Beauties* would describe Samuel's divorce as a sort of slave auction, with Samuel taking the part of the master selling his slave/wife, Sara: "[F]rom the auction mart of a western court, Mr. F. gave out three warnings; cried – 'Going! – going!! – gone!!!' and legally knocked down his wife with the hammer of divorce."[69]

Parton v. Fleming; or, Fanny Fern v. Mrs. James Parton

After *Life and Beauties* exposed Fanny Fern's "true" identity (and her status as a divorcee and the name of her ex-husband), she made this exposure work to her advantage by making public and visible the connection between the embodied author and her print manifestation in her sketches. On January 5, 1856, she married a third time, to James Parton, and, having learned from her experiences, she entered into a prenuptial agreement to create a separate estate for her literary properties. The agreement specifies the property that Sara Payson Eldredge held as a feme sole before their marriage ("Funds invested and to be invested, Stock in Bank or corporate institutions, the Copy right of and to Books & publications, Contracts and other effects and interests"), and James Parton "covenants and agrees to and with" his soon-to-be wife that "Sara shall have, hold, possess, own, manage, use, control, and enjoy" her property "and the income, profits, interest, dividends and payments" accruing from the property "as if she were a feme sole."[70]

69 *Life and Beauties*, 30. *Life and Beauties* actually assigns the role of deserter to Samuel and claims that Samuel "advertised" his wife in the *Boston Daily Bee* after he had moved to Chicago. If this were true, he would have met the Illinois residence requirement for divorce early enough to divorce her before she signed her contract with Derby. However, the *Bee* advertisement lists his residence as Boston.

70 Settlement on the intermarriage of Sara Payson Eldredge and James Parton, 5 Jan. 1856, James Parton Papers, bMS Am 1248.3 (p. 2), Houghton Library, Harvard University. Quotations by permission of the Houghton Library, Harvard University. A portion is quoted in Warren, *Fanny Fern*, 153. Designation of a trustee was not a legal necessity in New York under the 1848 and 1849 New York married women's property statutes. The statutes are reprinted in Norma Basch, *In the Eyes of the Law: Women, Marriage and Property in Nineteenth Century New York* (Ithaca: Cornell University Press, 1982), 233–4. However, the contract designates Oliver Dyer as trustee. On 16 June 1856, a codicil named Lowell Mason, Jr., as cotrustee with Oliver Dyer. As trustee, Dyer is the "party of the third part" of the contract, as fully a party to the agreement as soon-to-be husband and wife. Warren edits the agreement so that it appears that Sara Payson Eldredge and James Parton are the only parties to it, even though she mentions Dyer's trusteeship in a footnote.

Projecting into the future, the contract also grants Sara the same degree of control over "all property which may hereafter arise or accrue to her by reason of any new works which may be prepared by her." Another contract, with *New York Ledger* publisher Robert Bonner, guaranteed her a handsome salary as compensation for contributing a weekly column to the *Ledger*, a paper that did not discourage newspaper exchange reprinting of Fern's sketches, but which made sure the world knew that Fern only "wrote for" the *Ledger*. Her personal and professional lives in good order, Sara Parton *became* Fanny Fern. Her sketches protected by copyright and proprietary control vested in her as if she were a feme sole, Fern would, in ensuing years, regularly publish book collections of these sketches, and she was not subjected a second time to unauthorized book reprinting of her sketches.

Even though Fanny Fern's personal and professional lives from 1856 onward are stable and tranquil in comparison to the turbulent years of 1851 to 1855, no author in the antebellum United States was guaranteed complete protection from unauthorized exploitation of literary property. On July 26, 1856, the *New York Ledger* warned its readers against a recently issued work illegitimately bearing the name of its famous columnist. Deriding the "ungrammatical preface and chapter headings" of "Fanny Fern's Family Cook Book," issued by Philadelphia publisher William Fleming, the *Ledger* protests that Fern had not authorized the book and that its publication was "an outrageous imposition" upon both Fern and her readers. "Suppose that this Philadelphia publisher were a popular author himself," asks the *Ledger*, "how would he like some one to use his name and place it on a book that he had never seen or heard of, in order to make it sell?" In short, the publisher had used Fanny Fern's name as a trademark without her consent and thus had misled the public into believing that she was the source of the cookbook.

In 1856, comfortably ensconced at the *Ledger*, Fanny Fern responded to this incursion into her territory in ways both typical and atypical of her earlier attempts to police her authorial persona. In her early career, she had no legal means to stop such incursions, and she cleverly turned this disadvantage into an advantage, capitalizing on those incursions by making them the subject of her columns. In 1856, however, Fern both took legal action *and* made the violation and her action against the violator the subject of a column, "A Premonitory Squib before Independence." Under the signature "Fanny Fern," the satirical voice of "Fanny" describes Sara Parton's successful suit against the infringing publisher. The "Fanny" who sparred with her adversaries in print in the *Olive Branch* thus merges with "Fanny Fern," who merges with Sara Parton. The suit and her column about it attest to her arrival as a unitary authorial subject capable of proprietorship.

Or do they? Nicole Tonkovich argues in her analysis of *Parton v. Fleming* that names reveal "the inherently arbitrary and unstable connection of the signifier and signified at the point of personal identity," and an author who wants to establish a claim to her literary property must create at least the appearance of a stable connection between the author's real name, the author's pseudonym, the author's body, and her intellectual progeny/property.[71] For a woman writer, whose name shifts as she first bears the name of her father and then the name of her husband (or, in the case of Fern, three husbands in succession), the problem of naming presents both challenges and opportunities. She can exploit a variety of personae, but she must also, Tonkovich argues, maintain a uniformity of "textual character" to retain legal title to her work.[72] Fern's early periodical career introduces a further layer of complication to this gendered instability. In order to succeed in her claim against Fleming, Fern needed to represent her early career and her status as a literary proprietor during that early career as stable and unchallenged. *Parton v. Fleming* and her column about the suit are thus both part of the same project Fern initiated with *Ruth Hall* – stabilizing and policing "Fanny Fern" by writing out conflicting elements of her early history.

Fern incorporates into "A Premonitory Squib before Independence" a newspaper report that only briefly describes the legal basis to her claim of ownership of the Fanny Fern pseudonym[73]: "Mrs. Parton alleges that she is *the* 'Fanny Fern;' that all her writings are published under that name, and that she has acquired a special and only right to use it." The formal complaint filed with the court sets out in more detail the facts required to establish that possession: how and when she adopted the name, the sales of her books under that name, and the association in the public mind between the name and her literary productions that those sales created. As the complaint tells the court, Sara Parton "adopted the name or style of 'Fanny Fern' by which to indicate" her literary productions in June of 1851, and prefixed this name to "all the works composed by her . . . and the Copy Rights of several of her volumes [were] thus secured as if the same had been written by a person with the name of 'Fanny Fern.'"[74] She claims

71 Tonkovich, *Domesticity with a Difference*, 47–8. Note, however, that both she and Michael Newbury wrongly describe *Parton v. Fleming* as a copyright suit.

72 Ibid., 45.

73 An identically worded report appeared in the 11 July 1856 *Daily Pennsylvanian*, the day the suit was filed and a special injunction immediately issued. The version incorporated into Fern's column has a different title and first sentence and is dated 14 July 1856, so Fern apparently learned of the outcome of her suit from a reprinted notice in a New York paper. In any event, what Fern quotes is not, as both Tonkovich and Newbury assume, the court's opinion or order in the case. The court simply granted Parton's request for a preliminary injunction without an opinion, thus implicitly affirming the legal reasoning presented in the complaint.

74 Complaint, *Parton v. Fleming*, filed 11 July 1856, Eastern District of Pennsylvania Federal Court records, Mid-Atlantic Regional Branch of the National Archives, Philadelphia, PA.

that until the appearance of Fleming's cookbook, she had used the name "exclusively," and that the name thus was "well known among and recognized by Printers, Publishers and the Reading Public." Further, through those sales, her books had circulated extensively and continued to circulate extensively, bringing her "great pecuniary profit and reward," and her works "are regarded by those who deal in literary property as valuable and saleable and that the said Sara has acquired a special and sole right to use the said name or style of 'Fanny Fern' and to prefix the same to her compositions." Fleming's "ungrammatical, vulgar and commonplace" book, as the complaint describes it, will thus harm her financial interests because its low quality is "calculated to injure and depreciate the Literary reputation of the said Sara as such authoress and to diminish the popularity and sale of the works" published under her pseudonym. Furthermore, Fleming's book will "impair the value" of her pseudonym, a value built up over many years of exclusive use, and thus diminish her ability to use the name profitably on future publications.[75]

Throughout, the complaint grants centrality to the publication of Fern's works in book form, also attaching affidavits from Daniel Mason (of Mason Brothers, publishers of *Ruth Hall*), Oliver Dyer (formerly of the *Musical World*), and J. C. Derby attesting to her use of her name on books and the sales of her books. Just as Ruth is firmly in control of her self-representation at the end of *Ruth Hall*, the complaint presents Sara Parton as being in control of her self-representation, with Fleming's cookbook presented as the first disruption of this control. The complaint entirely avoids the multiple disruptions to her proprietary control from 1851 to 1855, failing to disclose the wide circulation of the Fanny Fern name in the periodical marketplace by others beyond her control (both attached to her writings and to the writings of others), the use of her name in the title of a book published without her authorization (*The Life and Beauties of Fanny Fern*), or the fact that the legal holder of the title to her literary properties as late as 1853 was her second husband, Samuel Farrington.[76] Thus the complaint's representation of the history of "Fanny Fern" is as artfully fictional in its rewriting of this history as is *Ruth Hall*.

These possible challenges to her proprietorship also do not appear in her representation of the suit in her column. Instead, "A Premonitory Squib"

75 Ibid.

76 At the time of the publication of *Life and Beauties*, there were no published decisions concerning the use of an author's name on a book featuring public domain materials. Later in the century, a court ruled that Washington Irving's heirs could not use a trademark claim in the title "Irving's Works" to prevent republication of his works after their copyrights had expired. *G. P. Putnam's Sons v. Pollard & Moss* (1880), in Wilma S. Davis and Mark A. Lillis, eds., *Decisions of the United States Courts Involving Copyright and Literary Property, 1789–1909* (Washington, DC: Copyright Office, 1980), 2127–9.

constructs another version of the narrative Elizabeth Cady Stanton read in *Ruth Hall* of a woman writing her way out of bondage and into independence and self-possession. Fern begins the sketch by describing (in the continuous present tense) resistance from lawyers she consults about the case, who tell her that she has no legal claim to her name: "'FANNY FERN is not my name, is it?' Let me tell you, that if I originated it, as a *nom de plume*, I have as much right to the sole possession of it, as I have to the one I was baptised by; and no one has any more right to appropriate it, than to take the watch from my girdle. 'Doubted?' – We shall see; I have listed to croakers before now, with my arms a-kimbo."[77] In the rest of the column, she pays tribute to herself and her triumph over both those doubters and William Fleming. The court confirms that her pseudonym is her personal property as much as that watch concealed in a pocket in her clothing. In her reading of the case, the court enforces both the law of property and rules of gentlemanly conduct, confirming that Fleming was not "honest, honorable, and chivalric" when he reached into that pocket and stole her name. In emphatic terms, she describes herself as a free and independent writing woman fully in possession of herself and her property: "Listen! All you who wear (blue) bonnets, and down on your grateful knees to me, for unfurling the banner of Women's (scribblers) Rights. Know, henceforth, that Violet Velvet, is as much your name (for purposes of copyright and other rights) as Julia Parker, if you choose to make it so."[78] Like the women at the Seneca Falls Convention who drafted the Declaration of Sentiments by adapting the rhetoric of the Declaration of Independence to proclaim the independence of women from the tyranny of men, Fanny Fern declares her independent right to her name as property.

In a related and typically complex and topical pun, Fern refers obliquely to the Eastern District of Pennsylvania federal court in which she brought suit and to the record of the judge in her case, Judge John Kintzing Kane, in a famous Fugitive Slave Law case: "What is the use of being a woman, if you can't carry a point? Are bonnets to be trampled on by boots? Judge

77 *New York Ledger*, 2 Aug. 1856.

78 Ibid. Despite Fern's invocation of "copy-rights" here, such a misappropriation of an author's name was not (and is not) an infringement of copyright, and the complaint filed in the case makes it clear that her lawyers did not argue that Fleming's appropriation of her name constituted copyright infringement. See George Ticknor Curtis, *A Treatise on the Law of Copyright* (Boston: Charles C. Little & James Brown, 1847), 299. See also Bret Harte's successful suit against a publisher who sold a book including sketches by Harte and sketches not by Harte, presenting the volume as if Harte was the source of the entire volume's contents (*Harte v. DeWitt* [1874], in Davis, *Copyright Decisions*, 1201–2); and Mark Twain's failed attempt (much like that of Irving's heirs) to use trademark law to prevent a publisher from publishing some of his uncopyrighted newspaper sketches in a book bearing the name Mark Twain (*Clemens v. Belford* [1883], in Davis, *Copyright Decisions*, 647–51).

Kane says No. May he live to Pass-more such decrees." At about the same time that her suit was before Judge Kane, Passmore Williamson filed a suit against Judge Kane in Pennsylvania state court. In his suit, Williamson, a white abolitionist, charged that Kane's imprisonment of him for contempt of court (after he refused to produce fugitive slaves he was suspected of harboring) violated Pennsylvania state law.[79] Judge Kane deprived Passmore Williamson of his freedom for his efforts to free slaves, and Williamson sought to have Kane imprisoned for his violation of his civil rights under Pennsylvania state law. By deploying the "Pass-more" pun, Fern figures herself both as slave and master. She is the slave, trampled by the boots of William Fleming and forced into involuntary servitude by his appropriation of her name and identity, and whom Kane now grants independence by passing his decree in her case. However, she is also the master, the party whose legal interests Kane protected under the Fugitive Slave Law, and Kane has decreed that her fugitive property (her "title") must be returned to her, its rightful owner.

But just as Fanny Fern seems to step forth as an authorial subject in full possession of herself and as the proprietor and source of her works, she slips away. Her declaration of independence for herself and her scribbling sisters stands in silent conflict with the caption of the reprinted newspaper report of the proceedings incorporated into her column: "'FANNY FERN' BEFORE JUDGE Kane – In the United States District Court at Philadelphia, before Judge Kane on Friday, James Parton and Sara P. Parton, his wife, made application for a special injunction." The traditional blue paper wrapper for the manuscript case file swallows up her separate identity even more completely than the caption of the printed report, captioning the case "James Parton & wife v. Wm. Fleming." Both Fanny Fern and Sara P. Parton disappear into the person of James Parton, becoming the unnamed appendage, "wife." Her declaration of independence is an illusion. Her third husband filed on her behalf the suit that purportedly grants her "independence" because she as a wife has no separate legal existence. Despite the prenuptial agreement that exhaustively cataloged the rights that she could exercise over her separate estate and the marital rights over her property that James Parton agreed not to exercise, she still could not bring

79 Richard Hildreth included an account of the Passmore Williamson case as an appendix to his American edition of *Atrocious Judges* (New York: Miller, Orton & Mulligan, 1856). See also Paul Finkelman, *An Imperfect Union: Slavery, Federalism, and Comity* (Chapel Hill: University of North Carolina Press, 1981), 255–65. A *Philadelphia American Courier* article (2 Aug. 1856) reports Williamson's suit against Kane in Delaware County Court. The *Philadelphia Sunday Dispatch* (27 July 1856) reports Williamson's visit to Moyamensing jail on the anniversary of his incarceration. Kane was, of course, also the district judge impaneled with Justice Grier to hear *Stowe v. Thomas* (see Chapter 3). For a brief biography of Kane, see John. H. Frederick, "John Kintzing Kane," in Dumas Malone, ed., *Dictionary of American Biography* (New York: Scriber's, 1961), 5:257–8.

suit against Fleming without her husband's consent and full cooperation. In the eyes of the law, he retained control over her person, and a court could only enforce a judgment against her through him. Even if she *might* have been able to file the suit independently, her lawyers took the cautious route, anticipating and deflecting a possible conservative reading of her status.

Even here in the later stage of her career, Fern's attempt to establish absolute proprietorship fails, her status as a married woman undermining that claim; I want to suggest, in closing, however, that her inability to claim full proprietorship made her more typical than atypical as an author in the 1850s and 1860s. Although Judge Kane may have decreed in *Parton v. Fleming* that "bonnets" were *not* "to be trampled on by boots," in the 1850s authors still remained, for the most part, in the position of "bonnets," susceptible to being trampled on by those having more power in the literary field and wearing heavy boots (namely, publishers and readers).

A threat to Benjamin Shillaber's literary proprietorship illustrates this point. In 1853, Shillaber's Mrs. Partington newspaper sketches were subjected to unauthorized publication in a book that also included "counterfeit" Mrs. Partington sketches. This one book subjected Shillaber to the offenses Fern suffered in two separate incidents – *Life and Beauties* reprinted her newspaper sketches without authorization, while the *Fanny Fern Cook Book* attached her name to text she had not written. In its report on this doubly offensive counterfeit publication, the *Olive Branch* makes Mrs. Partington stand in for Shillaber and describes such unauthorized publication as a violation of her person:

> Mrs. Partington has been the subject of one of the most heinous outrages ever perpetrated upon a female woman. Some shabby book-publisher in New York thrust his hand into her ridicule [a Partington-ism for "reticule"], selected a few of her choicest sweets, and buried them among a heap of old Joe Miller's and other stale rubbish, the shape of a volume, to which he had the audacity to attach the old lady's name as god-mother! We would warn our readers against the counterfeit book, entitled "Mrs. Partington's Carpet-Bag of Fun," and notify them that the old lady has collected her sayings and philosophizings together, and a Boston publisher will soon give them to the world in a handsome illustrated volume.[80]

Like William Fleming, who would take Fanny Fern's name from a hidden pocket in her dress, much as if he had taken a watch, the piratical New York publisher accosts Mrs. Partington on the street and takes her property (her sketches and the reputation attached to her name) from her handbag, and then resells this property in a way designed to tarnish her reputation. All that

80 *Olive Branch*, 31 Dec. 1853.

Mrs. Partington (and Shillaber) can do, however, is hope that readers will recognize and respect the "real" Mrs. Partington and her literary progeny, rejecting the spurious god-child as inferior. The anecdote thus implies that to be an author of newspaper sketches is to be like Mrs. Partington, a woman alone in public carrying a purse and particularly susceptible to thieves.

During all of the years of Fern's literary career, authors repeatedly petitioned and lobbied Congress in favor of international copyright and Congress repeatedly rejected their entreaties, while in the press, copyright advocates and opponents fiercely debated how the law should structure the relationship between authors and their intellectual property. Indeed, after the Civil War, as discussed in Chapter 3, Fern's third husband, author James Parton, helped to organize the International Copyright Association and became a recognizable voice on the procopyright side. Before the Civil War, in late 1857, Fern took her own public stand on the international copyright issue in a *New-York Ledger* column. Protesting the inaction of Congress and the President, she lambasts European publishers who "[put] their forefinger and thumb into my pocket, and [help] themselves." "It is the unprincipled principle of the thing," she protests, "the cool impudence of it – it is the idea that what's yours *isn't* yours."[81] Fern, like all American authors, had recourse to the law to stave off the depredations of American publishers (at least if they or their publishers properly registered copyrights in their works); foreign publishers, however, could pick authors' pockets with impunity. Readers who followed Fanny Fern through her manifold periodical and book appearances would have seen a constant oscillation between Fern's authorial self-possession and dispossession and between her appearance and disappearance as a literary proprietor (whether she "disappeared" as a proprietor because her works were not property in the absence of copyright or because she "disappeared" into a husband, the single legal subject of marriage). She constructed a more stable authorial self after the first few years of her career and deployed this self to proprietary advantage, but her relationship to her literary property remained tenuous and deeply problematic. This problematic relationship ultimately did not interfere with her financial success as a writer. In the periodical marketplace, she capitalized on these "problems," turning unauthorized circulation to her advantage. In the book marketplace, even when, as in *Parton v. Fleming*, she declared that she had triumphed over her womanly disabilities in relation to her property, the inevitable surfacing of her problematic relation to property as a married woman only made her seem *more* like an author rather than less. At a time when literary proprietorship was

81 *New York Ledger*, 28 Nov. 1857.

seldom secure, when all authors, like married women, could simultaneously claim their literary property and find themselves dispossessed of it, a woman whose legal status similarly oscillated between possession and dispossession through marriage, between being a property owning subject and being the property of her husband, was particularly suited to the role of author in America.

Chapter 5

A "Rank Rebel" Lady and Her Literary Property: Augusta Jane Evans and Copyright, the Civil War and After, 1861–1868

In his 1884 memoir, New York publisher J. C. Derby relates the story of the publication of Augusta Jane Evans's arch-Confederate novel *Macaria; or Altars of Sacrifice* in the North and South during the Civil War. In Derby's telling, after the beginning of the war, which had the effect of "temporarily suspending the publication of books of fiction," he "heard occasionally through the lines from the gifted young authoress, who sent [him] in 1863 [*sic*], by a blockade-runner, *via* Cuba, a copy of her novel entitled 'Macaria,' published by West & Johnson [*sic*], then, as now, well-known booksellers in Richmond, Virginia. The volume was printed on coarse brown paper, the copyright entered according to the *Confederate States of America*, and dedicated 'to the brave soldiers of the Southern Army' "[1] (emphasis original). Unbeknownst to her, he continues, he arranged with Philadelphia publisher J. B. Lippincott to issue a Northern edition (Derby's own publishing house Derby & Jackson had failed shortly after the beginning of the war). When New York publisher Michael Doolady announced a competing edition of the work, Derby approached Doolady, who claimed "that the author being an arch rebel was not entitled to copyright and would receive none" (p. 394). Derby and Lippincott called on Doolady together and persuaded him to pay all royalties in trust to Derby, while Lippincott agreed to withdraw his edition. Derby recalls with even greater relish Evans's appearance on his New York doorstep "[l]ate in the Summer of 1865" (that is, not long after the end of the war) "closely veiled," wearing a dress whose fashion is many years out of date, reluctant to stop long at his office because her brother, "very badly wounded" during the war, waited outside (pp. 394–5). When he told her for the first time "that she had a considerable amount subject to her order, for copyright received on *Macaria*" (p. 395), she suddenly could afford both a new wardrobe and proper medical attention for her brother.

Derby's retrospective narration of events during the years 1863 through 1865 is very much an artifact of the post-Reconstruction era. His account of his postwar encounter with Evans in 1865 is a classic of the genre that

1 J. C. Derby, *Fifty Years among Authors, Books and Publishers* (New York: G. W. Carleton & Co., 1884), 392–3 (hereinafter cited in the text).

historian Nina Silber has labeled the "romance of reunion." In a narrative repeated obsessively in the postwar North, dramatists, fiction writers, and journalists described marriages between Northern men and Southern women, romantic unions designed to cement a reconciliation between North and South (a reconciliation to which the South, as the female partner in the "marriage," consented but in which "she" also consented to her subordination to the masculine North). Northern novelist and Union army officer James De Forest inaugurated the genre in 1867 with his novel *Miss Ravenel's Conversion from Secession to Loyalty*, but as Silber argues, this particular metaphor for sectional reconciliation became commonplace only after the failure of Reconstruction.[2] Although Derby and Evans did not marry, he portrays himself as the gallant Northern hero and Evans as the passive Southern lady rescued from poverty and destitution (the gentlemen publishers of the South had failed her – her Confederate publisher, West & Johnston, could not even manage to pay her royalties for the Southern publication of *Macaria* in nearly worthless Confederate currency). Although she previously and ardently supported the Confederacy by offering up her writing, her nursing skills, and her brother's health on the "altars of sacrifice," Derby and Lippincott effectively recaptured her womanly talents and emotions for the North and the Union. "And this is the story of 'Macaria,'" Derby concludes with evident satisfaction, "and how it came to be published in the *United States of America*" (p. 395) (emphasis original).

Derby's story has come to define both Evans's authorship and the fate of Southern literature during the war, but the true story of Evans and her literary property during and after the war as reconstructed in this chapter is far more complex than Derby's narrative suggests. As Derby notes, the copyright in Evans's novel was registered according to Confederate law, a fact that in retrospect he refers to ironically, suggesting to his postbellum, post-Reconstruction readers the absurdity of the Confederate Congress's establishing a legal basis for literary proprietorship. Scholars have paid exceedingly scant notice to the Confederate copyright law, and one might easily, like Derby, find the law quixotic and trivial in light of the fact that the

2 Nina Silber, *The Romance of Reunion: Northerners and the South, 1865–1900* (Chapel Hill: University of North Carolina Press, 1993), chap. 2. The genre has pre–Civil War antecedents, such as in *The Planter's Northern Bride* (1854), in which author Caroline Hentz defended the South and slavery by depicting a marriage between a male Southern planter and a female New Englander. Gregory S. Jackson considers the shift in political theory underlying the difference between Hentz's prewar romance and another postwar De Forest novel, *The Bloody Chasm* (1881). "'A Dowry of Suffering': Consent, Contract, and Political Coverture in John W. De Forest's Reconstruction Romance," *American Literary History* 15, no. 2 (2003): 276–310. Jane Turner Censer analyzes Southern women writers' uses of the genre as an instrument of Southern self-critique in the 1870s and 1880s. "Reimagining the North-South Reunion: Southern Women Novelists and the Intersectional Romance, 1876–1900," *Southern Cultures* 5 (1999): 64–91. Kathleen Diffley analyzes a broader genre she calls the "romance of union" and finds examples as early as the war years. *Where My Heart Is Turning Ever: Civil War Stories and Constitutional Reform* (Athens: University of Georgia Press, 1992), chap. 2.

war decimated the South's relatively small publishing industry and made the protection of literary property largely a moot point.[3] The Confederate copyright law was, indeed, a lost cause within The Lost Cause, but, as Drew Gilpin Faust argues in *The Creation of Confederate Nationalism*, "the struggle for achievement of nationalism often becomes itself the occasion of its fullest realization." That is, a struggle to establish a nation that ultimately fails can, nevertheless, give rise to a fully realized nationalist ideology; and, as Faust argues, scholars must analyze Confederate nationalism "in its own terms – as the South's commentary upon itself – as its effort to represent southern culture to the world at large, to history, and perhaps most revealingly, to its own people."[4] Furthermore, as Alice Fahs argues in *The Imagined Civil War*, the war "catalyzed a rethinking of prevailing beliefs about the connecting links between literature and society and between individual and nation."[5] Evans was an ardent supporter of both the Confederate nation and its copyright law, and the laws passed at Evans's instigation are an important part of "the South's commentary upon itself" and, in particular, its articulation of a vision of the roles of literature, authors, readers, and the literary market in the construction of the Confederate nation.

The story of Augusta Evans's copyright activism and literary proprietorship during and after the Civil War brings into sharper focus the story told in Chapter 2 about the relationship between women authors and nationalism and between literature and nationalism in the 1820s through the 1840s. Copyright advocates in the antebellum United States argued that a truly "American" literature was necessary to build and sustain the young nation's status as a nation, holding up Catharine Sedgwick as a model literary producer. The Confederate Congress (spurred in part by Evans's lobbying)

3 The longest discussions of the Confederate copyright statutes appear in articles of a documentary or antiquarian bent. On the only copyright infringement case tried under the Confederate copyright law, *Goetzel v. Titcomb*, see Thomas Conn Bryan, "General William J. Hardee and Confederate Publication Rights," *Journal of Southern History* 17, no. 2 (1946): 263–74. On Confederate copyright registration records, see Raymond Robinson, "Confederate Copyright Entries," *William and Mary Quarterly* 16 (1936): 248–66. For very brief (and sometimes inaccurate) mentions of the law, see E. Merton Coulter, *The Confederate States of America, 1861–1865* (Baton Rouge: Louisiana State University Press, 1950), 508; Elisabeth Muhlenfeld, "The Civil War and Authorship," in *The History of Southern Literature*, ed. Louis D. Rubin et al. (Baton Rouge: Louisiana State University Press, 1985), 180; William C. Davis, *A Government of Their Own: The Making of the Confederacy* (New York: Free Press, 1994), 252; Lawrence F. London, "Confederate Literature and Its Publishers," in *Studies in Southern History*, ed. J. Carlyle Sitterson (Chapel Hill: University of North Carolina Press, 1957), 83; and Aubert J. Clark, *The Movement for International Copyright in Nineteenth Century America* (Washington, DC: Catholic University of America Press, 1960), 84. The standard history of Southern Literature fails to even mention the copyright statute. Jay Hubbell, *The South in American Literature 1607–1900* (Durham: Duke University Press, 1954).

4 Drew Gilpin Faust, *The Creation of Confederate Nationalism: Ideology and Identity in the Civil War South* (Baton Rouge: Louisiana State University Press, 1988), 6–7.

5 Alice Fahs, *The Imagined Civil War: Popular Literature of the North and South, 1861–1865* (Chapel Hill: University of North Carolina Press, 2001), 18.

attempted to enact the literary nationalistic program previously argued for by copyright advocates in the United States. Neither the literary nationalist program envisioned by antebellum copyright advocates nor the one envisioned by the wartime Confederate copyright advocates was ever fully realized. In the prewar United States, international copyright repeatedly failed in Congress. In the Civil War South, such legislation succeeded, but failures of diplomacy and wartime material constraints prevented the realization of the legislation's goals. Sedgwick and Evans thus negotiated different legal and cultural terrains. Sedgwick cannily exploited the possibilities of a market structured by a law that resisted authorial proprietorship, while Evans helped to bring into being a law strongly supporting authorial proprietorship and (if only briefly) exploited the system she had helped to create. Evans's lobbying thus locates her and her works within the sphere of a hoped-for self-sustaining Confederate nation that would both produce and consume literary works suitable to its newly independent status.[6]

The Confederate copyright law also, however, regulated literary trade between the Confederacy and other nations. My focus on the divergence in the legal regulation of literary property between North and South complicates Alice Fahs's interpretation of the nature of Southern literary nationalism. Focusing on the similarities between Northern and Southern popular wartime literary texts, Fahs challenges Confederate claims that its wartime literature was "essentially different from the North's – despite all evidence to the contrary." Instead, she labels such claims of distinctiveness as "a performance of political difference that may have been the most distinctive aspect of Southern literary culture" (p. 9). That is, Southern *claims* of difference *constituted* a difference that can be located nowhere else in the literary culture. Certainly, Fahs's discovery that Southern periodicals reprinted unrevised stories from *Harper's Weekly* as though they were original Southern tales of the war demonstrates that some differences were more "imagined" than real. However, by passing an international copyright law, the Confederacy sharply and concretely differentiated its regulation of literary property and

6 Based at least in part on Derby's account of the novel's publishing history, almost all modern readings of *Macaria* have focused exclusively on Evans's designs on Confederate readers. William Perry Fidler's analysis assumes that the readers requiring propagandizing by the novel are Southerners. "Augusta Evans Wilson as Confederate Propagandist," *Alabama Review* (1949): 32–44. All of Drew Gilpin Faust's work on Evans and *Macaria* analyzes the text as one designed for an audience of Confederate women. "Altars of Sacrifice: Confederate Women and the Narratives of War," *Journal of American History* 76, no. 4 (1990): 1200–28; *Mothers of Invention: Women of the Slaveholding South in the American Civil War* (Chapel Hill: University of North Carolina Press, 1996), chap. 7; "Introduction: Macaria, a War Story for Confederate Women," in *Macaria; or, Altars of Sacrifice* (Baton Rouge: Louisiana State University Press, 1992), xiii–xxix. See also Jennifer Lynn Gross, "'Lonely Lives Are Not Necessarily Joyless': Augusta Jane Evans's *Macaria* and the Creation of a Place for Single Womanhood in the Postwar South," *American Nineteenth Century History* 2, no. 1 (2001): 33–52; and Suzy Clarkson Holstein, "'Offering Up Her Life': Confederate Women on the Altars of Sacrifice," *Southern Studies* 2, no 2. (1991): 113–30.

thus its literary culture from the North's. By passing an international copyright law, the Confederacy announced to other nations (particularly Britain) that the Confederacy was an ethical nation that respected the property rights of foreign nationals and that deserved respect from other nations. By lobbying for international copyright, Evans thus participated in the Confederacy's articulation of its nationalist ideology in the international arena, where the Confederacy sought, ultimately without success, recognition of its status as an independent nation.

This chapter begins with the events of 1861, tracing Evans's involvement behind the scenes in the Confederate Congress's passage of a copyright resolution and statute, and then considers at greater length the logic of the Confederacy's adopting international copyright provisions at its moment of origin as a nation. I argue that Evans's promotion of Confederate copyright followed the logic of Confederate nationalism as experienced by the two heroines of *Macaria*. Like Evans herself, Irene Huntingdon and Electra Grey engage in the project of nation building through cultural production while taking advantage of unprecedented opportunities for female self-possession and independence made possible by the war. That is, Evans's copyright activism served both the Confederacy's interest and her own interests as an author. The second half of the chapter turns from the 1861 copyright act to its revision in 1863 and to the publication of *Macaria* in both the South and North in 1864. In 1863, as Evans was preparing to publish her Confederate nationalist novel, she sought to consolidate her legal position in the Confederacy through technical, but significant, amendments to the copyright law. However, she also, as my reconstruction of the publishing history of *Macaria* makes clear, *sought* a Northern audience (and Northern royalties) rather than having them imposed on her unwillingly and unknowingly. The chapter closes with a reading of her novel *St. Elmo*, written and published after the war but set before it. In contrast to *Macaria*, in which the dual heroines remain unmarried, *St. Elmo* features a popular author-heroine, single and independent, who finally succumbs to marriage. As an unmarried woman until 1868, Evans's property was entirely at her disposal, but in *St. Elmo* she deploys coverture to advantage as a narrative device. Through her author-heroine, Edna Earl, who disavows authorship and surrenders to marriage and coverture in the novel's final pages, Evan strategically staged her own authorial dispossession and reassimilation into the American literary market. Although one might expect to find Evans's career as devastated by the war as was her erstwhile nation, the exact opposite was true. Despite temporary dislocation and discontinuity, Evans effectively reconsolidated her position in the Northern market and, it seems likely, lost little or no money on the sales of her novels. In my reconstruction of Evans's activities during the 1860s, she emerges not as a passive victim of the war and its aftermath but as a canny player in the literary field, who understood and exploited the possibilities of shifting national narratives shaped by copyright law.

"A glorious redemption from Yankee bondage": International copyright and the articulation of Confederate nationalism

Evans became strongly identified with the Confederacy at the onset of the Civil War, but her career as a published author began six years before secession. Evans wrote her first novel, *Inez: A Tale of the Alamo*, when she was fifteen years old. The novel intertwined romance and anti-Catholic critique with the historical events surrounding the famous battle that eventually led to Texas breaking ties with Mexico and becoming an independent republic. Harper & Brothers, a large New York publishing house, published the novel in 1855, when Evans was twenty, but her name did not appear on the title page. Sales were low during the 1850s, and the novel received little critical attention.[7] In 1859, Evans approached J. C. Derby, of Derby & Jackson, with the manuscript of *Beulah* (a novel about an orphan's intellectual and spiritual journey from skepticism to Christian faith) after another New York publisher, D. Appleton, declined it. On the recommendation of his wife and other women in his family, Derby published the novel (*Fifty Years*, 389–90). Although *Beulah* was not a bestseller on the scale of *Uncle Tom's Cabin*, it sold largely enough to earn Evans considerable royalties, to establish her reputation with readers (she published this novel under her own name), and to ensure that she would find a publisher for her next novel.[8]

The Civil War, of course, intervened. During the first days of the Confederacy in early 1861, after secession but before the commencement of hostilities with the Northern states, hundreds of interested spectators thronged Montgomery, Alabama, in February to witness the labors of the provisional Congress as it drafted a provisional constitution and enacted laws.[9] Among those spectators was Augusta Evans, then unmarried and residing in Mobile, Alabama, with her family. As a literary celebrity and prominent Alabamian, Evans was a sought-after guest at the many social events prompted by the presence of the Confederate Congress, and she sought and obtained introductions to some of the Congressmen. During this period,

7 William Perry Fidler, *Augusta Evans Wilson, 1835–1909: A Biography* (Tuscaloosa: University of Alabama Press, 1951), 40–5.

8 The last edition of the novel under Derby's imprint appeared in early 1861, with the notation "25th Thousandth." According to Susan Geary's reading of market circumstances in the 1850s, such sales would qualify the novel as a commercial success, if not a best seller. "The Domestic Novel as a Commercial Commodity: Making a Best Seller in the 1850s," *Papers of the Bibliographical Society of America* 70 (1976): 365–93.

9 Narrative accounts of the early days of the Confederacy in Montgomery that have influenced my very brief account here include Clement Eaton, *A History of the Southern Confederacy* (New York: Macmillan, 1954); Emory M. Thomas, *The Confederate Nation, 1861–1865* (New York: Harper & Row, 1979); George C. Rable, *The Confederate Republic: A Revolution against Politics* (Chapel Hill: University of North Carolina Press, 1994); and Davis, *A Government of Their Own*.

she first met J. L. M. Curry, then a provisional and later a formally elected representative from Alabama to the Confederate Congress, with whom she corresponded extensively during and after the war. She was also introduced to Thomas R. R. Cobb, representative to the provisional Congress from Georgia, where she was born and where her father's family still resided. Curry and Cobb both participated in the drafting of the provisional and permanent constitutions of the new nation. Many secessionists claimed that the new Confederacy was loyal to the *true* intentions of the founding fathers of the United States, and they demonstrated this claim of descent by making their new constitution track the U.S. Constitution closely in most of its provisions. Reproducing exactly the copyright and patent clause in the U.S. Constitution ("To promote the progress of science and useful arts, by securing, for limited times, to authors and inventors, the exclusive right to their respective writings and discoveries"), the Confederate Constitution reserved copyright and patent law to the Confederate national government rather than allowing the individual states to legislate on the subject.[10]

Mimicking the U.S. Constitution's copyright clause reserved to the Confederate Congress the *power* to enact copyright laws, but by actually taking the trouble to do so when many more pressing matters required attention, the Congress signaled that copyright was a serious matter of national concern, as important a part of the project of nation building as the other matters occupying the Congress at that time, such as establishing an army, a postal system, and courts of law. Southern author William Gilmore Simms lobbied William Porcher Miles, his friend and a Confederate congressional representative from South Carolina, in favor of international copyright by explaining how such a move would serve to represent Southern culture to Europe and the Northern states and to establish a new national identity to which literature was central. "Do not forget the interests of Literature in the formation of the new Government," he wrote on February 20, 1861. "Have it decreed that all Nations, States or Confederacies in amity with this Gov. and giving to its people the privileges of Copyright, as possessed by their own, shall enjoy the same rights & securities as our own people – *but no other States!* The leading men of letters at the North are all abolitionists, with

10 Confederate States of America, *Provisional and Permanent Constitutions, Together with the Acts and Resolutions of the Three Sessions of the Provisional Congress of the Confederate States* (Richmond: Tyler, Wise, Allegre & Smith, 1861), 20. Charles Robert Lee, Jr., usefully lines up the U.S. and CSA constitutions as parallel texts. *The Confederate Constitutions* (Chapel Hill: University of North Carolina Press, 1963), Appendix C. For the long and contentious historiographical debates about the relation of Southern secession to the American Revolution and the U.S. Constitution, see George C. Rable, "Beyond State Rights: The Shadowy World of Confederate Politics," 135–53; and Michael Les Benedict, "A Constitutional Crisis," 154–74, in *Writing the Civil War: The Quest to Understand*, ed. James M. McPherson and William J. Cooper (Columbia: University of South Carolina Press, 1998). Suffice it to say that the U.S. Constitution is unambiguously the source of the intellectual property clause in the Confederate Constitution.

very few exceptions. Such a measure will astonish them!"[11] At this optimistic early moment in the history of the Confederate States of America (CSA), Simms imagines Northern literary men (but not women), all strong advocates of international copyright but few sympathetic to slavery, being astounded by the justice and generosity of the Confederate nation toward authors and their interests (but, of course, such protection would not be extended to U.S. citizens, whose government was not "in amity" with the Confederacy).

On March 7, anticipating the imminent departure of the Confederacy's first diplomatic mission to Europe, the Congress passed "A Resolution in Relation to International Copyright." The resolution urged the President to instruct his commissioners to "enter into treaty obligations for the extension of international copyright privileges to all authors, the citizens and subjects" of Great Britain, France, Prussia, Saxony, and any other European nation that had passed laws enabling reciprocal copyright protection.[12] However, it was not Simms's friend Representative Miles, but Representative T. R. R. Cobb who introduced this measure, and strong circumstantial evidence suggests that he did so as a result of lobbying by Augusta Evans. In a letter to his wife dated February 26, he reports that "Miss Evans, the author of 'Beulah'," had insisted on being introduced to him and that she flattered him concerning a speech he had made in Athens, Georgia, in 1857.[13] Just a few days later, in a letter dated March 1, he writes that he intends to introduce a bill "granting international copyright privileges to the authors of France and Great Britain, because those Nations have granted these rights to our authors."[14] After the bill's passage on March 7, he boastingly describes to his wife his three-pronged plan to win European recognition for the Confederacy, the three prongs being his three legislative initiatives: international copyright, a scheme for regulating the cotton trade, and a prohibition of Sunday mail delivery. These three initiatives would, he believed, bring together the authors, workers, and Christians in support of the Confederacy: "In my opinion [the international copyright resolution] will operate strongly to bring the literary world, especially Great Britain,

11 William Gilmore Simms to William Porcher Miles, 20 Feb. 1861, in *The Letters of William Gilmore Simms, Vol. 4: 1858–1866*, ed. Mary Simms Oliphant et al. (Columbia: University of South Carolina Press, 1955), 329–30. Simms also proposed a much longer term of copyright than granted in the United States (fifty years with a fifty-year renewal term), but neither Miles nor any other Confederate Congressman ever proposed such a long term of protection in the CSA.

12 Confederate States of America, *Provisional and Permanent Constitutions*, 81. Note, however, that the departing Confederate diplomats were not specifically charged with negotiating a copyright treaty. James D. Richardson, ed., *A Compilation of the Messages and Papers of the Confederacy, Including the Diplomatic Correspondence, 1861–1865*, 2 vols. (Nashville: United States Publishing Co., 1906).

13 T. R. R. Cobb to Marion Cobb, 26 Feb. 1861, "Correspondence of Thomas Reade Rootes Cobb, 1860–1862," *Publications of the Southern History Association* 11, no. 4 (July 1907): 242.

14 T. R. R. Cobb to Marion Cobb, 1 Mar. 1861, ibid., 247–8.

to sympathize with us against the Yankee Literary Pirates. Our cotton will bring the working world to the same point and my Sunday amendment if I can pass it will bring the religious world. With these three on our side we can bid defiance to potentates and powers."[15] In retrospect, Cobb's assurance that a copyright initiative might bring Great Britain over to the Confederate side seems quixotic. However, at this early stage, ambitions for the Confederacy were riding high – few expected war, and most expected that other countries, especially Great Britain, the primary consumer of the South's primary source of wealth, cotton, would immediately recognize the Confederacy as an independent nation. In all likelihood, Augusta Evans persuaded him to propose the measure to the Congress using exactly the logic that he suggests to his wife – that international copyright would act as diplomatic leverage with Britain.

Two months later on May 21, after hostilities had commenced at Fort Sumter and in the final rush of legislative activity before the government relocated from Montgomery to Richmond, Virginia, the Congress enacted a copyright statute that made the issue of negotiating international copyright by treaty moot. Like the copyright clause in the Confederate Constitution, the Confederate statute mirrors the U.S. statute closely on matters such as term, renewal, and registration (the statute also mirror's the U.S. statute's use of the masculine pronoun to refer to authors and copyright proprietors).[16] It departs significantly from the U.S. model, however, by allowing protection for noncitizens and nonresidents. "[A]ll rights and privileges allowed" by the act to "citizens of the Confederate States" are also extended to "citizens or subjects of any foreign state or power" if that foreign nation grants like rights to citizens of the Confederacy.[17] The Confederate Congress thus adopted

15 T. R. R. Cobb to Marion Cobb, 7 Mar. 1861, ibid., 257. On Cobb's three-pronged plan for the nation and its faults, see William B. McCash, *Thomas R. R. Cobb (1823–1862): The Making of a Southern Nationalist* (Macon, GA: Mercer University Press, 1983), 215–18. In retrospect, Cobb's program seems ludicrous, but in February and March of 1861, his confidence appeared reasonable and typical rather than misplaced, and Evans's targeting of him as an ally was shrewd and successful. Charles M. Hubbard summarizes the reasons for the eventual failure of Confederate diplomacy to achieve its objective of recognition of the CSA as an independent nation by European governments. *The Burden of Confederate Diplomacy* (Knoxville: University of Tennessee Press, 1998), x. As he also makes clear, in 1861 and 1862, there was a very real possibility of the CSA actually achieving recognition. See also Coulter, *Confederate States*, chap. 9, and Thomas, *Confederate Nation*, chap. 8.

16 Before the Civil War, the U.S. amended its original 1790 Copyright Act on a piecemeal basis without drafting a comprehensive revision. Thorvald Solberg, ed., *Copyright Enactments of the United States, 1783–1906* (Washington, DC: Government Printing Office, 1906). The Confederate statute does not reproduce the provisions of a single U.S. statute, but it effectively rationalizes and consolidates seventy years of U.S. legislation, with a few slight departures (e.g., giving jurisdiction to district rather than circuit courts, which the Confederacy never established, and not providing postage-free transmission of deposit copies).

17 Confederate States of America, *Provisional and Permanent Constitutions*, 106. The records of the Confederate Congress do not identify any particular Congressman as sponsor of the copyright statute. However, once they had acceded to the logic of the international copyright resolution sponsored by

international copyright thirty years before the U.S. Congress, which actively resisted it from the 1830s up until the war and continued to resist it until 1891. Although the provision never took effect because no nation ever recognized the Confederacy as an independent nation, the CSA made this gesture at a moment when it fully believed that recognition was imminent and that the provision of this statute would take effect. Thus through this statute, the new nation "represent[ed] southern culture to the world at large, to history, and . . . to its own people" as crucially different from the United States, and Augusta Evans played a key role in articulating this new nationalist ideology.

What nationalist narrative did the Confederacy (and Evans) seek to construct through the passage of an international copyright statute? For a variety of reasons, the Confederate press did not leave behind anything like the voluminous commentary on copyright issues found in the antebellum U.S. press. In the Confederacy, there was no heated battle between opposing positions played out for decades in Congress and the press, but simply the quiet enactment of international copyright with little debate. Deeply suspicious of a centralized concentration of governmental power, the Confederacy never adequately funded a government printing program to print and distribute records of the Confederate Congress or even its statutes,[18] and thus within the Confederacy, even the existence of the international copyright provisions escaped some in sympathy with the law's aims.[19] The excitement of secession and then the bloody drama of war also displaced potential public discussion, and the press soon ran into production difficulties, including shortages of paper and type.[20] Still, from a small quantity of contemporary commentary and from the larger, well-developed discourse of Southern literary nationalism, we can trace the law's logic and, implicitly, Evans's motives for lobbying for its enactment.

The 1861 international copyright provision in the Confederate statute had the potential to produce three classes of results, all of them clearly dear to Evans's heart: to spur the production of a new national literature reflecting Southern values, to represent the Confederacy to other nations, and to

Cobb, including international copyright in the copyright statute would simply be a logical extension of a policy already accepted.

18 When Confederate Congressman J. L. M. Curry answered an inquiry from a constituent concerning the CSA's patent law, he enclosed a copy of the statute but advised him that copies of a revision to the statute were likely to be scarce and found only in the hands of the Congressmen themselves. J. L. M. Curry to T. B. Cooper, 20 Jan. 1862, J. L. M. Curry Papers, Library of Congress.

19 See, e.g., "The Literary World," *Southern Illustrated News*, 8 Nov. 1862, 2–3, "predicting" the future passage of an international copyright statute eighteen months after the passage of the law.

20 See Fahs's excellent discussion of the challenges faced by the Southern press, both materially and philosophically, as it attempted to articulate a new Confederate nationalist vision after secession. *Imagined Civil War*, 21–41. Fahs supplants the previous standard account by Hubbell. *South in American Literature*, 447–62.

secure the financial interests of authors who were citizens of the Confederacy. As described in Chapter 2, before the war, international copyright advocates, North and South, argued that international copyright would promote the full development of American literature. In the absence of international copyright, so the argument went, works by American authors were at a disadvantage on the market in competition with cheap, unauthorized reprints of British works. Copyright reform would level the playing field, doing justice to British authors, but, more importantly, encouraging more Americans to write works suitable for an American audience, thus pushing out of the market British works that promoted aristocratic values antithetical to the best interests of readers in a democratic republic.

Even before the war, many Southerners claimed that *Northern* literature and its values similarly monopolized the *Southern* literary market and forced readers to consume alien values (although the South claimed the aristocratic values of the "Cavaliers" as its own while seeking to repel the "Yankee" and "Puritan" values and antislavery sentiments of the North).[21] Evans herself made such arguments in a series of four anonymous articles on "Northern Literature" and "Southern Literature" published in the *Mobile Advertiser* in 1859, just as *Beulah* was about to appear from the presses of Derby & Jackson and as the sectional conflict was heating up with John Brown's raid on Harper's Ferry.[22]

In the first two articles, Evans focuses on the flaws of Northern literature, particularly Northern periodical literature. She devotes the most space and heat to criticizing literature published in weekly papers such as Robert Bonner's *New York Ledger*, home of Fanny Fern and E. D. E. N. Southworth (she does not name the *Ledger*, but clearly identifies it with her reference to the oddity of "the gifted [Edward] Everett" appearing in a paper "whose hydra head is a thousand times more self prolific than that of the Sernaen Serpent").[23] However, she also turns her attention to "a Northern Monthly issued in Modern Athens" (clearly the *Atlantic Monthly*, which was in the midst of serializing Harriet Beecher Stowe's third novel, *The Minister's Wooing*) and its criticisms of Democratic President Franklin Pierce. She asks rhetorically, "Can *anything* redeem a Magazine whose influence under the falsely assumed guise of a lofty literary object, is directly subversive of that

21 Jay Hubbell, "Literary Nationalism in the Old South," in *American Studies in Honor of William Kenneth Boyd*, ed. David Kelly Jackson (Durham: Duke University Press, 1940), 175–220.

22 William Perry Fidler claims authorship for Evans on the basis of style, tone, and references in her correspondence at the time to her contributions to Mobile papers. "Augusta Evans Wilson as Confederate Propagandist." Elizabeth Moss also discusses these articles at some length. *Domestic Novelists in the Old South: Defenders of Southern Culture* (Baton Rouge: Louisiana State University Press, 1992), 163–7. See also Naomi Z. Sofer, *Making the "America of Art": Cultural Nationalism and Nineteenth-Century Women Writers* (Columbus: Ohio State University Press, 2005), chap. 2.

23 "Northern Literature," *Mobile Daily Advertiser*, 10 Oct. 1859, [2]. Edward Everett's *Mount Vernon Papers* were serialized in the *Ledger* in 1859.

respect for the character of our rulers, veneration for our laws, and confidence in the constitution established by our fathers, which form the ground work of the main pillars which support our social and political fabric? What sort of national literature is that which seeks to render all classes of society dissatisfied with their normal condition, whose every breath infuses some deadly poison into the vitals of the nation whose literature it claims to represent?"[24]

Her first article on "Northern Literature" attacks the abolitionism of Northern periodicals only indirectly, referring ominously and cryptically to the consequences for the South of "drifting unconsciously in the wake of a vessel which, if it continues its course, will soon dash to fragments and all on board will be involved in a common destruction." In her second article, she takes direct aim, attacking Northern weekly papers in which "the low sensual African is dragged up from his normal position and violently thrust into an importance which the Creator has denied him by indications as strong as physical inferiority and mental incapacity could make them. The demons of pandemonium are actually prowling through the Northern States, making efforts to tear down fabrics which genius, guided by the wisdom and experience of past ages, have [*sic*] erected."[25] Sounding the same note as William Cullen Bryant and other international copyright advocates in the antebellum North, who decried British literature as "poison" and "trash," she criticizes Northern literature's "decided tendency toward evil" and asks, "What excuse can possibly be given for deluging the world with such monstrous trash?"[26]

Unlike Bryant, J. G. Palfrey, and other procopyright, literary nationalist Northerners who protested the evils of *British* literature, however, Evans does not locate the evil in alluring representations of aristocratic life unsuited to a plain, republican people in a society with the potential for class mobility. Instead, in her articles on "Southern Literature," she proudly claims a (slightly modified) aristocratic status for the Southern planter class, which she characterizes as particularly qualified to act as a bulwark against the social chaos overtaking the North: "Next to the British aristocrat, we know of no position in the world more desirable than that of the Southern planter. The one represents the most favorable feature of that government known as a limited monarchy; the other the most favorable feature of that government known as a representative republic. . . . There is no other class which at present can command time to attend properly to the interests of the country, and there is no class from which we have a clearer right to demand contributions which shall reflect credit upon our literature."[27] While arguing for the salutary effects of the greater participation of Southern elites in literary culture, she also warns against the "provincial" and "localizing" tendency

24 Ibid. 25 "Northern Literature," *Mobile Daily Advertiser*, 16 Oct. 1859, [2] 26 Ibid.
27 "Southern Literature," *Mobile Daily Advertiser*, 6 Nov. 1859, [2].

in Southern literary production, noting her "dislike to the principle which would lead Southerners to praise and even glorify everything Southern, regardless of quality."[28] She instead argues that Southern writers should produce works according to the strictest standards of taste, and thus participate in the building and strengthening of a "*national* literature" equal to that produced during the great age of periodical literature in eighteenth-century England.[29]

Once the Southern states seceded and the nation was "dashed" into two large "fragments," the Union and the Confederacy, Evans and other Southern literary nationalists necessarily shifted their argumentative ground to recognize that their "province" had claimed the status of a nation. Thus Evans ends *Macaria* with its heroines, Irene and Electra, founding a school of design for Southern women, which they envision as promoting a Southern cultural nationalism entirely separate from Northern cultural influences. Irene, who finances the undertaking, echoes Evans's prewar ideas about the South and American cultural nationalism when she opines that "the planters of the Confederacy . . . have wealth, leisure, and every requisite adjunct, and upon them, as a class, must devolve this labor of love – the accomplishment of an American Renaissance – the development of the slumbering genius of our land."[30] However, she quickly turns from this ideal of an "American" cultural rebirth to a recognition of the difference that secession and its aftermath makes: "As we are distinct, socially and politically, from other nations, so let us be, intellectually and artistically" (p. 410).

Similar calls for Southern cultural nationalism appeared regularly throughout the war in Confederate periodicals, from the well-established monthly the *Southern Literary Messenger* to new literary weeklies and small daily newspapers. Although these articles seldom link the call for literary nationalism to the Confederacy's copyright law, they share with copyright advocacy published in the antebellum United States an understanding that literature is essential for a nation to establish cultural independence from another nation that once controlled it. Much as Evans did in 1859, Confederate magazinists attack literature published in Northern periodicals, such as the *New York Ledger* and *Harper's Monthly*, and decry *Uncle Tom's Cabin* and its negative effect on the South's reputation in Europe. Ella Swan, writing for the *Southern Field and Fireside* in 1861, for instance, castigates its readers for freely circulating "'Uncle Tom's Cabin,' Dred Scott [*sic*], and other works as poisonous as the deadly Upas tree . . . while Southern authors have met with little encouragement at your hands."[31] An anonymous article in the

28 "Southern Literature," *Mobile Daily Advertiser*,30 Oct. 1859, [2].

29 "Southern Literature." *Mobile Daily Advertiser*, 6 Nov. 1859, [2].

30 Augusta Jane Evans, *Macaria; or, Altars of Sacrifice*, ed. Drew Gilpin Faust (Baton Rouge: Louisiana State University Press, 1992), 409 (hereinafter cited in the text).

31 Ella Swan, "Southern Literature," *Southern Field and Fireside*, 13 July 1861, 60.

same weekly also celebrates "the secession of intercourse with the North" as a blessing, providing the south with

> blessed . . . relief from an avalanche of trash, which every mail poured into our borders – the production of a frightful tribe of superannuated females and penny-a-lining denizens of garrets – which our generous and hospitable people have taken into their homes in the name of Literature. Thank God! the sons and daughters of the South can be no longer be lured and contaminated by the lackadaisical fiddle-faddle of Bonner's *Ledger* or the "counterfeit presentments" of *Harper's Weekly* and *Leslie's Illustrated*. In these particulars we are "free and independent," which is no mean step toward a glorious redemption from Yankee bondage.[32]

Others, again echoing antebellum literary nationalistic attacks against British literature, label Northern literature as trash, poison, and impure food that the South was well rid of.[33] The *Southern Illustrated News* calls the firm that published Augusta Evans's first novel, Harper & Brothers, "Sharper & Brothers," thus punningly criticizing the firm for its "sharp" and dishonest business practices in failing to compensate British authors for American reprinting of their works.[34]

Confederate periodicals repeatedly proclaim Southern independence an opportunity for the South to free itself from "a state of colonial vassalage" in manufactures, literary and otherwise.[35] Although Confederate literary nationalists revile Northern literature, authors, and publishing practices, they do not, as some antebellum copyright advocates did, revile British literature and authors. Instead, they embrace the values of British culture and honor British authors. Boasting of the royalty payments made by the West & Johnston to Southern authors as evidence of "the salutary result of our liberation from Yankee bondage," the editor of the *Southern Literary Messenger*, for instance, also praises the firm for having made arrangements with English firms "to remunerate English authors for their labours. Hitherto foreign writers have been robbed, by Yankee swindlers, of the fruits of their genius; so that the American book trade was regarded as a system of legalized piracy; but we are glad to learn that the disgraceful proceeding is no part of Southern practice or legislation."[36] Indeed, some clearly hoped that the international

32 "Southern Enterprise – Southern Literature," *Southern Field and Fireside*, 2 Nov. 1861, 188. See Fahs on this paper's unacknowledged reprints from *Harper's Weekly* in 1863 and 1864. *Imagined Civil War*, 5, 37.

33 See, e.g. "Yankee Literature," *Southern Illustrated News*, 13 Sep. 1862, 5, which calls Northern literary productions "the opprobrium of the Universe," "an abomination," and an "abortion," and cites "Uncle Tom's" pernicious influence abroad.

34 "The Literary World," *Southern Illustrated News*, 8 Nov. 1862, 2.

35 "Yankee Literature," *Southern Illustrated News*, 13 Sep. 1862, 5.

36 "Editor's Table," *Southern Literary Messenger*, Feb. 1863, 117–18. The *Messenger* also reprinted a portion of Goetzel's letter to Bulwer discussed in more depth later.

copyright provisions of the law would entice British authors – and the British government – to embrace the Confederacy. Just as, before the war began, T. R. R. Cobb imagined his international copyright resolution eliciting the "sympathy" of British literary men and William Gilmore Simms imagined British authors being "stunned" by the generosity of the Confederacy for enacting international copyright, other Confederate ideologues deployed the international copyright statute as diplomatic leverage after the commencement of hostilities. Evans, a keen observer of international politics, almost certainly understood the law's dual potential as an instrument of both literary nationalism and Confederate diplomacy.[37]

A series of articles in the *Index*, a weekly newspaper published in London during the war and covertly financed by the Confederacy, and, closer to home for Augusta Evans, some clever maneuvering in the public press by Mobile publisher S. H. Goetzel demonstrate how the Confederacy's international copyright statute could be put to use in the campaign for British recognition. The *Index* began publication in 1862, by which time the 1861 Confederate copyright act was old news, but publisher Henry Hotze seems to have intuited the value of the legislation for propaganda purposes. In the third issue of the paper published in May 1862, an anonymous article (probably written by Hotze himself) on "Southern Feeling towards England" argues, "The South, for generations back, has been proud of its closer affinity of blood to the British parent stock, than the North, with its mongrel compound of the surplus population of all the world, could boast of it."[38] As evidence of this feeling, he claims that Southern gentlemen before the war refused to aid the Northern publishers in their "wholesale piracy" of English books. Instead, "the Southern gentleman prided himself upon paying five times the price for an English edition, than that same book would have cost in a 'Yankee' dress." Considering this affinity with and respect for England, Southerners are justly puzzled, in his estimation, by the reluctance

37 For evidence of Evans's knowledge of international politics, see Irene's abstruse discourse in the closing chapters of *Macaria* responding to the European critique of secession (pp. 365–7), as well as Evans's public letter to John Lothrop Motley, author of a much admired history of the Dutch Republic, responding to his criticism of the Confederacy's version of republicanism. "To John Lothrop Motley. Historian of the Dutch Republic and United Netherlands," *Mobile Advertiser and Register*, 21 Aug. 1861, [2]. It was published as by "A Confederate Woman," but see Augusta Jane Evans to Rachel Lyons, 20 Aug. 1861, in Rebecca Grant Sexton, ed., *A Southern Woman of Letters: The Correspondence of Augusta Jane Evans Wilson* (Columbia: University of South Carolina Press, 2002), 35–6.

38 "Southern Feeling Towards England," *Index*, 15 May 1862, 40. For Hotze's propaganda activities, including his founding of the *Index* and his presumed authorship of many articles, see Charles P. Cullop, *Confederate Propaganda in Europe, 1861–1865* (Coral Gables, FL: University of Miami Press, 1969). See also Frank Lawrence Owsley, *King Cotton Diplomacy: Foreign Relations of the Confederate States of America* (Chicago: University of Chicago Press, 1931), 166–75; and R. J. M. Blackett, *Divided Hearts: Britain and the American Civil War* (Baton Rouge: Louisiana State University Press, 2001), 144–5.

of England to recognize the Confederacy as "a new nation claiming admission into the family of nations."[39]

A few weeks later, the *Index* published another anonymous article, "The South as a Literary Market," and this second article dangles the prize of Southern readers as paying literary consumers more directly before British economic self-interest. The article, written from the (most likely assumed) perspective of an Englishman, begins by stating the obviousness of the "interest of commerce" in the South as a market for British goods and as a supplier of raw materials for British industry. The "independence of the South," claims the writer, opens "to unrestricted free trade a market of fabulous capacity for production and consumption" that "would be equal to the discovery of another India, and that an India discovered for our special benefit and enjoyment, without the drawback of its costing us large standing armies, and equally expensive machinery of government."[40] The writer's invocation of India as a point of comparison to the South is no accident – in the years leading up to the war, England attempted to substitute its own colony for the southern United States as a source of cotton for its mills. However, India's climate proved inappropriate for the production of the faster growing, more cheaply produced short staple cotton (grown in most regions of the southern United States), and the land tenure system under which Indian peasants worked provided little incentive for increased production to meet the demands of British mills.[41] Shifting to his true object, literature, the writer of the article in the *Index* paints an imperial fantasy of the South as a potential highly profitable literary colony of England rather than as an independent cultural producer freed from its "bondage" to the North. Describing in detail the losses suffered by British authors and publishers under the "wholesale and systematized piracy practised under sanction of law in the United States," the writer holds out as an antidote an independent Confederate nation and its international copyright law. The Confederacy "enlarges the appreciative and remunerative audience of every man who lives by his pen, or who plies it from choice or fame, by some six or seven millions of his own race and language, eager to receive intellectual instruction from the parent source of their language and literature."[42]

39 "Southern Feeling," 40. 40 "The South as a Literary Market," *Index*, 5 June 1862, 89.

41 For Britain's failed prewar attempts in India, see Owsley, *King Cotton*, 1–8. For a variety of complex reasons, the British textile industry managed to weather the absence of Southern cotton, and cotton thus had no power as a diplomatic weapon. See also Frenise A. Logan, "India – Britain's Substitute for American Cotton, 1861–1865," *Journal of Southern History* 24, no. 4 (1958): 472–80. Whatever historical retrospection tells us, however, at the time that Hotze invoked India here, such an argument would not have seemed pointless or ridiculous.

42 "The South as a Literary Market," 89. Actually, the article reproduces the text of the March 1861 international copyright resolution rather than the statute that superseded it, demonstrating the lack of publicity given to legislation, but nevertheless publicizing the intent of the relevant portion of the statute.

While recognizing that the Southern states may eventually produce their own literature, the writer promises that they "will not for many years be able to supply their own literary wants, or to give an equivalent for what they must receive from Europe." Nor will the South be willing to consume Northern cultural products, leaving an "immense vacuum" for British publications to fill.[43]

In early 1863, Mobile publisher S. H. Goetzel & Co. publicly demonstrated exactly what the *Index* hypothesized – that the Confederacy was a paying audience for British authors – and cleverly turned this demonstration into a bid for diplomatic recognition. Goetzel was one of the largest publishers of *belles letters* in the Confederacy,[44] both Southern and reprinted European, and in late 1862 he reprinted Sir Edward Bulwer-Lytton's novel *A Strange Story* (first serially in parts, and then complete in a single volume). In early 1863, at about the time Evans was finishing up *Macaria* and negotiating with West & Johston for the novel's publication in the Confederacy, Goetzel cleverly used the *Mobile Advertiser and Register* and the exchange system to publicize his intention to pay "a free-will international copyright" royalty to Bulwer-Lytton of ten cents a copy on 10,000 copies issued. In his "letter" to the British author, he claims to have resorted to publishing private business correspondence in the newspaper only because of "Mr. Lincoln's" refusal to let even correspondence with the "neutral nations of Europe, Asia, and Africa" through the blockade. However, this posture is transparently disingenuous. By choosing Bulwer – a man who was, not coincidentally, both a popular novelist and a Member of Parliament – as an object and by publishing his letter to him in the newspaper, Goetzel publicly represented the Confederacy to Bulwer-Lytton and his constituents as scrupulously ethical in its protection of private property and thus deserving of recognition:

> This is the first time to our knowledge that a republication of an English work has been attempted in the Southern States, and we think not to err if we assure you that our practice is merely a small sample of Southern commercial dealings generally, and that all the other publishers of the South will act in the same spirit of justice and humanity. Notwithstanding that the people of the Confederacy are outraged to an abominable degree – to a degree which defies the description of an illustrious pen like yours, most honored Sir – order reigns in our territories, and all sorts of property is properly protected; at any rate, more than amongst our unprincipled, savage invaders. Hence it is not extraordinary that the property of the mind, which is of the highest in creation, should be more highly respected here than amongst our enemies.

43 Ibid., 90.

44 For the best accounts of Goetzel's Civil War era publishing activities, see London, "Confederate Literature," and John Tebbel, *A History of Book Publishing in the United States, Vol. 1: The Creation of an Industry, 1630–1865* (New York: R. R. Bowker, 1972), 473–7.

> It is very much to be regretted that the great nations of Europe are not properly informed (certainly not impartially) of all the circumstances of the Confederate States of America.[45]

In his 1842 *North American Review* article in favor of international copyright, J. G. Palfrey cited Bulwer's first novel *Pelham* as an example of antirepublican literature for which Catharine Sedgwick's didactic novellas provided an antidote (see Chapter 2). J. G. Palfrey had little use for the man who inaugurated the so-called "silver fork school" of British fiction, and he hoped that the effects of international copyright would effectively push Bulwer out of the American market. In contrast, Goetzel uses promised royalties earned from Confederate readers to appeal to Bulwer as a natural ally of the Confederacy. When Bulwer wrote *Pelham* in the 1830s, he created a new literary and social type, what one modern critic calls "an outrageously flippant and cynical dandy aristocrat, who nevertheless had a hidden social conscience and who was utterly dedicated to noble political and aesthetic ideals."[46] In the 1830s, Bulwer was also a reform-minded Whig MP, but by the time of the American Civil War, he had inherited his mother's estate (and the hyphenated surname Bulwer-Lytton) and moved far to the right, becoming a Conservative and a critic of the movement toward universal male suffrage in England.[47] As Charles E. Shain notes, Bulwer, like many British aristocrats, was no lover of the United States; even though he did not publicly support secession and the Confederacy, he was not sorry to see the Union weakened by being split in two because he was disturbed by the "spectacle of a huge rival Anglo-Saxon population unled and unleavened by any county families."[48] Considering the Confederacy's claims to the aristocratic heritage of the Cavaliers and Bulwer's increasing conservatism and investment in his own aristocratic status, Goetzel's choice of Bulwer for this literary diplomatic maneuver is ingenious.

Goetzel frames the letter with a claim that "by some means unknown to us, newspapers now and then have found their way over the ocean," and, indeed, his letter made its way across the ocean to England, where it was published in the *London Standard* and favorably commented on in the *Reader*. Then, within a matter of months, Goetzel's letter and British

45 S. H. Goetzel, "Sir E. Bulwer Lytton, M. P., London," *Mobile Advertiser and Register*, 26 Feb. 1863, [2].

46 Allan Conrad Christensen, *Edward Bulwer-Lytton: The Fiction of New Regions* (Athens: University of Georgia Press, 1976), 223.

47 James L. Campbell, *Edward Bulwer-Lytton* (Boston: Twayne, 1986), 11–13, 16–19.

48 Charles E. Shain, "The English Novelists and the American Civil War," *American Quarterly* 14, no. 3 (1962): 403. See also Owsley, who says that in 1861, "Even Bulwer-Lytton thought that now was England's opportunity to make permanent the division of a rival that had grown too arrogant and strong." *King Cotton*, 205.

comments on it found their way back across the Atlantic to the offices of the *American Publisher's Circular & Literary Gazette*, a New York trade journal. The *Publishers' Circular* reported with relish Bulwer's denial of having received royalties from a Confederate publisher and his praise of Harper & Brothers for paying Bulwer and his publishers a substantial voluntary royalty £750 ($3,750) for its serialization of *A Strange Story* in *Harper's Weekly*. Overstating its case as much as Goetzel overstates his, the *Circular* goes so far as to claim that "the South has rarely published a book" and that Bulwer's novel was "never reprinted in Mobile or any other place in the South."[49] Whatever the facts concerning Bulwer's compensation for "American" sales, both sides attempt to occupy the same rhetorical ground, insisting that their nation's publishers respect British authors and British property.

As the articles in the *Index* and Goetzel's letter in the *Mobile Register* demonstrate, international copyright promoted (white, educated) Southerners to Britain as paying literary consumers and as aristocratically disinterested "cavaliers," whose claim to national status should be respected. By lobbying for an international copyright law, Evans participated in creating this particular version of Confederate ideology, a particular story that the new nation told other nations and itself about the values that constituted this nation. However, international copyright also potentially opened England as a paying market for Southern producers and thus served Evans's authorial self-interest at the expense of the interests of Confederate readers. A lone voice publicly criticizing international copyright (in the *Mobile Register* in 1861) advocated the "right" of Southern publishers to appropriate British literary property on behalf of Southern readers. This critique brings into sharp relief by way of contrast how international copyright participated in the articulation of the dominant version of Confederate nationalism, which represented the Confederate nation as commercially disinterested, agrarian, and aristocratic in opposition to the commercially motivated, industrialized, and plebian "Yankee" North.[50] In this anticopyright article, almost certainly

49 "American Publishers and English Authors," *American Publishers' Circular & Literary Gazette*, 1 June 1863, 143–4. The *Circular* resorts to half-truths and exaggeration to rebut Goetzel's half-truths and exaggerations. In England, the novel was serialized in Charles Dickens's magazine *All the Year Round*, and as Dickens explained to Bulwer in a letter dated 4 Dec. 1860, "For the transmission of proofs to America week by week for simultaneous publication – of course without damage to copyright here – I could get you (as our American transactions are on a very good footing) £300 – three hundred pounds." Victor Alexander George Robert Bulwer-Lytton, *The Life of Edward Bulwer, First Lord Lytton* (London: Macmillan, 1913), 2:344.

50 For a summary of the Cavalier versus Yankee dichotomy fully developed by 1860, see William R. Taylor, *Cavalier and Yankee: The Old South and American National Character* (New York: George Braziller, 1961) 15. As Taylor makes clear in his study, this dichotomy was always a myth (what Drew Gilpin Faust would later call an "ideology") rather than an accurate description of social reality, but it was a myth that had real political effects. One other early 1861 newspaper article takes a similar stance to the *Register* article but ultimately focuses on patents and says nothing about international copyright. "Patents and Copyrights," *Montgomery Weekly Advertiser*, 27 Feb. 1861, 3. See Chapter 3 for Henry

read by Augusta Evans herself on her return from her visit to the Confederate Congress and her introduction to T. R. R. Cobb, the author praises Cobb's motives for proposing international copyright but faults him for failing to contemplate the "practical effect of the application of that theory" to the situation of the Confederacy.[51] As a nation that exported "cotton and not books and statues," the Confederacy would gain only increased prices for British books. As a nation in its infancy, the Confederacy had no authors who could compete with British ones. While waiting for the development of a national literary culture, urged the *Register*, "Let us freely avail ourselves of the science and the thought of other nations, especially those whom Providence has made the depositories of the noble acquisitions of our race.... Let us buy their books cheap and make them accessible to the mass of the people." Noting that a common language made British literature particularly accessible, the article proclaims that the South had "an inherited right" to British-authored texts "as members of the Caucasian race."

These arguments made by the *Register* were not new; instead, they replicated, with only slight variation, highly effective arguments made against international copyright by Northern publishers from the 1830s on, such as members of the book trade who petitioned the U.S. Congress against international copyright in 1842, describing British literature in their petition as an inherited "birthright" that should remain "free as the vital air, untaxed, unhindered," a "vital river of knowledge" that should not be damned.[52] In the Confederacy, however, such arguments represented an ineffective minority voice, calling on a version of nationalism out of synch with the Confederacy's movement away from populism and democracy. The *Register* article criticizes international copyright because it "would benefit but a few – and only a very few – of our literary men." However, the nation was at war to defend the property interests of a planter class representing a small fraction of the total population, and thus calls in the language of what conservatives of the era would label "agrarianism" for the rights of "the people" to convert private property to the public good fell on deaf ears. Augusta Evans's second novel, *Beulah*, had found an audience, if not a

Carey's 1868 analysis of the regional inflections of antebellum copyright advocacy – although he does not mention and likely did not know of the Confederacy's international copyright provisions, he seems to have accurately diagnosed the anti-common-reader, aristocratic bias of the antebellum Southern thinking about international copyright as evidenced in the Confederacy's decision to legislate international copyright.

51 "Mr. Cobb's Resolution and Southern Literature," *Southern Confederacy* (Atlanta, GA), 18 May 1861. I quote from a reprint crediting the article to the *Mobile Register* because no issues of the *Register* from the months leading up to its merger with the *Advertiser* in June 1861 survive.

52 Senate, *Memorial of a Number of Persons Concerned in Printing and Publishing, Praying an Alteration in the Mode of Levying Duties on Certain Books, and Remonstrating against the Enactment of an International Copy-Right Law*, 27th Cong., 2nd sess., 13 June 1842, S. Doc. 323, 1–2.

paying one, in England before the war, demonstrating her ability to compete successfully with British authors. She almost certainly saw the advantage of international copyright to her own financial interests as an author in the early stages of planning her third novel, *Macaria*.[53] Evans, one of the South's "literary women" rather than its "literary men," helped to create a copyright system designed for her own benefit as one of the "the very few" at the expense of "the mass of the people."

"I am I assure you, greatly indebted for the passage of the Act securing Copyrights": Augusta Evans lobbies for Confederate copyright revision

Augusta Evans's efforts to shape the Confederacy's copyright law did not end with international copyright in 1861. As *De Bow's Review* astutely observes in its brief report concerning the 1861 act, a provision of the act requiring copyright registration in the Confederacy within four months of foreign publication "sets free all works hitherto copyrighted at the North."[54] Although such an "emancipation" of Northern property was a potential boon for Southern publishers, who could then legally reprint Northern books, such a provision was potentially problematic for loyal Confederate authors who had transferred outright or contracted away rights in their property to Northern publishers, as most Southern authors necessarily had in the prewar years because there were very few Southern book publishers. Again, as *De Bow*'s queried, "Those [copyrights] of authors residing within the Confederate States, we presume, may be saved by a reissue, though we do not see this in the act."

Evans seems not have recognized the negative implications of the original statute for her own interests immediately after its passage. However, the difficulties faced by S. H. Goetzel when he published in Mobile a Confederate edition of Col. W. J. Hardee's *Rifle and Infantry Tactics* (difficulties well publicized in Mobile newspapers from June 1861 through the end of 1862) may have alerted her to the loophole in the law and prompted her to lobby Curry for an amendment to the law. The U.S. Army originally commissioned Hardee's *Tactics* when Hardee was a U.S. army officer, and Lippincott and Grambo published it in Philadelphia in 1855. Shortly after secession, Hardee joined the Confederate army and lightly revised his *Tactics*. He then contracted with Goetzel to publish this revised edition for

53 Saunders, Otley & Co. published *Macaria* in England in 1864 (advertised in the *Index* 27 Oct. 1864 and reviewed 1 Dec. 1864). Evans very well may have arranged this British edition with Saunders, Otley & Co. just as she did a Northern edition with Derby.

54 "The Southern Confederacy," *De Bow's Review*, Sep. 1861, 315.

the Confederate market, and Goetzel registered the first Confederate copyright to protect his edition. Almost simultaneously, however, other Confederate publishers, in competition with Goetzel and Hardee, brought out reprints of the 1855 Philadelphia edition. In response, the *Mobile Advertiser and Register* published an indignant editorial protesting the shoddy ethics of the piratical publishers. In addition, Goetzel's ads for the book feature prominent warnings to buyers not to be fooled into buying the "spurious" and "mutilated" editions and threaten to sue infringing publishers and booksellers under the Confederate copyright law. Hardee had never properly secured a U.S. copyright registration for the first edition, however, with the result that it had fallen into the public domain before the war. As a result, the Confederate courts would not enjoin Confederate publishers from reprinting the 1855 Philadelphia edition, and Goetzel's 1863 suit against a Mobile bookseller failed. Goetzel and Hardee ultimately resorted to private legislation to secure a special Confederate copyright for Hardee's *Tactics*.[55]

As Goetzel and Hardee's battle with piratical Confederate publishers played out on the stage of the *Mobile Advertiser and Register*, Evans was hard at work writing the novel that became *Macaria*. Wartime production difficulties delayed the publication of *Macaria* until 1864, but she had begun writing the novel perhaps as early as 1861 and continued writing through 1862.[56] On February 22, 1863, she wrote Richmond publisher West & Johnston accepting their terms for publication of the novel, "namely $1000 cash and ten percent on every copy published; with the understanding that as soon as you deem it advisable you will republish 'Beulah,' allowing me the same percentage."[57] In late 1862 (before Goetzel's suit trying to suppress Confederate reprinting of *Hardee's Tactics* had failed, and when, one can infer from the surviving correspondence, Evans had begun her negotiations with West & Johnston), her good friend J. L. M. Curry first introduced in the Confederate House of Representatives "A bill to secure copyrights to authors and composers, citizens of the Confederate States, whose works

55 Goetzel's registration for *Hardee's Tactics* in the District of Alabama court is dated 4 May 1861. Robinson, "Confederate Copyright Entries," 255. Goetzel's ads for *Hardee's Tactics* ran regularly in the *Mobile Advertiser and Register* for much of 1861 and 1862. The *Advertiser and Register*'s editorial expressed especial horror that Southern publishers should show as little or even less "honor" than Yankee publishers. "A Mobile Book-Copyright," *Mobile Advertiser and Register*, 27 June 1861, 2. See Bryan, "General William Hardee," for a complete account of the suit and private legislation.

56 In Aug. 1861, she reported that "Mr D." (probably J. C. Derby) had safely received "my precious MS" and was "much pleased with it!" Augusta Jane Evans to Rachel Lyons, 20 Aug. 1861, in Sexton, *Southern Woman*, 35. Events described in the later chapters of the novel take place in the summer of 1862, so she clearly continued writing into late 1862. Elsewhere, I fully reconstruct this chronology and lay to rest the idea that there was an 1863 Confederate first edition of *Macaria*. "The Publishing History of Augusta Jane Evans's *Macaria*: Unwriting Some Lost Cause Myths," forthcoming in *Mississippi Quarterly*.

57 Augusta Jane Evans to West & Johnston, 22 Feb. 1863, in Sexton, *Southern Woman*, 53.

were copyrighted under the laws of the United States."[58] On its first introduction, the bill disappeared into the Committee on the Judiciary, never to reappear, but after the bill's second introduction in January of 1863,[59] the Committee reported favorably on it. After a friendly amendment, it was passed into law in April 1863, nearly two years after the passage of the original Confederate copyright statute.[60]

The first section of this bill provides for exactly what *De Bow's* earlier suggested – that Confederate authors would be entitled to a "reissue" of their U.S. copyrights in the Confederacy. The second section went even further, allowing authors to take back copyrights that they had contracted or signed away before the war. The friendly amendment to the bill qualified the rights under both sections somewhat, specifying that authors could take back their copyrights and sue for infringement only if such a recapture did not interfere with an interest held in such a copyright by another loyal Confederate citizen and did not interfere with the right of the Confederate government to dispose of sequestered physical copies of books printed by Northern publishers.[61] After the passage of the new act, Evans wrote to Curry, "To your friendly interest and perseverance, I am I assure you, greatly indebted for the passage of the Act securing Copyrights; which is (as far as I am capable of judging,) sufficiently protective, and perfectly satisfactory. Accept my grateful acknowledgments for its successful accomplishment."[62]

Like Irene, the heroine of *Macaria*, who asks her friend Dr. Arnold to propose her plan for financing public education to the state legislature because "I do not wish to be known at all in the affair. It is not a woman's business to put forward legislative bills" (p. 276), Evans clearly directed Curry to draft and propose legislation to remedy what she had come to see as a defect in the law while preserving the public appearance of detachment from the business of government. But what, specifically, did Evans have to thank him for? Recall that Evans had negotiated with West & Johnston for the publication of a new Confederate edition of *Beulah*. Although Hardee's *Tactics* was not protected by a U.S. copyright registration, U.S. copyright law did fully protect *Beulah*. Evans had assigned her copyright to J. C. Derby before publication, however, leaving her novel open for Confederate reprinting without authorization from or compensation to her – at least until Curry successfully amended the law to suit her. Indeed, even the language of the

58 *Journal of the Congress of the Confederate States of America*, 1861–1865 (Washington, DC: Government Printing Office, 1904), 5:360. (House, 9 Sep. 1862).

59 *Journal of the Confederate Congress*, 6:35 (House, 21 Jan. 1863).

60 *Journal of the Confederate Congress*, 6:402 (House, 22 Apr. 1863).

61 *Statutes at Large of the Confederate States of America, Passed at the Third Session of the First Congress; 1863*, ed. James M. Matthews (Richmond: R. M. Smith, 1863), 113–14. See Coulter for the CSA's sequestration acts, both passed in 1861. *Confederate Nation*, 123–4.

62 Augusta Jane Evans to J. L. M. Curry, 15 July 1863, in Sexton, *Southern Woman*, 65. Sexton erroneously glosses this letter as a "thank you" for the passage of international copyright.

act strongly hints that Curry specifically designed it to meet the needs of a rare Southern woman author who had published a commercially successful novel in the North before the war but who in 1863 was a loyal Confederate. The original 1861 Confederate copyright act, like the U.S. copyright statutes, uses the masculine pronoun exclusively to refer to authors and other copyright proprietors. In contrast, the first two sections of the Confederate copyright revision act manage to avoid gendered pronominal references entirely, but the third section of the act specifies, "Any author, designer or publisher, who may become entitled to the benefit of the provisions of the first section of this act, shall have all the remedies for any infringement of *his or her* copyright, which may have occurred before the passage of this act, which would exist had such infringement occurred subsequent to its passage" (emphasis added). Decades later, J. C. Derby imagined Evans sitting helplessly in the South during the war and relying on his active exertions in the North on her behalf. In reality, however, Evans was working quietly behind the scenes in the South to wrest the copyright to *Beulah* out of his control, at least in the Confederacy. That is, while Derby was preparing for Miss Evans's conversion from secession to loyalty, Miss Evans was actively working for the Confederacy and her own economic interests as a loyal citizen of that Confederacy, even when her interests directly conflicted with Derby's.

Evans's self-possession and independence working behind the scenes on behalf of Confederate copyright intersect with the self-possession and independence of the heroines of the novel she was writing simultaneously with her copyright lobbying. In her novel, she advocates that women act disinterestedly to promote the Confederacy's national interests, but, as she did in her own life, she recognizes the possibility that women who dedicated themselves to serving the Confederacy might also come to own and master themselves as they could not in the prewar South. As Drew Gilpin Faust persuasively argues, through *Macaria* Evans promoted the idea that Confederate independence represented an opportunity for single women like the novel's two heroines to find "both true personal independence and fulfillment" outside of marriage: "Women, Evans suggests . . . need not simply endure the war but might justly celebrate its unprecedented opportunities for self-realization. Through Confederate nationalism these women thus may truly find themselves. In 1864, with nearly half the white male population of the South wounded or killed, the single life was for many inevitable. Evans felt she could dare to make it seem desirable."[63] Both heroines of *Macaria*, primary heroine Irene and secondary heroine Electra,

63 Faust, *Mothers of Invention*, 172. But see also Holstein, "Offering up Her Life," and Gross, "Lonely Lives." Sofer emphasizes the continuities in Evans's project of defining and justifying women as artistic producers in a high cultural mode rather than finding *Macaria* exceptional. *Making the "America of Art,"* chap. 2.

repel the marital advances of men they do not love but who claim the right to "master" and "own" them. Refusing to honor her father's promise to his dying sister that their infant children (cousins) will marry when they become adults, Irene Huntingdon tells her father, "You have the right to guide me, to say what I shall not do without your consent, but I am a free-born American, thank God! I do not draw my breath in Circassia, to be bartered for gold by my father. I, only, can give myself away.... Is one of God's holy sacraments to become a mere pecuniary transaction? – only a legal transfer of real estate and cotton bales?" (p. 200). Electra similarly rejects the attempts of painter Mr. Clifton, her teacher and guardian, to "claim" her as his marital property, proclaiming, "I will stand alone" (p. 133).

In a complex (and sometimes contradictory) set of interlocking images, when Evans's heroines refuse to submit to the "tyranny" and "bondage" of masculine authority and the marriage market, they simultaneously become figures of the new Southern nation that will justifiably overthrow the "tyranny" and "bondage" of the North (even when, as is the case with Irene, she resists the authority of a Southern patriarch of the planter class, her father). Irene and Electra reject the prospect of loveless marriages because both love the same man, Russell Aubrey, whom Irene will not marry because her father forbids it, and whom Electra cannot marry because Aubrey loves only Irene. Russell Aubrey, describing to Electra his presumption that Irene will marry a man she does not love (the governor's son) because her father wills it, sarcastically opines that love "is not necessary to latter-day matrimonial contracts.... She [Irene] is bound hand and foot, and her father will immolate her on the altar of money.... I pity the woman whose fate rests in his iron grasp" (p. 215). Shortly thereafter, in a campaign speech in an election for the state legislature in which Irene's father is the opposing candidate, Aubrey prophesies, "The period was rapidly approaching when the Southern states, unless united and on the alert, would lie bound at the feet of an insolent and rapacious Northern faction" (p. 228). When describing the state secession convention (in which, naturally, both Aubrey and Mr. Huntingdon serve, but in opposite factions), Evans, speaking as the narrator, writes: "Bitter differences sprung up at the very threshold on the *modus operandi* of Southern release from Yankee-Egyptic bondage" (p. 299). On the one hand, then, Irene's situation is an analogue of the image of the (female) South bound at the feet of the rapacious, commercially motivated North; on the other hand, she lies (metaphorically speaking) bound at the feet of her greedy, tyrannical, Southern father, whose authority is congruent with the authority of the Confederacy and Southern patriarchy. Even when her father joins the Confederate army and goes off to fight for the "right" side of the conflict, he will not fully forgive Irene for refusing to submit entirely to his patriarchal authority.

In the end, Irene escapes both her father's will and her own desire to submit willingly to the bonds of marriage to the man she loves. Conveniently, her father dies a heroic death in the war, forgiving Aubrey and admitting his errors with his dying breath. Aubrey does not survive his nemesis long enough to marry Irene, however. He, too, dies a heroic death in the war, leaving both Irene and Electra independent and dedicated to the Confederacy. Irene nurses wounded soldiers and runs an orphan asylum, while Electra aspires to paint the first great work of Confederate art. Irene also commissions Electra to be the principal of a school of design for Southern women, an institution Irene creates so that Southern women who have lost the support of actual or potential husbands killed in battle will be able to learn skills that will enable them to support themselves. Looking forward to the Confederacy's ultimate victory so that they may stand independently rather than lie bound at the feet of the North, Irene and Electra also vow not to submit to marital bonds. "Remember," Irene counsels Electra, "the woman who dares to live alone, and be sneered at, is braver, and nobler, and better than she who escapes both in a loveless marriage" (p. 413).

"[H]owever repugnant it may be to loyalty to learn that such a rebel book can find publisher and readers in the North": *Macaria* and Evans's literary property in the North during the war

Through the heroines of her novel, Augusta Evans articulates a vision of the Confederacy and Confederate womanhood as standing entirely apart from the North in all things, including trade and culture. Discussing the future of the Confederacy with Electra, Irene argues for a "free trade" policy, with "our ports . . . open to all markets of the world, except Lincolndom," so that "the rigid laws of political economy [may] forge links of amity" with Europe (pp. 366–7). One might expect, then, that Evans would not wish to forge her own links of literary trade with Lincolndom at the height of the Civil War; however, evidence suggests otherwise. By attempting to reclaim the copyright of *Beulah*, Evans consolidated her position as a Confederate author writing for Confederate audiences, but she also had designs on the Northern market. Certainly, her status as a loyal Confederate made her ability to control the circumstances under which her novel would be published in the North tenuous at best. The Union considered Confederate loyalists to be "citizens in rebellion" rather than "enemy aliens," but secession and the war placed Evans, for all practical purposes, in the same position in relation to the Northern market as American authors to the British market and British authors to the American market before the war. In the absence of international copyright statutes or treaties, publishers in the United States could and did, with perfect impunity, republish the works of British authors without their permission and without payment of royalties to them. Although American authors could obtain copyright protection in England under certain highly limited circumstances, American authors were, in most instances, as vulnerable to unauthorized reprinting in England as English authors to unauthorized reprinting in America (as discussed in Chapter 3, Harriet Beecher Stowe received no compensation for the substantial English sales of *Uncle Tom's Cabin*).

In the North, it did not take long for enterprising publishers to recognize that Confederate authors might be treated as Stowe had been in England or Charles Dickens in America. As the *New-York Tribune* reported in a long article on a book trade auction of stereotype plates in 1862 (an auction featuring the entire stock of the recently defunct firm of Derby & Jackson), "Miss Evans's Beulah ran through 40 editions in its day, but the plates were bought by a Mr. Scott for $205, and there is small chance of there being much copyright paid to the authoress hereafter, for the [*sic*] is a rank Rebel, and a nurse in a Southern Hospital."[64] A stereotyped book could be printed from the plates as needed for years, or even decades, without the necessity of re-typesetting the book. In the 1850s, as the cost of stereotyping books went down, stereotyping became routine. Under normal (prewar) conditions, a publisher who acquired existing stereotype plates (at an auction like the one reported here or through a private sale) also assumed the original publisher's contractual obligation to pay royalties on all copies printed from those plates.[65] However, the *Tribune* predicts that Northern publishers will ignore such obligations incurred before the war to an author such as Evans who has become a "rank rebel." Indeed, the *Tribune* goes beyond prediction, positively encouraging Northern publishers to ignore such obligations to Southern authors. It is a small step from ignoring a contract signed before the war to ignoring a rebel author's literary property rights in a work created after secession.

Placed in such a position, Evans did precisely what American and British authors had done before the war to attempt to gain some benefit from sales of their books in the opposite country despite the lack of statutory protection – she forwarded an advance copy (either a complete prepublication copy or unbound advance sheets sent in installments as they came off the press) to a "foreign" publisher, on the understanding that he would

64 "Literary Intelligence.... The Book-Trade Sale – the Great Auction of Stereotype Plates," *American Publishers' Circular and Literary Gazette*, 1 Nov. 1862, 115 (identified as a reprint from the *New-York Tribune*). In modern bibliographical terminology, the "editions" here would be labeled "printings." Rather than switch confusingly between nineteenth-century quotations and modern bibliographical terminology, I use "editions" in the nineteenth-century sense in describing the subsequent printings from the plates of Evans's novels.

65 On trade practices with respect to stereotype plates, including copyright, see Michael Winship, "Printing with Plates in the Nineteenth Century United States," *Printing History* 5, no. 2 (1983): 16–26.

arrange for publication of an "author's edition" and would voluntarily pay her royalties on sales. (In this case, she chose a "foreign" publisher in New York, J. C. Derby, who, reminiscing years later, glossed over the commercial significance of Evans's sending him a copy of her novel; instead, he represents the copy as if it were a gift of friendship across the lines and as if the impulse to see the book published in the North were entirely his own). As would have been the case with a British edition of an American author's work, however, such an author's edition would only be profitable for Evans as long as other publishers observed "courtesy of the trade," an extralegal arrangement whereby the first publisher to announce an edition of a book by a foreign author was considered to have an exclusive right, even in the absence of statutory copyright protection.[66] Evans, Derby, and Lippincott all seem to have understood that they were proceeding according to this model, as demonstrated by Lippincott's announcement in the Northern trade press in December of 1863 that he would be publishing an unnamed "new work by the author of 'Beulah'".[67] That is, with her novel not yet in print in the Confederacy (Evans was still reading proof in December 1863), she had contacted Derby about Northern publication, and Derby had already made arrangements with Lippincott. Although Derby later recounted making arrangements with Lippincott for the publication of a Northern edition after receiving the complete Confederate edition through the blockade, evidence suggests that Derby acted without a complete printed text (or even, perhaps, the novel's title) in hand.

Lippincott's announcement to the trade had no legal effect – he was relying on their professional courtesy not to preempt the priority of his claim. Nevertheless, he forged ahead, announcing his edition of *Macaria* as "in press" by early May 1864, several weeks after the long-delayed Richmond publication. However, as a June 1, 1864, review of the Northern edition of another Confederate-authored novel, Sally Rochester Ford's *Raids and Romance of Morgan and His Men*, wryly observed, "There is no reason why the Confederacy, as it is called, should not have its war literature as well as ourselves, and the enterprising publishers of New York are reproducing it for us quite freely."[68] As early as May 19, 1864, John Bradburn, just such an "enterprising publisher of New York," was informing the trade of *his* plan to publish *Macaria* by advertising the book in the *New-York Daily Tribune* as "in press." A few weeks later, in its "Notes on Books and Booksellers," the *American Literary Gazette and Publishers' Circular* reported, "MR. JOHN

66 This account of trade practices necessarily oversimplifies. See James J. Barnes, *Authors, Publishers, and Politicians: The Quest for an Anglo-American Copyright Agreement, 1815–1854* (Columbus: Ohio State University Press, 1974), chaps. 3 and 7; Eugene Exman, *The Brothers Harper* (New York: Harper & Row, 1965), 52–9; and Tebbel, *History of Book Publishing*, 208–9.

67 "Announcements," *American Literary Gazette and Publisher's Circular*, 15 Dec. 1863, 146.

68 *American Literary Gazette and Publishers' Circular*, 1 June 1864, 87.

BRADBURN, of New York, is steadily and effectively adding to his list. He is now putting through the press a new novel entitled 'Macaria,' by Augusta J. Evans, author of 'Beulah,' 'Inez,' &c. He expects that it will be largely successful, and it is stated that orders already received exhaust the first supply."[69]

Bradburn and Michael Doolady (the man Derby later identified as the piratical New York publisher) were not full business partners and did not publish any books under a joint imprint, but these enterprising publishers shared a New York office address and collaborated on several Civil War era publishing ventures, including the first New York edition of *Macaria*.[70] *Macaria* was not the only Evans-authored literary property to which Bradburn and Doolady had "helped themselves." They had earlier acquired Harper & Brothers' stereotype plates for Evans's anonymous first novel, *Inez*, which Bradburn began advertising for sale in January 1864. They undoubtedly relished buying the stereotype plates from Harpers, probably at very low cost, at a time when they could safely ignore Harpers' promise to pay Evans royalties on sales (the 1854 contract between Evans and Harper & Brothers specified a royalty of "ten per cent, on their trade list price for each copy sold . . . over and above one thousand . . . during the terms of the copyright"[71]). Although *Inez* originally appeared without Evans's name on the title page, Bradburn's edition added a byline, "by Miss Evans, author of 'Beulah,'" thus exploiting Evans's greater success with *Beulah* to wring some additional commercial value out of the seemingly valueless stereotype plates of her anonymous first novel. To add insult to injury, Bradburn's early advertisements were so vague and ambiguous as to allow purchasers to assume that the book was new and featured Civil War content.[72] (One can only imagine Evans's dismay in February 1864 when she read an item in the *Mobile Advertiser and Register* reprinted from the *Chicago Times*, reporting, "A new novel, by Augusta J. Evans, authoress of 'Beulah,' entitled 'Inez; a

69 "Notes on Books and Booksellers," *American Literary Gazette and Publishers' Circular,* 15 June 1864, 113.

70 Bradburn's edition of *Macaria* designates him "successor to Michael Doolady," and Doolady filed for copyright registration of *Macaria*. However, Doolady's name continued to appear as a publisher's imprint during and after 1864, and New York City directories list both men (separately rather than together) at 49 Walker Street in1864 and 1865. Both publishers have largely flown under the radar of publishing history. For very brief (and inaccurate) sketches of their careers, see David Dzwonkoski, "M. Doolady," and Theodora Mills, "John Bradburn," in *American Literary Publishing Houses, 1638–1899*, part 1, ed. Peter Dzwonkoski (Detroit: Gale, 1986), 137, 63.

71 Memorandum of Agreement between Augusta Jane Evans and Harper & Brothers, 1 Nov. 1854, in Sexton, *Southern Woman*, [189].

72 See, e.g., an advertisement that ambiguously sandwiches the line "A Splendid New Story of the War" between an announcement of the imminent publication of *Inez* and an announcement of the imminent publication of *The Rival Volunteers, or, The Black Plume Rifles* by Mary A. Howe. *New York Tribune*, 13 Jan. 1864. In a sense, *Inez* actually was a Civil War book; on the novel as a transparent allegory of the sectional conflict, see Moss, *Domestic Novelists*, 154, 157.

Tale of the Alamo,' is announced by John Bradburn, of New York. The last heard of Miss Evans she was nursing rebel soldiers in Mobile."[73]) Thus by June of 1864, Bradburn and Doolady had appropriated two-thirds of Evans's existing oeuvre, turning her and her works into items on their Civil War list and under their control in the Northern market. They even went so far as registering U.S. copyrights as proprietors of *Macaria* and *Inez*, lending an air of legitimacy to their appropriation.[74]

So just what interests, personal and political, did this "rank rebel" author and these multiple Northern men in the publishing business serve in their efforts to give Northern readers access to *Macaria*? Augusta Evans was certainly looking out for her own financial interests when she made arrangements with Derby to publish her novel in the North, but in ensuring that a Northern audience had access to her novel, she also worked in tandem with the efforts by the Confederate government to manipulate Northern politics. Throughout the war, the Confederacy covertly supported Northern political elements (the so-called Peace Democrats and Copperheads) that wanted to see the war end immediately without a Northern military victory or a concomitant Southern surrender. Evans's novel potentially bolstered such Northern sentiments. At times in *Macaria*, Evans attacks the North in the strongest terms, but she also celebrates the Confederate nation and its values and portrays all elements of that nation, rich and poor, black and white, men and women, as united in support of the war effort. Planter-class Irene's efforts receive the most attention, but Mrs. Baker, a poor, white woman living on Factory Row, declares, "I am a poor woman, Miss Irene, but no soul loves the Confederacy better than I do, or will work harder for it" (p. 312). Loyal William, a slave who serves as the family cook, willingly follows his master, Mr. Huntingdon, into battle, and, in the words of his dying master on the battlefield, "he followed me so closely that he was shot through the head.... Poor fellow! he was faithful to the last" (p. 336). For Northerners who longed for an end to the bloodshed, such a portrait of the Confederate cause reinforced the message of those who claimed that the war was unjust and should cease immediately. A reviewer in a New York Copperhead newspaper, the *Day-Book Caucasian*, understood the import of the novel for Northern readers in precisely this way: "It asserts the dignity and earnestness of purpose characteristic of that people, and suggests them in the light of men and women who are worthy of the condition of the rights of freedom, and are determined to have them. This idea conflicts

73 "New Novel," *Mobile Weekly Advertiser and Register*, 27 Feb. 1864, in the Augusta J. Evans clipping file, Museum of Mobile, Mobile, Alabama.

74 Michael Doolady filed a copyright registration for *Macaria* in the Southern District of New York on 21 June 1864 and deposited a copy with the clerk on 2 July 1864. J. B. Lippincott & Co. filed for copyright registration in the Eastern District of Pennsylvania on 12 May 1864 and deposited a copy (apparently of Bradburn's edition) on 30 June 1864. John Bradburn's 1864 edition of *Inez* features a copyright notice claiming an 1864 Southern District of New York registration.

with current notions in many parts of the North, while it would seem that the southerners are regarded as an ignorant and low minded class of ruffians."[75] The covert efforts of the Confederate government to support the peace movement in the North had the ultimate goal of Lincoln's ouster from the presidency in the fall 1864 election by the election of a Democratic president. A Democratic president would, they believed, immediately call an armistice and begin negotiations with the Confederacy. After the stunning Union victory at Gettysburg in July, such efforts failed. However, Evans's novel hit the bookstores in New York at a moment when Peace Democrats were a powerful force on the verge of success and Lincoln and his Republican Party were in danger of being toppled.[76]

Why, however, would two sets of Northern publishers compete for the right to republish Evans's novelistic attack on the Union on Union ground? Bradburn's and Doolady's lists from this time reveal them to be political opportunists, at least in their professional roles as publishers. Playing both sides of the aisle, their heavily war-related lists included everything from Copperhead pamphlets attacking Lincoln and defending slavery to pro-Union abolitionist tracts.[77] If Evans had been a foreign citizen, the U.S. copyright law would have permitted and, indeed, even *encouraged* New York publishers to appropriate her literary property. However, the United States never acknowledged the legitimacy of secession, so Southerners loyal to the Confederacy were not, in the strictest technical legal sense, citizens of a foreign nation. Instead, Evans was a "citizen in rebellion," making her property, including intangible property, subject to confiscation and sale to finance the war effort. Private citizens who instigated confiscation suits were, however, only entitled to a percentage of the value confiscated, with the

75 "Macaria: A Novel," *New York Day-Book Caucasian* (weekly ed.), 20 July 1864, 5.

76 For the political climate and events of 1864 as described in this paragraph, see James M. McPherson, *Battle Cry of Freedom: The Civil War Era* (New York: Ballentine, 1989), chaps. 23, 25, and 26.

77 A few examples of Civil War–related materials published by each man during the war years demonstrate their political flexibility. Bradburn published Sir Arthur James Lyon Fremantle's *Three Months in the Southern States; April–June, 1863* (1864) (a sympathetic account by an Englishman who served in the Confederate army); John H. Van Evrie, *Subgenation: The Theory of the Normal Relation of the Races: An Answer to "Miscegenation"* (1864) (a Copperhead defense of slavery and black subservience as grounded in nature); Thomas Shepard Goodwin, *The Natural History of Secession; or, Despotism and Democracy at Necessary, Eternal, Exterminating War* (1864) (a critique of Southern slavery by a Northern minister as fundamentally incompatible with American democracy). Doolady published *Interior Causes of the War; The Nation Demonised, and Its President a Spirit-Rapper* (1863) (a satirical attack on the Lincoln administration); Richard Grant White, *Revelations: A Companion to the "New Gospel of Peace." According to Abraham* (1863) (a satirical attack on the Copperheads and Peace Democrats); and Oliver B. Bunce, *Reconstruction* (1862) (advocating an end to the war and reconstruction with autonomy for and continuance of slavery in the South). That two printings (dated 1864 and 1865) of the Godwin title appeared under the Derby & Miller imprint produced from the same plates as the Bradburn edition suggests that Derby & Miller and Bradburn and Doolady may have had more cordial relations than Derby recalled decades later.

lion's share going to the government.[78] In essence, Bradburn and Doolady confiscated Evans's literary property extralegally for their own benefit rather than for the war effort.

Although J. C. Derby, writing well after the war, presents himself as gentlemanly and chivalrous, his own actions with respect to Evans's novel were legally suspect on other grounds and demonstrate his own political and commercial opportunism. In his memoirs and as part of his narrative of the publication of *Macaria*, Derby claims that he was forced out of the publishing business in 1861 because the market required only schoolbooks and military manuals rather than the novels that were his stock and trade. He further claims that he did not return to publishing until well after the war.[79] However, Derby either misremembered or misrepresented his activities. As reported in the trade press and documented by extensive advertising, Derby, in early 1864, reentered the publishing business in partnership with his former partner N. C. Miller as Derby & Miller, and the firm commenced publishing a list made up entirely of war-related, pro-Republican pamphlets and books. Prominent on their list were Lincoln's collected "State Papers," which reviewers recognized as campaign propaganda for Lincoln in the upcoming presidential election.[80] Considering that Derby & Miller began advertising books for sale under the new joint imprint in February 1864,[81]

78 For the standard historical account of the U.S. law and its effects, with a specific focus on legal proceedings in New York, see Henry D. Shapiro, *Confiscation of Confederate Property in the North* (Ithaca: Cornell University Press, 1962). The Union passed two separate confiscation statutes, one in August 1861, and the other in July 1862. Although the 1861 act provided only for confiscation of property used in support of insurrection, under the 1862 act, "title to property owned by Confederates was vested in the government of the United States upon even tacit support of insurrection by a Southern owner" (p. 46). Under the 1862 standard, Evans's property was clearly subject to confiscation, and the fact that it was intangible property represented no obstacle to confiscation. Most of the suits filed in New York sought the confiscation of another sort of intangible property, specifically financial instruments, such as stocks, bonds, and notes.

79 On Derby's career, see Walter Sutton, "The Derby Brothers: 19th Century Bookmen," *The University of Rochester Library Bulletin* 3, no. 2 (1948): 21–9; and Robert S. Becker, "J. C. Derby and Company," in *American Literary Publishing Houses, 1638–1899*, ed. Peter Dzwonkoski (Detroit: Gale, 1986), 116–17 (*Dictionary of Literary Biography*, vol. 49). Both take Derby at his word. According to Madeleine B. Stern, "in the '60's, Derby and his former partner, Norman C. Miller, were again united for a time in the publication of books." *Books and Book People in 19th-Century America* (New York: R. R. Bowker, 1978), 14.

80 "Notes on Books and Booksellers," *American Literary Gazette and Publisher's Circular*, 15 Feb. 1864, 268. Among the books that were advertised or appeared under their joint imprint in 1864 are William D. Jones, *The Mirror of Modern Democracy. Being a History of the Democratic Party, from its Organization in 1825, to its Last Great Achievement, the Rebellion of 1861*; Julian K. Larke, *General Grant and His Campaigns*; and Henry J. Raymond, *History of the Administration of President Lincoln* (also called "Lincoln's State Papers"). They were also New York agents for Horace Greeley's *History of the American Conflict*. On the State Papers as Republican propaganda, see a review in *American Literary Gazette*, 15 June 1864, 120. See also its review of *Mirror* as an anti–Democratic party diatribe, "Book Notices. . . . Politics and Questions of the Day," *American Literary Gazette*, 15 Mar. 1864, 341.

81 J. C. Derby & N. C. Miller, Advertisement, *American Literary Gazette*, 15 Feb. 1864, 283.

they must have been planning their joint enterprise by late 1863 when Derby set the wheels in motion for Northern publication of a certain Confederate novel. (And, despite her disavowal of trade with "Lincolndom" through Irene, Augusta Evans clearly knew Derby's political sympathies; writing in February 1861 to friend Rachel Lyons, she remarks, "You ask of *Mr Derby* in your last. I hear from him frequently – had a letter *yesterday*. . . . Mr. Derby is of course a *Union Man*; and thinks *Secession* is a grave sin. He is much distressed because *I* am so *very warm* a *Secessionist*, and believes southern rights might have been obtained *in* the *Union*; *which we* at the *South* know to be *impossible*.")[82]

In his memoirs, Derby claims that he asked Lippincott to publish *Macaria* because he himself was no longer a publisher and because Lippincott, in his capacity as a wholesaler, had dealt largely in copies of Derby's edition of *Beulah*.[83] However, it seems equally or more plausible that Derby wanted to avoid accusations of Confederate sympathies that might have interfered with his Republican Party alliances inside and outside of the publishing business. Derby held two political appointments under Lincoln's Republican administration, as Librarian of the Department of State in 1861 and Despatch Agent for the City of New York in 1865.[84] J. B. Lippincott was also a Union man and a Republican (he was a founder of the Philadelphia Union League).[85] However, as a large, general publisher rather than a narrow specialist as Derby was during this phase of his career, he was probably subject to less political risk for publishing a single Confederate novel. Whatever their political and commercial motivations for trying to publish a novel designed to subvert all of the aims of the Republican administration they both supported, both Derby and Lippincott subverted the spirit, if not the letter, of the Union's confiscation laws by holding royalties in trust for Evans. By doing so, they helped Evans profit from Northern business dealings and evade confiscation of those profits to support the Union war effort.

Considering some of the reactions to the publication of *Macaria* in the North, Derby and Lippincott may have been grateful that Doolady and Bradburn preempted their plans. Well after the war and after the failure of radical Reconstruction, Derby boasted of their honorable protection of

82 Augusta Jane Evans to Rachel Lyons, 2 Feb. 1861, in Sexton, *Southern Woman*, 31.

83 On Lippincott's book wholesaling business, the largest in the United States and perhaps the world in the nineteenth century, see J. Stuart Freeman, Jr., *Toward a Third Century of Excellence: An Informal History of the J. B. Lippincott Company* (Philadelphia: J. B. Lippincott, 1992), 5–16.

84 For Derby's political appointments, see Sutton, "Derby Brothers," 23. He also claims that Derby "spent most of the war years in Washington," a claim that Derby's publishing activities in New York in 1864 would seem to belie.

85 "Joshua Ballinger Lippincott," in *Appleton's Cyclopaedia of American Biography*, ed. James Grant Wilson and John Fiske (New York: D. Appleton, 1888), 3:734–5.

the interests of a rebel lady, but during the war their original plan to publish *Macaria* went unremarked, while reviewers wrote scathingly of Evans and "her" Northern publishers. The *Evening Post*, a strongly pro-Union and Republican paper, describes the book and the controversy caused by its sale: "Miss Evans, the author of 'Beulah,' is a Southerner, and has embraced with an enthusiasm amounting to malignity, the ultra political views of her section of the country. Thus imbued, she has written a novel called 'Macaria' – published in this city by John Bradburn – in which she gives full scope to her political vagaries. The work originally appeared in Richmond, and is so rampantly disloyal in the tone and utterance, that the booksellers of a western town returned to the publisher here all the copies they had received from him."[86] Damning the book with faint praise, the *Post* concludes its review: "As a literary production, 'Macaria' is at least equal to Miss Evans's previous works, and however repugnant it may be to loyalty to learn that such a rebel book can find publisher and readers in the North, yet it must be said this is the most carefully written novel – we might say, too, the most pretentious one – that the war has suggested to the novelists of either side." Whereas the *Post* found the novel "pretentious" and thus easily resistible, another strongly pro-Union paper, the New York *Sunday Dispatch*, found the novel to be alarming because it was seductively compelling. Describing the novel from the "powerful pen of the author of Beulah" as "peculiar, forcible, eloquent . . . riveting and enchaining the interest from the outset," the reviewer describes the appeal of Evans's uncommon, highly individual characters, who "haunt you replete with magnetism." Readers, "eyes blinded" and "following with [their] heart[s]," awake abruptly from this seductive dream at chapter 27 of the novel when they are "plunged head and ears into the whirl and tumult of Secession." The reviewer is repelled by Evans's support for the "monstrous birth" of secession, "whose nourishment has cost us so vastly much of life and peace. . . . Strip aside the mask of entertaining fiction with which the intent before us is veiled, and you behold the cunning appeal for aid and sympathy for an ill, a horror that has in its wake the ultimate death of the country's prosperity. 'A house divided against itself cannot stand.'"[87]

Before and after this critical backlash, Bradburn advertised the book in New York papers across the political spectrum, from Republican (the *Post*, Horace Greeley's *New York Tribune*, and the *Dispatch*) to "War Democrat" (the *World*) to Copperhead (the *New York Day-Book Caucasian*). Rather than back off from his promotion of the novel after critics characterized it as seductively traitorous and as promoting the doctrines responsible for the division and ruin of the nation, Bradburn responded by *advertising* the controversy. Bradburn's early ads say nothing about the content of the novel

86 "New Novels. Confederate, English and Federal," *Evening Post* (New York), 25 July 1864, 1.

87 "New Publications," *New York Dispatch* (Sunday ed.), 17 July 1864, 3.

but puff Evans's established reputation and use the common tactic of advertising sales already achieved as a means to promote further sales.[88] His ads breathlessly claim, "The publisher deems the bare announcement of a book by the author of 'Beulah,' sufficient to insure the largest advance orders of any novel of the season.... The first edition of Five Thousand is fast passing through the press... orders already received exhaust our first supply."[89] In July, however, Bradburn began quoting *negative* reviews in his advertisements and otherwise drawing attention to the novel's war content and Confederate loyalties. Ads feature the *Post*'s "repugnance" at the mere fact of the book's publication in the North and its reports of Western booksellers returning copies of the novel as badges of honor.[90] They also proclaim *Macaria* a "Great Southern Novel" rather than simply a "new novel by the author of 'Beulah.'" Bradburn also solicited and published a defense of Evans's novel by Mary Howe, a Northern woman whose Civil War novel, *The Rival Volunteers, or The Black-Plumed Rifles*, he had just published. In her defense of Evans and "her publisher," Howe implicitly contrasts *Macaria*'s reception with the U.S. and foreign reception of Stowe's *Uncle Tom's Cabin*:

> As to its political bearing, although I have no secession sympathies, and should bitterly mourn the day ushering in the final dismemberment of our once happy and prosperous land, I yet think the free press of a free people in a most anomalous condition, when Abolitionism, (in my humble opinion, rank treason toward both the spirit and letter of the Constitution,) is tricked out – the public applauding the echo – in the most gorgeous dyes of romance, throughout our most popular fictitious literature while a word, even in a novel, against the fanatical demagoguism that has brought our country to the verge of ruin, is visited with threat and rebuke upon publisher and author.[91]

From Mary Howe's perspective, Bradburn deserved praise for vigorously exercising the freedom of the press worthy of a free people, and Evans, though misguided in her secessionist sympathies, presented far less of a threat to the national union than Stowe.

88 For the development of this promotional strategy in the 1850s, see Susan Geary, "The Domestic Novel as a Commercial Commodity: Making a Best Seller in the 1850s," *Papers of the Bibliographical Society of America* 70 (1976): 365–93.

89 John Bradburn, Advertisement, *New York Dispatch* (Sunday ed.), 5 June 1864, 8.

90 See, e.g., John Bradburn, Advertisement, *New-York Daily Tribune*, 2 July 1864, 2.

91 Howe's endorsement appeared in ads before the *Post* review, as well as after. See, e.g., John Bradburn, Advertisements, *New-York Times*, 23 July 1864, 5; *New York Day-Book Caucasian* (weekly ed.), 30 July 1864.

"[A]s I lost my property (negroes and Confederate bonds) during that revolution, I must attend to the 'question of bread and butter'": *St. Elmo* and Evans's literary property in the reunited nation

Within a year of Mary Howe's defense of Evans as an author and Bradburn as a publisher, the Civil War was over. The Union was re-membered, if not fully politically reconstructed or happy and prosperous; and Augusta Evans, "blissfully unaware" of the Northern tussle over her novel (at least so J. C. Derby thought), showed up on Derby's doorstep in New York and was given access to substantial royalties held in trust for her. Thus Derby gives to the story of Evans's authorship of *Macaria* the same moment of narrative closure that Fanny Fern gives to her eponymous heroine in *Ruth Hall*, with the crucial difference that Derby ascribes agency exclusively to himself and Lippincott, while the female author remains a passive object. When he tells Evans to buy a new dress, she answers, "Mr. Derby, my father has lost everything; the slaves have been freed, and all our property confiscated. I have no money with which to replenish my wardrobe" (pp. 394–5). Not even an independent adult woman, she is a dependent daughter, doubly dispossessed – the North took everything from her father, and thus she has lost even her secondary relationship to property.

Modern scholars have not challenged (and Evans herself did not challenge) Derby's account, but, as is often the case with Evans, the ladylike pose of submission and deference to masculine authority masks a calculated strategy to achieve her own ends. One might pause to reflect here on her motivations for visiting Derby's office – was she in New York solely to find medical care for her brother and was coincidentally making a social call on her old friend, as he seemed to think, or had she arrived at Derby's place of business with the specific intention of collecting royalties from the man to whom she had entrusted the publication of her novel in the North? She may have been "blissfully unaware" of the particularities of the imbroglio involving Derby, Lippincott, Bradburn, and Doolady, but she was *not* blissfully unaware of standard publishing trade practices. Sensibly, rather than waiting in the devastated city of Mobile for publishers to write her, she went to them. Her appearance on Derby's doorstep thus implies that rather than being a passive victim of circumstances, Evans was executing the first step in her comprehensive campaign for reoccupying the Northern market.

A few months after her New York visit, in the fall of 1865, she wrote to her friend, former Confederate Congressman J. L. M. Curry, once again presenting herself as stripped of all property (including slave property, but this time representing herself as the wronged proprietor rather than her father). Declaring authorship to be a financial necessity in the wake of Southern defeat, Evans describes to Curry her intention to write a history of the

Confederate government (a plan she later surrendered when former vice president of the Confederacy Alexander Stephens announced his intentions to do so), as well as a novel (the incipient *St. Elmo*): "[A]s I lost my property (negroes and Confederate bonds) during that revolution [the Civil War], I must attend to the 'question of bread and butter,' and I am trying to write out a novel, the plan of which has been vaguely straying through my mind for some time. My history, I intend to make the *great end of all my labors* in the realm of letters, and while I gather the requisite materials, I must continue to draw a support from my inkstand."[92] She goes on to describe the difficulties of finding time to write when she is "doing her own work" because of the "advent of the Yankees, and consequent hegira of our negroes." She humorously and elaborately describes her labors over a hot stove in the heat of a Mobile summer, thus indirectly, but nevertheless pointedly, drawing attention to her new status as "slave" in her own household.

In her presentation of her dilemma to both Derby and Curry, she claims that she is radically dispossessed (although to Curry, she presents herself, rather than her father, as having been a proprietor in the past). Literary property, either an unanticipated interest in Northern property during the war (the copyright in *Macaria* protected by Derby) or an anticipated new property to be created in and protected by the law of the reunited nation (the incipient *St. Elmo* as a future source of "bread and butter), is a means to restore her status as a proper Southern lady. With it, she can buy a new dress or hire a new cook. Both of Evans's self-representations in 1865, one preserved in Derby's memoir and the other more directly in her letter to Curry, are strategically incomplete, however, allowing two men, one a Northern Republican and the other a conservative Confederate, to mobilize the figure of the Southern lady to ends appropriate to their contrasting ideologies. Derby can "save" her, the helpless, defeated woman, from the ill effects of the war and bring her back into the Union. Strategically, she *omits* from her letter to Curry her visit to Derby and his payment to her of substantial royalties on the Northern sales of *Macaria*. Instead, she tells him that she went with her brother to consult a "celebrated German physician of celebrity" and refused to speak with "*prominent* Republican leaders who wished to see me," accepting visits only from men "who had proved their detestation of the war party and policy."[93]

Despite her proclaimed detestation of Northern men and institutions, she could not hope to make "bread and butter" in the postwar United States as an author without them. Through her literary texts (*Macaria* and *St. Elmo*), as well as through her meetings with publishers, Evans negotiated

92 Augusta Jane Evans to J. L. M. Curry, 7 Oct. 1865, in Sexton, *Southern Woman*, 107.

93 Augusta Jane Evans to J. L. M. Curry, 7 Oct. 1865, in Sexton, *Southern Woman*, 108. On Evans's decades long love-hate relationship with the cultural world of New York, see Sofer, *Making the "America of Art,"* chap. 2.

her authorial identity and established herself as a proprietor under radically different circumstances. A reconstruction of Evans's activities in 1865 and 1866 makes clear the scope of her ambition as she moved from one narrative of proprietorship to another. Her visit to J. C. Derby (and her decision to send *Macaria* North to him in the first place) ensured that she benefited handsomely from Northern sales of *Macaria* during the war. In his memoir, Derby quotes another recollection from Evans of the 1860s, a recollection that sheds light on her other activities during that 1865 trip to New York:

> With reference to my present Publisher, G. W. Carleton, I should like the world to know how noble and generous he has always been to me. When purchasing the stereotype plates of my earlier books, he told me that he was obliged to pay so much for the plates of "Macaria" that he could only allow me a moderate percentage on the future sales. We agreed upon the terms and signed the contract, which specified a certain percentage on "Macaria." Subsequently, after "St. Elmo" and "Vashti" [her fifth novel] had been published, I one day received a letter from Mr. Carleton, saying that the sales of the volumes justified him in increasing the percentage on "Macaria." From that period until now, in making his annual settlement of copyright, he has paid me a larger percentage on "Macaria" than my original contract specified, and this increase was his own voluntary generous impulse, for I had never solicited any change of terms. Verily, a Prince of Publishers! (p. 397)

In typical fashion, she presents these facts in praise of her chivalrous publisher rather than as a tribute to her own business acumen, leaving unstated a crucial link in this chain of events: precisely how G. W. Carleton became her postwar publisher, the man fortunate enough to publish one of the nineteenth century's great best sellers, *St. Elmo.* It seems likely that on her 1865 New York trip, Evans made calls on two publishers, both Derby and Carleton. Furthermore, she did not approach Carleton at random – he, as much as Bradburn, had become "her" publisher in the North during the war. Recall the mysterious "Mr. Scott" who bought the stereotype plates for *Beulah* at a publisher's trade sale in 1862, a trade sale that featured the entire stock of plates owned by the then defunct firm of Derby & Jackson. By 1863, these plates had made their way from Mr. Scott to G. W. Carleton, who began featuring *Beulah* in his advertisements as "a novel of great power and interest."[94] Carleton did not have the strong Republican party ties of J. C. Derby, but in partnership as Rudd & Carleton, he had published the Wigwam edition of the *Life, Speeches, and Public Services of Abraham Lincoln*, the popular campaign biography for Lincoln's first run for President in 1860. During the war, he published many war-related titles,

94 *New Books and New Editions Recently Issued by Carleton, Publisher* (New York: Carleton, 1863).

leaning heavily to the Republican side, with occasional titles from opposing points of view.[95] By 1864, probably anxious to avoid Evans's Confederate sympathies, the firm's advertisements described *Beulah* as "a very powerful *American* novel"[96] (emphasis added).

Perhaps Evans found a copy of *Beulah* in a New York bookstore under Carleton's imprint, or perhaps she saw an advertisement in a Northern newspaper or magazine. Through whatever means Evans became aware of Carleton's edition of her second novel, it seems likely that, armed with this information, she approached him with a threefold purpose: to seek payment of royalties from his sales of *Beulah*, to propose that he publish her next novel, and to suggest that he acquire the plates for *Macaria* and *Inez* from Bradburn and Doolady. Carleton acted the part of the honorable gentleman – and took advantage of the connection that the plates of *Beulah* gave him to the popular author. Carleton, like Derby before the war, had developed a profitable specialty in women's novels. He also published Mary Jane Holmes and Miriam Coles Harris in 1865, and he would soon add Mary Virginia Terhune (another former Derby & Jackson author) to his list. Evans proved to be a logical and highly profitable addition to his stable of women novelists.

Bradburn and Doolady, however, were not cut out for the role of gentlemen publishers. With the war over, would they continue to pay royalties, either through Derby or directly to Evans? With the prospect of a new Evans novel on the horizon, would they squeeze as much money as they possibly could out of Carleton in return for the plates of *Macaria*? And what about *Inez*, the profits from which they had been enjoying, apparently royalty free? As Evans attested in the 1880s, Carleton ransomed the plates for *Macaria* from Bradburn and Doolady at a high price. By acquiring these plates, Carleton was able to offer *Beulah*, *Macaria*, and *St. Elmo* together on his list for 1866–67 holiday season and throughout the rest of the century. Bringing *Inez* out under the Carleton imprint took a little longer because Bradburn and Doolady continued to control use of the Harpers' plates and to issue editions through 1870, thus exploiting the exponentially increased value of Evans's name and reputation in the wake of *St. Elmo*'s phenomenal success. The first G. W. Carleton edition of *Inez* finally appeared in 1871, printed from the original 1855 Harpers' plates, with the plates and the book remaining under the control of Carleton and his successors until the copyright expired in 1897. G. W. Carleton and his successor, G. W. Dillingham,

95 Tebbel, *History of Book Publishing*, 346. His partnership with Rudd ended in 1861. For Carleton's career, see also Stern, *Books and Book People*. His publications ranged politically from Epes Sargent's novel *Peculiar* (1864) (abolitionist/Republican), to Dennis A. Mahony's memoir *Prisoner of the State* (1863) (about his imprisonment in Washington, DC, in 1862 for his opposition to the Lincoln administration's interpretation of the Constitution), to a reprint of West & Johnston's Confederate edition of Raphael Semmes' *Cruise of the Alabama and the Sumter* (1864).

96 Carleton, Publisher, "Advertisement – New Books," *New-York Daily Tribune*, 9 Apr. 1864, 8.

continued to publish Evans's copyrighted works, both old and new, through the early twentieth century (Dillingham published her last novel, *Devota*, in 1907).[97] Thus, through astute maneuvering in the postwar period, Evans ensured that all of her books eventually came under the stewardship of one publisher, who kept them in print and paid her royalties regularly for the remainder of the century.

"To-day I snap the fetters of your literary bondage": Slavery, copyright, and Augusta Jane Evans's representation of female authorship in *St. Elmo*

Macaria, a story of single blessedness in support of the Confederacy, continued to sell after the war, but for many years it sold in editions printed from John Bradburn's plates. These plates omitted Evans's dedication, which reads, in part, "To the Army of the Southern Confederacy, who have delivered the South from Despotism, and who have won for generations yet unborn the precious guerdon of constitutional republican liberty." After Confederate nationalism became a lost cause, the narrative represented by both *Macaria* and Evans's personal and professional life became less desirable and less marketable. She seems to have understood the superior usefulness of the narrative of her literary proprietorship offered in Derby's account of her wartime activities over the counternarrative of her copyright activism. She clung to her secessionist sympathies, but she also endorsed and praised the "chivalry" of Derby and Lippincott's efforts on her behalf. Derby quotes her as writing to him: "I have always felt profoundly grateful to Mr. Lippincott, but fate has never indulged me in an opportunity of adequately thanking him, for his generous and chivalric action, in behalf of an unknown rebel, who at that period was nursing Confederate soldiers in a hospital established near 'Camp Beulah'" (p. 395). She also dedicated *St. Elmo* "to J. C. Derby, in grateful memory of many years of kind and faithful friendship." *St. Elmo* was also Evans's greatest commercial success, one of the very few American novels to even come close to *Uncle Tom's Cabin* for sales on the

97 After printing the 1864 edition of *Inez* from the Harpers' plates, Bradburn printed another edition in 1865. In 1868, the plates found their way back briefly to their original home, when "W. I. Pooley, Harper & Brothers Bldg." issued an undated edition (the identification of Evans on the title page as "the author of St. Elmo" dates it to 1866 or later). The Pooley edition was also advertised in Mobile newspapers in January 1868 (clipping in the Augusta Jane Evans file, Historic Mobile Preservation Society, Mobile, AL). *Inez* was then issued under Michael Doolady's imprint in 1870, before it finally appeared under Carleton's imprint in 1871, with subsequent editions by Dillingham in 1887 and 1888. The first postwar edition of *Macaria* from the Bradburn and Doolady plates appeared under Carleton's imprint in 1867, with subsequent printings by Carleton in 1868 and 1869, and under Dillingham's imprint in 1888. In 1896, Dillingham issued a revised edition. See Faust's "Note on Editions of *Macaria*" (xxviii–ix) on the nature of the revisions.

American market before the twentieth century.[98] Evans achieved such a rapid recuperation of her popular reputation with Northern readers (who, considering the economic devastation of the South, necessarily made up the bulk of those phenomenal sales) both through business decisions about publishing and through the narrative design of the novel. With her slave property emancipated and her identity as a female Confederate nationalist outmoded in the South and unappealing in the North, she focused her labors on creating new literary property and a new authorial identity, both constructed through the means of *St. Elmo*, a novel that features a popular author as its heroine.

At the close of *St. Elmo*, the reformed rake title character proclaims to Edna Earl, his newly acquired bride, "To-day I snap the fetters of your literary bondage. There shall be no more books written! . . . And that dear public you love so well, must even help itself, and whistle for a new pet. You belong solely to me now, and I shall take care of the life you have nearly destroyed, in your inordinate ambition."[99] In St. Elmo's view, literary ambition has enslaved Edna to the public, and he will offer her freedom, but a freedom within the sphere of "belonging" to him and the home over which he will preside. Although the figure of slavery takes center stage at this crucial moment and at two other moments in the novel, the reality of African chattel slavery (and the "future" war to be fought over it) remains unrepresented. The novel is set in some ill–defined antebellum time and vaguely Southern location. Shadowy characters called "servants" quietly inhabit the background of grand southern houses, and St. Elmo's "plantation" is at a distance, a place to which he escapes and where neither Edna nor the novel follows him. Indeed, it is only in the last chapter of this very long novel that Evans makes it clear that the novel is set before the war[100] and, only by implication, that those "servants" are slaves. In *Disarming the Nation: Women's Writing and the American Civil War*, Elizabeth Young argues

98 Both of the standard works attempting to document the relative popularity of literature in the American market include *St. Elmo* on their lists of top-sellers. Frank Luther Mott, *Golden Multitudes: The Story of Best Sellers in the United States* (New York: Macmillan, 1947), 126–7, 309. James D. Hart, *The Popular Book: A History of America's Literary Taste* (New York: Oxford University Press, 1950), 118–20, 308.

99 Augusta Jane Evans, *St. Elmo. A Novel* (New York: Carleton, 1867), 568 (hereinafter cited in the text).

100 The narrator describes Edna as contemplating the coming "storm of 1861" and the (not yet accomplished) "threatened secession of the South" (p. 561), thus implicitly dating the end of the novel to late 1860. Sofer presents a quite different, but compelling, reading of Evans's choice of a prewar setting. On a personal level, Evans "retrospectively rewrites history, giving Edna both her own political and aesthetic ideas and the social influence among Northern intellectuals that Evans herself lacked," while on a broader, political level, Edna's triumph stages a Southern victory over the North on a cultural level despite the South's recent military and political defeat. Specifically, she argues that Edna's triumph enacts the prewar cultural nationalist program outlined in Evans's 1859 *Advertiser* articles. *Making the "America of Art,"* chap. 2.

that women writers have deployed "the Civil War as a multivalent cultural symbol as well as literal setting" in order to "represent internal rebellions, conflicts, and fractures" and to "symbolically energiz[e] a war within against the terms of civility."[101] Young's formulation accurately characterizes the disruptive energies released for Irene and Electra in *Macaria*, but Evans avoids precisely this sort of disruption by placing Edna in a prewar setting. From a novel in which two heroines sidestep the "bondage" of marriage and dedicate themselves to a war in support of Southern social and economic institutions (including slavery), Evans moves forward (or rather backward) to a novel set in a lightly specified, seemingly slave-free antebellum South in which her author heroine escapes "bondage" to a mass reading public through married service to her husband.

Early readers of the novel in 1866 and 1867 clearly conflated Edna and Evans. As "Mobilian" wrote in a long review in the *Mobile Advertiser and Register*, "Edna Earl, with head drooped over her manuscript, and light of a sad, weary smile creeping over her face as she soliloquized 'will my readers see it as I see it?' . . . is Augusta Evans, as to her estimate of herself, and her hope of her readers."[102] Evans anticipated this identification between heroine and author and deployed it to advantage as she resituated herself and her literary property in the postbellum field. Like Fanny Fern and Mary Virginia Terhune, Evans significantly revised her own experiences when she created her author-heroine. In Evans's case, she wrote out the Civil War contexts and political questions so crucial to her personal and professional life from 1861 to 1865. In *St. Elmo*, Edna Earl's first publication is an anonymous article titled "Who Smote the Marble Gods of Greece"; in 1862, Evans herself anonymously published an article on the same theme in the *Gulf City Home Journal* under the title "The Mutilation of the Hermae."[103] Edna's article consists entirely of scholarly speculation on who smashed the famous marble statues of Hermes in ancient Greece. In contrast, Evans's article uses the ancient iconoclasm primarily as a pretext for an assault on the North. Positing a future era as distant from 1862 as 1862 was from ancient Greece, Evans imagines "the curious historiographer groping through the dust of dead aeons . . . [stumbling] upon a 'Mutilated Image,' and [proclaiming] that in the nineteenth century a rude Iconoclasm shook the American Nation

101 Elizabeth Young, *Disarming the Nation: Women's Writing and the American Civil War* (Chicago: University of Chicago Press, 1999), 17. In light of her public political commentary during the war, Sarah E. Gardner finds puzzling Evans's failure to express in print her anger at Reconstruction as she did in private letters to Confederate loyalists, but this bifurcation seems to me perfectly logical and in keeping with Evans's postwar self-fashioning. *Blood and Irony: Southern White Women's Narratives of the Civil War, 1861–1932* (Chapel Hill: University of North Carolina Press, 2004), 45–6.

102 Mobilian, "Miss Evans and 'St. Elmo,'" *Mobile Advertiser and Register*, 13 Jan. 1867.

103 "The Mutilation of the Hermae," *Gulf City Home Journal*, 9 Nov. 1862. The article is preserved as an enclosure in a letter to J. L. M. Curry. Augusta Jane Evans to J. L. M. Curry, 10 Nov. 1862, J. L. M Curry Papers, Library of Congress.

to its centre and over-threw the noblest government which the wisdom of the world ever established." The idol smashed is, of course, the U.S. Constitution, and the iconoclast "the North, which has consummated the utter desecration of our political fane, and hurled Liberty, our tutelar [*sic*] Goddess, from her lofty pedestal." The true principles of liberty embodied in the Constitution, she writes, have been "enshrined in the Southern Confederacy," which is waging war against "Black Republicanism" and "Abolitionism" to protect its sanctity. In *St. Elmo*, when Edna publishes "Who Smote the Marble Gods," the Confederacy Evans defended in "The Mutilation of the Hermae" does not yet exist. Instead, Edna's article becomes the occasion for a long series of clashes between Edna and St. Elmo over women's intellect and women as authors, a struggle that finally ends on the steps of the church when St. Elmo snaps her fetters to the public and claims her as his possession in marriage. Modern feminist critics have found Edna's capitulation to marriage at the end of the novel both disappointing and fundamentally in contradiction with Edna's character and Evans's plotting of Edna's life. Even those critics who find the entire plot arc and character development of the novel consistent rather than contradictory are brought up short by the violence and domination of St. Elmo's language as he transforms Edna into a proper wife by breaking the fetters that bind her to her reading public.[104] However, in the context of Evans's career and her engagements with literary proprietorship, this cluster of images and Edna's narrative trajectory from *feme sole* author to domesticated married woman "owned" by a husband follows a strategic logic. As discussed in Chapters 1 and 2, what troubled authors and their allies in the antebellum United States in their fight for international copyright was the notion that property could cease to be property, that an author could find himself one moment a proprietor and the next moment propertyless. Writing after the war, George Haven Putnam, a Union veteran and heir to his father George Palmer Putnam's publishing business and copyright advocacy,[105] directly links the question of copyright reform to the institution of slavery that he had fought a war to abolish. His remarks are a response to a resolution issued in 1872 by a

104 On the ending as hopelessly contradictory, see Susan K. Harris, *19th–Century American Women's Novels: Interpretative Strategies* (New York: Cambridge University Press, 1990), 76; Diane Roberts, "Introduction," *St. Elmo* (Tuscaloosa: University of Alabama Press, 1992), xviii–xix; Anne Goodwyn Jones, *Tomorrow Is Another Day: The Woman Writer in the South, 1859–1936* (Baton Rouge: Louisiana State University Press, 1981), 57, 59–60; Mary Kelley, *Private Woman, Public Stage: Literary Domesticity in Nineteenth-Century America* (New York: Oxford University Press, 1984), 191–2. On the coherent logic of the ending, see Karen Tracey, *Plots and Proposals: American Women's Fiction, 1850–90* (Urbana: University of Illinois Press, 2000), 82, 103; Bradley Johnson, "Dueling Sentiments: Responses to Patriarchal Violence in Augusta Jane Evans' St. Elmo," *Southern Literary Journal* 33, no. 2 (2001): 25–6; and Sofer, *Making the "America of Art."*

105 Ezra Greenspan, *George Palmer Putnam: Representative American Publisher* (University Park: Pennsylvania State University Press, 2000).

Philadelphia book trade anticopyright association: "That thought, unless expressed, is the property of the thinker . . . when given to the world, it is as light, free to all. . . . As property it can only demand the protection of the municipal law of the country to which the thinker is subject"[106] (Henry Carey's critique of copyright clearly influenced their resolution; see Chapter 3). Putnam scoffingly replies,

> The property which would, if it still existed, most nearly approximate to such a definition as this is that in *slaves*. Twenty years ago, an African chattel who was worth $1000 in Charleston became, on slipping across to the Bermudas, as a piece of property valueless. He had no longer a market price. It is this ephemeral kind of ownership, limited by accidental political boundaries, that our Philadelphia friends are willing to concede to the work of a man's mind, the productions into which have been absorbed the grey matter of his brain and perhaps the best of his life. (pp. 21–2)

An author whose ownership evaporates is thus a powerless author, who himself, because his property "escapes," has been pressed into a sort of involuntary servitude to the reading public. In Putnam's words, "Authors are laborers, and their works are, as fully as is the case with any other class of laborers, the results of their own productive faculties and energies. Literary laborers lay claim, therefore, to the same protection for a full and free enjoyment of the results of their labors as is demanded by those who work with their hands" (p. 3).

Until 1891, however, the U.S. Congress valued wide distribution of cheap books to educate the democratic masses over authors' claimed "rights." Copyright was not an absolute property, like a bale of merchandise, but a "*property* of a peculiar character" that had status as property only as the result of domestic regulation.[107] That is, authors existed only to serve readers, and Congress had the power to decide whether or not authors got paid. Furthermore, in a twist Putnam does not consider, not only did the books of women writers, like those of their male contemporaries, cross the Atlantic where publishers appropriated their "property" without their permission, but women writers themselves became a sort of property in marriage and lost the self-possession that is a prerequisite to ownership. During the war years, Augusta Evans was additionally subjected to such "appropriation" of her literary property when it crossed the contested political border between North and South, between Union and Confederacy. Evans's fictional narrative of female authorship in *St. Elmo* reflects these anxieties about author-reader relations in nineteenth-century America and resolves these conflicts in a way

106 George Haven Putnam, *International Copyright Considered in Some of Its Relations to Ethics and Political Economy* (New York: G. P. Putnam's Sons, 1879), 20–1 (hereinafter cited in the text).

107 Senate Committee on Patents, *Report to Accompany Senate Bill No. 32*, 25th Cong., 2nd sess., 25 June 1838, S. Doc. 494, 2.

that both appealed to readers' interests and consolidated Evans's interests as a woman author attempting to reintegrate herself into U.S. national legal and cultural structures.

Edna's first book, an effort already under way when she publishes "Who Smote the Marble Gods," is an analysis of the unity of all mythology and religions, presented in the form of a novel. This ambitious choice is appropriate for a woman who sees authors as invested "with peculiar sanctity, as the real hierophants anointed with the chrism of truth" (p. 167). Her second book, *Shining Thrones of the Hearth*, tempers her original impulse to write in a learned, high-cultural mode with a dose of her domestic moral authority as a woman. Despite the psychic conflict between womanly domestic duty and her public role as an author dramatized and resolved in her final surrender to St. Elmo, Edna makes herself perfectly comfortable in the literary marketplace for most of the novel. When Edna begins her first book, the narrator approvingly describes Edna's intention to prove her mind a "mint, where all valuable ores are collected from the rich veins of a universe – are cautiously coined, and thence munificently circulated" (p. 168). Edna fears the critics and other authors, but she does not fear her readers, despite warnings from her male literary advisors. After she refuses St. Elmo's first proposal of marriage, he tells her that "the masses" will trample her in her pursuit of fame. Does she know, he asks, that "'*literati*' means literally the branded? The lettered slave! . . . *Literati*! A bondage worse than roman slavery!" (p. 340). But "the masses" wholeheartedly accept Edna and her works. "While critics snarled, the mass of readers warmly approved," reports the narrator. Edna clearly understands the market and how it is regulated by copyright, among other things. Explaining to Felix, her pupil, about charges of plagiarism against her by critics, she tells him, "If it is necessary in well-regulated municipalities to have inspectors of all other commodities, why not of books, also? I do not object to the rigid balancing – I wish to pass for no more than I weigh" (p. 455).

However, Edna does *not* remain in the well-regulated municipality of the republic of letters (a republic not yet disrupted by the Civil War), nor does she remain within the extended family of her readers. Instead, as Edna lies prostrate on a sofa, having fainted during her wedding to St. Elmo, he severs her ties to the literary market for her. Within the logic of the novel and its metaphors, Edna's final surrender to St. Elmo in marriage is the exchange of one form of bondage for another; as an author, her readers own her, and as a wife, St. Elmo will own her. Similarly, Edna progresses as an author, as well as a woman, toward domestic space, as she first restricts herself to domestic topics and then is restricted to the home. In this movement further into domestic space, Edna does not so much disappear as an author as exchange service to a mass audience in the marketplace for service to an audience of one, St. Elmo, in the confines of the home.

As the author of *Macaria*, Evans was a feme sole woman in sole possession of her literary property and a citizen of the Confederate nation, a nation that pledged itself to protect the rights of foreign property in transit through its borders. As the author of *St. Elmo*, Evans offered herself up to readers in the reconstructed United States as property to be appropriated rather than as a proprietor. Although Evans earlier aligned herself with an expansive and ambitious program for increasing authorial power by promoting international copyright in the Confederacy, we find her occupying in 1866 the same authorial ground as Sedgwick in the 1830s and Stowe in the 1850s and 1860s. Through her didactic fictions, Sedgwick represented authors (herself included) not as proprietors, but as servants to readers, who transform an author's works (and implicitly the author herself) into their own "best property" in their homes.[108] Through Edna Earl, Evans similarly represents authorship as a form of service. After losing *Stowe v. Thomas*, Stowe became the victim heroine of international copyright reform. Similarly, Evans aligns Edna as an author (and, implicitly, herself) with slavery rather than mastery. First, readers are Edna's masters, and then her husband is her master – she is first a "lettered slave" and then her husband's possession. St. Elmo may "snap" the fetters that attach her to her reading public, but he clearly snaps on a new set of fetters that chain her to him during her coverture.

With the war still fresh in the memory of readers and Evans's identity as a Confederate partisan well known, one might expect Northern reviewers to associate Evans and her novel with the war and to criticize her for these associations. However, just as St. Elmo claims Edna Earl as his own, Northern readers easily claimed Edna and reclaimed Evans as their own. Northern reviewers criticized Evans's outlandish displays of erudition in the novel and the Byronism of her hero, but they also easily reincorporated her and her novel into "America." The *New York Times*, for instance, laments that her "power" was "misapplied," but it unambiguously labels her an "American novelist" and omits any reference to Evans's Southernness or the war.[109] The Roxbury, Massachusetts, *Journal* notes that she "destroyed" the reputation she had established with *Beulah* by publishing *Macaria* and going "with her section," but it notes approvingly that she "avoids all reference to the war or

108 On Jewett's continuation of this tradition of representing author-reader relations, see Melissa J. Homestead, "'Links of Similitude': The Narrator of the Country of the Pointed Firs and Author-Reader Relations at the End of the Nineteenth Century," in *Jewett and Her Contemporaries: Reshaping the Canon*, ed. Karen L. Kilcup and Thomas S. Edwards (Gainesville: University Press of Florida, 1999) 76–98.

109 "Miss Evans' New Novel," *New York Times*, 5 Jan. 1867, 2. *St. Elmo* was reviewed almost exclusively in newspapers rather than magazines, although Evans clearly aspired to the high-cultural status monthly or quarterly magazine reviews conferred. The other Northern newspaper reviews quoted from are reprinted excerpts from "Notices of St. Elmo," *Mobile Advertiser and Register*, 11 Jan. 1868, 1.

to politics" in *St. Elmo* and labels it "the best of its author's books." Similarly, the Norwich, Connecticut, *Bulletin* informs readers that while "the plot of the story is located in Tennessee, and though the some of the names and localities have been made familiar by the war, there is nothing of the cannon drum, or bugle in the volume, or anything that pertains even remotely to the great rebellion."[110]

Evans's gambit of retreating to the antebellum South in her novel succeeded. Although Edna consents to submit to a Southern rather than a Northern gentleman in marriage, Edna's surrender, like that of the romance of reunion, gave Northern readers the satisfaction of witnessing a willful Southern woman and her property brought under masculine control. (Evans herself succumbed to the bonds of matrimony in the wake of *St. Elmo*'s astonishing success. In 1868, she married Lorenzo Wilson, a wealthy man more than twenty-five years her senior, whose substantial investments outside the Confederacy had escaped wartime confiscation.[111]) Despite this facade of willing surrender, however, this plot of containment empowered the "real" author behind the fictional one. Evans's novel, which closes by effacing the female author as economic agent, was enormously popular with readers, thus allowing Evans to fully exploit the commercial value of her literary property in the newly reconstituted American nation.

110 *Debow's Review*, reflecting its Southern character, laments that Evans expected war-weary Southerners "standing now midst the ashes of fair homestead and national discomfiture, with every energy taxed to retrieve our fallen fortunes" to "[ascend] Mount Parnassus" with her in *St. Elmo*, but they do not criticize her decision to set her novel before the war. Instead, they wish that she had painted a truer picture of "Southern life ere the rude hand of Radicalism completely obliterated the delicately tinted lights and shadows." "St. Elmo," *Debow's Review*, Mar. 1867, 270.

111 Fidler, *Augusta Evans Wilson*, 150.

Epilogue: Belford v. Scribner *(1892) and the Ghost of Mary Virginia Terhune's* Phemie's Temptation *(1869); or, The Lessons of the "Lady-Writers" of the 1820s through the 1860s for Literary History and Twenty-First-Century Copyright Law*

In Chapter 1, I stated that no court ever issued an opinion explicitly ruling on the implications of the intersection between coverture and copyright for a married woman's literary proprietorship – which is not to say that no party to a litigation ever asked a court to rule on the issue. In an ironic twist of fate, the intersection between coverture and copyright became a key issue in a copyright infringement suit involving a work by Mary Virginia Terhune, the author of *Phemie's Temptation*, the novel that figures prominently in my analysis of coverture and copyright in Chapter 1. The Supreme Court issued the decision that finally resolved the case in 1892, thirty-four years after *Godey's Lady's Book* began serializing *Phemie's Temptation*. Although I will not attempt to delve as deeply into the legal and social climate of the 1880s, 1890s, and beyond as I have into that of the 1820s through the 1860s, this dispute suggests the continuing importance of the intersection between coverture and copyright – as an ongoing reality for women authors in the late nineteenth century, as a force in twentieth-century constructions of literary history of the nineteenth century, and as a cautionary tale for the continuing expansion of copyright in the twenty-first century.

When Mary Virginia Terhune began writing *Phemie's Temptation* in 1867, she had been a popular novelist for thirteen years and a married woman for eleven (her first novel, *Alone*, published in 1854 in Richmond, was so successful that J. C. Derby republished it the following year in New York; she married Edward Payson Terhune in 1856).[1] Her publisher from 1863 on,

1 Throughout this chapter, I rely on Karen Manners Smith, "Marion Harland: The Making of a Household Word," PhD diss., University of Massachusetts, 1990, for the events of Terhune's life. However, Smith does not include any mention of *Scribner v. Clark* or *Belford v. Scribner*, nor does she reference Terhune's correspondence with Charles H. Scribner. Smith has also generously shared with me ideas and resources from her research. Mary Kelley also does not reference the Terhune-Scribner correspondence, perhaps because it was not yet fully processed and available at the time of her research. *Private Woman, Public Stage: Literary Domesticity in Nineteenth-Century America* (New York: Oxford University Press, 1984). Terhune's authorial self-conception looks quite different in light of this correspondence than it does through her correspondence with lifelong friend Virginia Dance Eppes, Kelley's primary manuscript source.

Sheldon & Co. (which stepped into the breach left by the failure of Derby & Jackson at the beginning of the Civil War), happily republished in book form most of her serialized novels and novellas that first appeared in *Godey's Lady's Book*, where she was the lead contributor. Indeed, the serial installments of *Phemie*, consisting of twelve numbers, occupied the lead position in *Godey's* for the entire year of 1868. Her payments from *Godey's* and the royalties paid by her book publishers handsomely supplemented her husband's salary as a Presbyterian minister.

At the height of her success as a writer of women's fiction, Terhune significantly shifted her literary production. Although she never entirely stopped writing fiction (and continued to write for *Godey's* intermittently until Louis Godey sold the magazine in 1883), she turned to other genres, but particularly cookbooks and domestic advice writing. In 1870, she published her novel *At Last* with G. W. Carleton, but when she approached Carleton with a plan to publish a cookbook, he declined the opportunity, reportedly laughing at the idea that such a book would sell as well as her fiction.[2] If it is true that Carleton laughed off her proposal, Charles Scribner's Sons, which published the book instead of Carleton, had the last laugh. The book, titled *Common Sense in the Household: A Manual of Practical Housewifery*, interspersed "familiar talks" on domestic themes with recipes, and it went through eight editions and sold one million copies during its fifty years in print.[3] By 1879, the stereotype plates manufactured in 1871 were so worn that Scribner's asked Terhune to prepare a revised and corrected edition, for which they cast new plates and registered a new copyright on publication of the revised edition in 1880.[4] In his 1884 memoir, J. C. Derby claims that Terhune

2 Kate Sanborn, ed., *Our Famous Women* (Hartford, CT: A. D. Worthington Co., 1884), 637. J. C. Derby also reports Scribner's decision, but without the laugh. *Fifty Years among Authors, Books and Publishers* (New York: G. W. Carleton & Co., 1884), 566–7. Carleton did continue to publish her fiction through the 1870s and 1880s, replacing Sheldon in this capacity.

3 Smith, *Marion Harland*, 328.

4 Deposition of Mary Virginia Terhune (6 Nov. 1884), 40–1, 43, in *Belford, Clarke & Co. et al. vs. Charles Scribner*, Appeal from the Circuit Court of the United States for the Northern District of Illinois to the U.S. Supreme Court, Oct. Term, 1891 (hereinafter *Belford, Clarke*). Also Deposition of Mary Virginia Terhune (17 Nov. 1884), 52; and Deposition of Charles Scribner (30 Dec. 1884), 87, both in *Belford, Clarke*. For all documents related to both the Circuit Court and Supreme Court proceedings in this case (with the exception of the published opinions of the courts), I cite from the printed record submitted to the Supreme Court (Case No. 13,287), using the pagination from this printed record. These documents are available in bound volumes at the Supreme Court library and on microfilm at the Library of Congress Law Library. The circuit court documents (in manuscript, typescript, or print) are also part of the original case file for *Scribner v. Clarke* at the National Archives, Great Lakes Region Branch (Record Group 21). Throughout, I synthesize and simplify aspects of the case, focusing on the relevant information and conflicts for my analysis. For instance, there was actually more than one defendant in the original action because Scribner's sued both the book's publisher and the printer with whom the publisher had subcontracted for the printing of the book. Additionally, various persons give slightly different accounts of key facts and events, including the events surrounding the discovery of the various infringing volumes, the titles of volumes discovered, and the dates of discovery.

had made "a sum equal to three years salary of the Governor of New York" (about $30,000) in royalties from sales of the volume, and in court depositions in 1884, Terhune herself reluctantly disclosed that royalties paid to her for sales of the book were no less than, and some years considerably more than, $2,000 a year.[5]

At first blush, the narrative trajectory of Terhune's career represents the apotheosis of the domestic woman. She may have written a surprisingly bitter and caustic novel about the legal condition of married women and the particularly ludicrous situation of a woman author who suffered under the law, but the novel was clearly not a roman à clef. Although she and her husband had conflicts and tensions in their marriage, they presented to the public an image of idealized marital unity. As Mary Forrest describes the Terhune marriage in *Women of the South Distinguished in Literature*, "It is said that a more complete refutation of the slanders generally heaped upon 'literary domesticity' can scarcely be imagined, than that afforded by the happy home of our author. United to a man of ripe scholarship, sound judgment, and tastes and sympathies kindred with her own, she invariably appealed to him in all important matters. His is the first reading and only revision of her MSS. before they are given into the hands of the printer."[6] One can only wonder what Edward Terhune said if and when he was the first reader of *Phemie's Temptation*, but with her turn to cookery and domestic advice, his wife seemingly obliterated even the *appearance* of a breach in the marital unity of the couple. Whatever her legal status as a married woman (and by 1870, almost all of the Northern states had enacted sweeping statutory reforms of the common law of coverture), her functional marriage to a supportive husband and their unity of purpose behind her pubic career as an author would seem to have made such questions moot as she continued publishing both in magazines and in book format – more cookbooks and domestic advice, as well as travel writing, history, and fiction.

But the story of the Reverend Dr. Terhune, Mrs. Terhune, and the copyrights in Mrs. Terhune's works took an unexpected turn in the 1880s. In late 1883, Mary Virginia Terhune's sister in St. Louis sent her a copy of a book titled "D. Crawford's Economy Cook Book, edited by B. Bush," which copied verbatim a significant portion of *Common Sense in the Household* by "Marion Harland." Publishers Belford, Clarke & Co., of Chicago, produced and printed the cookbook, which was designed to be an inexpensive volume that department stores throughout the country could present as their own. Department stores ordered the cookbook from Belford with a custom title

5 Derby, *Fifty Years*, 567. Smith translates his claim to $30,000. *Marion Harland*, 336, 609n. Cross–Examination of Mary V. Terhune (30 Dec. 1884), in *Belford, Clarke*, 79.

6 Mary Forrest, *Women of the South Distinguished in Literature* (New York: Charles B. Richardson, 1866), 198–9. See also Karen Manners Smith for the private tensions in the Terhune marriage.

page, and through this device, *Common Sense in the Household* by Marion Harland also became "Ehrich's Economy Cook Book" (New York), "Towle & Buxton's Economy Cook Book" (Dubuque, Iowa), and "Lord & Taylor's Economy Cook Book" (New York) (and likely others undiscovered).[7] Mary Virginia Terhune was, as she wrote to Charles Scribner in January 1884, "seriously annoyed and alarmed by the persistent thrusting of such quantities of these piratical productions upon the market and willing to second you to the utmost of my power in your spirited resistance of the injustice." Mr. Forbes of Forbes & Wallace, the local department store owner from whom she had obtained copies of one version of the infringing book, told her that Belford shipped him copies "by the wagon-load" and assured him that reports of any legal difficulties with the books were untrue.[8] Scribner had asked her to examine copies of various versions of the volume in order to complete her affidavit for the suit, and her displeasure escalated several days later when Mr. Forbes provided her with a copy of "How to Cook. By Marion Holmes," yet another iteration of the volume. "Externally," she wrote, "it is but a deceptive copy of the 'Kitchen Edition of Common Sense in the Household' [the authorized low-priced edition of *Common Sense*]. Internally, it is verbatim a reproduction of 'The Economy Cook-Book.' A friend who has just come in has taken up 'How to Cook' from my desk with the exclamation, 'Another of your series!' I am *angry*!"[9] As her friend's response to the volume demonstrated with painful clarity, the "author's" name on the title page of *How to Cook* ("Marion Holmes") was designed to trade on the commercial value of her pseudonym ("Marion Harland"), just as the text inside the volume infringed the copyright in the work she had authored.[10] Incensed by this doubled violation, she placed notices in newspapers in Springfield, Massachusetts, and Newark, New Jersey. Having executed the necessary affidavits for her publisher, who was the copyright owner and thus the plaintiff, she assumed that the matter was effectively closed, but she could not have been more wrong. Scribner's filed suit in the Federal Circuit Court of the United States, Northern District of Illinois (the defendant's corporate domicile), in January 1884, but matters dragged on for years in Chicago before the judge issued a decision. The defendant's appeal to the Supreme Court added yet more years to the process.

7 Bill of Complaint (18 Jan. 1884), in *Belford, Clarke*, 7–10.

8 Mary Virginia Terhune to Charles H. Scribner, [12 Jan. 1884], Archives of Charles Scribner's Sons, Author Files, Manuscript Division, Department of Rare Books and Special Collections, Princeton University Library (the archive as a whole hereinafter "Scribner's Archive"). Quotations published with permission of the Princeton University Library.

9 Mary Virginia Terhune to Charles H. Scribner, [15 Jan. 1884], Author Files, Scribner's Archive. Terhune was normally scrupulous in her correspondence with Scribner, and it is telling that she failed to date these two letters among the hundreds preserved. I have fixed approximate dates based on copies of letters from Scribner to Terhune, to which she is clearly responding.

10 Bill of Complaint (18 Jan. 1884), in *Belford, Clarke*, 9–10.

The case presented a number of substantive copyright law issues. Were recipes entitled to copyright protection at all, or did they so effectively merge unprotectable idea with the language embodying the idea that copyright law should not protect recipes as literary works? Similarly, did the table of contents and organizational scheme of *Common Sense* deserve copyright protection? And, finally, considering that the defendant rearranged and revised the copied portions of *Common Sense* and reproduced less than half of the text as a whole, did their taking rise to the level of copyright infringement? As is often the case in copyright infringement suits, however, the defendant argued the case on all fronts, attempting to have the case thrown out of court on more technical grounds, as well as arguing the substance. If, for instance, the defendant could prove that Scribner's had no legitimate title to the copyright for *Common Sense*, the defendant's copying became irrelevant because Scribner's had no standing to sue. Belford attacked Scribner's claim to title of the copyright for *Common Sense* on a number of grounds, but the one relevant here is their attempt to invalidate the transfer from author to publisher of the right to publish her manuscript. In their original bill of complaint, Scribner's describes "M. Virginia Terhune" as "a gentlewoman, wife of Edward P. Terhune, and a citizen of and resident of Springfield, in the State of Massachusetts, [who] has been and now is an authoress." In tracing the chain of title in the copyright of *Common Sense*, the publishing firm explains,

> [B]y an agreement with the said M. Virginia Terhune, [Scribner's] undertook and became interested in and assumed the risk and responsibility of the publication of said work; [and] that said agreement was duly made and entered into in said city and State of New York and was performed in said State between the parties thereto, and by the laws of said State of New York the said M. Virginia Terhune, being a married woman, was duly authorized and empowered to enter into and execute said contract in the same manner and to the same extent as if she had been a *feme sole*.[11]

Sensing a vulnerable point in the chain of title, the defense counsel used the depositions of Mrs. Terhune and her publisher to gather facts that might undermine the validity of the contract between the married woman author and her publisher. The peripatetic nature of the Reverend Dr. Terhune's career as a minister potentially raised as a genuine question which state law rightfully determined his wife's ability to hold and dispose of property separately from him. From 1856 through 1884 (i.e., from Mrs. Terhune's first collecting the materials from which she wrote *Common Sense* through Scribner's filing suit), the minister's family resided in no fewer than four states. Mrs. Terhune began collecting recipes in 1856, the first year of their marriage, during which the minister served a church in rural Virginia. When

11 Bill of Complaint, in *Belford, Clarke*, 2, 3.

Mrs. Terhune formally wrote out her collected recipes for publication as a cookbook in 1870 and when she entered into her first contract with Scribner's in 1871, the Reverend Dr. Terhune held a pastorate in Newark, New Jersey. In 1874, New Jersey was one of the last Northern states to pass a comprehensive and progressive married women's property law. Under New Jersey's earlier statute of 1852, Mrs. Terhune's copyright in *Common Sense* may *not* have been considered her separate property, and even if the copyright had been recognized as her separate property, the 1852 statute would not necessarily have given her the right to enter into a contract respecting it.[12] When she executed the contract for the revised edition of *Common Sense* in 1880, her husband had moved on to a church in Springfield, Massachusetts. When her sister sent her the infringing cookbook from St. Louis in 1883, the Terhune family was in transition. The Reverend Dr. Terhune had resigned his pastorate in Springfield for one in Brooklyn, New York, but his wife remained behind in Springfield to close up their house. The family thus did not finally establish its joint residence in New York State until 1884. New York was an early, progressive reformer of married women's property laws, and under the provisions of its 1860 statute, as Scribner's complaint states, the copyright of the married "authoress" would have been her separate property, and she was fully empowered and authorized to enter into a contract respecting it.[13] However, she was *not* a New York resident in 1870 or 1880. Furthermore, throughout these years, the family maintained a summer home in Pompton Lakes, New Jersey.

The shifting residence of the Terhune family raised important questions, but even after a determination of which state law applied, the outcome might depend on whether or not Mr. Terhune had inserted himself into these transactions. Had he, in the language of the law, sought to "reduce to [his] possession" the copyrights, contracts, and royalties of which his wife was the nominal owner? Belford's lawyers thus sought to determine who actually handled the ongoing business transactions with the publisher with respect to Mrs. Terhune's cookbook. From 1871 on, testified one employee of Scribner's, regular royalty payments to "Mrs. E. P. Terhune" appeared in

12 John F. Kelly, *A Treatise on the Law of Contracts of Married Women* (Jersey City, NJ: F. D. Linn & Co., 1882), 448–54. This nineteenth-century treatise summarizes the law as it stood at almost precisely the moment that this lawsuit arose and during the decades leading up to that moment. The summary of earlier law was necessary because lawyers needed to know the state of the law in given jurisdictions during earlier years to determine the status of contracts signed during those years. The need for a nearly 600-page volume on the subject in 1882 complicates the assumption that by the 1880s, married women were full legal subjects under the law, capable of contracting with regard to their property just as their husbands could. The chronology of composition, publication, revision, and republication can be traced through Terhune's depositions (6 and 14 Nov. 1864) in *Belford, Clarke*, 38–57.

13 Kelly, *Treatise*, 455–62.

the records of the firm. Defense counsel, on cross-examination, asked for clarification on this point:

Q: Do you know the husband of Mrs. Terhune?
A: I know him by sight; I am not acquainted with him.
Q: Did he receive any of this money?
A: Not from me.
Q: Did he make the collections personally?
A: No sir; not as a general thing. There may have been a case where he received a check, but it was not customary.
Q: Do you know about that, whether he ever did receive a check or not?
A: Not positively. My impression is that once or twice part of that amount was handed him by her direction, but I couldn't say positively.
Q: You think on some occasions part was paid to him by her direction or not; do you know that?

Mr. CRANE [plaintiff's counsel]: He did not say that.

Q: I asked him if he knew certain occasions when he received money.
A: I can't say positively, but my impression is that he did receive a check once or twice.[14]

In February 1884, nearly a year before this December deposition but after the court issued a preliminary injunction, Charles Scribner declined a settlement offer of $500, explaining to the firm's attorney in Chicago that the sum was "inadequate . . . for the damages which we have sustained, and they should pay much more [$2,500] for the use of their pirated material for the year during which they have sold their book."[15] Still waiting for the master in chancery to issue his report based on the pleadings and depositions of 1884, Scribner wrote to that same attorney in early 1886, complaining, "I'm afraid that bills are all we shall ever get out of this suit. I hope it is costing Belford something."[16] The court did not finally hear the case until 1888. At the 1888 hearing, defense counsel used the uncertainty suggested by the multiple state residences and the lack of clarity concerning Mr. Terhune's involvement in his wife's literary business affairs to attack the validity of the original transfer of the copyright to Scribner's in 1871. "It was objected at

14 Deposition of Frederick B. Mead (2 Dec. 1884), in *Belford, Clarke*, 63–4. For the text of the 1860 New York statute, see Basch, *In the Eyes of the Law*, 234–7.

15 Charles H. Scribner to Walter C. Larned, 14 Feb. 1884, Scribner's Archive, Charles H. Scribner Letter Books, part 1, vol. 9, p. 34.

16 Charles H. Scribner to Walter C. Larned, 12 Apr. 1886, Scribner's Archive, Charles H. Scribner Letter Books, part 1, vol. 11, p. 117. He later reported to Terhune that the bills had reached $400 and finally nearly $2,000, the amount of damages awarded. Charles H. Scribner to Mary Virginia Terhune, 29 Oct. 1887; and Charles H. Scribner to Mary Virginia Terhune, 15 Nov. 1890, Scribner's Archive, Author Files.

the hearing," Judge Blodgett writes in his opinion, "that the complainant could not recover in the case, because the proof shows that Mrs. Terhune, the author of this book, whose *nom de plume* is Marion Harland, was a married woman at the time the copyright in question was taken, and that by the common law her husband is entitled to the benefits of her literary work, as well as any other proceeds of her industry during coverture."[17]

Judge Blodgett refused to seriously entertain this challenge to the validity of the plaintiff's copyright, but his reasoning does not fundamentally disturb the legal proposition behind Belford's argument. He reasons that because both editions of *Common Sense* appeared with the Scribner's firm name listed as proprietor in the copyright notice and because Mrs. Terhune accepted regular payments of royalties from Scribner's, "the court will presume that her legal title as the author of these books was in some due and proper manner conveyed and vested in the persons who secured the copyright thereof." In particular, he does not accept the defendant's contention that only Mr. Terhune could legally transfer the right to publish his wife's book to Scribner's, but *not* on the ground that coverture had been legislated away. Instead, he reasons,

> Acquiescence for so many years by all the parties in this claim of proprietorship in the copyright is, it seems to me, enough to answer this suggestion of Mr. Terhune's possible marital interest in his wife's earnings. It is certain that if there is any ownership in this work by copyright at all, it is in the complainant, in whose name the copyright was taken and now stands, so far as is shown by the proof of this case. If the law of the domicile of Mrs. Terhune entitles her husband to any part of her earnings, that is a matter to be settled between her husband and the complainant, and which the defendants cannot interpose as a defense to a trespass upon the complainant's property rights in this copyrighted book.[18]

In short, he leaves open the door for other *husbands* of female authors to interfere with their wives' rights to manage and dispose of their literary properties, but he refuses to allow the *defendant* to assert *Mr. Terhune's* rights in order to escape liability for their own wrongdoing.

Belford was not, however, ready to accept the circuit court's judgment. Instead, they filed an "Assignment of Error by Appellants" with the U.S. Supreme Court in 1888, arguing that the circuit court erred in finding "that the complainant was the owner of the copyright to the book" because "the proofs in this cause show that he never was the proprietor of said book nor

17 *Scribner v. Clark* (Circuit Court, N.D. Illinois – April 9, 1888) 50 F. 473, in Wilma S. Davis and Mark A. Lillis, eds., *Decisions of the United States Courts Involving Copyright and Literary Property, 1789–1909* (Washington, DC: Copyright Office, 1980), 2352.

18 Ibid.

of the copyright therein."[19] That is, Belford claimed that Scribner's did not own the copyright in *Common Sense* and thus had no standing to sue Belford for copyright infringement. Although Belford only raised the issue during oral arguments at the circuit court level, in their appeal brief to the Supreme Court, Belford sets out their legal reasoning in writing:

> At common law a married woman has no interest in personal property acquired by or through her during marriage, but it belongs absolutely to her husband. No proof was introduced of the provisions of the laws of New York or of New Jersey or of Massachusetts, where it was stated said M. Virginia Terhune resided at the time said bill was filed and no proof was submitted to show that the laws of either of said states differed from the common law; and the presumption is that the common law is in force in the different states unless the contrary is pleaded and proved. [citation omitted] "But in case of personal property acquired after marriage by her means, such property belongs absolutely to the husband; so that if a legacy should be given to the wife during coverture, and the husband should die before it is paid or due, it would not belong to the wife, but the husband's executor." Reeve's Domestic Relations, 134 (60). It does not appear that Mrs. Terhune had any right, to sell her husband's property or to make contracts in regard to it, and it would seem that the suit in question ought to have been in his name as complainant therein.[20]

Rather than respond to the appellant's reasoning, the Supreme Court quoted and approved the circuit court's holding on this point as correct,[21] but that the appellant even made this argument is revealing. Despite decades of statutory reform, argues the appellant, the common law of coverture is the rule that governs marriages, and any state statutes would merely carve out exceptions to the rule. Therefore, if the specific provisions of the applicable state statutes are not submitted to the court, the common law holds sway.

In support of their interpretation of the common law that they claim rightfully determines the status of Mrs. Terhune's literary property, they cite Tapping Reeve, whose influential 1816 treatise *The Law of Baron and Femme; of Parent and Child; of Guardian and Ward; of Master and Servant; and of the Powers of the Courts of Chancery* summarized for American law students, lawyers, and judges both the English common law of coverture and equitable

19 Brief and Argument for Appellants, *Belford v. Scribner*, U.S. Supreme Court, Oct. Term, 1891, 13. Belford actually presented an interlocking set of reasons that Scribner's did not own the copyright, but they are highly technical and not relevant to my analysis here. Furthermore, if the court had held that the challenge based on coverture was legitimate, this cause alone could have been sufficient to invalidate Scribner's title.

20 Ibid., 17–18.

21 *Belford v. Scribner* (United States Supreme Court – Submitted March 24, 1892 – Decided April 11, 1892) 144 U.S. 488. 12 S.Ct. 734. 36 L.Ed. 514, in Davis, *Decisions*, 210–11.

exceptions to coverture.[22] By the 1880s, treatises derived from his influential summary had partially shed the original archaic title, flying under the flag of *Reeve's Domestic Relations* in citations in legal arguments such as Belford's. However, the slightly modernized full title as it appears on the title page of 1880s editions of the treatise was still *The Law of Husband and Wife, of Parent and Child, Guardian and Ward, Master and Servant.* Furthermore, the example cited from Reeve on the effect of coverture on personal property acquired by the wife drives home the point I made in Chapter 1 – that a copyright's nature as a piece of personal property is highly peculiar and eccentric. Certainly, in 1871, Mrs. Terhune's common law copyright for *Common Sense* (her right to publish, or withhold from publication, her manuscript cookbook) was a "personal property acquired after marriage." However, Reeve's example of the operation of law on a "typical," unspecified item of personal property is fundamentally incommensurate with the example of Mrs. Terhune's literary property. Reeve's specific example is a "legacy," some kind of personal property (not a piece of real estate, for which different rules applied) willed to a married woman "during her coverture." His hypothetical wife does not earn the property; instead, a third party bestows it on her. Let us imagine an item of personal property that clearly does fit into this scenario – a valuable piece of antique furniture. In what sense is an armoire bequeathed to our hypothetical married woman by her uncle equivalent to a copyright in a work authored by a married woman, a property that comes into existence as a product of her authorial labor? If we attempt to read Reeve's logic onto Terhune's situation, she appears entirely detached from herself, her literary labors, and her literary property, which are transformed into properties originating outside the marriage and of which her husband (or her husband's estate) can rightfully take possession. Recall that in Terhune's novel *Phemie's Temptation*, the redoubtable spinster Miss Darcy describes the legal situation of abandoned author-wife Phemie as "simply and ludicrously hopeless!" Terhune effectively predicted the legal analysis of her own situation as an author-wife, in which the total effacement of the writing wife's legal agency makes her situation as a married woman and literary proprietor appear simply and ludicrously hopeless.

Of course, Belford lost the case, and neither the circuit court nor the Supreme Court applied this suggested interpretation of the implications of coverture to Mrs. Terhune's situation as a married woman author; however, the case demonstrates the intransigence of coverture as both a legal and cultural construction, a construction that would not die and that continued

22 Norma Basch discusses Reeve's uneasy rapprochement with the common law of coverture as summarized by Blackstone, finding that he did not fully accept the legal fiction of marital unity. *In the Eyes of the Law: Women, Marriage and Property in Nineteenth-Century New York* (Ithaca: Cornell University Press, 1982), chap. 2. However, as the cited principle from Reeve suggests, such a philosophical difference did not necessarily lead to different results.

to haunt married women who labored with their pens.[23] Indeed, coverture was as intransigent as the lawsuit and the infringement that gave rise to it. By 1890, Belford, Clarke & Co. had gone bankrupt, and, as discovered by one of Mary Virginia Terhune's friends, poet Mary Riley Smith, someone was disposing of remaining copies of the enjoined infringing books by selling them in Mexico.[24] When Belford filed the appeal in 1888, the firm was required to give bond for the $2,000 in damages due to Scribner's under the circuit court decision, but by 1891, lawyers arguing the appeal were protecting the interests of the ghostly corporate shell of a bankrupt company. In the wake of the Supreme Court's decision in favor of Scribner's and against the defunct Belford, Terhune wrote the novella "The Articles of Separation" (1894), which revisits and revises *Phemie's Temptation* in the context of the literary culture of the 1880s and 1890s.[25] The novella suggests both Terhune's own continuing frustration with the legal status of the married woman author and her astute prediction of the imminent disappearance of herself and other popular antebellum women novelists from literary history.

Before turning to the implications of this story, let me briefly review the fate of the copyright debates in the postwar United States and the place of women in these debates. Throughout most of the nineteenth century, organized efforts to reform the copyright law washed over American literary culture in waves. In each coordinated movement, a group of men of letters gathered to express a common outrage at the lack of international copyright, formally organized an association and elected officers, wrote magazine articles and pamphlets in favor of reform, and lobbied Congress, but when lobbying failed, as it invariably did for most of the century, the group lost momentum and disbanded. In one such wave of activity in 1886, the new American Copyright League, heir apparent to the International Copyright Association that James Parton helped organize in the late 1860s, solicited "letters" from prominent American authors on the international copyright

23 Ellen Weinauer's analysis of how coverture produces the married woman as a gothic subject spurred me to think about haunting and ghosts in relation to Terhune's later career, although my analysis does not directly depend on hers. "Property Writes: Authorship and Ownership in America, 1848–1870," PhD diss., Indiana University, 1993, chap. 2.

24 Mary Virginia Terhune to Charles H. Scribner, 11 Nov. 1890, Scribner's Archive, Author Files. Charles H. Scribner to Mary Virginia Terhune, 15 Nov. 1890, Scribner's Archive, Charles H. Scribner Letter Books, part 1, vol. 14, p. 368.

25 The story appears in a volume titled *Mr. Wayt's Wife's Sister* (New York: Cassell, 1894), 251–314. Thanks to Karen Manners Smith for suggesting that I read this story because of its relationship to *Phemie's Temptation*. The story may have appeared in a magazine before 1894, although I have been unable to locate such an appearance. However, on the basis of evidence from the story itself, especially names of people with whom and places with which Terhune did not come in contact until the early 1890s, Smith is of the opinion that Terhune wrote the story no earlier than the early 1890s. No correspondence preserved in the Scribner's Archive documents that the company notified Terhune of the court's decision in 1892, and the decision was not reported in the *New York Times*. However, it is clear that in the 1890s Terhune conducted some of her business in person with Scribner.

question to be published in the sympathetic *Century Magazine* under the title "International Copyright: Plain Speech from American Authors" (in 1888, the League republished the series as a pamphlet titled *What American Authors Think About Copyright*).[26]

The authors' sentiments expressed under the aegis of the American Copyright League represent a fair sampling of authorial thinking on the international copyright issue at a moment when copyright advocates were closer than they had ever been to actually achieving the goal of reform. Still, anyone who surveys and samples documents from the American copyright debates from the 1830s through the 1880s soon discovers that the same arguments appear over and over again, showing, at best, incremental repetition inflected by changes in the larger society rather than creativity or originality of thought. "What American authors thought about copyright" in the 1880s differs little from what American authors thought about copyright in 1842, 1853, or 1867. Reflecting ongoing calls for perpetual copyright protection as well as international copyright, William Dean Howells proclaims, "I am in favor of any and every device for securing to the foreign author that property in his writings which our country nobly bestows on native authors for forty-two years before suffering them to become public pillage" (p. 6). Mark Twain, continuing the long tradition of jeremiads on the detrimental influence of the foreign values embodied in foreign literature on American readers, laments the "semi-annual inundation from Zola's sewer" that washes over American readers in cheap editions (p. 10). In a similar vein, Brander Matthews complains that authors suffer from unfair competition, while readers suffer because they do not get the best American books and get only "cheap and nasty" reprints of British works (p. 7). Thomas Wentworth Higginson, like his antebellum predecessors in the copyright movement, concerns himself with the damage to an author's reputation caused by the "garbling" of an unprotected book, "a loss not to be measured in money" (p. 6). Thomas Bailey Aldrich simply declares himself to be so angered by the "shameful" state of affairs that he cannot even bring himself to comment on it (p. 4).

In a decided departure from antebellum copyright advocacy efforts, however, the American Copyright League gave women authors a platform (at least in print), so that they could be active agents of copyright reform rather than passive objects of sympathy. The International Copyright Association did obtain signatures of some women authors for its 1868 petition to Congress. Among those who signed the 1868 petition were Augusta Jane Evans (not yet married to Colonel Wilson; she had lobbied for international copyright in 1861 Confederacy, so why not sign a petition to the U.S. Congress in 1868?), "Grace Greenwood" and Mary A. Denison (both of

26 American Copyright League, *What American Authors Think About International Copyright* (New York: American Copyright League, 1888) (hereinafter cited in the text).

whose copyrights had been registered by their husbands as proprietors in the 1850s), Frances Kemball, Mary Jane Holmes, Metta Victor, and Fanny Fern (uncharacteristically signing the petition organized by her husband as "Mrs. James Parton," her name following that of her husband, who was the secretary of the new organization).[27] However, the International Copyright Association pamphlet distributed with copies of the 1868 petition reproduced speeches made and statements read at their public meeting in New York, and women either did not seek or were not offered the platform. In contrast, in 1886 the American Copyright League offered women authors the opportunity both to sign a petition and to add their voices in print to the cause. Women's letters are only six of the fifty-three published, and some women very well may have declined to have their opinions published, letting their signatures speak without explanation.[28] Among those who signed but did not submit letters were Louise Imogine Guiney, Miriam Coles Harris, Helen Hunt Jackson, Constance Fenimore Woolson, Mary Noales Murfree, Harriet Prescott Spofford, Adeline D. T. Whitney, Mary Virginia Terhune, and Sarah Orne Jewett. Five of those who did contribute letters participate wholeheartedly in the call for international copyright and use the same arguments and adopt the same tone as their male peers. Rebecca Harding Davis adopts the same nativist stance as Mark Twain, lauding immigration laws that allowed the United States to exclude undesirable immigrants and criticizing Congress for not passing laws that would effectively exclude literary undesirables (p. 5). Elizabeth Stuart Phelps identifies international reprinting as a kind of theft; punning on the title of her recently published comic novel *Burglars in Paradise* (1886), Phelps opines, "There can be but two opinions on such a matter, and that they cannot be unlike those of the burglar and of the burglar*ee*" (p. 8). Frances Hodgson Burnett, carefully using gender-neutral language, calls on the classic Lockean argument concerning the right of "one" to the products of "one's" brain labor: "A right to the control and the protection of one's brain, it seems to me, cannot be questioned from any point of view in an age which recognizes in so many other ways the liberty of the individual. For any country to say that its subjects may use, without proper compensation based on a mutual agreement as to its value, the results of the intellectual activity of those of another, is but a remnant of those barbaric times when physical strength was the sole basis of right, and government only an organized power of

27 International Copyright Association, *International Copyright: Meeting of Authors and Publishers, at the Rooms of the New York Historical Society, April 9, 1868, and the Organization of the International Copyright Association* (New York: International Copyright Association, 1868). See pp. 42–6 (appendix) for the petition and signatures. If this petition was officially submitted to Congress, Congress did not order it to be printed in its records.

28 Forty-four letters of the letters in the pamphlet originally appeared in the *Century* in Feb. 1886, while nine additional statements by authors, some excerpted from other sources but all by men, were added to the pamphlet.

oppression" (p. 4). Mary Mapes Dodge uses similar rhetoric, but she fails to note the irony of the gendered language of her call for reform: "It is high time that on this question our law-makers should cease to interpret the 'rights of *man*' as meaning only the rights of Americans" (p. 6; emphasis added).

Only Louisa May Alcott, in a pithy, one-sentence reply to the solicitation of her opinion on the subject, draws attention to the still problematic relationship of women to property and political power in late nineteenth-century America. "If women are allowed a vote in the matter," Alcott writes archly, "I decidedly cast mine for International Copyright" (p. 4). By the 1880s, coverture was (allegedly) a dead letter, its power eliminated (or at least heavily diluted) by legislative reform. In many states, married women could acquire, hold, and transfer property, they could sign contracts, and they could enjoy the fruits of their own labors in the form of wages. However, coverture still had power over the lives of all American women, married or unmarried, because it continued to rationalize the exclusion of women from full participation in political life. Because a married woman's identity merged into her husband's upon marriage, so the story went, granting a married woman the right to vote (and to serve on juries, and to be a lawyer) would endanger that sacred marital unity; marriage was the natural and proper state for all adult women; therefore *all* women should be excluded from exercising political agency.[29] Alcott, who never married and who therefore could unambiguously exercise full control over her literary properties as a *feme sole*, nevertheless recognized the irony of the American Copyright League soliciting her opinion and her signature to be presented to Congress – she, like (almost) all women, still could not vote, even if her position as a best-selling author on both sides of the Atlantic gave her a clear incentive to support copyright reform.

In 1891, on hearing of the passage of the International Copyright Act, Sarah Orne Jewett (who signed the 1886 American Copyright League petition) wrote in a letter to Annie Fields that she wanted to memorialize the new law by purchasing and engraving a piece of silver plate so that tangible evidence of the triumph could be "handed down": "Yes, it is quite magnificent about the copyright bill, and I like to have my country honest at last about the Spoliation Claims. I told Mother yesterday that she must buy a piece of plate and have it marked French Spoliation Claims, 1891, and have

29 As Nancy Cott argues, the status of married women under coverture led to the "fixing [of] all women, not only wives, in a position of minimal citizenship." "Marriage and Women's Citizenship in the United States, 1830–1934," *American Historical Review* 10, no. 5 (1998): 1453. See also Joan Hoff, "Constitutional Discrimination, 1872–1908," in *Law, Gender, and Injustice: A Legal History of U.S. Women* (New York: New York University Press, 1991), 151–91. States controlled access to the franchise, even for federal elections, and thus a few Western states did allow women to vote in the late nineteenth century, but not Massachusetts, Alcott's state of residence.

it handed down."[30] By referring to the "French spoliation claims" against America, she focuses on the situation of French authors, most likely because of her friendship with Madame Marie Therese Blanc ("Th. Bentzon"), for whom she acted as an informal American agent, and because French law granted copyright protection to *all* authors, regardless of their nationality. She thus implicitly accuses American readers and publishers of "spoliation," the act of plundering an adversary's property during a time of war, implying that American readers have been at war with French authors and have unjustly taken their property under the pretext of wartime suspension of international property relations.

But what was "handed down" through literary history as the story of the "triumph" of authors in 1891 was told and retold? Mary Virginia Terhune supported international copyright with her signature in 1886, and her depositions in the *Common Sense* case demonstrate her strong sense of herself as a righteous literary proprietor. However, her story "The Articles of Separation," published three years after the International Copyright Act and two years after the Supreme Court's decision in *Belford v. Scribner*, demonstrates her awareness, either conscious or unconscious, that the supposed triumph of "the author" was not a triumph for "lady-writers" like herself. "Articles" bears a complex, intertextual relation to *Phemie's Temptation* and its narrative of a married woman's literary proprietorship. Recall that in *Phemie's Temptation*, when the eponymous heroine's husband deserts her, she is unable to enforce her rights under a publishing contract she entered into as a married woman. When, as a deserted wife, she continues to publish in order to support herself and her daughter, her husband periodically reappears and claims "his" royalties from the publication of her books, and she is absolutely powerless to prevent him from doing so. Finally, and only very reluctantly, she divorces him, and the novel ends. "The Articles of Separation" features a similarly mismatched marriage between a noble woman author (Agnes Welles) and a caddish husband (Barton Ashe). For most of the novella, the couple is married and cohabiting (if not happily). Like Phemie, Agnes secretly writes and publishes a novel, even though her husband has decreed that she must not be a "literary woman" after their marriage. She gives birth to her novel shortly before she gives birth to her daughter (with the book-as-baby analogy made excruciatingly clear). The stress of keeping her secret and her full understanding of just how repulsive her husband would find the revelation of her authorship bring on the brain fever that kills Agnes. Her infant daughter survives her by only a few days. In the last few paragraphs of the novella, which the narrator proclaims has no "conventional moral," we find out that Barton Ashe has remarried, to a "beautiful society girl with a tolerable fortune." The new Mrs. Ashe gets the last word(s) of the

30 Sarah Orne Jewett to Annie Adams Fields, [undated, 1891], in *Letters of Sarah Orne Jewett*, ed. Annie Fields (Boston: Houghton Mifflin, 1911), 55.

novella: she languidly dismisses another woman's veneration of some distinguished authors by calling them "Bohemians" who are, at most, "nice" (p. 314).

On the level of overplot, the novel and novella appear to have little in common – one woman's marriage ends in divorce, while the other woman's marriage ends with her death. However, Terhune's repetition of key names makes it clear that *Phemie*, written decades earlier, was very much on her mind in the 1890s, and, I believe, that *Belford v. Scribner* had brought *Phemie* back from the dead and made the issues she tackled in the novel live again for her. In *Phemie*, the heroine's maiden name is Rowland, and in "Articles," a publisher named "Mr. Rowland" makes a significant appearance. He appears at the Ashe residence to implore Agnes to write "one of a projected series of popular novels" (p. 280), and his request precipitates a marital crisis. Barton is infuriated because he believes that his wife has prearranged the visit but made it appear to be a surprise. Agnes does not publish with Mr. Rowland the novel that she writes subsequent to this visit, but when she does publish *The Story of Walter King*, she uses the pseudonym "John Hart." The writing wife thus ironically takes on the surname of the villain of *Phemie's Temptation*, James Hart, the man who abandons the writing wife.

So why return to the same conflict and characters at this moment, and why do so with such drastically different results for the married woman author-heroine? In one sense, Terhune and her female author peers had outlived the plot of *Phemie* – whatever the status of the copyrights in Terhune's works produced in the 1850s, '60s, and '70s, in the state of New York and in most states in the 1880s and 1890s, a married woman author could truly claim her copyrights as her own property and contract with a publisher independently if she so chose. In another sense, as I indicated in my analysis of Louisa May Alcott's letter in support of international copyright, coverture was very much alive as a way to understand the marital relation and the places of both husband and wife in it, but particularly the place of the wife. As the narrator of "Articles" describes the change produced in the transition from unmarried pair to husband and wife, "The turn of the bridal pair from the altar symbolizes a reversal in their mutual relation. The bonds that have held the lover in vassalage – very sweet bondage, perhaps, but still not liberty – are with the utterance of the nuptial benediction transferred to the woman he holds by the hand. Barton Ashe was very much in love, but he was a very man. His wife was now his property" (pp. 260–1). Despite the legislative reform of coverture, a doctrine that came close to transforming wives into their husbands' chattel, a "very man" like Barton has not let go of the ideas behind the legal strictures that have been softened or eliminated. Phemie and Agnes, separated by decades, nevertheless resemble each other as writing wives whom their husbands regard as their property.

"Articles" begins on the eve of the wedding of Barton Ashe and Agnes Welles, with a conversation between Barton and his uncle, the Honorable

Simeone Barton, a forty-year-old bibulous bachelor Congressman.[31] The Congressman rails against the participation of "the writing woman" in feminist reform and warns his nephew that he is in danger of being introduced socially as "Mrs. Agnes Ashe and husband." Barton Ashe refutes this charge by presenting his uncle with their newly engraved calling cards for "Mr. and Mrs. Barton Ashe," and he promises his uncle that if his prediction is true, "I shall employ you to draw up the articles of separation" (that is, he will hire his uncle to act as his divorce lawyer) (pp. 254–6). Thus the question posed by the story at its opening is, will Agnes allow her identity to be fully merged into that of her husband, or will she assert her individual identity and agency as a woman writer? Through a different plot, Terhune contemplates in "Articles" essentially the same issue raised by *Phemie* and then raised by the infringing publisher in *Belford v. Scribner*: what are the consequences when a married woman author creates a literary property and contracts independently for publication of her work?

Both of Terhune's literary texts and Terhune herself bear a relationship to feminism so contradictory that they appear schizophrenic. The narrator of "Articles" often aligns herself with traditional ideas of marriage, saying apparently without irony, for instance, that the Ashe marriage "made [them] one – in law and gospel" (p. 272). Furthermore, the story was published the year that Terhune officially lent her name and reputation to the movement opposing women's suffrage.[32] The story also seems to hold masculine misogyny (as represented by the Honorable Barton Simeon) and a crude variety of feminism (as represented by Miss Mary Marvell, a reincarnation of Miss Darcy from *Phemie's Temptation*) equally responsible for the failure of the Ashe marriage and for Agnes's untimely demise. Barton's uncle's prediction that the marriage will fail makes Barton feel insecure, while Miss Marvell's proclamations that the "private good" of his marriage is a "public disaster" (p. 261) and that Barton may be mobbed some day "for imprisoning the eagle and stilling the song of the lark" antagonize him (p. 274). As a result, he cannot see what is plainly true: that his wife is entirely capable of being *both* a proper, domestic wife *and* an author.

By forbidding Agnes to fulfill her dual destinies, Barton forces her into secrecy and her own form of schizophrenia. After her husband reads her novel aloud to her without knowing she is the novel's author, Agnes comes to believe, quite literally, that her novel is as much her baby as her baby daughter (named Agnes) and that she has orphaned her brainchild: "She was the unsuspected mother of a foundling. In secret and in fear, she had

31 During this conversation, the Congressman repeatedly refers to his conversations with his colleague "Jones of Illinois" as authority. By locating Barton's views on married women as authors geographically in this way, she may be gesturing toward Belford and their arguments in *Belford v. Scribner*, which originated in Illinois.

32 Smith, *Marion Harland*, 504–5

laid the new-born baby at a stranger's door. He had cared for, fostered, and clothed it, and on this New Year's Day, her husband had ignorantly adopted the waif and led it, a beautiful child, to her, bespeaking her [*sic*] admiration for it" (p. 291). Agnes briefly fantasizes that the family can reconcile and that her husband will take in the child that had been "fostered" by another man (her publisher) and that embodies the other self she put into writing it. However, her fantasy quickly dissipates when her husband proclaims that if a woman wrote the novel (which he doubts because of its "virile" rather than "feminine" qualities), he "should *not* like . . . to know a woman who could write" such a novel (pp. 296–7). In the wake of this conversation, after her husband leaves for a late night at his "club" (yet again), Agnes sneaks away from her nurse to find her "baby" and to destroy the manuscript evidence of her authorship. She succeeds in taking the printed volume to her bed, but in leaving her desk open and her papers scattered around the library, she sets the stage for her husband to discover her authorship by discovering her publishing contract. Tellingly, Terhune "reproduces" the opening paragraphs of the text of the contract in the story:

> MEMORANDUM OF AGREEMENT made this 6th Day of August, 188–, between AGNES WELLES ASHE of New York City, and RHINE, RHONE & CO., Publishers of New York City.
>
> Said AGNES WELLES ASHE being the author and proprietor of a work entitled, "THE STORY OF WALTER KING, BY JOHN C. HART," in consideration of the covenants and stipulation, etc. etc. etc. (pp. 310–11)

After reading this document, which proves both Agnes's authorship and her independent assertion of her legal agency as a proprietor, Barton decides that he *will* ask his uncle to draw up divorce papers; because she has not properly made herself one with him, they should legally be two. However, such a step proves to be unnecessary. Just as he is writing a note to his uncle about his intention to divorce Agnes, he feels someone (clearly Agnes's ghost) pass him as he sits at the library desk where she wrote the novel, "so close that he [feels] the wind from floating garments" and smells the fragrance of her favorite roses (p. 312). He need not complete and send the instructions to his uncle because, as the doctor announces, his wife has just died.

The contract that Terhune signed with Scribner's in 1871 arranging for publication of *Common Sense* became a public document as an exhibit in *Belford v. Scribner.*[33] In 1888, Belford had the entire record of the proceedings in the Circuit Court, including the contract between Terhune and

33 Agreement between Mrs. E. P. Terhune (Marion Harland) and Charles Scribner & Co., 1 Apr. 1871, as Complainant's Exhibit H and K (2 Dec. 1884), in *Belford, Clarke*, 99. The language of the contract in "Articles" is not identical to Terhune's contract for *Common Sense*. In fact, the 1871

Scribner's, printed, and this printed record accompanied Belford's appeal to the Supreme Court. In 1892 (the year after Congress passed the International Copyright Act), the Supreme Court read and considered that record in deciding the fate of Belford's appeal. The Supreme Court declined to declare Terhune's contract with Scribner's invalid, but the questions presented to the court about this contract are an essential context for understanding Agnes Ashe's death and how that death speaks to Terhune's situation and the situation of the nineteenth-century married woman author at the century's end.

Both in the nineteenth century and in modern scholarship, the effects of marriage for women under the common law have been labeled a kind of "civil death." That is, on entering the state of coverture, a woman so thoroughly loses her ability to act as a legal subject in the civil sphere that she is essentially dead to that world. In *Phemie's Temptation*, the author-heroine spends most of the novel civilly dead but abandoned by the husband whose legal identity is supposed to "cover" hers. When she attempts to assert "her" proprietary rights, she is, metaphorically, a ghost of whom the law takes no cognizance. In "The Articles of Separation," which is quite specifically set in the 1880s, coverture as an obstacle to the writing wife's literary proprietorship loses its force. However, the disruption of marital unity produced by her exercise of the right to contract for the publication of her book *literally* produces the death of the writing wife. And, in both novel and novella, Terhune devotes her narrative energies to the wife's literary production within her unhappy marriage, rather than to imagining and describing her continuing production after the marriage's end. In Fanny Fern's novel *Ruth Hall*, when Ruth's daughter asks her if she herself will also be an author when she grows up, Ruth answers, "God forbid . . . no happy woman ever writes. From Harry's grave sprang 'Floy.'"[34] In the context of Fern's novel, the statement testifies to the fact that the death of Ruth's husband produces her authorial career under the pseudonym "Floy" – she writes because, unhappily, she is a widow and has been deprived of the economic support of her husband. Terhune's plotting of women's authorship confirms the truth of Ruth's statement through an ironic inversion – *un*happy *married* women *do* write, but Terhune cannot narrate the possibility of their lives beyond marriage as happy, single, writing women. *Phemie's Temptation* ends with Phemie's divorce, while at the close of "Articles," only the ghost

contract describes her as "author" only, not explicitly assigning her the label "proprietor" of her text, although her proprietary status is implicitly relied on. Terhune's decision to specify Agnes's status as "proprietor" so prominently both calls up her own contract at issue in the suit and draws attention to the central legal issue in a way that the actual contract does not.

34 Fanny Fern, *Ruth Hall and Other Writings*, ed. Joyce W. Warren (New Brunswick: Rutgers University Press, 1986), 175.

of the unhappy married woman author still walks (or floats) the earth, while the ornamental society wife who took her place remains, a bodily presence seemingly devoid of intellect or heart.

Something else remains alive, if dismissed by the society wife, at the end of "The Articles of Separation." A literary woman whom Terhune pointedly calls "Queen Mab" (the reigning spirit of death in Percy Bysshe Shelley's poem of the same name) tells the new Mrs. Ashe, "I have gone out to few large assemblies this seasons. . . . But I have greatly enjoyed certain conclaves of choice spirits, to which I have been admitted. Evenings with the Laurence Huttons, the Brander Matthewses, and Mrs. and Mrs. William Dean Howells are something to be remembered forever with pride and delight" (pp. 313–14). The married woman author is a ghost, but author, editor, and critic William Dean Howells, the "Dean of American Literature," remains alive, with two of his fellow writer-critics. Their wives are also at home, but their identities are fully merged into those of their husbands, the persons in the marital pairs who have public identities as writers.

So what lessons does the ghost of Agnes Ashe offer for literary history and the future of copyright? More broadly, how does the nineteenth-century literary landscape look different if we account for all of the stories of women's literary proprietorship in nineteenth-century America I have recovered in this book? And what lessons does this refigured landscape hold for ongoing twenty-first-century debates about the continuing expansion of copyright? The ghost of Agnes Ashe hovers at the border between life and death, gesturing backward to her life history and forward to a literary landscape from which she has departed. Her ghost gestures back to the earlier years of the nineteenth century, a time during which women's authorship flourished under a law that granted authors a modest and limited status as proprietors while privileging the interests of readers. She gestures forward to the 1890s and the twentieth century, years in the wake of the triumph of international copyright during which those who advocated for the continuing expansion of copyright would, implicitly and explicitly, devalue authorial achievements such as those of both the actual Terhune and the fictional Agnes and Phemie.

Narratives of literary history (and histories of other forms of cultural production) have always been tools in advocacy for the expansion of copyright. If the current law provides inadequate incentives for cultural production, then the body of work produced under the current legal regime testifies to the law's inadequacy. In such logic, history testifies to the need for additional reform in the future by devaluing or discounting what the "inadequate" law enabled. The historical narratives deployed in copyright advocacy thus often ignore or disparage the interests of those whom the existing law served well, namely, publishers, readers, and those authors who prospered in the face of supposedly inadequate protection of their property rights. In the nineteenth century, advocates of international copyright often argued that a new age of American literary production would begin as soon as Congress passed an international copyright law. However, after nearly a century of debate and activism, the forces marshaled behind the cause of international copyright did not disband to sit back and watch the literary flowering of America. Instead, publishers and authors soon turned to the question of copyright term extension, arguing that international copyright was not enough and that the expansion of the author's proprietary domain across space and geographic boundaries needed to be complemented by an extension of the author's domain across time. But even when the Copyright Act of 1909 extended the maximum possible copyright term from forty-two to fifty-six years, copyright advocates soon moved on to new issues, always seeking to "perfect" copyright by making it more like other forms of property and less like a limited government grant of privilege designed to spur production for the benefit of the broader public interest.

These changes at the end of the nineteenth and the beginning of the twentieth century have often been interpreted as a triumph for authors' rights, but the expansion of copyright is seldom what it seems. As Christopher Wilson argues in *The Labor of Words*, although authors believed that the passage of the International Copyright Act would lead to increased freedom and power for authors, publishers instead increasingly "managed" authorial production. Because each work could potentially find a (paying) worldwide rather than just an American market, publishers increasingly intervened in the artistic process, putting authors on advance contracts and specifying subject matter, in order to ensure a marketable and thus valuable product.[35] A seeming expansion of author's rights was thus ultimately a triumph of corporate interests.

For most of the twentieth century, unlike the nineteenth century, there was no well-organized opposition to copyright expansion arguing for readers' and other cultural consumers' interests. Although nineteenth-century publishers in some respects used readers' interests as a cover for their own commercial interests, publishers articulated a powerful and cohesive rationale for how American copyright should regulate the field of production so that it served readers' interests first and foremost. In the absence of such a coherent and widely publicized rationale, today's American cultural consumers and their representatives in Congress have repeatedly acquiesced to demands that the property rights of copyright owners be more fully and properly "recognized." In 1998, Congress extended the term of copyright protection yet again, from the previous term of the life of the author plus fifty years to the author's life plus seventy years, and the Supreme Court refused to strike down the law as unconstitutional.

35 Christopher Wilson, *The Labor of Words: Literary Professionalism in the Progressive Era* (Athens: University of Georgia Press, 1985), chap. 3.

One might hope that in the late twentieth century, the gendered "widows and orphans" rhetoric that fueled the first extension of the term of U.S. copyright protection in 1831 would no longer hold sway on the floor of Congress. However, in a perversely fitting turn of the historical screw, on the death of Sonny Bono, erstwhile singer and songwriter and finally congressional representative from California, his widow Mary Bono was elected to fill the unexpired portion of his Congressional term. She thus became heir to both his copyrights and to his advocacy of copyright term extension in Congress. After being elected to a full term of Congress in her own right, Mary Bono spoke on the floor of the House of Representatives on October 7, 1998, in support of the Sonny Bono Copyright Term Extension Act. Merging her roles as widow and legislator, she told her Congressional colleagues,

> Copyright term extension is a very fitting memorial for Sonny. This is not only because of his experience as a pioneer in the music and television industries. The most important reason for me was that he was a legislator who understood the delicate balance of the constitutional interests at stake. . . . He was active on intellectual property issues because he truly understood the goals of Framers of the Constitution: that by maximizing the incentives for original creation, we help expand the public store-house of art, films, music, books, and now also, software. It is said that "it all starts with a song," and these works have defined our culture to audiences world-wide. Actually, Sonny wanted the term of copyright protection to last forever. I am informed by staff that such a change would violate the Constitution. I invite all of you to work with me to strengthen our copyright laws in all of the ways available to us. As you know, there is also Jack Valenti's proposal for term to last forever less one day. Perhaps the Committee may look at that next Congress.[36]

Exactly how did the United States reach this point at which Congresswoman Bono, without irony, can interpret the Constitutional provision directing "[t]o promote the progress of science and useful arts, by securing for limited times to authors and inventors the exclusive right to their respective writings and discoveries" to mean that copyright protection for individual works could last more than 100 years, or even "forever less one day"?

Some antebellum copyright advocates understood and genuinely believed that copyright protection was a limited reward to authors for their service to readers, and as a result, they merely asked that Congress grant this reward to residents and nonresidents alike (I would class Catharine Sedgwick in this group). However, many modern copyright advocates (and Mary Bono is a fair specimen) only superficially speak the language of copyright as an incentive and reward for creative activity. Instead, the logics of property and

36 Statement of Mary Bono, in 144 *Congressional Record* H9946, 9952 (7 Oct. 1998).

entitlement ultimately drive the policies they support.[37] How, for instance, would protection lasting "forever less one day" increase the stock in the "*public* storehouse" of culture? The public domain, that body of works that were never or are no longer protected by copyright, is the true "public storehouse"; so what happens to the public interest when cultural goods that otherwise would enter the public domain remain in private (and largely corporate) hands (almost) forever? Mary Bono, widow of Sonny Bono, who was once a small-time songwriter, perfectly represents the cover story of the continuing expansion of copyright – that artists need to eat, and that when they die, their copyrights should still be alive so that the widows and orphans of the artists can drink from the royalty stream. But the reality is, and always has been, far different: U.S. copyright law has always granted protection to "authors and proprietors," and proprietors, corporations holding copyrights as assets rather than individual creators, hold the lion's share of valuable copyrights.

Others (such as Siva Vaidhyanathan and Lawrence Lessig) have recently and powerfully critiqued the implications of the growth of copyright for freedom of speech and democratic cultural exchange in the United States, and I direct readers to their critiques.[38] However, in closing, let me bring my "lady-writers" to this debate. For much of the twentieth century, literary history and copyright advocacy shared a similar logic and value judgments about the nineteenth century: the law failed to reward adequately the efforts of truly "great" authors, while those whose literary labors found handsome financial rewards could safely be discounted as hacks or scribblers. Literary history and the logic of copyright advocacy have diverged with the late twentieth-century revaluation of the works of popular women authors in literary history. This revised literary history is thus now in the position to challenge the logic of copyright advocacy by drawing attention to what the nineteenth-century law enabled for authors, readers, and publishers rather than focusing exclusively on what the law (allegedly) frustrated for some authors.

If it were possible to raise my nineteenth-century "lady-writers" from the dead to bring them to the floor of Congress to testify about their experiences, what would they recommend for the future of U.S. copyright law? Would they agree with my reading of the significance of their experiences? Catharine Sedgwick would, I believe, agree that the public interest should prevail and that granting modest proprietary rights to authors is sufficient.

37 Paul Goldstein's elaboration of this strain of thinking seems to me to be the most egregious. *Copyright's Highway: From Gutenberg to the Celestial Jukebox* (New York: Hill & Wang, 1994). Edward Samuels gives the same rationale an even more popular gloss and dresses it up with pictures. *The Illustrated Story of Copyright* (New York: St. Martin's, 2000).

38 Siva Vaidhyanathan, *Copyrights and Copywrongs: The Rise of Intellectual Property and How It Threatens Creativity* (New York: New York University Press, 2001); Lawrence Lessig, *The Future of Ideas: The Fate of the Commons in a Connected World* (New York: Vintage, 2002).

Clearly, her signature on the 1838 "Citizens of New York" petition to Congress demonstrates her support for recognizing such modest protection for authors internationally, but she understood that authors have no natural, eternal property rights in their literary texts and that such a reading of authorship conflicts with the values of a democratic republic. Terhune, Harriet Beecher Stowe, and Augusta Evans might be wary of making self-interested demands in the halls of Congress, while Fanny Fern would feel no compunction, but all four authors very well might argue for the continuing expansion of authorial proprietorship on the same grounds as does Mary Bono. All four, like Sedgwick, expressed public support for international copyright at least once during their lives: Evans and Fern signed the 1868 American Copyright Association petition, Terhune signed the 1886 International Copyright Association petition, Stowe wrote to Horace Greeley at the *Tribune* in support of international copyright, and Fern wrote her *New-York Ledger* column on the subject. And, as my case studies demonstrate, all four had far-reaching proprietary ambitions, even if their ambitions were frustrated and the extent of their ambitions did not become widely publicly known: Stowe filed *Stowe v. Thomas*; Evans was the architect of Confederate copyright; Fern aggressively and creatively policed her proprietary domain throughout her career, and Terhune both expressed her (admittedly conflicted and confused) outrage at the effects of coverture on married women's literary proprietorship in *Phemie's Temptation* and "The Articles of Separation" and did everything in her power to aid her publishers in their suit against the infringers of her cookbook. In short, the ladies might speak in unison with Mary Bono, complaining that cultural producers have not gotten their due and that they are entitled to a term of protection for their literary property of "forever less one day."

But is the purpose of copyright law to fulfill completely the desires of authors and to give them everything to which they believe they are entitled? If, magically, we could go back to the early nineteenth century and give early copyright advocates what some of them demanded, protection for literary property that was not bounded by time or space and that was global and eternal, how would the cultural landscapes of the nineteenth and twentieth centuries have been transformed and today be transformed? Sedgwick, Stowe, Evans, Fern, and Terhune, both the authors and their works, are products of a copyright climate that did not fulfill such fantasies. If such fantasies had been fulfilled, would they have been able even to enter the field and play such an important role in the development of a mass market and reading public in America, or would Mary Bono's "public storehouse" be filled with a small quantity of cultural goods controlled absolutely and eternally by a few corporations, while the public domain did not exist at all? If granting literary texts the status of property under the law and making authors into proprietors is the key to spurring creativity for the benefit of readers, then how do we account for the productivity and popularity of women who held the title to their literary properties only imperfectly, or not at all? In bringing the stories of the "lady-writers" to debates over the future of copyright, I make their experiences speak against what they imagined were their own interests, but I also seek to value what they achieved and the public-interest-driven copyright policy that enabled their achievements.

Index

LaVergne, TN USA
16 August 2010
193396LV00003B/36/P

9 780521 154758